The Bible

The Bible

Respectful Readings

George Anastaplo

LEXINGTON BOOKS
A division of
ROWMAN & LITTLEFIELD PUBLISHERS, INC.
Lanham • Boulder • New York • Toronto • Plymouth, UK

LEXINGTON BOOKS

A division of Rowman & Littlefield Publishers, Inc.
A wholly owned subsidiary of The Rowman & Littlefield Publishing Group, Inc.
4501 Forbes Boulevard, Suite 200
Lanham, MD 20706

Estover Road
Plymouth PL6 7PY
United Kingdom

British Library Cataloguing in Publication Information Available

Library of Congress Cataloging-in-Publication Data

Anastaplo, George, 1925–
The Bible : respectful readings / George Anastaplo.
p. cm.
Includes bibliographical references (p.) and index.
ISBN-13: 978-0-7391-2498-7 (cloth : alk. paper)
ISBN-10: 0-7391-2498-6 (cloth : alk. paper)
ISBN-13: 978-0-7391-2499-4 (pbk. : alk. paper)
ISBN-10: 0-7391-2499-4 (pbk. : alk. paper)
1. Bible—Criticism, interpretation, etc. I. Title.
BS511.3.A53 2008
220.6—dc22 2007046973

Printed in the United States of America

∞™ The paper used in this publication meets the minimum requirements of American National Standard for Information Sciences—Permanence of Paper for Printed Library Materials, ANSI/NISO Z39.48–1992.

To the Memory of Seven *Religieux*
whose Good Works testified to
their salutary Faiths:

Reverend Robert L. Bowman (1923–1976)
Reverend Kermit Eby (1903–1962)
Rabbi Monford Harris (1920–2003)
Sister Candida Lund, O.P. (1920–2000)
Father R. Eric O'Connor, S.J. (1907–1980)
Rabbi Richard W. Winograd (1935–1974)
Rabbi Maurice B. Pekarsky (1905–1962)

Contents

Chapter One

On Taking the Bible Seriously Again

'Tis the gift to be simple, 'tis the gift to be free;
'Tis the gift to come down where we ought to be;
And when we find ourselves in the place just right,
'Twill be in the valley of love and delight.

Simple Gifts[1]

I

We are constantly challenged today by intellectual and social developments that have permitted, perhaps even encouraged, a vigorously-promulgated atheism to become familiar. Thus, we have become accustomed to hearing, especially among the more sophisticated, systematic disparagement of the texts and doctrines upon which religious allegiances in the Western world have long depended.

At the same time, even the most vigorous "non-believers" among us invoke standards of right and wrong that go back for centuries, if not for millennia, in the West. But questions can be raised (partly because of such intellectuals) about how much respect *should* be paid to the "absolute" standards of right and wrong, good and bad, that we have inherited.[2]

Compare, by way of contrast with current inclinations among intellectuals, this somewhat unfashionable introduction, a half-century ago, to a study of political philosophy: "We shall not shock anyone, we shall merely expose ourselves to good-natured or at any rate harmless ridicule, if we profess ourselves inclined to the old-fashioned and simple opinion according to which Machiavelli was a teacher of evil."[3] It often seems that it is the more educated, or at least the most "advanced," among us who are most likely to be so ungentlemanly as to be heard questioning aggressively both the pieties of the day and the old-fashioned notions we have inherited about good and evil.

However this may be, is it not prudent to assume that most people, especially in a long-established community, want to be right and to do good?[4] Indeed, most people would much prefer to find themselves, in their everyday conduct, "in the place just right." The useful respect of the community at large can be secured and maintained by its leaders only if it should be evident that they are indeed "where [they] ought to be."

Essential here can be informed and sustained instruction directed to that education which recognizes that the community does tend to rely mostly upon familiar notions about right and wrong.[5] Systematic instruction in traditional literature and philosophy, as well as in our ever-changing natural sciences, can help "reconnect [students] to a glorious past and promote thoughtful contemplation on our collective future."[6]

II

Philosophy and literature courses sometimes draw upon the Bible. Of course, the Scriptures present themselves as something more than literature, but they *are*, to a considerable degree, literature—and sometimes great literature at that.[7]

That the Bible is vital to the heritage of the West would be hard to deny. It could once be taken for granted, along with the works of William Shakespeare, as part of the "equipment" of the statesman.[8] This is evident in the career and words of Abraham Lincoln, who could speak of "the good old maxims of the Bible" as being "truly applicable to human affairs."[9]

The Bible has long been considered essential among us for moral instruction, for rhetorical training, and for the development of the ability to identify the circumstances that call for prudential judgments. It should not need an extended argument, therefore, to persuade anyone familiar with the history of the West to acknowledge the importance of the Bible among us.

Even so, the Bible is generally much neglected these days, however fervent its champions may be in some quarters. Certainly, a teacher (say, in a law school) should not expect the typical college graduate to have more than a vague familiarity with the Bible.[10]

Critical to any effort to induce students, as well as citizens at large, to take the Bible more seriously than they otherwise might is to help them see how interesting it can be. This can be done by our showing each other that the Bible may be read in a way that challenges even someone who cannot regard it as divine revelation, however much the same reading deepens the faith of the faithful.[11]

III

The discussions of the Bible collected in this book were developed by me on a variety of occasions over decades. What was said on each occasion (drawing, it is hoped, on a consistent overall understanding of such things) was likely to be influenced, naturally enough, by the audience and the circumstances.[12]

A tremendous amount of biblical scholarship has long been available to the interested reader. Most of it, however, is too specialized for use here. The things I offer are hardly the last word on the biblical passages I discuss. But perhaps they provide a useful first word for readers who might not otherwise be inclined to look into the Bible. The wary reader should be assured that I do not attempt to address questions of faith in this book: that is, I do not presume to say here either what "really happened" on this or that momentous occasion two to three millennia ago or what one should "believe."

There are things in the biblical passages I discuss which readers should be encouraged to notice, including what are considered by a biblical author to be problems of evidence or of the relevant moral questions or of the proper mode of examining his materials. Particularly useful for all of us is the training offered here in *how to read carefully*, which includes the refinement of an awareness of the purposes and presuppositions of the accounts that one may happen to be presented as a human being or as a citizen or as a scholar from time to time. More often than not, in the admittedly "amateur" discussions offered here, each biblical text dealt with is read primarily on its own.[13]

ADDENDUM

Blaise Pascal reported, "The last thing one settles in writing a book is what one should put first." I have decided, upon finishing this book, to suggest something about the experiences I have brought to my subject.

I draw here on the privilege of growing up among Southern Baptists in a small town in southern Illinois, even attending as a child one of their Sunday schools for several years. Of course, our family remained very much part of the Greek Orthodox community in St. Louis, Missouri (where my two brothers and I were born). My experience with American Protestantism has included a six-decades-long marriage to a Texas Presbyterian whose maternal grandfather had been a minister.

During the Second World War and immediately thereafter I served as a U.S. Army Air Corps aerial navigator. These flying duties took me as far west as Formosa, as far south as Liberia, and as far east as Saudi Arabia. Thereafter I was trained academically as a student at the University of Chicago and as a teacher at the University of Chicago, Rosary College (now Dominican University), the University of Illinois (Chicago), the University of Dallas, Lenoir-Rhyne College, Rochester Institute of Technology, and Loyola University Chicago School of Law.

My friendships over the years have also been instructive, including my intimate associations with Jewish teachers and fellow students, especially at the University of Chicago. My friends have ranged in political orientation from Ramsey Clark (a law school classmate, who became attorney general of the United States and since then a fervent champion of international human rights) to Gus Zuehlke (a conscientious Midwestern banker who remains a devoted champion of Senator Joseph McCarthy). I came to know Mr. Zuehlke when he attended adult education seminars I conducted at The Clearing in Door County, Wisconsin. His associations both with Senator McCarthy and with me are described in a recently-published book, *Call Me Gus* (by Kristin Stankewicz).

I have benefited, in preparing this book, from the encouragement provided by the *Oklahoma City University Law Review* when it published in 1998 an earlier version of the material in this book. That publication included a generous foreword by Robert H. Henry, who is now Chief Judge of the U.S. Court of Appeals for the Tenth Circuit. The newest material in this book may be found in the appendices, which examine questions and issues suggested by my examination of various books of the Bible.

One can see, by comparing this book with its law journal predecessor, what needs to be done to convert into books the two dozen other book-length collections that I have published in law journals during the past two decades.

Chapter Two

On Prophecy and Freedom[14]

> God is not a man, that He should lie; neither the son of man, that He should repent: When He hath said, will He not do it? Or when He hath spoken, will He not make it good?
>
> Balaam[15]

I

Why do things happen the way they do? Are things truly the way they seem to be?

One explanation naturally available to us—that is, available without the aid of any divine revelation—is that there are "cause and effect" relations that account for the way things happen. Critical to these relations are the characters and choices of diverse human beings.

Any recourse to *chance* in accounting for what happens among us adds uncertainty, if not even mystery, to the stories that we may depend upon. Chance may reflect our limited grasp of the whole.

The role of prophecy in an account may seem to compound whatever mystery chance or coincidence contributes to the "situation." Prophecies can remind us of our limitations in either controlling or understanding both our actions and the actions of others.

But may not prophecy also help us see that the world makes sense? Does it not suggest that there is somehow a purpose, if not even a "predictable" scheme or an overall sense, to what happens?

Certainly, prophecy can help us notice aspects of actions, as well as connections among them, that we otherwise might not notice or notice as well. A tragedy may be enhanced when the audience knows what is going to happen. It has been pointed out, for example, that Jean Anouilh, in his *Antigone*, makes sure that his audience knows from the outset of the play how that very old story goes. In the *Iliad*, also, Homer keeps anticipating for us what is going to happen, beginning with his opening lines. And Aristotle noticed in the *Poetics* that old (and hence familiar?) stories formed the basis of the best tragedies.[16]

Although prophecies may help account for what happens, things rarely happen *because* of prophecies. That is, the reasons things happen and have their effect on any particular occasion are independent of prophecy. Consider how the prophesied things, once they happen, appear to those who do *not* know of the relevant prophecy. Moreover, it does not seem that the relatively few things that are prophesied are intrinsically different in character from the bulk of things that do happen and that have no known prophecy connected with them.

II

A prophecy, for our purposes here, is simply a prediction about what is going to happen or about how someone will act. Our initial concern is not with the prophet as a political leader or moral guide. In the Greek stories, for example, it is often left uncertain why the prophecy is provided or is available.

Prophecy can be distinguished, for our immediate purposes, from miracles (aside from whatever there may be miraculous about the availability of any prophecy). Also, genuine prophecies can be distinguished from apparent prophecies: there have always been among human beings many "prophetic" utterances, but most of them are not truly prophecies—that is, most of them are mistaken or ill-founded. Jocasta, in Sophocles' *Oedipus Tyrannus*, voices a common skepticism about much of what passes for prophecy; Croesus, in Herodotus' *History*, takes the precaution of arranging for test runs on the celebrated oracles available in his day.[17]

Prophecy can be understood to "report" in advance what could thereafter be reported in retrospect, especially if the causes and consequences of actions should be (as they usually are) independent of the prediction. This is something like predictions by economists and meteorologists, as well as by chemists and physicists (including cosmologists). A physicist's account of massive movements in distant galaxies, for example, may appear much the same whether he is anticipating the future or discovering the past.

In principle, it can be said, all human events could be subject to prophetic accounts, even if only a few are thus predicted or accounted for.

III

We are particularly concerned here with prophecies that take the form of predictions about what is going to happen because of something determined by the divine or by fate or by some other apparently intelligent power. It may be difficult, if not impossible, in any situation, to figure out either the basis of the prophesied determination or the reason why that particular determination has been disclosed to the parties most obviously affected by it.

We usually get the impression, when a prophecy is involved in a situation, that the parties primarily dealt with have no effective "choices" about critical things, however much may be left to them in selecting the mode of fulfilling that which is prophesied. We can be troubled if it should seem that someone is completely in the grip of his "fate." Interest in a story as story is likely, at least among us, to be undermined by this.

But, it should again be noticed, only a very few (albeit, in some cases, terribly important) things in a human being's career may be prophesied. If everything is known in advance, then the "actual" life is but a "rerun"—and our attention might well be directed instead to trying to understand that life as it developed "the first time around"—that is to say, in the mind of whatever intelligent power may have ordained it or at least anticipated it in such detail.

IV

It seems likely that if genuine prophecy is available with respect to human affairs, then all that one does is in principle predictable (that is, is subject to prophecy), including the choices that one is likely, if not even bound, to make. Thus, the sequences of events prophesied are caused (or can be accounted for) in the same way as the sequences that are not prophesied. There need be no difference between them: they can all be considered subject to the same rules, whether or not we can ultimately understand such rules or the way the world is.

Why some things are prophesied and not others may be related to the character or circumstances of the principal parties involved. In the best stories, perhaps, the prophecy may follow "naturally" from the kind of human being one is. Otherwise, the story may really be about the character and motives of the ordaining power—and that can be much harder, if not impossible, to get at or, perhaps, to remain interested in. Difficulties suggest themselves if the observer must resort to a kind of inspiration or prophecy of his own in order to begin to understand what is going on. John Adams observed, in an 1812 letter to Thomas Jefferson, that "nothing is clearer from [the Scriptures of Christians] than that Their Prophecies were not intended to make Us Prophets."[18]

With or without prophecy in a story, we may still have the problem of determining why it is that someone chooses, or is moved, to act as he does. There has always been something mysterious or incomprehensible and at the same time compelling about this discovery, leading to familiar inquiries into determinism, freedom, and fatalism.

V

The scope of the ordaining power I have just referred to may bear upon whether there is a prophecy in any particular situation. It need not, probably should not, bear upon how the human being described is destined to act. This is especially so if the ordaining power is wise and just. Is it not difficult to imagine such a power other than that? Or, at least, is it not difficult to take it seriously for long if that ordaining power (as a moral being) should not truly know what it is doing?

I have suggested that the ordaining power in these situations is uncovering or revealing more than it is making or shaping. But even if it is considered to be making, or choosing, must it not still take various principles or ends into account in much the way that the thoughtful human being should? If it does not, the story told (however true it may be) can become meaningless.

Would not the ordaining power be unlike human beings in that it would not be moved by passions? The Olympian gods of the Greeks (and perhaps of the Romans) do seem to be moved by passions, which requires that something else must hold sway over the matters which they are involved in or are interested in—and this we see in (and is seen by?) Homer. Nor would the ordaining power be dependent upon time in working things out. This may be another way of saying that an ordaining power has no passions.

If the Olympians were completely dispassionate, however, they might not be needed in a story. Certainly, they would not need to be multiple. The more perceptive poets who employ such gods find them useful in dramatizing stories about the way human beings act and perhaps should act. The usefulness of the Olympians includes the role they play in bringing prophecies to light, prophecies about events that (we can notice, upon close inspection) they themselves often cannot control, however much they may happen to want to do. In this respect, poets can be very much like the ordaining power, which finds it salutary to make prophecies available with a view to teaching lessons to the human race.

If we should conclude that everything is ordained, might we not still wonder why things have been ordained as they are? It is, I have suggested, substantially like the inquiry as to why human beings act as they do, although it may be easier to address the human things directly than to attempt to get at them by way of the mind or the will of an ordaining non-human power. I have further suggested that the ordaining power, in anticipating the career of a human being, must *try* to figure out (and, if wise enough, should *be able* to figure out) what a human being will do in a variety of circumstances when his or her time comes.

The key lesson taught us when we contemplate stories in which prophecies loom large is that one should always try to do the right thing. That is, it can be said, where virtue and true freedom lie. If the gods do not agree with this lesson, so much the worse for them—for does not the ultimate ordaining power or standards govern and judge them also?

VI

Consider, as illustrative of my arguments here, the prophecies in the *Iliad* with respect to Achilles and Troy. Those prophecies sometimes hang heavy over warriors and cities. Such fates are intimately related to what people are like and how they conduct themselves.

When Troy carries on as it does, especially with respect to Helen and Paris, it can expect the fate it suffers. We should not be surprised that this city's choices lead to its destruction. We are familiar with such a pattern from the Bible, where prophecy often takes the form of spelling out the political and social consequences of religious and moral misconduct.

Nor should we be surprised by Achilles' fate. He runs risks by staying at Troy, especially considering how he is both expected and willing to expose himself as much as he does to battle. It is certainly safer for him to go home. He wins great glory at Troy. Does not this glory presuppose considerable freedom on his part? Otherwise he would not deserve the recognition he does get. Achilles is not merely an instrument of some fate; his spear, for example, is an instrument in his service, but this fact does not suffice to win glory for that spear.

There is little that Achilles does that is dependent upon any prophecy about him, however much various prophecies can throw light on Achilles' state of mind. The prophecies here, whether about Troy or about Achilles or perhaps about any other character, do not affect much, if at all, our understanding of the story that is told by Homer. It *can* affect our understanding of what Homer believes that his audience needs to know if it is to grasp, or fully to enjoy and to learn from, the story that he tells. The greater the role of gods and prophecies, it can be said, the more limited the characters (if not even the audience itself) may be understood to be.

VII

Consider again, as further illustration of my arguments, the prophecies relating to Oedipus. Sophocles' use of prophecy in his Oedipus plays appears more complicated than is Homer's use in the *Iliad*, at least at first glance. Much *seems* to depend in Sophocles' account upon Oedipus' desperate efforts to avoid the grim fate revealed to him at Delphi.[19]

The precise things done by Oedipus to his parents, however, do not depend directly upon prophecy. The indirect dependence of his acts upon prophecy is another matter, as may be seen when one considers what Laius and Jocasta did to their infant son because of a prophecy. But it should be remembered that children are given up by their parents for a variety of reasons, and that can lead to troublesome complications. Thus, Oedipus' acts, as well as those of Laius and Jocasta, can be understood in human terms. The prophecy at work here may be no more mysterious, or no more difficult to grasp, than what the story of Oedipus would have looked like without any prophecy having been made known (in advance of his critical actions) either to him or perhaps to his parents. That is to say, chance or coincidence can seem mysterious, or at least worthy of comment, even to the most skeptical.[20]

Powerful prohibitions with respect to patricide and incest remind us that what Oedipus did is not unimaginable. Inadvertent offenses are not unknown here, and their consequences (especially upon exposure) can be devastating.[21] Neither prophecy nor divine intervention is needed to make a story about these matters powerful. People do become aware, as perhaps Oedipus did, of questionable passions that they must deal with. And people sometimes do have notions, after the fact if not before, about what was "bound to happen" to them. We can even hear it said, "This could have been prophesied." Are we not all familiar with developments that we have somehow contributed to that are very much like what we have always wanted to avoid?

How would the Oedipus story be understood if no prophecy had ever become public knowledge, especially if it had never been revealed to Oedipus? The coincidences would appear to be remarkable, of course, but still comprehensible. Would not the worst things that happened to Oedipus be then seen as largely due to the kind of man he was? For one thing, Oedipus may not know when one should leave bad enough alone. (Is not incest somehow "appropriate" for a man who wants to know more and more, if not even more than he is capable of dealing with?) Prophecy may help us see what is otherwise discernible as well—that there are critical limits to a man's ability to control his fate. The career of Oedipus dramatizes what happens when someone presumes to believe that he understands more than he does. It could be instructive to imagine the questions Socrates would have pursued in Oedipus' circumstances, just as he had had questions about the Delphic oracle pertaining to Socrates' wisdom.[22] The riddling character of some of the more notorious Delphic oracles should alert us to the fact that prophecies can be as puzzling as life itself and perhaps for the same reasons.

VIII

Whether it is a typical instance of prophecy (as in the *Iliad*) or an atypical instance (as in the *Oedipus Tyrannus*), the sequence of events dealt with in a properly-wrought story should be susceptible to our analysis and understanding. No real mystery need be involved, or at least no more than confronts us in everyday life as we try to understand why things (sometimes quite dreadful things) happen the way they do.

I again notice that a prophecy may do no more than say in advance what a reporter would say in retrospect—or that the audience can expect or "say" when it hears a story the second time. The fundamental irrelevance of timing may be seen in the test run by Croesus in Herodotus' *History*: it is assumed there that the oracle which has power to foretell the future accurately should also be able to tell the present at a distance.

Prophecy, I have argued, is distinctively a matter of timing, or at least primarily a matter of timing, not a matter of causation. The ordaining power reveals beforehand the story which the poet or historian will be able to tell afterwards. (Time, I again notice, can be without intrinsic significance for the divine.) One's insight, as to what accounts for the way things are or as to how things hang together, may count for more than when the events are anticipated or when they happen.

Insight, or understanding, is far more important here than power, even the power of prediction. The timing of one's awareness of what is happening is related more to one's prowess as a magician than it is to one's thoughtfulness. When it came down to a contest, we are told in *Exodus*, both God and Pharaoh had magicians to employ. But, we are also told, Moses (with the aid of Aaron) is much more than a magician; he would not be remembered as he is if he had simply been a "super-magician" who was able to best the Pharaoh's magicians at their trade.[23]

IX

I mention briefly three texts that could well be considered for further instruction about the matters I have touched upon here.

The first text is Moses Maimonides' *The Guide of the Perplexed*, where the great medieval Jewish scholar explains that the prophet must be a man of surpassing intelligence and outstanding moral stature. Related to this explanation is his suggestion that God does not ever act, change, or move in His dealings with human beings. Is it implied there, or at least in my readings of him, that if one understood what nature does and requires, genuine prophecy would pose no problem?[24]

The second text is Thomas Aquinas' treatise, *On Truth*, where he considers whether the commandments of God are due to will alone. No, he argues, the will and the intellect are coextensive in God. And, he adds, it is blasphemous to assume that there are not good reasons for what God ordains.[25]

The third text to be considered is found in still another 1812 letter from John Adams to Thomas Jefferson:

> [Certain contemporary prophets] made themselves sufficiently known to me when I was in the Government [that is, when he was Vice President or President?]. They all assumed the Character of Ambassadors extraordinary from The Almighty: but as I required miracles in proof of their Credentials, and they did not perform any, I never gave publick Audience to [any] of them.[26]

We are reminded by this quotation of a major question we moderns would probably have in confronting any alleged prophecy. It is a concern that seems far less a concern in the ancient accounts that we have: How did the prophecy come and what validated or legitimated this or any other revelation? Of course, there *is* the test of time: Did the prophecy prove to be valid? But even here there is the question of the reliability of the report that there *had* been a prophecy beforehand and that it had been fulfilled afterwards. In such matters, it seems, the evidence alleged with respect to any aspect or at any stage of the matter would be subject to the same kind of question. Perhaps this should remind us of the mutual irrefutability there may be between reason and revelation. This may be something that I have not taken sufficient account of in my examination thus far of the nature and uses of prophecy in literature. We should be reminded also that prophecy is made use of by those, such as poets and priests, who may ultimately seem to rely more upon divine inspiration than upon deliberate inquiry.

Chapter Three

On Biblical Thought[27]

I want to begin with the remark that I am not a biblical scholar.

Leo Strauss[28]

I

So extensive is the literature that has been inspired by the Bible that one cannot hope to do more than deal on any occasion with a small fraction of it, making a few suggestions about whatever one may have been privileged to notice that is not generally noticed in one's own time, however often it may have been noticed in the past.

The Bible and things biblical very much shape and permeate our way of life. These are matters learned at the maternal knee and reinforced by much that is encountered in everyday life. Even non-believers can be influenced by the Bible in many more ways than they suspect. Consider, for example, how an aggressively atheistic Marxism "naturally" drew for its vitality upon the moral vision of the Bible.

However much I (because of my heritage) may make use of the New Testament (that is, the Greek Bible), I will be primarily concerned at the outset of this inquiry with the Hebrew Bible, the Bible of the Jews, as it has come down to us in its conventional or canonical form. It is difficult enough even for Jews to understand much of that Bible, including Jews who know ancient Hebrew well and who have immersed themselves in the background and way of life of their people. Much of the subtlety of the Bible is likely to be lost upon the rest of us. How unprepared we can be for reading ancient texts is suggested by the difficulty we have in appreciating a line given by Euripides to Hippolytus: "My tongue swore, but my mind took no oath."[29] The ill-fated Hippolytus says this when he threatens to reveal the shameful proposition on behalf of his passionate stepmother Phaedra that he had been tricked into having sworn he would keep to himself. Our difficulty in appreciating this line is testified to by our inability to grasp why ancient Athenian audiences should have considered Hippolytus' statement to be as outrageous as they evidently did.

This great affront to piety was not mitigated, it seems, by the subsequent refusal of Hippolytus to repudiate his oath, a refusal which contributed to his untimely death. The difficulty we have in understanding the outrage of the Athenians about such matters (another is the savage popular response to the failure of the victorious Athenian navy to recover the bodies of its dead after the battle of Arginusae) should suggest to us how far we have moved from ancient piety in the way we think, in the way we believe, and in the way we think about the diverse ways that people do happen to believe.[30]

We as students of the Bible must venture, therefore, into what is bound to remain largely strange territory. We are implicitly licensed in our efforts here, however, by an observation made by Moses to his people as he prepared to take his leave of them:

> Behold, I have taught you statutes and ordinances, even as the Lord my God commanded me, that ye should do so in the midst of the land whither ye go in to possess it. Observe therefore and do them; for this is your wisdom and your understanding in the sight of the peoples, that when they hear all these statutes, shall say: "Surely this great nation is a wise and understanding people." For what great nation is there, that hath God so nigh unto them, as the Lord our God is whensoever we call upon Him? And what great nation is there, that hath statutes and ordinances so righteous as all this law, which I set before you this day?[31]

That is, it is expected by Moses that other peoples can pass judgment of sorts upon what the people of Israel both have and do.

What the Israelites have in the Bible are the story of their emergence as a people and accounts of their encounters with the Divine. In those encounters a critical issue, which arises again and again for them, is the question of their fidelity to the God that has singled them out for special attention. There are, for example, repeated relapses by many of them into idolatry, the most notorious instance being their experiment with the Golden Calf even as Moses was securing the Ten Commandments from God. Since the divine presence in the lives of this people can often seem to be established largely by inference, the challenge of idolatry must be taken very seriously as a counter-argument of sorts. If idolatry had been simply absurd, or completely distinguishable from the true worship, that forbidden form of worship would not have appeared as often as it evidently did among the Israelites.[32] Nor would it have aroused the deadly opposition that it did among the more pious, including the terrible thing that Moses and his allies did to the worshipers of the Golden Calf. On the other hand, laws, power, and sanctions would not have sufficed to sustain Judaism down to our day if there had not been something sublime, if not even ineffable, about the vision of the divine to which the people of Israel seem to have been dedicated almost from the outset.[33]

II

Inferences of what we, not the Israelites, would call the supernatural can be instructive. Consider Shakespeare's *Macbeth*, with its account of the bloody career of a usurping nobleman who kills his king and then a comrade (Banquo) whom he sees as a threat to his ill-gotten crown, and thereafter others of good character whom he regards as unreliable. Macbeth's career is anticipated by prophecies given to him and Banquo at the outset of the play by witches encountered after a battle—and that career is further illuminated for him by subsequent prophecies by the witches when he seeks them out.[34]

We, as the audience, see and hear as much of the witches as Macbeth does. They do not pretend to be personally responsible for what happens to Macbeth. Nor are the witches shown as intervening to change the course of events. But what they say, and how Macbeth and Banquo think and act in response to what they hear from the witches, can help us better understand what happens.

Consider, now, how Macbeth's career looks to the people of Scotland who (aside from Banquo and Lady Macbeth) know nothing, so far as we can tell, about any of Macbeth's encounters with the witches. His career seems to be comprehensible to them, as comprehensible as any career of a bloody tyrant can be. This suggests that the witches do not add anything essential to the action, however much they may dramatize (for us, perhaps also for Macbeth) what is happening. The witches, and the responses to them of Macbeth and Banquo, may help us to see better than we otherwise might a moral dimension of the action of this play. At the very least, the witches throw light into the dark corners of the souls of Macbeth, his wife, and perhaps Banquo.

But, I repeat, the people of Scotland (including Macduff) do not need any such visitations in order to be able to "understand" what they have to deal with. Unfortunately, things like this do happen "all the time"—and peoples have grasped them for what they are with or without inferences of divine intervention and with or without the aid of unnatural beings such as witches.

III

We, in contemplating the story of the people of Israel provided us by the Bible, are privileged as are the audiences of *Macbeth* in viewing the action. It is taken for granted, if not shown, in one action after another reported in the Bible, that divine intervention, or at least some kind of divine attention, must be reckoned with.

This may be seen, from the outset of the account of this people in the Hebrew Bible, with the career of Abraham. We will find that it may also be seen toward the end of the biblical account of this people with the career of Mordecai. Very early in the life of the people of Israel is the story of the Binding of Isaac.[35] No one around Abraham, it seems—not the servants who accompany him, not his wife Sarah, not even his son Isaac—hears (*or perhaps ever learns of*) the word from God that Abraham somehow hears. The action, as witnessed by outsiders (among whom we too can be numbered), consisted of Abraham wakening one morning, his long trip to the appointed place, his handling (mishandling?) of Isaac, and his sacrifice of the ram that then "happened" to become available. Nothing was done in this sequence, as witnessed by outsiders, that does not go on every day, even what can seem (in *other* circumstances) as incomprehensible child abuse.

The way these everyday doings are understood, however, reflects the thought of the Bible—for it is that thought which accounts for, and interprets, the actions of a people and its leaders, whether founders, prophets, or kings. Biblical thought may be seen in the doctrines or argument of the books of the Bible, doctrines and arguments that inform the accounts of the actions that are recorded.

Biblical thought may also be seen in the way of life laid down for the people—that way of life summed up in and reinforced by various rules. These are the statutes and ordinances of which Moses spoke, and to which we shall return.

Biblical thought may be seen as well in the consequences of the teachings and the ways of life promoted by the Bible. Long-term consequences include the Jews of our time, a people who remain faithful to a way of life—or at least to a name and the aspirations implied by that name. They are, by most accounts, a highly civilized people, however much the God of their Bible can be condemned, as in a current Jordanian high-school textbook, "as a God who is bloodthirsty, fickleminded, harsh and greedy."[36]

IV

The consequences of the influence of the Bible include, in the short run, the state of mind as well as the way of life of the Jews at the time of Jesus. That was a century or two after the Hebrew Bible, as we know it, was completed. That Bible and the way of life grounded in it, along with the influence of the Roman occupation, contributed to the conditions that Jesus' generation encountered in the Holy Land. Jesus himself, we should not need to be reminded, was very much a Jew—and his interests and expectations, and the way he and his companions talked about them, were those of Jews, not those of Romans or Greeks or, say, those of Chinese or Hindus. Much of what may be found in the Greek Bible (or the New Testament), it can be said, is *one* of the ways that the Hebrew Bible "naturally" led to when the Israelites encountered the Greek and Roman world.

What were the people of Israel accustomed to by the time of Jesus? Certainly, a considerable number of practices, rituals, and institutions were taken for granted by that people, as well as a sometimes-heated way of talking about them. Furthermore, remarkable feats of healing seem to have been regarded as so routine that they were both believable and yet not fully persuasive as to one's divine credentials. If the accounts in the Greek Bible are to be believed, the healing done by Jesus was obvious enough, so obvious that questions could be raised about, for example, the propriety of his healing on the Sabbath. Questions could also be raised, of course, about the source of anyone's extraordinary powers in these and other matters. Something out of the ordinary was routinely looked to in such circumstances, whether divine or diabolic.

Indicative of the temper of those remarkable times was the troubled response of King Herod upon hearing of the wondrous things reported about Jesus, including the healings. Speculations abounded in Herod's court and elsewhere as to what *was* going on. Herod himself may have wondered, or so we are told, whether this was John the Baptist come back to life, the man whom the king had ordered beheaded and whose head he had thereafter seen on a platter.[37] It was, it seems, a world in which this sort of thing could happen—or, at least, it was a world in which this sort of thing was believed to be possible. Apocalyptic literature was evidently common in Judaism at that time.

We should notice that, however much interest was exhibited in afflictions and their healing, the emphasis did seem to be placed at the time of Jesus not upon the distinction between the healthy and the unhealthy, but rather upon the (perhaps related) distinction between the clean and the unclean. The same can be said about the dietary and related laws of the Hebrew Bible, however much the rationalists of our day sometimes account for them as health and sanitation measures. An emphasis upon *health* looks more to *nature* as a guide, which is simply not the way of the Hebrew Bible (nor, for that matter, the way of the Gospels in the Greek Bible either). On the other hand, an emphasis upon *cleanliness* looks more to the moral dimensions of things, including to that preeminent biblical virtue, *piety*, especially in the form of unquestioning obedience to God's decrees.[38]

V

Piety in the Hebrew Bible, more so than in the Greek Bible, looks to conduct in the context of one's life as part of a people. It is in ancient Judaism, more than seems to be true in Christianity, the piety of members of a community, less so the piety of an individual soul concerned primarily for its personal salvation. Of course, there is something of these two forms of piety in both the Greek Bible and its Hebrew predecessor—but the emphasis in each does seem critically different to me.

Whatever the significant differences may be between the two books (or between the two sets of books), there is much of course that is similar. Illustrative of fundamental similarities is how miracles are approached in both the Hebrew Bible and the Greek Bible. The typical biblical assumption is that nothing comes from nothing. The one major exception to this assumption may be the initial creation of the world. But such creation out of nothing, if that is how *that* event is intended to be regarded, is obviously rare if not even unique. In principle, the Creation could not be witnessed by any human being or, perhaps, ever understood: there is no place human beings can "stand" from which to "see" it. To say "creation out of nothing" is to say that things somehow *are*. It is also to say that we must proceed from our awareness of the world as it is and, so far as we can tell, as it has long been and will long (if not forever) continue to be.[39]

However one understands the Creation, the "typical" biblical miracle (including resurrections?) must work with *something*. Jesus, for example, does not conjure up from nothing the food with which he feeds the multitudes. That is, he is not merely a magician. Rather, he transforms, one way or another, a few loaves and fishes into even more loaves and fishes, just as he had needed something (that is, water) from which to make wine during the wedding feast at Cana.[40] Consider also the variety of means usually employed by Jesus in his healing miracles. This is made explicit in his response to his disciples, when they asked him why *they* had not been able earlier to cast demons out of a man whom Jesus had just cured: "This kind can come forth by nothing, but by prayer and fasting."[41] That is, Jesus teaches them, effective healing requires both accurate diagnosis and appropriate treatment, with a specific remedy evidently required for each affliction.

Nor is Moses himself primarily a conjuror, however one understands his contests with Pharaoh's magicians in Egypt. The same can be said, of course, of the God of Moses. Consider, for example, how He explains to the people of Israel how He will drive the Hivites, the Canaanites, and the Hittites out of the land that the Israelites have been promised: "I will not drive them out from before thee in one year, lest the land become desolate, and the beasts of the field multiply against thee. By little and little I will drive them out from before thee, until thou be increased, and inherit the land."[42] That is, the land is not to be put "on hold" by God, awaiting the ability of the Israelites to enter and manage it. Rather, God has to arrange for the interim; there are what *we* would call "natural processes" to be reckoned with.

The miracle of miracles, for our immediate purposes, may be the parting of the sea in such a way as to permit the Israelites to escape the pursuing Egyptians. Here is the account in *Exodus*: "And Moses stretched out his hand over the sea; and the Lord caused the sea to go back by a strong east wind all that night, and made the sea dry land, and the waters were divided."[43] Consider how different this would sound if the strong east wind, blowing all night, had not been included by the author (or by his editors). The account, as given, invites inquiry, including consideration of a vital question: What is possible? Such an inquiry, which seems to be promoted by the Hebrew Bible (as one can see by delving into the Talmud and other extended and often ingenious exercises in biblical interpretation), affects how one reads a number of stories and how one understands the encounters with the Divine that human beings may on occasion have. It may be impossible for us to exaggerate the sublimity of the intimations of the Divine found in the Bible.

A recent *New York Times* story reports scientific findings that bear upon what happened with Moses and his people. That article begins:

> Applying an expert knowledge of wind over water, two oceanographers have developed what they say is a plausible scientific explanation for the parting of the waters that enabled the Israelites to make their miraculous escape from Egypt in the biblical story of the Exodus.[44]

This account of the parting of the sea was anticipated by historians who could speak of the fortuitous concatenation of events that permitted the Israelites to cross the water and thus escape the Egyptians.[45]

What, then is a miracle? There are, I have been told, three words for *miracle* in biblical Hebrew: *nes* (sign), *ot* (sign), and *mofat* (wondrous sign). That which we call *nature* does not have to be invaded by an outside force for a miracle to occur. A miracle, it seems, is a sign of the ultimate governance of the world (perhaps by an intelligent being) as manifested in something out of the ordinary that has happened. The historian or the oceanographer can make instructive inquiries into the facts surrounding the sea-parting matter under review—but there still remain such questions as how Moses knew when to stretch out his hand (or when to do something else) and how others knew what to make of all this.

We as modern rationalists should take to heart here the observation by that prince of modern rationalists, Niccolò Machiavelli, who reported that a grave accident in a city is always preceded by a sign.[46] Perhaps we, working from his authority, might add that one may be able to reason back to miracles (or to a divine interest in the fate of a people) by considering how things have indeed come out.

VI

All this bears upon how biblical prophecy is to be regarded. Prophecy means not only predictions of things to come but also (perhaps even more) interpretations of the things that are happening or have happened (including, of course, dreams and other visitations). An overall problem here, for us perhaps but not (it seems) for the authors of the biblical books, is what it means to say, "The Lord said . . ." Divine messages, it also seems, are conveyed many ways—just as there are many ways among human beings for imagining and otherwise thinking about things.

Prophecy, at least in the Hebrew Bible, seems to be intimately connected with ruling or with preparing a people for proper rule, which may include restoring them to a better condition than that into which they have fallen. It has been argued: "The American tradition of popular government in the person of [Abraham] Lincoln [can be] seen to depend upon the statesman as prophet. And prophecy, as [one can learn] from [Leo] Strauss, who had it from Maimonides—and ultimately from Plato's Athenian Stranger [in the *Laws*], was the political name for political science."[47] The rhetorical aspects of prophecy are evident here, contributing as it does to effective rule.

The faith or doctrines, or even the stories, of the Hebrew Bible may be hard for outsiders to assess properly. But we have seen, on the word of Moses himself in the fourth chapter of *Deuteronomy*, that other peoples would be impressed by the way of life—the ordinances and statutes—of the Israelites. Evidently those measures are in themselves comprehensible by others; they do not depend upon the stories in the Bible about the relations between God and human beings, or even upon any special knowledge of God. Other peoples, however limited they may be in their grasp of the language and the history and perhaps the circumstances of the Israelites, should be able (Moses indicates) to recognize the wisdom of the arrangements by which his people live.

We can leave for another occasion the significance of the fact that many of those arrangements, pronounced by Moses and his God to be unchangeable, are no longer observed by most Jews around the world, and not only those arrangements which deal with sacrifices or require the long-destroyed Temple and its institutions. In this respect, the Jews of our time have become much like the other peoples of the world that Moses speaks of. Modern Jews, like thoughtful Gentiles, can observe the Israelites' statutes and ordinances from afar, admiring them perhaps but *not* (because of their circumstances, if not also because of their inclinations?) adopting them as fully their own. In this, as in many other ways, many (perhaps most) modern Jews have become like the bolder members of that ancient Jewish sect we now know as the first Christians, considering many of the ancient prescriptions laid down by Moses to be no longer applicable to everyday life.

VII

The *Deuteronomy* celebration of the Mosaic ordinances and statutes anticipates, for a people still wandering in the desert, a settled life in the Promised Land, the place where that temple will be built around which much of the life of the community can be organized into what *we* call a "religion." All this, I have noticed, is at the beginning of the life of the Israelites as an organized people, a life described and provided for in the Torah.[48]

At the other end of the Hebrew Bible chronologically is *Esther*, one of the last books included in the canon. There has always been some question about the inclusion in the Bible of a text that has in it no explicit references to God. Mordecai does tell his niece Esther that if she did not help save her people, then help would "come from another place."[49] I have been told that the word here for place—*makom*—is one of the terms associated with God. But here, as elsewhere, God is no more than hinted at. And yet *Esther* has always been a very popular book, accounting for that "topsy-turvy world of exile" reflected in the Purim festival, a festival that still has a wide appeal.[50]

It is useful to be reminded, in preparation for my concluding remarks in this introduction to biblical thought, of the story of *Esther*. There is (we are told by a modern scholar) first the plotting of Haman and how he is foiled:

> When Ahasuerus, the great Persian king [Xerxes?] was looking for a successor to Queen Vashti whom he had deposed at a drinking party for being disobedient, he finally chose the Jewish maid, Esther, or Hadassah (however, he did not realize that she was Jewish). Mordecai, the uncle who had raised her, had once saved the king's life but had never been rewarded for it ([*Esther*] chs. 1–2).

After Haman son of Hammedatha, the king's prime minister and a mortal enemy of Mordecai, had persuaded the king to permit a pogrom in which all Jews—men, women, and children—would be killed and their property plundered on the 13th of the month of Adar, Mordecai persuaded Queen Esther to risk execution by appearing before the king, unannounced, to intercede for her people (chs. 3–4). Though Esther broke the law by appearing before the king unannounced, she was warmly received by him; and he eagerly accepted her invitation to attend, along with Haman, a dinner for the three of them at her quarters. At that party the king, who was in the mood to grant Esther virtually any wish, was asked only one thing: that the three of them attend another party there the next day. While returning home, Haman was infuriated to see Mordecai the Jew still refusing to bow down to him. At home, at the suggestion of his wife, Zeresh, Haman decided to have a stake constructed at his place and the next morning to ask the king for permission to impale the defiant Mordecai on it (ch. 5).

But that night the king, unable to sleep, had the court records read to him and so learned of how Mordecai had saved him—and yet had gone unrewarded for it. Thus, the next morning when asked by the king what the king should do to honor "a certain" benefactor, Haman, thinking that the king had Haman himself in mind, recommended that a high-ranking official lead the king's "friend," clothed in the king's robe and riding on the king's horse, through the streets of Susa, calling everyone's attention to the king's benefactor. Ahasuerus accepted Haman's advice. But to Haman's chagrin, Haman had to do all that for Mordecai! (ch. 6)

Later that day, when Ahasuerus, Queen Esther, and Haman were at Esther's second party, Esther finally revealed to the king that she, along with her innocent people, the Jews, were to be annihilated because of Haman. Realizing that he had been grievously misled, the king bolted from the room in a rage, only to return shortly and find Haman "pawing" the queen, begging for her forgiveness. Haman, of course, was executed immediately, being impaled on the very stake he had constructed for Mordecai (ch. 7).[51]

Then there is our scholar's follow-up to the destruction of Haman:

Mordecai, whose relationship to the queen was revealed then by Esther, was rewarded by being made prime minister. Moreover, because the first edict instituting the pogrom against the Jews could not be revoked, Mordecai was allowed to draft a new royal edict, whereby the Jews were encouraged to defend themselves against their enemies on the 13th of Adar. Many pagans, including government officials, began to side with the Jews (ch. 8).

On the appointed day, 75,000 people who took up arms against the Jews throughout the empire were killed, plus 510 people in Susa, including Haman's ten sons. (However, nowhere was there any plundering by the Jews.) While the Jews throughout the empire celebrated their great victory the following day (i.e., on the 14th of Adar), the Jews living in Susa, thanks to Esther's further inter-

> cession to the king on their behalf, were granted permission to use that day for exposing on the city wall the corpses of Haman's sons and for routing out and killing the last remnant of their enemies, 300 in number. Thus, the Jews of Susa could not celebrate their victory until the 15th of Adar.
>
> Eventually, the story of Esther, Mordecai, and Haman was officially commemorated, by order of Mordecai and Esther, on the 14th and 15th of Adar and was known as the festival of Purim, the name coming from the fact that earlier Haman had cast *pûr*, or lots, to determine the most propitious day for his pogrom (ch. 9). Thus were the Jews saved by Queen Esther, and as prime minister Mordecai continued to serve well both the king and the Jewish people (ch. 10).[52]

Are there not in the story of Mordecai echoes of the story of Joseph in Egypt?[53]

I mention in passing that there are, in an ancient Greek version of *Esther*, six extended passages (107 verses in all) that have no counterpart in the traditional Hebrew text. And, it has been noticed, "the most striking addition in the Greek text [of *Esther*] is God himself, the word or his name occurring over fifty times."[54] This addition, I venture to suggest, reflects an understanding of things significantly different from that in the traditional Hebrew text, whatever the Hebrew source may have been upon which the Greek text is based.

VIII

Esther is an Exilic book, telling a story of Jews in the Diaspora (in this case, in the Persian Empire). The almost fiendish delight at the fall of Haman exhibited by Jews down to our day during Purim celebrations can be understood to reflect the dreadful treatment Jews have suffered at the hands of Gentiles for more than two millennia now. An unsympathetic Martin Luther wrote that the Jews "love the book of *Esther* which so befits their bloodthirsty, vengeful, murderous greed and hope."[55]

Our observations about how the career of Macbeth appears to the people of Scotland who know nothing about the witches he encountered should help us see better the story of *Esther*, if not the entire Hebrew Bible. There is in the *Esther* story, about the fate of another bloody tyrant, no reference either to prayer or to God. That is, here too there is nothing equivalent to Macbeth's witches made available to the community at large. There *is* in *Esther* a reference to fasting by the threatened Jews.[56] It is evident that those Jews are still identifiable as such, following as they do rules different from the Persians, so much so that Haman can accuse them to the king of being a seditious enclave in the country, following their own laws rather than the laws of the king.[57] Still, it is a highly assimilated Jewish community: even the names of Mordecai and Esther are not Hebrew; her name, a Talmudic commentator suggests, is derived from that of the goddess Ishtar.[58] Those who insisted upon this book for the long-established canon may have sensed that it aptly dramatized the circumstances and choices that most Jews (many of whom were by then in the Diaspora) would confront for some time.

This is the way things happen in exile, at least in that exile which follows upon the people having once been established in the Promised Land. The hand of the Divine is far less evident in exile than it would have been either in the Holy Land or on the way there. Also, Exilic Jews do not have authoritative guides (such as the Temple authorities) who can direct their daily activities, interpret their experiences for them, and shape their opinions about both the highest and the lowest things.

Esther shows how things *can* look from the outside. Thus, as we have seen, the insomniac king asked to be read to, and the account read is of a service done him by a man who had not been properly acknowledged—and this helped topple the murderous Haman. Earlier, Mordecai had said to Esther: "[W]ho knoweth whether thou art not come to royal estate for such a time as this?"[59] Would not such elements—the insomnia of the king, what was read to him, and the status of a Jewish woman in the Persian court—once have been explicitly identified as the doings of God?

That kind of conclusion is now left to inference. But, we can see, the events that prove decisive do seem to be intimately related to the characters of the people involved. Things follow naturally, we would say, because of the characters of the participants in this drama. That this is the way things work out would once have been understood as manifestations of the divine ordering of the world, however the form of the story or of the storytelling is changed because of circumstances.

Esther, then, *is* for a people in exile—and so it may seem quite relevant today to much of the Jewish people in Diaspora. But one caution is in order here: Jews today, in the West, find themselves in quite different circumstances from those of their ancestors in ancient Egypt, Babylon, Persia, and Rome. The dominant religion of the people among whom they now live is itself grounded in Judaism. Indeed, we may well wonder, what would the general understanding of Judaism be like today (including among most Jews) without Christianity throwing light back upon it? There are, we know, a multitude of non-biblical sects all over the earth, many of them larger than the Jewish sect, which do not get the attention worldwide (both favorable and unfavorable) that Judaism does.

IX

I have considered how the episodes in *Esther* would have been described if they had taken place either in the Holy Land or in much earlier times. If, for example, they had been described as various events are in *Kings* and *Chronicles*, Mordecai would perhaps have been cast as a prophet and Esther as a Rebekah-like figure (somehow inspired by God) concerned for the interests of her loved ones.

If the episodes of *Esther* had been described in the old-fashioned manner, with explicit divine interventions in one form or another, we as moderns might then have been encouraged to ask: What really happened? It would probably be assumed, in our answer to that question, that there is usually a kernel of truth to a biblical story, however fanciful that story may seem to the modern rationalist.

The kernel of truth that "everybody" might well accept in the *Exodus* sea-crossing account is that the desperate people of Israel did manage to cross that sea in a memorable way. The Israelites in Egypt had already experienced a series of remarkable episodes that led to their liberation—and that series, and the eventual outcome, could usefully be put in terms of divine providence. However, neither this "success story" nor that in the time of Mordecai is more remarkable, in critical respects, than that of the Jews in the latter half of the twentieth century. Who would have thought that any people that had been subjected to something as devastating as the Nazi reign of terror would be able to establish, for the first time in almost two thousand years, a vigorous country of their own in the Holy Land? Is not this so amazing that it can plausibly be identified as miraculous?

We have already noticed that the miracles of the Bible usually presuppose the presence and workings of the matter that is transformed or otherwise dealt with. How does God work His will? Perhaps in the somewhat curious way that the king does in *Esther*. The decree he had originally issued, looking to an organized assault upon the Jews, "cannot" be revoked even by himself after the exposure and death of Haman. But another decree permits the Jews to prepare themselves for battle and hence to defend themselves against the consequences of the prior decree. Thus, things set in motion continue to work as they "naturally" do—and other things have to be depended upon to counter them. (This way of proceeding does have the advantage, for the Jews, of permitting them to identify and hence to be able to destroy many of their enemies.)

How much of the Bible, we can well wonder, could be retold in the more secular mode of *Esther*?[60] What differences would such refashioning make? We learn from Jesus, with his uses of parables, that messages often need to be adapted to one's audiences. Was he not in this, as in many other ways, very much a Jew, an understandably prudent Jew?

In considering what the best way is of describing the various episodes and the centuries-long development found in the Hebrew Bible, we may again be drawing upon the political implications of prophecy. The question of "what really happened" is one that is asked both by the pious man and by the metaphysician—and the effort to answer such questions encounters that tension between Reason and Revelation which is longstanding and which may be reflected as well in the perennial struggle between Philosophy and Poetry. An underlying question here is: Was God at work on any particular occasion? What do both this question and any answer to it mean?

We have learned, from watching modern physicists at work, how critical minute signs may be, the measurement and interpretation of which can lead them both to breathtaking cosmological speculations and to puzzling conjectures about fundamental particles. The rest of us, partly because of what we have learned from watching our physicists, can ask: What are the things that we see happening in the world, both in nature and in history, signs of? Further questions here are the following: What signs are there today that a believer could, not implausibly, interpret as God's providence at work? Is the world such, because of a Ruling Mind, that things usually somehow work out sensibly? How, for example, *should* the fate of modern Israel be understood—or is a half-century not enough time for a reliable judgment?

I have noticed similarities between Judaism and Christianity and their reliance upon one another. I have also noticed some critical differences. It is revealing that the Hebrew Bible again and again records episodes in which a precarious presumptuousness on the part of the people of Israel takes the form not only of failing to do what had been ordained by the statutes and ordinances of God but also of doing more than what had been ordained by those statutes and ordinances. The latter misconduct may be seen, for example, when an ill-fated Uzza touches the Ark when it is about to fall and when an ill-fated Saul offers sacrifices when Samuel is not available.[61]

The Greek Bible, on the other hand, seems more receptive to those who would do much more than is commanded. Consider, for example, how Jesus extends the commandment against adultery to an injunction even against lustful thoughts.[62] To what extent does this kind of interpretation of the Mosaic code anticipate, if it does not facilitate, a depreciation of that political order to which prophecy in the Hebrew Bible is in large part dedicated?

It is revealing that Jesus' healing on the Sabbath can be said to have first moved his critics to try to destroy him.[63] That is, the community can be threatened by benevolent efforts that undermine the established order and point ahead to a breakdown in a salutary discipline, especially in the tumultuous times that Jesus encountered. Whether the souls refined by these efforts are elevated thereby and whether the political order being protected was already in the course of ultimate dissolution are questions that can be, and indeed have been, much debated. A suggestive parable is offered us here by the wily Machiavelli:

> One reads in the ancient things of the Venetian Republic that when a Venetian galley returned to Venice there arose certain differences between those on the galley and the people. Whereupon the tumult came to arms, and neither the force of ministers, nor reverence for the citizens, nor fear of the magistrates, could quiet the thing, when suddenly a gentleman, who had been their captain a year before, appeared before those sailors and through love of him they were parted and abandoned the fight. This obedience generated such suspicion in the Senate, that a little afterwards the Venetians, either through prison or through death, assured themselves of him. I conclude then that [this kind of procedure] is useful in a prince and pernicious in a citizen. [It is pernicious, in a citizen] not only to the fatherland but [also] to himself: to the [fatherland] because these modes prepare the way to tyranny, and to himself because his city, in suspecting his mode of procedure, is constrained to assure herself to his harm.[64]

Machiavelli's Venetian (Uzza-like) gentleman evidently had not "intended" anything subversive of the Venetian Republic. Was it not imprudent of him, however, not to be aware of how his intervention would look? Should he, in self-defense, have gone ahead with a usurpation of power once he had intervened? Is it not significant that Machiavelli leaves the gentleman anonymous? Had that Venetian, once "exposed," foolishly failed to exploit the opportunity he had had to make a name for himself?[65]

The tension displayed here by Machiavelli between *love* and *duty* is prudent to keep in mind as we think further not only about the lessons of both the Hebrew and the Greek Bibles but also about the lessons generated by the confrontation between, on the one hand, the Old Way that was somehow responsible for (and that may be in some ways redefined by) the New and, on the other hand, the New Way that remains somewhat dependent upon the Old. The signs here invite, perhaps require, respectful if not even reverent interpretation.

Chapter Four

Cain and Abel[66]

> Every art and every inquiry, and likewise every action and choice, seems to aim at some good, and hence it has been beautifully said that the good is that at which all things aim.
>
> Aristotle[67]

I

It is with considerable gratitude that I once again find myself with an opportunity to acknowledge a teacher of almost a half-century ago. I studied with Malcolm P. Sharp in my first year at the University of Chicago Law School in 1948–1949, taking his three-quarter course in contract law and preparing a paper (in the legal writing course) on his then-recently-published article on aggression.[68] Decades later I was to study with him again when he, after retiring from law school teaching, joined the faculty of Rosary College, something that the imaginative leadership of Sister Candida Lund, then president of this college, made possible.

Mr. Sharp's "Aggression" article remains challenging and hence instructive. It is very much concerned with what he describes as "our propensity to lethal hostility."[69] Mr. Sharp, in his valiant efforts here, was a spiritual descendant of the first man in the Western world who is known to have concerned himself with the enduring problem of "our propensity to lethal hostility," the author of the story of Cain and Abel in *Genesis*. Mr. Sharp came to regard the Sermon on the Mount as the culmination of the remedy implicit in the *Genesis* account. Such an approach as that found in the Sermon might have prompted the author of our story of fratricide to ask: "Do we have to say, if we recognize Cain to be truly bad, that Abel was simply good?"

A celebrated anthropologist of our day cautions us about how to approach the opening chapters of *Genesis*:

> No one of adult mind today would turn to the Book of Genesis to learn of the origins of the earth, the plants, the beasts, and man. There was no flood, no tower of Babel, no first couple in paradise, and between the first known appearance of men on earth and the first buildings of cities, not one generation (Adam to Cain) but a good two million must have come into this world and passed along. Today we turn to science for our imagery of the past and of the structure of the world, and what the spinning demons of the atom and the galaxies of the telescope's eye reveal is a wonder that makes the babel of the Bible seem a toyland dream of the dear childhood of our brain.[70]

This is a salutary caution, if only that it reminds us of the effort that is required to perceive what is truly serious and challenging in our ancient inheritance.

We all know the story of Cain and Abel. It is frequently alluded to, even in the popular press. (One may wonder how the name of Cain has come to be adopted by some families in recent centuries.) So pervasive is the reputation of Cain that disturbed men can identify themselves with Cain, as may be seen in a crime story recently published by an alumna of Rosary College. Her book is about a young man who killed a couple in Winnetka, Illinois. This young man included, in a testament he wrote, these observations:

> Remember that I am the Adversary, the Interloper. . . . Remember that I am the second son of Adam and Eve. Remember that I rose up in front of god and slew my brother Abel out of greed. Remember it all, but if you should somehow forget some of it, just remember this, My name is Cain and I kill people.[71]

There is here a revealing slip: Cain is not "the second son of Adam and Eve." This slip does suggest, however, how Cain must have felt—that he had been demoted with respect to his brother.

We all sense, at least in the Western world, that the story of Cain and Abel is fundamental to human nature and to social relations. A thoughtful commentator upon *Genesis* has this to offer us about the significance of fratricide:

> The theme of brother killing brother is a common beginning for many peoples. The most famous is the story of Romulus and Remus. It is by no accident that

> in this case we are more familiar with the Roman myth than with any corresponding Greek myth. The political, in the most common usage of the word, played a higher role in Rome than it did in Athens. In the Bible, too, the fratricide is committed by the founder of the first city. The myth or account is an essentially political account, though the fratricide itself is an essentially prepolitical act. The founding of a city requires a leader, and yet there is a natural equality among brothers. The awareness of this difficulty seems to lie behind both accounts. Greek myth, on the other hand, deals more with patricide, which ultimately means the attempt to become one's father by replacing him. Motivations for erasing one's own origins, or rather becoming one's own origins, lie in the attempt to assert one's own complete independence of being. In that sense patricide is essentially an apolitical act.[72]

The political aspects of fratricide are exposed to view in civil war. I draw upon the passions of domestic strife in the opening passage of my commentary upon the Amendments to the Constitution:

> The greatest wars fought by the American people have been civil wars. The first was the struggle between Patriots and Loyalists from 1774 to 1784; the second was the struggle between Northerners and Southerners from 1857 to 1865. . . . Civil wars tend to be exceptionally destructive, partly because the cost for each victory is paid twice over: the victor suffers not only his own casualties but those of his fraternal opponent as well. The Patriots could refer, as in the 1776 Declaration of Independence, to their "British Brethren." And in the 1863 Gettysburg Address the reference to the "brave men, living and dead, who struggled here" unites the desperate enemies of that battlefield.[73]

Malcolm Sharp attempted to bring all this up-to-date with these controversial observations in his 1947 "Aggression" article:

> When one has watched two world wars and the threat of a third, he may become impressed with the importance of a relatively simple generalization. Independent of all the rational considerations, it appears that the desire to surpass, the impulse to dominate, and simple hatred, combined, perhaps with an impulse to kill, however vicariously, which are constant factors in wars, have together a distinct force which creates for our society its outstanding problem. This is the force which is needed to release the destructive energy of the new weapons. The first, and perhaps a sufficient, means toward solution of our problem seems to be clear recognition of the nature of this force and a simple but strong determination to discount and control it in the conduct of international affairs.[74]

Even so, it is perhaps not insignificant that the story of Cain and Abel does *not* seem to play a dominant role in traditional biblical studies.

II

What happens in the story as it has come down to us? Here is the account in chapter IV of *Genesis*:

1. The man [Adam] knew his wife Eve and she conceived and bore Cain saying, I have acquired a male child with the help of the Lord.
2. She bore his brother Abel. Abel became a keeper of sheep and Cain became a tiller of soil.
3. And in process of time it came to pass, that Cain brought of the fruit of the ground an offering unto the Lord.
4. And Abel, he also brought of the firstlings of his flock and of the fat thereof. And the Lord had respect unto Abel and to his offering:
5. But unto Cain and to his offering He had not respect. And Cain was very wroth, and his face fell.
6. And the Lord said unto Cain, Why art thou wroth? And why is thy face fallen?
7. Surely if thou doest well there will be a lifting: And if thou doest not well, sin lieth at the opening. And unto thee shall be his desire, and thou shalt rule over him.
8. And Cain said to his brother Abel . . . and when they were in the field Cain arose and killed his brother Abel.
9. And the Lord said unto Cain, Where is thy brother Abel? And he said, I do not know; am I my brother's keeper?
10. And He said, What hast thou done? The voice of thy brother's blood crieth unto me from the ground.
11. And now art thou cursed from the earth, which hath opened her mouth to receive thy brother's blood from thy hand;
12. When thou tillest the ground, it shall not henceforth yield unto thee her strength; a fugitive and a vagabond shalt thou be in the earth.
13. And Cain said unto the Lord, my punishment is greater than I can bear.
14. Behold, Thou hast driven me out this day from the face of the earth; and from Thy face shall I be hid; and I shall be a fugitive and a vagabond in the earth; and it shall come to pass, that every one that findeth me shall slay me.
15. And the Lord said unto him, Therefore whosoever slayeth Cain, vengeance shall be taken on him sevenfold. And the Lord set a mark upon Cain, lest any finding him should kill him.
16. And Cain went from before the face of God and dwelt in the land of Nod, east of Eden.

17. And Cain knew his wife; and she conceived, and bore Enoch: and he builded a city, and called the name of the city, after the name of his son, Enoch. . . .
25. And Man [Adam] knew his wife again: and she bore a son, and called his name Seth: For God, said she, hath appointed me another seed instead of Abel, whom Cain slew.
26. And to Seth, to him also there was born a son: and he called his name Enosh: then began men to call upon the name of the Lord.[75]

This Genesis account is summed up in this way for the modern reader in the opening paragraph of an *Encyclopedia of Religion* entry:

> *Cain and Abel*, the first two sons of Adam and Eve, the progenitors of the race according to the Bible, after their banishment from the garden of Eden (*Genesis* 4). Cain (Heb., *Qayin*), the elder, was a farmer; Abel (Heb., *Hevel*) was a shepherd. The biblical text jumps from their birth to a later episode when both made (apparently votary) offerings to the Lord: Cain presented a meal offering of his fruits and grains, while Abel offered up the firstlings of his sheep. The offering of Cain was rejected by the Lord, and that of Abel was accepted. No reason for this is given, and generations of pious attempts to justify this event have been made by contrasting the intentions of the donors and the nature and quality of their donations. Cain's despondency led to a divine caution to resist the temptation to sin (*Genesis* 4:6–7); presumably this refers to the jealous urges and hostile resentments Cain felt. But the elder brother was overwrought and killed his brother in the field. This led to the punishment of Cain: like his father, he would not farm a fertile earth; and, like him, he would be banished "eastward of Eden." Fearing further retribution, Cain was given a protective "sign," whose aspect delighted the fancy in later legends and art. There is a deliberate reuse of the language of the temptation and punishment of Adam and Eve (*Genesis* 3) in the ensuing account of the temptation and punishment of Cain (*Genesis* 4:1–17).[76]

One more passage, by way of recapitulation before I venture upon commentary of my own, is offered us by Maimonides:

> Among the things you ought also to know and have your attention aroused to is the manifestation of wisdom constituted by the facts that the two children of *Adam* were called *Cain* and *Abel*; that it was *Cain* who slew *Abel in the field* [*Genesis* 4:8]; that both of them perished, though the aggressor had a respite; and that only *Seth* [the third son of Adam and Eve] was vouchsafed a true existence. *For God hath appointed me another seed*. [*Genesis* 4:25] This has already been shown to be correct.[77]

I note at the outset of my commentary that of the three births explicitly connected with Adam and Eve (Cain, Abel, and Seth), it is only with respect to

Cain that Eve is somewhat boastful. Adam is mentioned as having conceived children, but not any more than that is said about him in connection with them. (Later, in the biblical stories, we sometimes see mothers dominate the upbringing and careers of their children. The greatest case of that in the Hebrew Bible is the series of interventions by Rebekah in the lives of Jacob and Esau. The greatest case of that in the Greek Bible is the part played by Mary in the life of Jesus.) We may well wonder whether we are intended to believe that Cain inherited Eve's deviousness while Abel inherited Adam's gullibility. Both Adam (in the Garden) and Abel may be primarily keepers or tenders rather than farmers; both suffer from relying upon craftier relatives.[78]

Thus, Abel followed Adam's pre-Expulsion calling, that of tending; Cain followed the calling of the farmer, to which Adam was relegated after his expulsion from the garden. But Cain suffered the fate that many farmers have encountered down to our day: the soil stopped yielding its strength—and he moved to the city. Is the life of a city dweller essentially that of a "vagabond" in that one is not really rooted in any soil?

There are a number of all-too-human features, including the blighting effect upon Cain of what he had done to his brother. Such an effort may be seen, much later, in Shakespeare's *Hamlet*, when Claudius, who had killed his brother to get his throne and his wife, recognizes the primal curse of Cain upon him.[79] But Claudius, unlike Cain, goes on from one misdeed to another, until he is destroyed.

III

The Cain Complex may be intrinsic to human nature, at least as a recurring condition. Both what he is and what he does seem to depend upon the knowledge human beings have, after the Garden, of good and bad. That the Cain Complex may be intrinsic to humanity is suggested by the fact that the first social actions performed outside the Garden culminated in a murder. Just as in the Garden the first deaths seem to have been killings—the killings of animals for the skins with which God clothed Adam and Eve—so outside the Garden the first death was also a killing.

So much is killing a problem that the first positive law promulgated among human beings outside of the Garden is God's injunction against the killing of the guilty Cain. People have to be restrained, it seems, from doing what they would otherwise be inclined to do to him. Neither Cain nor people at large have to be *told* that killing of the innocent is bad; they do have to be told how they should, and should not, respond to it.

A curious feature of Cain's psyche is that he does care, perhaps too much or in the wrong way, what God thinks of him. He seems to believe that it is good that God approve of him, even though he does seem ignorant of the extent of God's power (for example, as to what God already knows about the fate of Abel). Indeed, God seems to be regarded by Cain as the source of all good. Perhaps he has been influenced by the stories that he, as the first son, got from his parents after their expulsion from the Garden.[80]

The Cain Complex is such, moreover, that the first violent crime committed by human beings is intimately connected with "religious" differences. This points up how critical one's standing before God can be for the human being. This is evident, later, in the Israelite opinion that it is piety above all which matters—and this does not depend upon investigation but ultimately upon submission. Abel, for one, seems to be rather simple; it is Cain who thinks and worries (just as later Judas Iscariot may have been disturbed at not being sufficiently appreciated by the Divine).[81]

IV

Thinking and worrying promote innovation. Cain is one of the greatest innovators in the Hebrew Bible, contending for top honors with pioneers such as Abraham and Moses. Certainly, he is the greatest non-Israelite innovator in the Hebrew Bible, except of course for God.

We can count the ways in which Cain innovated, beginning with his recourse to sacrifice. This was *not* (so far as we know) at God's suggestion; nor is anything said about the ritual followed or of the use, if any, of a shrine or an altar. It is as if as little as possible should be said here about how this sacrifice was conducted, something that is to be properly provided for later. (Was there something anticipating paganism about the way Cain, if not also Abel, proceeded?) Still, Cain does sense that it is important for the human being to "get right" with God—and this he tries to do, but with disastrous consequences, perhaps in part because he wants to be in control. (Was Abel saved here by being a follower, something that may be usual for, if not essential to, true piety?)

Cain is also an innovator in expressions of pride and envy. He as the older son may consider it his inherent right, if not even his duty, to take the lead.

This leads to the innovation of homicide. This may include the presumption of attempting to change the divinely ordained order of things.[82]

The central innovation here may be that of deception—the deception by Cain of Abel and then by Cain of God. In this he has pre-Expulsion models: first the Serpent and then Adam and Eve. The questions put by God to Adam and Eve and then to Cain may seem somewhat deceptive as well, insofar as they suggest that God does not know the answers to his questions. The questions are: "Where art thou?" and "Where is thy brother Abel?"[83] But were not these questions designed not to mislead but rather to make Adam and Eve and then Cain face up to what they had done and what they had become?

Then Cain, who had been an innovator in homicide, became an innovator in apprehensiveness lest he be killed in turn. Adam and Eve, before him, had not been similarly apprehensive following upon their misconduct (which they did try to conceal?). Cain misses here, however, the opportunity to be an innovator in confession once God had questioned him, a response which might have helped to redeem him.

This apprehensiveness seems related to the innovation of Cain as city-builder. Perhaps he had come to recognize that the more aggressive human being needs a city both to restrain him before he goes bad and to protect him from the undisciplined vengeance of others once he is widely regarded as bad.[84]

Finally, Cain is an innovator in the arts, at least by laying the groundwork for them and fathering a line of innovators in the arts. Do those arts include poetry, and if so does this anticipate the role of revelation in human affairs? It is poetic inspiration (sometimes in the form of revelation?) which permits us to discern and to learn what might have happened and why in the relations between God and man.

Is Cain as much of an innovator as he was primarily because he *was* first among the male human beings born outside of the Garden? That there may have been something special about him is suggested by our suspicion that Abel, even if he had been first, would not have had the temperament of the innovator. Is this why Abel the Follower (a born follower?) perishes while Cain survives, at least for a while? Is all this related to the martyr-like quality of Abel, something that later made him appealing among Christians as an exemplar of the passive virtues? (*Following*, we have noticed, may be essential to piety. It can be good to be a follower if the right things are followed. But Abel followed Cain into the fields as well as into sacrificing. Proper leadership may be needed for the most useful piety. But can the true leader, the genuine innovator, be pious himself in this sense?)

V

Whatever the many innovations of Cain, what we know him best for—or, should we say, worst for?—is one of them, the killing of his brother. In this Cain may have, knowingly or not, imitated Abel. That is, Cain seems to say, if blood-sacrifice is what clearly satisfies God, then here it is in its most dramatic form!

In proceeding thus Cain obviously does not understand God or proper sacrifice or what God might have wanted. In short, he (unlike Abel?) has no reliable notion of what God is like. Yet he is more than once in direct communication with God (just as Noah, Abraham, and Moses were to be afterwards). Direct communication with God seems to be something that both Cain and the author of *Genesis* take for granted.[85]

Up to the time that Cain kills Abel, he had had to settle in his piety for killing (that is, harvesting) vegetation—unless, of course, he had been willing to sacrifice his own life. Suppose this had occurred to him. Would God have stopped him in time (as He was later to stop Abraham from sacrificing Isaac)? But, it seems, this never occurred to Cain: he was too much moved by the desire for self-preservation, as well as for self-assertion, to sacrifice himself.

We need not concern ourselves with whether Cain "really" dealt directly with God, or with whether God concerned Himself with the affairs of Cain and his family, or with whether human beings can know what God thinks and does. Nothing that happens in the story of Cain and Abel requires the divine actions reported there, but rather the opinions of human beings that God exists and conducts Himself somewhat as reported there. What is also needed, and what the author relies upon to make the story comprehensible, is a reliable moral judgment. Such moral judgment can carry the reader a long way, however many obscurities there may remain in the account we have.

VI

That there are challenging obscurities in the story of Cain and Abel should become apparent to the careful reader who dwells upon their story. We cannot begin to be confident that we have a reliable sense of this account if we do not at least recognize its obscurities for what they are. These obscurities take the form of various things that are not reported which the reader might, not unreasonably, expect to be reported. An inventory of these omissions is now in order, some of which omissions commentators across the ages have tried to supply one way or another.

The first omission, already touched upon, is an explanation of why God respected Abel's sacrifice and not Cain's. Or, if much of this is primarily in Cain's imagination, why is it that Cain believed that God respected Abel's sacrifice and not Cain's? Is there something about killing and blood and perhaps the roasting of flesh (if that is what was done by Abel) that makes animal sacrifice seem more awesome and hence elevated? Cain would have learned from the sacrifice by Abel, if he did not already know, that killed things stay lifeless—and this can be awe-inspiring.[86]

Some commentators, including some very early rabbis, suggested that while Abel sacrificed the firstlings of his flock, Cain did not use his finest crop. But then, are not firstlings easier to recognize than variations in one's crops? Or was it not what Cain offered, but rather the spirit in which he offered it, that proved troublesome?

There have also been speculations about the relative merits of herding and farming in the Bible. Shepherds move over considerable territory; they need not claim any plot of land. Farmers, on the other hand, are apt to be more possessive; they are more godlike in shaping, or reshaping, the land. This may be seen most dramatically in the building of cities, to which Cain "graduates." It is in cities, by the way, that wickedness reaches its depths in the Bible, such as in Sodom and Gomorrah.

The callings of the brothers are introduced with that of Abel, the younger, mentioned first as if the life of the shepherd is superior. The great men of the Hebrew Bible—such as Abraham, Moses, and David—tend to be shepherds.[87] Still, the emphasis in the story does seem to be upon how "well" Cain should do. Cain senses that he was judged "personally" by God—and that he was found wanting. That is, it can be said, he was discerned (or "prophesied") by God to be the kind of man who would kill a rival who seems to surpass him.

However engaging such speculations may be, the critical lesson here may be that it does not matter what God's basis was for distinguishing between Cain and Abel. There are, we are taught, bound to be differences (if only in perception) among the blessings that a human being has or is denied. The key question is, then, how one responds to the differences, whatever their basis and however they are perceived. Each case will be different in its details, but the principal lesson brought to it from the story of Cain and Abel should be the same.

VII

Another omission of something that we would expect to be told is what Cain said to Abel before he killed him. It is clear from the Hebrew, scholars tell us, that something *said* is required in the sentence, something which appears to have dropped out (if not even been suppressed) in the transmission. Some editors have attempted to supply the omission, the most popular (from antiquity) being "Let us go into the fields." Other editors spare their readers any problem here by saying only that Cain talked with Abel, with no indication that what they had talked about had ever been in the text. It may not be insignificant, by the way, that there is no indication that Abel said anything on that occasion. Some commentators simply confess themselves at a loss as to what was said by Cain.

I venture the suggestion that the author might have (from the beginning) deliberately left the account the way it now is, thereby inviting his readers to think about what Cain said to Abel. One's answer to this question may depend upon how other questions are answered. One's conjectures here could draw upon suppositions about the character of the two brothers, their relations, and the circumstances.

Can we not begin to get some idea about how Cain talked to Abel from what we know about the conversation of his that *is* recorded, what he said to God? He had asked God, "Am I my brother's keeper?" He may have been asking God, in effect, "Do you want me to be Abel's Abel?" (Does Cain dare imply that *God* should have been Abel's keeper, if not also Cain's?) And, we have noticed, Abel as a keeper of animals had killed for his sacrifice the life entrusted to *him*. (It is only occasionally, by the way, that we regard *harvesting* as *killing*.)

One's speculations here could extend to having Cain require Abel somehow to disavow God, thereby negating God's rejection of Cain. Abel thus would have been a martyr to his faith, refusing to side with Cain against God at least to the extent of agreeing that Cain had a proper grievance against God.

An extreme in speculation here, which I have anticipated, would have Cain asking Abel: "If God prefers animal sacrifices, why should *you* not be next?" This suggestion could even foresee Abel's blood enriching the soil, as some pagans were later to do, in order to improve its fertility and to increase its yield. Thus, Abel would be "planted" to advance the interest of agriculture.

This extreme form of speculation could have Abel recognize that he had expended his passion in blood sacrifice, passion related perhaps to exclusion from the wonderful Garden that their parents had once enjoyed. This exercise in speculation could even have Abel *offering* himself as a sacrifice, to help Cain purge his own passion in turn. Would there be something Christ-like in such self-sacrifice? Or would it expose Abel as someone who does not understand what is good for Cain? These questions remind us of how little we know, or perhaps can ever know, about Abel.

Once we have canvassed these and like speculations, we may be obliged to return to the conclusion that the author does not believe it matters what Cain said to Abel or Abel to Cain. Rather, the reader is taught, one simply should not do what Cain did in the circumstances in which he found himself.

VIII

Still another omission, or set of omissions, has to do with details that literal-minded readers find troublesome, such as where Cain found his wife, or who the other people are that Cain is afraid of. (Had Cain already been exposed, therefore, to births and deaths?) We are thus back to the historicity questions we avoided upon opening this discussion. It is obvious that this kind of question does not seem to trouble the author of *Genesis* at all—nor is it very interesting.

Similar omissions include an explanation of how people elsewhere are supposed to know that Cain had killed Abel. Cain's fear may be primary here. Perhaps he believes that other people will find out, as God had found out (and as Eve found out), that Cain had killed Abel. This could be another way of suggesting that Cain does not truly know what God is like. Yet God responds as if there *is* something to Cain's concern about his own safety.

Similar omissions include an explanation of what the life-protecting mark was that Cain carried. On the other hand, the more blighted Cain appears because of what he has done, the less likely it should be that anyone else would want to imitate him by killing Cain.

The omissions of these and like details and explanations, including such things as the instrument used by Cain for the killing (had it been the one Abel had used for *his* sacrifice, or was it a farmer's tool?), suggest that the reader was expected to know the overall story of which the author had given enough of an indication to serve his immediate purposes. This is not an exercise by the author in biology, in history, or in geography; it is instead a study in character and in morality, especially perhaps in piety.[88] An attempt is made thereby to explain how and why the world is the way it obviously is, with violence "always" intrinsic to human society. It is a world, the reader knows, in which men *are* killed and thereby permanently lost to view—and divine intervention cannot be depended upon to avert or to reverse such things. In this way the author teaches, with neither distracting detail nor formulaic concealment, what the circumstances of human beings in this world are truly like. It is not divine intervention that must be looked to for help here, except perhaps in the form of promoting the moral probity which human beings are taught to cherish.

IX

The greatest omission in this story for the modern reader, perhaps, is the lack of any explanation of how Cain (or others elsewhere) could have been expected to know that Cain's killing of Abel was clearly bad. The original misconduct of Adam and Eve had depended upon an explicit prohibition laid down by God about eating of a designated Tree. Not so in Cain's case: he was expected to know better without any explicit prohibition with respect to killing another human being.

It is (to use a post-biblical term) the *naturalness* of the human awareness of what is bad that the doctrinaire modern might find troublesome. Unfortunately, this natural awareness does not suffice to guide and restrain everyone all of the time—and so both the laws of cities and the commands of God are needed to promote human virtue and happiness. This is especially true when the natural acquisitiveness, as well as the natural aggressiveness, of human beings has to be contended with.[89]

That there is something natural about the human awareness of the good as well as of the bad is suggested, without of course the use of the term *natural*, in Moses' leave-taking of the people of Israel. We have seen that he predicts that peoples who hear all the statutes laid down for the Israelites will say, "Surely this great nation is a wise and understanding people."[90] That is, Moses suggests, other peoples will recognize, without the help of the true divine revelation transmitted by Moses (and by others), the merits of the way of life provided by God for the Israelites.

Similarly we, in circumstances far different from those of Cain and Abel, can recognize the merits of how God dealt with Cain in his dreadful extremity. We are reminded that the "propensity to lethal hostility" is deep-rooted in the human race. One form that "lethal hostility" takes is the determination that all too many of us in this country have to kill those who have killed others, something that may be seen in the far greater use of capital punishment in the United States than in any other nation in the Western world today. Malcolm Sharp would have had us notice that even such a mass murderer as Cain—a mass murderer in the sense of the multitude Cain cut off when he killed Abel—even such a mass murderer as Cain was spared the often-corrupting flattery of having others imitate him in his lethal hostility.[91]

Chapter Five

Rebekah, Isaac, and Jacob[92]

Veni, vidi, vici.

Julius Caesar[93]

I

Abraham Lincoln, who was an early supporter in this country of "women's rights"—especially the right of suffrage—opened his famous "House Divided" speech, in 1858, with the observation, "If we could first know *where* we are, and *whither* we are tending, we could better judge *what* to do, and *how* to do it."[94] That speech expressed a concern, a century and a half ago, about the policy of the United States with respect to slavery. But it can be understood as throwing light as well upon women's issues today.

In order for us to know where women are and whither they are tending, it would be useful to determine where they have come from and why they were wherever they were. This might be particularly useful since much *is* made by feminists of the opinions inherited from earlier decades and centuries that affect the status of women down to our day. These inherited opinions are condemned as arbitrary and outmoded. How we identify such opinions, and what we make of them, may very well affect how carefully we can think about the serious questions here.

II

A major influence in the West upon the status of women has been, of course, the Bible. The Greek Bible is often seen as somewhat egalitarian in its teaching (whatever various churches may have done in practice), since women are portrayed as often decisive in the life of Jesus (with his mother, of course, receiving special recognition in some quarters). The Hebrew Bible is another story, being often regarded as generally oppressive of women. Consider, however, the implications of the opening verses of the fifth chapter of *Genesis*: "This is the book of the generations of Adam. In the day that God created man, in the likeness of God made He him; male and female created He them; and blessed them, and called their name Adam, in the day when they were created."[95] Although we must leave discussion of these lines for another occasion, they should at least put us on notice that things may not be as simple as they may usually seem with respect to these matters. But, still, it is striking how this is put: "Male and female created He them . . . and called their name Adam."[96]

I should now like to consider one of the lives in the Hebrew Bible—that of Rebekah, the wife of Isaac, the mother of Esau and Jacob. It is important, I believe, to begin by looking at such stories for themselves alone, guarding thereby against the limitations inherent in the reading of any such story that is done with a view to some use (including polemical use). That is, one should begin by carefully reading the story as much as possible on its own terms. Only when one grasps the enduring teachings of such a story may one be able to apply them sensibly to one's transient concerns.

At the very least, then, we can exercise ourselves thereby in how to study the evidence available in a well-crafted report.

III

That much (some would say, too much) is made of males and maleness in the Hebrew Bible is obvious. Perhaps decisive in revealing the biblical orientation is the fact that the God of the people of Israel can be routinely spoken of as "the God of Abraham, Isaac, and Jacob." Indeed, the most critical way of identifying that people, down to this day, is to speak of them as the descendants of these three men.

It is important, for what we will be looking into here, to notice that it will not do simply to speak either of the descendants of Abraham or of the descendants of Isaac. For Abraham has had through Ishmael, and Abraham and Isaac have had through Esau, many descendants who have not been Jews. Critical, then, in making the Jews who and what they are has been the generating by Jacob, but a Jacob who is very much a descendant of Abraham and Isaac.

IV

Is it not evident to any perceptive reader of chapters 24–33 of *Genesis* that the traditional description could just as aptly be (for some purposes), not "Abraham, *Isaac*, and Jacob" but rather "Abraham, *Rebekah*, and Jacob"? That is, is it not evident that the interventions of Rebekah seem to have been decisive in providing for the transfer of the divine promise given to Abraham and thereafter assumed by Isaac—for the transfer of that promise from Isaac to Jacob rather than (as Isaac seems to have intended) to Esau?

But however decisive Rebekah was in the transfer of the promise, and hence of the authority, it is not her name, but rather that of her husband, which is honored. Indeed, she can sometimes be disparaged as having been underhanded in what she did, even though the Jacob whom she favored has always been considered vital to the character and success of what we now know as the Jewish people.

This bears looking into. We turn to what we can consider "the inside story" of the Jewish people, *the* People of the Torah.

V

This is so much the inside story of the Jewish people that it is to be found at the very heart of the *Book of Genesis*, which recounts the anticipations and the development of that people, leaving it to the next book, *Exodus*, to make a new beginning with Moses. The central verse of *Genesis* may well be verse 40 of chapter 27.[97] This comes at the conclusion of the story of Jacob's deception of Isaac, depriving Esau of the blessing which his father had intended to give him and leaving him instead with a second-best blessing.

Leading up to the center of *Genesis* are the stories of the marriage of Isaac and Rebekah, the births to them of the twins Esau and Jacob, the sale by a hungry Esau of his birthright to Jacob, the marriages of Esau to foreign women, the scheming of Rebekah with Jacob whereby the blind Isaac gives the blessing to Jacob instead of to Esau, and the consequent anger of Esau. Following upon the center of Genesis are the stories of the flight of Jacob from his brother's wrath, the deals made by Jacob with Laban (his mother's relative) whereby Jacob gets Leah and then Rachel in marriage, the dozen children born to these sisters and to their servants (with Jacob as the father), the tricks played by Laban on Jacob to protect Leah's interests and then by Jacob on Laban to protect Jacob's interests, the flight of Jacob with his family and wealth, and his return home to a reconciliation with Esau, some twenty years after his original flight.

Critical to all of these stories prior to the flight of Jacob from home is, of course, Rebekah, his mother, the wife of Isaac.

VI

Isaac is, of the three founding patriarchs (who include his father Abraham and his son Jacob), the only one to remain monogamous. Why was this? His pleasures, as we shall see, were simple. Besides, he was rather passive and, as we shall also see, Rebekah was quite a handful.

The passivity of Isaac goes way back. It is evident in the submissiveness which laid him open to being sacrificed by his father Abraham (upon God's request).[98] And it may be seen that his marriage was arranged for him by a servant of Abraham, if not by God Himself. Once the marriage *is* arranged, it seems that Rebekah runs things thereafter.

Abraham, it can be said, did not trust Isaac to choose a wife for himself. Nor did he want him to return to the land of Abraham's kindred for a wife, lest he not return to the land promised Abraham and his seed. So a trusted servant is sent instead. (When Jacob and his quite large family left that land to go to Egypt, in the time of Joseph and the famine, it took a considerable effort for the Israelites to get back.)

The story of how Rebekah was chosen is told, in effect, four times. Critical to the story of Rebekah at the well are her offers of water for both the servants of Abraham and for their camels. It is a charming story of an eager and excited girl who may well have had her eyes opened to the possibilities of this world when she was exposed to the wealth displayed by the visitors. Her responses at the well seem almost in conformity with some prophecy.[99]

The passivity of Isaac, on the other hand, is further evident in the fact that one of the few accomplishments in his very long life was to dig *again* the wells which had been dug by his father—and these he called by the same names used by his father.[100] Thus he is, at least at first glance, no more than a conduit; certainly, he is not an innovator.

VII

It so happened that the first-born, to whom God's promise would ordinarily be transmitted, was one of twins. These were the only children Isaac ever had, born to him (at age sixty) twenty years after his marriage began. Even while the twins were in Rebekah's womb, the children contended with each other.[101] So marked was their contention, it seems, that their mother sought an explanation from the Lord and was given a prophecy that the younger was to supplant his brother (hence the name, Jacob). Each of her sons, she was told, would found a people.[102]

The fact that it is reported that Rebekah had been given this prophecy—that "the Lord [had] said [these things] unto her"[103]—is often neglected in assessments of what she does, as is the fact that Jacob is several times spoken to by the Lord after he secures his father's blessing.[104] Of course, it will be said by some, experiences of divine revelation are subjective things—but no more so, one might reply, than the importance and consequence of receiving a paternal blessing.

VIII

In any event, it is not mere subjectivity that leads the reader to distinguish Esau from Jacob. Since they *were* born at virtually the same time, and of the same father, it is hardly likely that Rebekah would prefer one to the other merely as "the baby of the family" (in the way, say, that Jacob came to prefer Joseph and Benjamin, who had the added attraction for him of having been the children of Rachel, the woman he loved most).

Esau and Jacob seem to be two quite different kinds of men, from early on. One is a hunter, of a rough and ready sort; the other, more sedentary, a tender of flocks. The life of Jacob, then, is steadier, and is reflected in the fact that he has a more reliable source of food than does Esau, who on one occasion has to barter away his birthright ("despising" it) in order to get something immediately to satisfy his appetite.[105] Esau eats voraciously on that occasion, which suggests something about his lack of self-control, and hence about his ability to rule himself and others.

IX

There are, then, vital differences between Esau and Jacob on the basis of which one might sensibly choose between them. It is not unreasonable to suppose that Rebekah preferred Jacob for the very reasons that the typical reader of *Genesis* can prefer him. Perhaps it should be added that in preferring him, Rebekah preferred someone much like herself in shrewdness, a timely shrewdness which may not be unrelated (in its development) to one's formally subordinate position in society.

No reasons are given explicitly by the author for Rebekah's preference. Perhaps the reader is invited to work out the reasons for himself, developing thereby some of the shrewdness exhibited by Rebekah. But we are not left with any doubts as to why *Isaac* prefers Esau. That he is the first-born is, at least for him, obviously important. But it can also be reported: "Now Isaac loved Esau, because he did eat of his venison; and Rebekah loved Jacob."[106] Thus, we see, Rebekah is less transparent than Isaac. To say that she preferred Jacob may be saying no more than that she believed him better qualified to serve as the heir of God's great promise.

That Isaac's preference for Esau is considerably influenced by his appetites is to be seen also when the time came for the blessing to be imparted. Isaac did not want to do this without indulging himself once again in the venison dish that he loved—and this meant that Esau had first to go hunting.[107] This gave Rebekah the time she needed for the great substitution. Isaac was guided by his appetite when he gave his blessing, as Esau had been earlier when he sold his birthright.

X

Rebekah's critics are generally prepared to concede that Jacob was superior to Esau for carrying forward the promise given by God to Abraham. Even so, they do not like the deception she practiced in getting her way (or is it in getting God's way?).[108]

What should she have done? It is sometimes said that she should have tried to reason with Isaac, in order to persuade him to defer to Jacob.[109] But there is no indication that Isaac was open to such an approach—and if it should have failed, it might have put him on his guard and thus foreclosed another approach. Besides, time seemed to be short.

Rebekah had to move fast. She improvises well, anticipating various problems. Jacob, we see thereafter, can also improvise. He was very much his mother's son, as Esau seemed to be his father's.[110]

Thus, Rebekah is in certain ways superior to both Sarah (Abraham's principal wife) and Rachel (Jacob's favorite wife). She knows what is going on; she knows what is needed; she knows what to do about it. In short, she is the *knowing* one.

XI

And so it came to pass that the blessing was conferred by Isaac on Jacob, with a curse on whoever cursed the recipient.[111] Did this mean that Isaac would have cursed himself by cursing Jacob upon discovering the ruse? We notice that no name was used when the blessing was conferred, but rather "my son." In any event, when the ruse is exposed Isaac does not remonstrate with either Jacob or Rebekah.[112] It is as if he somehow appreciated the good sense of what had happened, whatever he may still be moved to try to do for Esau. But then, Isaac *is* a great one for going along with what has been done to and for him.

Isaac goes on to give Jacob still another blessing, this time upon his departure from their home.

XII

Jacob leaves home, on the advice of Rebekah, because of the wrath of Esau who proposes to kill Jacob as soon as Isaac dies.[113] (It seems that Esau cannot bear to offend his father while he is still alive.) That Rebekah *cares* for Esau is indicated here, for she says she does not want to lose both of her sons in one day, which would happen if one should be killed and the other should be condemned as a murderer.[114]

Rebekah is acting, to some extent, as a mother, not as a statesman for the people. And it is here, for the only time, that we see the formal references (but not by her) to "Esau her elder son" and to "Jacob her younger son."

XIII

The departure of Jacob must be explained to Isaac. Isaac is told by Rebekah that Jacob must make a better marriage than Esau had, who had married local women of foreign birth.[115] This is a point on which, it seems, Isaac and Rebekah agree; and this is still another indication of Esau's unsuitableness as successor to the promise made to Abraham by God. Perhaps this recognition helps reconcile Isaac to the consequences of the deception practiced upon him.

But in assigning this reason for Jacob's departure, Rebekah again deceives Isaac. (Would his sensibilities have been hurt if he had learned that one of his sons wanted to kill the other?) Or was this Rebekah's true reason for sending Jacob away, and not the one given to Jacob? That is, had Rebekah been concerned lest Jacob contract as unfortunate a marriage as had Esau? In short, did she deceive Jacob also—for the good of the people (and hence for his enduring good)?

We are reminded by these questions that motives may usually be mixed in any great decision.

XIV

It would now be useful to consider the price paid by Rebekah for the deceptions she engineered.

For one thing, as I have anticipated, she has not fared well with some modern commentators. Indeed, she has sometimes been harshly condemned by them, especially those of a Protestant inclination.[116] Are Christians generally more apt to be "purists" in such matters? In any event, I do have the impression that Jews are more apt to be sympathetic to her. They may have always been more inclined, than were (say) the early Christians, to be concerned with the problems and needs of the community in this world.[117]

Some commentators make much of the despair of Esau and Isaac upon discovering the deception. But was it not better for everyone involved that the feelings of Esau be "hurt" than that the great legacy be put into the wrong hands? Sentimentality in such matters is no substitute for statesmanship. Certainly, the appetites of Jacob seem superior to those of Esau, as does his stamina, as may be seen in his willingness to work fourteen years to secure Rachel for his wife.[118]

XV

That Rebekah should pay a price for her part in the deception of Isaac is suggested by the author of *Genesis* as well. We never hear more of her, once she has launched Jacob. This may mean, among other things, that Jacob can "substitute" Rachel for his mother, as Isaac had once "substituted" Rebekah for his mother Sarah.[119] Had Rebekah underestimated how long Jacob would have—*or would want*—to be gone? We do hear a little more about Isaac; and, it seems, Jacob may have seen him again when he returned from his self-imposed exile twenty years later.[120]

But Rebekah evidently parts permanently from her favorite son when he leaves their home. She existed as the shaper of the family. Once she provides for the long future, and does so in a decisive manner, she drops out of the picture, leaving it to Isaac to claim the glory of a place in the authoritative formula: "Abraham, Isaac, and Jacob."

It also seems that Rebekah "makes up" for her imposition upon Isaac and Esau by living the rest of her life with *them*. There is no indication that she does *not* care for them. Nor is there any indication that they ever learned how much she was responsible for the deceptions practiced by Jacob upon his father.

XVI

Rebekah had been concerned that Isaac not make a grave mistake. She was prepared to deprive herself of her favorite son in order to protect the strength of the family and its promise, a family that would have been weakened by Isaac's acting on the basis either of his appetites or of the conventions of succession.

We are told about the death of Isaac.[121] We are even told about the death of Rebekah's nurse.[122] But we are not told of Rebekah's death. Does this indicate her eclipse? Or does the author thereby indicate instead that she lives on in the family to which she sacrificed so much?

XVII

With this question we can turn, however briefly, to an explicit consideration of the "women's issues" which have been touched upon thus far in this chapter.

We notice, first, that Rebekah comes across as a far stronger figure than women were supposed to be in biblical times. Of course, some will say, women have always been stronger than they were generally believed to be—and it is only because men have usually told, or neglected, their stories that they have not been given proper recognition. But, I ask in turn, does not *this* story, whether or not told by a man, display Rebekah as formidable?

More important, must there not have been something worthwhile about a way of life (albeit a way of life defined in critical respects by males) that could produce someone as sensible and attractive as Rebekah? Does not this question, and my discussion of the story thus far, suggest that the available evidence about the status of women heretofore may not always be properly assessed? Should we not expect that women will naturally make their preferences count, their opinions known, and their talents felt in any healthy community—that they will be at least as influential (one way or another) as their men in family matters?

XVIII

Still, some will say, the failure to give women their due, to recognize their rights, has compelled them to proceed as Rebekah did in heading off what her perhaps foolish husband would have done. Thus, it can be said of those times, as one scholar has: "The will of the husband is the will of the house; the woman must often act by underhand means and use cunning in order to have her way. A typical example of this kind of woman's cunning is when Rebekah makes the blind father give Jacob his blessing."[123]

But is not this to say that women, instead of relying either upon unexamined authority or upon mere brawn (in the fashion of men), are obliged by their circumstances to rely in family relations much more than do men upon their instincts and their wits?[124] This may promote in women a sensitivity and an astuteness with respect to such matters that men do not usually develop, however much the legacy that women like Rebekah should be concerned to see properly transmitted is a legacy that has (and naturally has?) a few men as its primary human sources. Furthermore, if men and women were substantially alike in such matters, one must wonder whether both would be significantly deprived of what the collaboration of dissimilar elements can properly provide. Or, put another way, one can ask what, if anything, do the female and the male distinctively contribute—not only physically, but also psychically—to a vital human and humane association.

XIX

It should at once be added that if a woman does have a superior position within the family—that superiority which comes from knowing her husband and children better than they know either her or perhaps themselves—it is in large part because women usually take the family more seriously than do men.[125] Concern with the family is less likely for them than it is for their men to be challenged by outside interests. It is not surprising, considering the requirements of pregnancy and nursing, to say nothing of the early years of childrearing, that women should traditionally have considered the family to be as important as they have.

Rebekah's superiority in family affairs is indicated by things both large and small. Thus, she is confident that she can so prepare Isaac's food that he will not be able to distinguish the lamb Jacob can immediately supply him from the venison Esau has gone out to find. (Does this suggest that hunting, with its uncertainties, can be more than adequately replaced?) Also, Rebekah has more practical sense than Isaac: she will not allow whatever "rules of the game" there may happen to be (about the succession, for instance) to govern everything. That is, she knows her children and knows what they are, and are not, capable of. This means that she may know better than Jacob that Esau will get over his anger. Jacob is very apprehensive upon meeting his brother, after years of separation, while Esau is moved to embrace him.[126]

Another way of indicating the natural differences between men and women, especially where the family is involved, is to say that God knew better than to ask of Sarah what he asked of Abraham, the sacrifice of a child that would test and ratify one's faith.[127]

Lest it be thought that it is only with a weak husband that a woman is shown by the Bible to get her way, it should be remembered that it was Isaac's mother who got her way with Abraham in getting him to drive out Ishmael for the sake of her son, Isaac.[128]

XX

What should we make of any protest that Rebekah is unjustly treated in that she is not given the recognition due her? In fact, some feminists would say, there is something all too familiar about this, in that the woman is obliged to sacrifice herself anonymously to the needs of the family in circumstances where her husband is apt to mess things up and yet it is he who is eventually given "credit" for what *she* has had to fix.[129]

That Rebekah is all too often denied due recognition is no doubt true. But is not such denial more of a deprivation for those who fail to recognize superiority than it is for the superior person? Are not men more apt than women to make more of a name, whereas women are more sensible (have they *had* to be more sensible?), preferring a substantial achievement to a mere name?[130]

XXI

Is not Rebekah recognized by those who count, by those who study with care the account in *Genesis* of what did happen between Isaac and her? Do we not "honor" ourselves by honoring her—which we can do only by reading with care what *has* been written about her?

It sometimes seems, by the way, that Rebekah is the only one (aside perhaps from Abraham) in the early line of the people of Israel who had decisions to make that indeed made a difference. It should also be noticed that there are only two places in the Hebrew Bible where Solomon is said to have been tested for his wisdom—and in both instances, women were involved.[131] With this reminder of the wisdom to which women are peculiarly open, or which they might inspire (even when not wise themselves), let us return to our story proper—to a few more observations about human issues (of which "women's issues" can be considered a significant part).

XXII

There does remain the question of whether deception should ever be resorted to.[132] Abraham, we see in the Bible, is capable of deception at times; and Jacob, later, has to resort to it—in a good cause—in dealing with his not altogether straightforward father-in-law.[133] We recall also Stephen A. Douglas's complaint, in the next-to-last of his famous debates with Abraham Lincoln in 1858, that Lincoln had "a fertile genius for devising language to conceal his thoughts."[134]

The story of a great deception is, as we have seen, at the heart of *Genesis*, suggesting thereby the desperate measures that may have to be resorted to in the foundation, or preservation, of a great people. Not too much should be made of such measures, of course; but neither should they be completely forgotten. Shrewdness is called for in dealing with the things of this world, we are taught with some discretion.[135] We are also taught, by this story at the center of *Genesis*, that prosaic matters such as family relations can be at the foundation of the most exalted institutions.[136] Certainly, the events at the beginning and at the end of *Genesis* are far more momentous in appearance than the transactions tucked away in the middle of it.

Perhaps more can be made of honesty at all costs if one's kingdom is not of this world.[137] Perhaps, then, deception in an emergency can be thought of in the Hebrew Bible as healing on the Sabbath is thought of in the Greek Bible—it is something which may be justified as an exception.[138] Besides, it should be noticed, Jacob identifies himself to the blind Isaac as "I am Esau thy first born."[139] May this have been technically correct in that Esau had cavalierly bartered away to Jacob his birthright? Besides, Isaac's credulity here is almost an invitation to Jacob. It may even suggest that Isaac *wants* to be duped into doing what, in his heart of hearts (that is, in Abraham's heart), he knows to be the right thing. This inviting credulity may be seen in Isaac's willingness to allow his sense of touch and his sense of smell to take precedence over his sense of hearing—and so he can say, upon feeling Jacob (who had had his smooth skin prepared for such a test by the resourceful Rebekah), "The voice is the voice of Jacob, but the hands are the hands of Esau."[140]

Does not the teaching of God for the people of Abraham, Isaac, and Jacob depend ultimately upon the hearing? Are not lessons taught the people, lessons that should govern actions to which one is likely to be drawn by the other senses?

XXIII

It is startling how much both the word of God beforehand to Rebekah and the word of God on several occasions afterward to Jacob (those words which seem to affirm, or at least to accept, what had been done in deceiving Isaac) can be disregarded by commentators. This story becomes for them merely a case of a mother favoring one child over another. They, in their sentimentality, do not appreciate that she is hard-headed, not soft-hearted. But, as I have already indicated, if the word of God is not taken seriously, why should any paternal blessing be significant?

Those who take divinity seriously might well ask: Why did not God have Jacob born first, if He wanted *him* to inherit the blessing? Perhaps, it can be answered, because the story as given does show that rules are not immutable and that good judgment cannot be altogether ruled out in applying rules that are ordinarily worthy of respect. This is a lesson of particular importance for a people who will be characterized by its substantial submission to the Law.[141]

XXIV

Still others who take divinity seriously might well ask: Should not Rebekah have relied upon God to achieve the prophesied role for Jacob, without resorting herself to dubious measures? God, we are reminded by the pious, will provide.

I am reminded here of a colleague's story about a preacher who put his faith in God. The floodwaters were rising and a National Guard truck came to his church. "Reverend," he was told, "You'd better come with us." "No," he replied. "I have faith in God. He will provide." The water rose higher, so much so that the preacher had to go to the balcony of the church. A voice from a Coast Guard boat could be heard calling outside the balcony window, "Reverend, you'd better come with us." "No," he replied. "I have faith in God. He will provide." Well, the waters rose still higher, so much higher that the preacher had to climb up on top of the church steeple. A police helicopter hovered overhead, with a rope ladder let down—and the preacher could hear from a megaphone, "Reverend, you'd better come with us." Again there was the reply: "I have faith in God. He will provide." When the water rose even higher, the preacher drowned. In due time, he found himself welcomed at the pearly gates by St. Peter himself. But before he accepted the invitation to go in, he entered a complaint to this effect: "I must say that you people don't know how to treat your friends. Here I had such great faith that God would provide—and what happened, I ended up drowning, and me a man with a family, too." And so, St. Peter was obliged to explain: "What, in the name of Heaven, did you expect from us? First we sent you a truck; then we sent you a boat; and then we sent you a helicopter. What were you waiting for, man, the Second Coming?"[142]

XXV

The workings of the divine in human affairs can be most mysterious. If trucks, boats, and helicopters can be instruments of the divine will—and who are we to say that they cannot—why not Rebekah also? Thus, Rebekah could be understood as recognizing that she had been told what she had about the destiny of Jacob and that she had been provided the talents and opportunities she had—she could recognize (as Esther was to recognize much later?) she had been put in the position she had—in order to be able to do something constructive when the need arose. After all, God had revealed the truth to *her*, not to Isaac. It was her duty as a human being—not only as a woman—to do what she could to ensure the soundness of the People that was to mean so much to the world.[143]

XXVI

These, then, have been some suggestions about how to read seminal materials that reveal where we have been, who we are, and where we might be going. To read materials of this caliber means, among other things, that one must be able to see the high in the low (as well as to do that which the sophisticated are, I am afraid, all too prone to do, to see the low in the high). Only if one can read carefully, and with the proper elevated openness, may one develop the largeness of soul, as well as the analytical ability, necessary to become and to remain a human being of stature.

Rebekah provides timely guidance to anyone who dares to be great. Is it not testimony to Jacob's stature both that Rebekah should have thought him worthy of her attention and that he should have responded as well as he did to her bold guidance? Do we not expose our own limitations if we should be unable to recognize in the story of the self-sacrificing yet eminently self-confident Rebekah the magnitude of both her aspirations and her statesmanship?

Chapter Six

Joseph[144]

> This field of glory is harvested, and the crop is already appropriated. But new reapers will arise, and *they*, too, will seek a field. It is to deny what the history of the world tells us is true, to suppose that men of ambition and talents will not continue to spring up among us. And when they do, they will as naturally seek the gratification of their ruling passion as others have done before them. . . . Towering genius disdains a beaten path. It seeks regions hitherto unexplored. . . . It thirsts and burns for distinction; and, if possible, it will have it, whether at the expense of emancipating slaves, or enslaving free men.
>
> Abraham Lincoln[145]

I

Joseph (Heb., *Yosef*), a son of Jacob and Rachel, full brother of Benjamin, and father of Epharim and Manasseh, is described in this way in a Jewish encyclopedia:

> An ancestor of the two most important tribes in Israel, Joseph figures largely in the narrative of *Genesis*, his life being narrated in a beautiful series of stories found in chaps. 30, 37, and 39 to 50. They run as follows: His father shows favoritism toward the first-born son whom his favorite wife (Rachel) had borne him in his old age. For this reason Joseph has ambitious dreams; he is cast into a pit by his jealous [older] half-brothers and then sold as a slave in Egypt. He repulses the advances of the wife of Potiphar, his master; she maligns him, and he is cast into prison. There he proves his skill as a diviner of dreams for the butler and baker of Pharaoh; and two years later when Pharaoh himself has a dream that needs interpretation, the butler recalls [Joseph's] previous success. Joseph

> is brought before Pharaoh, interprets the dream as predicting seven years of famine, and is made prime minister. He marries Asenath, the daughter of [an Egyptian priest], and uses the period of plenty to store up sufficient grain to protect Egypt against future famine.
>
> When the seven years of famine arrive, Canaan also suffers, and Joseph's [half-brothers] come down to Egypt to buy grain. They fail to recognize in the prime minister the Joseph whom they sold as a slave, but he recognizes them and proceeds to put them to a severe test—now appearing friendly, now changing to harshness, forcing them to bring his brother Benjamin [Rachel's other son] to Egypt, and arresting the latter on a false accusation to see if his brothers will defend him. Finally he reveals himself as their long-lost brother Joseph, asks after the health of his father, and invites the whole family to come to Egypt, where they settle in Goshen, in the northeastern part of the country. His father blesses him for this and expressly states that the descendants of Joseph's two sons shall in the future be reckoned as two separate tribes. When Joseph dies, his body is embalmed, and is taken along by the Israelites when they leave Egypt (*Exodus* 13:19) and eventually buried near Shechem (*Joshua* 24:32).[146]

Critical to the Joseph story are both the dreams that he has and the dreams of others that he interprets. His dreams, it can be said, serve to unify the various parts of his story.

Even so, the story of Joseph is *not* miracle-laden, perhaps the first major story in the Bible of which this can be said. As such it can guide us to see, in a light different from that immediately provided by the narrators of most of the other stories in the Bible, what those stories might look like without the embellishments that must have moved their original audiences. In this way we are instructed in a mode of dream interpretation that may be applicable to Revelation generally.[147]

The Joseph story in *Genesis* does not depend upon angels, theophanies, or prophecies, except insofar as dreams can be taken to be emanations somehow of the divine. A very helpful comment upon the dreams in the Joseph story, including the two dreams recounted by Joseph to his brothers, is provided by a learned professor:

> Even more potent a source of disharmony were Joseph's dreams. The strong feelings they aroused must be understood against the background of the times. Throughout the Biblical world, dreams were recognized as vehicles of divine communication. Several instances of this have already been encountered [heretofore in *Genesis*]. God revealed His will in dreams to Abimelech, King of Gerar [*Genesis* 20:3], to Jacob [*Genesis* 28:12, 31:11], and to Laban [*Genesis* 31:24]. In each experience the theophany is straightforward, and the message perfectly clear. This is not the case with Joseph's dreams [*Genesis*: 37:5–10], nor with those of the butler and the baker [*Genesis* 40:5] and Pharaoh [*Genesis*

> 41:1]. Here, the symbol, not the words, is the language of intelligence, and the dream is therefore enigmatic.
>
> Against this background, it is not to be wondered at that dreams are frequently productive of anxiety. To be ignorant of the true meaning [of a dream] is to be deprived of knowledge that might well be vital to one's welfare. Notice how in each of the cryptic dreams God does not figure explicitly in the content. Yet it is tacitly accepted that He is the ultimate source of the message being conveyed. This does not mean that the ancients did not recognize such a thing as an idle dream. They did, and that is why dreams in the Joseph biography always come in pairs, to prove their seriousness. . . .
>
> The accepted predictive aspect of dreams was cause enough for the brothers to take Joseph seriously.[148]

We all sense, even if we take dreams seriously, that most dreams *are* to be dismissed and forgotten. We have also heard of lying dreams—such a dream was sent by Zeus to Agamemnon in Homer's *Iliad*.[149]

Impressive as Joseph can be as dream interpreter, even more impressive is what Daniel does in the second chapter of the *Book of Daniel*, for there, the king (another foreign ruler) had demanded that his interpreters not only tell him what his dream meant, but also what the dream itself had been. Is there not something sensible, however formidable, in thus testing the abilities of a dream interpreter?[150]

II

Joseph is first distinguished not as a dealer in dreams but as the wearer of a special coat.[151] For that coat, a constant reminder of Jacob's deeply frustrated love for Rachel, is a kind of dream shared by Jacob and Joseph. Perhaps, also, a dream is like a coat, or a wrapper, to dress up (even as it conceals) what it covers.

I return to our learned professor for his useful report on Joseph's fateful coat:

> The narrative [of Joseph] opens with a picture of the seventeen-year-old Joseph who commands none of our sympathies. The "bad reports" of his brothers which Joseph brings to his father were certainly not calculated to endear him to them [*Genesis* 37:2f]; nor was the garment which Jacob presented him likely to ameliorate the brother's antipathy. Its precise nature eludes us, it being variously but uncertainly explained as "a coat of many colors," "a long sleeved robe," "an ornamental tunic"; there is no doubt, however, that it was a token of special favor and perhaps too, of luxury and lordship. In a later age it was the distinctive dress

of the virgin daughters of royalty. [2 *Samuel* 13:15] At any rate, to the brothers the coat was a hated symbol of favoritism and a cause of discord.[152]

It might also be noticed that, according to Maimonides, the distinctive garments of the priests of idolatrous tribes could help account for the "dress code" prescribed by Moses.[153]

Joseph's brothers may even have resented the disprizing of their own mothers by Jacob's glorification of Rachel's tale-bearing first-born.[154] Particularly galling for the brothers may have been the blatant designation of Joseph as the Chosen Son of one of the founders of the Chosen People.[155]

Be that as it may, garments (like dreams) can serve to unify the various parts of the story of Joseph. Just as a garment is vital in his original relations with his brothers, so is a garment vital in the false accusation made against Joseph by Potiphar's wife.[156] Still another garment figures in the investiture of Joseph with Pharaoh's power.[157]

III

We can now turn to the three pairs of dreams recorded in the Joseph story. The first pair—by Joseph himself—carries further the arrogance suspected by the brothers in the display of the special coat.[158]

Did not the brothers sense what we all can recognize, upon reflection, that human beings shape and otherwise control their dreams (even their most threatening dreams) to a considerable extent? The anger of the brothers assumes that one is largely responsible for one's dreams, or at least for telling them to others. (Is this another form of the young Joseph's impudent, if not also imprudent, habit of telling tales?)

Certainly, Joseph's brothers, as well as his father, can easily read Joseph's dreams. (None of the brothers, it seems, had the wit and perhaps the nerve to conjure up or, indeed, invent counter-dreams of his own.) I draw still another time upon our learned professor for useful comments upon this kind of situation:

> [I]nsofar as a dream was recognized to be inseparable from personality, it meant also that the dreamer somehow bore a measure of responsibility for his dreams. Joseph's visions of lordship, therefore, betrayed his true aspirations and contained, at the same time, the potentiality of fulfillment. This is why they could arouse hostility so intense as to culminate in a conspiracy to murder. [*Genesis* 37:5–20][159]

These two early dreams contribute directly to Joseph's enslavement. Such enslavement turns out to be the condition for his spectacular career, a condition that Joseph can later assure his brothers had been part of a grand divine plan.[160] *One* consequence of the kind of radical rejection suffered by Joseph is that the truly talented human being (if he can avoid crippling self-pity) is liberated to pursue a remarkably rewarding career of an unconventional character. We will consider further on how much this observation applies as well to the career of the Israelites as a people. We should also consider the possibility that the brothers, in resenting their subordination as they do, sense that Joseph's ascendancy would represent an unnatural (if not even a "foreign") rule over them. It is no accident, we suspect, that the rule of the House of Joseph over the Israelites, so spectacular in Egypt, must eventually give way, in the Promised Land, to the more patriotic rule of the House of Judah—and this despite the failings (including the sexual failings) of Judah, sexual failings that turned out to be critical to the development of Judah's most illustrious royal descendants.[161]

A truly prophetic element in Joseph's dreams may be the use of the reaper's sheaves of wheat,[162] which the typical dreamers among a herding people would not be likely to use. Later on, of course, the control of grain becomes the key to Joseph's great power in Egypt. It is fitting, therefore, that the opening and closing dreams of the six dreams in this series (Joseph's first dream and Pharaoh's second dream) should be about grain.[163]

IV

The second pair of dreams—by two Egyptian fellow prisoners of Joseph's—was prefaced by another abused garment, the one seized and misused by Potiphar's wife.[164] Just as Joseph's own dreams, back in the land of Canaan, were generated by his passions and circumstances, so perhaps were the dreams of Pharaoh's butler and baker, both men of some standing in Pharaoh's court.[165]

Joseph had gotten to know these men as fellow prisoners. Perhaps, also, he had come to learn enough about them and their circumstances to be able to grasp what their respective dreams meant. That is, their dreams (working with grapes and bread, respectively) may have reflected these servants' own assessments of (or "feel" for) their royal master's opinion of them.[166] Their dreams, therefore, may have been their ways of facing up to their situations, situations that could be expected to be settled (one way or another) upon the occasion of Pharaoh's birthday celebrations three days hence.[167] (Did the baker sense that he was in jeopardy?)

Joseph, by this time, evidently knows the Egyptian language, a skill that proves helpful to him not only as an administrator but also in dealing *incognito* with his brothers. No doubt, this helps him as well as in his capacity as a dream interpreter. Does his facility with dreams suggest that God speaks to all mankind in a universal language? Is it also suggested that God cares for all—or is He doing all this (including even inducing or at least permitting the impending famine in Egypt and elsewhere) for Joseph's sake or for the sake of Joseph's people?

However all this may be, the second pair of dreams may have been the key pair for Joseph's career, opening the way as it did to his decisive audience with Pharaoh.

V

The third pair of dreams in this story is also by an Egyptian, in this case, Pharaoh himself. Joseph speaks of this pair as one dream, adding that having two of them indicates that the matters forecast are imminent.[168] But this had not been so with respect to the youthful Joseph's two dreams.

Pharaoh's dreams may be the only pair of the three pairs of dreams that has an immediate effect upon actions: Joseph is appointed to high office. The other pairs of dreams had indirect effects, predicting events and affecting how people acted towards Joseph sometimes afterward. (All three sets of the events that were predicted, it could be said, would have taken place without the dreams or their predictions. One suspects, for example, that the brothers would have mistreated Joseph, with or without dreams—or that Joseph would have found other ways to provoke them into enslaving him. Perhaps, also, Joseph, like Mordecai in the *Book of Esther*, could have come in some other way to the attention of the foreign ruler.)

Why were Pharaoh's people not able to read the royal dreams? Were they closed off from God? Was there something about Egyptian life that impeded the deepest understanding of things? Or were Pharaoh's people afraid to invite and address the challenge that the dreams implied? (It might be worth considering how the Egypt of Joseph compares with the Egypt of Moses, including whether Joseph's agricultural policies permanently distorted Egyptian life.[169])

In order to assess properly Joseph's skills as a dream interpreter, one needs to know the relevant facts. Were there cycles of abundance and of famine in Egyptian history—and were there standard signs of shifts in climate approaching?[170] Did Joseph know enough to expect that any astute pharaoh, coming from a family long practiced in watching over Egypt, would have a "feel" for the relevant signs, which could then be organized and thereby considered by him in dreams?

The "dreams" that Joseph, like his father and brothers before him, is adept in reading are the total situations of the persons who do the dreaming. Indeed, it might even be said, Pharaoh was conducting a test, through his dreams, to determine who might be reliable enough to take on the formidable undertaking that he sensed would be required in the decade ahead.

VI

Joseph, perhaps more so than anyone else in the *Book of Genesis*, always had the capacity of getting into the good graces of human beings in authority. This capacity drew upon his charm and good looks, as well as upon his competence and reliability. All this meant, among other things, that he had a flexibility that permitted him to take advantage of the opportunities that happened to come his way.[171]

His ability to impress those in authority bore fruit in his dealings, in succession, with his father, his master (Potiphar), the prison warden, Pharaoh's butler, and finally Pharaoh himself. Joseph did more than interpret dreams: he then could be so bold as to suggest the measures called for, and he evidently did this in such a way (even presenting himself as divinely inspired) that Pharaoh was moved to discover that this gifted foreigner would be the best man for devising and executing the massive agricultural regulation that was called for.[172]

Joseph's adaptation to circumstances extended to his name-change, his dress (and shaving?), and his marriage (to the daughter of a priest for an idolatrous sect), all of which contributed to his brothers' inability to recognize in him the seventeen-year-old whom they had sold into slavery a generation earlier. Until they did recognize him, however, his rule over them—something that he had yearned for if his own dreams spoke truly—does not come until they recognize him as so much in control that he can forgive them and bestow prosperity upon them in a godlike manner, harkening back thereby to the young Joseph's second dream about celestial reconfigurations.[173]

VII

How has Joseph been recognized thereafter by influential Israelites once he buried the still doting father who had doubled the blessing he conferred upon the House of Joseph?[174] There is, among the prophets, silence with respect to Joseph. Other court Jews have fared better in how they are remembered, such as the Mordecai and Esther that the Feast of Purim celebrate.[175] After all,

Joseph's successes did contribute eventually to the enslavement of the Israelites in Egypt, an enslavement different in character from (as well as much longer than) the later Babylonian captivity.[176]

Why does Joseph have his family settle in Egypt? Does this settlement fulfill completely the dreams of mastery that Joseph had had? His brothers *had* been able to take food back to Canaan for Jacob and the others the first time they came to Egypt.[177] Besides, after seven years, the drought should have ended. Was it simply that the living was too easy in Egypt?[178] Even so, no dreams or prophecies are recorded as warning against the enslavement that would have to be endured in Egypt.

That there *were* problems with this family's removal to Egypt is indicated even during Joseph's lifetime. He has to assure his brothers that God would eventually deliver them from Egypt—and he exacts a promise that his bones would also return to Canaan. Did this assurance incorporate, in effect, the enslavement in Egypt of the Chosen People, something that had been anticipated as well by what God had told Abram, Joseph's great-grandfather?[179] Did the presence of Joseph's embalmed body—the body of the savior of Egypt—serve as protection for the people of Israel in that superstitious country, at least until the exploits of Joseph were forgotten?

Were the centuries in Egypt essential to the shaping of the Israelites? Was this subjugation vital to their character and self-consciousness?[180] Does *Genesis* describe the development of a people that would be ready for its exodus, liberation, and consequent exaltation? If there had been no Egypt, it can be argued, there might have been no Sinai.

Besides, was the remarkably fertile breeding ground of Egypt (a fertility apparent to this day) needed to permit the Israelites to become large and powerful enough to take over Canaan? And, in the process, that people were not only bonded together by their adversities, but also trained in agriculture and government because of Egypt and the Exodus. Just as Joseph was challenged and disciplined by enslavement, so perhaps were the Israelites. Still, there is Zionist criticism of Joseph today for having contributed to the enslavement of his people, just as there is criticism of the measures by which enslaved Africans were brought (culturally as well as physically) into a way of life now generally considered more advanced.[181]

Christianity makes far more of Joseph than do the Hebrew Scriptures subsequent to the *Book of Genesis*. The Christian Joseph—the husband of Mary, the mother of Jesus—was another dreamer who went to Egypt, but who did not stay long.[182]

Christianity itself very much depends upon the Hebrew Bible, including of course the *Book of Genesis* and the *Book of Exodus*. Such a record of the relations between God and the People of Israel would not have come from the way of life, whatever its purity, led by Abraham, Isaac, and Jacob. For the decisive record, which could be more or less reliably transmitted for centuries, the contributions of someone such as Moses were needed, a man schooled in the arts of Egypt. An access to the arts, if not also to the wisdom, of an already ancient Egypt had originally been made possible for many generations of Israelites by that enterprising dreamer of genius, Joseph, beloved son of Jacob and Rachel.

Chapter Seven

Moses in Egypt[183]

> But in order to come to those who have become princes by their own virtue and not by fortune, I say that the most excellent are Moses, Cyrus, Romulus, Theseus, and the like. And although one ought not to reason of Moses, he having been a mere executor of the things that were ordained by God, he ought yet to be admired, if only for the grace which made him worthy to speak with God.
>
> Niccolò Machiavelli[184]

I

The Ten Commandments open with God's reminder of His deliverance of the people of Israel from bondage in Egypt.[185] The story of that deliverance is told in the first fifteen chapters of *Exodus*. Reminders of that deliverance are found as well in many other places in the Hebrew Bible. It is anticipated when Abram is told by God:

> Know of a surety that thy seed shall be a stranger in a land that is not theirs, and shall serve them; and they shall afflict them four hundred years; and also that nation, whom they shall serve, will I judge; and afterward shall they come out with great substance.[186]

Other peoples hear one way or another of what had happened in Egypt, as may be seen in the somewhat confused remarks by a Philistine about "the gods that smote the Egyptians with all manner of plagues and in the wilderness."[187]

When the Israelites undertake, after a prolonged absence of Moses on Mount Sinai, to get themselves a Golden Calf to worship, they speak of

Moses having brought them out of Egypt.[188] Does God's self-identification as their rescuer dispose the Israelites to regard themselves, if on their own, as vulnerable to victimization? That is, do they regard vulnerability as *the* human condition, alleviated only when a people is somehow privileged to enjoy divine protection?[189] Indeed, do the Israelites depend, for their cohesiveness and perhaps for their identity, upon outside oppression? (This is a question often addressed in the United States by Jewish leaders who are troubled by the assimilationist tendencies promoted by American tolerance.)

God, upon first speaking to Moses, identifies himself thus: "I am the God of thy fathers, the God of Abraham, the God of Isaac, and the God of Jacob."[190] However vital Abraham is as the progenitor of the Israelites, it can seem to be Moses who places the decisive stamp upon this people (just as Abraham Lincoln, who echoes the story of *Exodus* in his Gettysburg Address, can sometimes be regarded as having done for the people of the United States).[191]

Abraham, like Moses and the Israelites, was mistreated in Egypt, albeit inadvertently by the Pharaoh of his day, from which plagues followed that moved Pharaoh to make amends.[192] But, unlike Moses, the patriarchs do not work miracles or exhibit signs, at least not as dramatically as Moses does (however prophetic they may have been). Nor, it seems, was much made of their stories, or of organized forms of worship, before Moses established the institutions he did. The people of Israel (so far as we are told) do very little to liberate, or even to explain, themselves before Moses emerges among them.

It is the career of Moses that is, in effect, celebrated during the Passover holiday. Even so, the Passover Haggadah barely mentions Moses by name.[193] This is consistent with the fact, reported in the Bible, that no man knows where Moses is buried.[194] In a way, it can be said, Moses is buried in the hearts of his people. In a sense, it can also be said, Moses came first, with the founding patriarchs dependent upon him.

II

The student of the Bible is pretty much restricted to the materials found there. Research into other materials is not likely to help one understand Moses. One has to think, that is, about what is available in the Bible, keeping in mind the caution that it is hard to exaggerate the subtlety of the stories found there.[195]

It remains quite mysterious how Moses was able to go from the palace to rule over the Israelites after championing their cause against the Egyptians. An account of his origins is provided, an account that suggests an explanation for his name.[196] He is born; he is deposited in the river; he is found, pitied, and saved by the princess, who adopts him as her own. Miriam, his sister, is instrumental in what happens to him: it is she who gets Moses' mother hired to take care of him.[197]

We may well wonder what this account, which can strike us as "mythical" in tone, is doing in the Bible. Is it needed to account for Moses' survival? If so, how are all the other males of his generation to be accounted for (or was there a gap in the Israelite male population)? Was the principal, if not the only, significant effect of the Pharaoh's condemnation of the newborn Israelite males to get Moses into the palace?

I do not believe that it is ever referred to again in the Bible that Moses came from the palace. Even so, are we not left to consider whether his marked difference from the Israelites that he leads is in part because of his palace origins?[198]

III

Moses' career as Liberator begins with his killing an Egyptian who is oppressing an Israelite.[199] We see here that it is not only Pharaoh who is oppressive, but perhaps also the Egyptians at large. Certainly, they are portrayed as benefiting considerably from the labor of a captive people. So when the plagues are inflicted upon all of the Egyptians, that may be fitting. Moses' killing of the Egyptian is like the Tenth Plague, the killing of the first-born of the Egyptians, leading to the Israelites' immediate deliverance.[200]

The spiritedness of Moses is evident here. Had he always been aware that he was an Israelite? It seems to be assumed, when Moses talks with God thereafter, that he knows that Aaron is his brother.[201] Abraham, we can see in *Genesis*, was more conciliatory in dealing with the people he had to "confront" early in his own career.[202]

When Moses tries thereafter to govern two quarreling Israelites, his authority is challenged.[203] He becomes fearful because his killing of the Egyptian is known, despite the precautions he had taken to make sure that his intervention against the Egyptian had not been observed.[204] So much is Moses' killing of the Egyptian known that Pharaoh and his officers are now after him. He flees to Midian, where he comes to be associated with Jethro's family.[205]

This means, as it turns out, that Moses had more than one exodus from Egypt. It also means that the quarreling Israelite's challenge had been critical: "Who made thee a ruler and a judge over us?"[206] Thus, it may be said, Moses fled to Midian not only to escape arrest by Pharaoh's officers but also to find an adequate response to this challenge of his leadership of the Israelites that he had heard.[207]

"Who made thee a ruler and a judge over us?"[208] If Moses pondered this challenge, he might well have wondered what indeed had moved him to assert leadership in the way he did. *Had* he acted on his own—and was he justified in doing so?

It was while he was serving as a shepherd that Moses saw the Burning Bush.[209] (We are not told how long he had been alone with his animals, thinking about things.) Muhammad is reported to have said: "He will never be a prophet who was not first a herdsman."[210]

It was on Mount Sinai that Moses saw the Burning Bush, the place to which he would eventually return with all of the people of Israel.[211] The thing which burned and yet was not consumed inspired wonder in him. He finds himself in the divine presence in a way, or to a degree, that he had never experienced before.

Why does God appear in this form to Moses? Is this manifestation of the divine a clear departure from Egyptian idolatry?[212] Thus, the God of Moses does not appear (and, it can be said, Moses does not have Him appear) in the form of an animal—or even in the form of a man or of an angel.

A burning that does not consume what is burned is an activity that we would call contrary to nature. Wonder is appropriate here. This *is* mysterious. Fire is again important at Mount Sinai while Moses is there, later on, with the people of Israel.[213] (On that occasion, too, is there something burning that is not consumed?)

IV

Moses—and perhaps even more important, the Israelites—got, as a result of the encounter with the Burning Bush, an answer to the question about who had made Moses a ruler and a judge: it was God Himself. Had Moses somehow intended this from the outset? Is that why he had intervened as he did against the oppressive Egyptian and then between the quarreling Israelites? Had Moses, in Midian thereafter, worked out on his own both what he had been moved by and what he was moving toward?

But he needed more in order for the Israelites to accept him—and perhaps also for Pharaoh to recognize him as the bargaining agent for the Israelites with the Egyptians. That is, he needed and got the Burning Bush—just as later he would need and get the teachings on Mount Sinai.

Some have argued that Moses was originally an Egyptian. Even if so, are not the Israelites as much his people as they are Abraham's? Abraham, it should be remembered, not only had no teaching to convey, at least not as systematically as Moses did, but he himself was originally a Chaldean.[214] It may not matter, for some purposes, whether "The Great Stranger" who undertakes to shape the Israelites is Moses or God.

Why is Moses chosen by God? We are not told, just as we are not told explicitly why Abraham was chosen. In both cases, how these two men conducted themselves—quite differently from all those around them—showed why they had been chosen. For God, the future is as much present as is the past. That is, He knows what men are like and what they will do.[215]

And so Moses receives his mission from God. God even anticipates that Pharaoh will not let the Israelites go at once.[216] God will first have to perform a series of wonders, by which the Israelites as well as Pharaoh will learn more about God. The Israelites, at the outset of Moses' "administration," may not know much about God, but they evidently know enough for Moses to be able to *talk* about their need to go away from the Egyptian in order to worship Him.[217]

V

Moses makes four sets of objections to God upon having been called to lead the Israelites out of Egypt.[218] The objections follow more or less plausibly, one after another. Can they be fully answered? Are not the objections put because Moses, an intelligent man who has been mulling things over, can find no satisfactory answer to them? Is that because there are never likely to be unequivocal answers available to such questions?

The objections relate to Moses' credentials, to how he will be accepted, and to how he will proceed. Moses begins by asking, "Who am I, that I should go unto Pharaoh, and that I should bring forth the children of Israel out of Egypt?"[219] This is, in effect, what the quarreling Israelite had asked Moses. After all, Moses had already tried to lead the Israelites—and he now had a killing to answer for. Perhaps it helps that he is the one man who is most likely, of all his people, to have ready access to the palace.

God's answer to the first objection is a curious one: "Certainly I will be with thee; and this shall be the token unto thee, that I have sent thee: when thou hast brought forth the people out of Egypt, ye shall serve God upon this mountain."[220] God seems to be saying, in effect, "*I* know you can do it—and you also will know it when you have done it."

Moses then begins to imagine how things will go when he undertakes his mission, beginning with the immediate response to be expected from his people: "Behold, when I come unto the children of Israel, and shall say unto them: 'The God of your fathers hath sent me unto you,' and they shall say unto me: 'What is His name?' What shall I say unto them?"[221] We move here from Moses' credentials to God's. The gods of other peoples, it seems, have names or have names given to them. But the God of the fathers of the Israelites is evidently not yet well enough known for them to have learned His name. Moses assumes that there is a name to be learned—and that it would be useful to know it. Something that takes the form of an answer is provided by God: "I AM THAT I AM . . . Thus shall thou say unto the children of Israel: 'I AM hath sent me unto you.'"[222] This is the brief answer to the objection. God continues with a much longer answer, repeating several times that He is the God of their fathers, the God of Abraham, of Isaac, and of Jacob, who would lead them, with some of the wealth of Egypt, into a land "flowing with milk and honey."[223]

Thus, the answer recognizes that the Israelites will be more impressed by what this divinity will do for them than solely by who He is. Indeed, it may be very difficult, if not impossible, to grasp who He is except in his capacity as Benefactor. The *I am that I am* name is provided for the first time on this occasion. I am told that the Hebrew used here can also be translated *I shall be what I shall be*. Either way, this is deeply mysterious, with perhaps God's *determination* paramount here. He is unpredictable, incomprehensible: this is a name that goes along with the mystery of the Burning Bush. God, therefore, is like the premise that must somehow be grasped if there is to be serious reasoning, a premise that cannot itself be proved or gone behind.[224]

Moses is then troubled by the problem naturally following upon revelation, however genuine it may be: How are those people to be convinced who are not privileged to have had the revelation made personally available to them also? And so he asks God: "But, behold, they will not believe me, nor hearken unto my voice; for they will say: 'The Lord hath not appeared unto thee.'"[225] Signs are then provided Moses to validate his message from God, two signs which are demonstrated at once (a rod turning into a serpent and a hand turning leprous) and a third sign which is to be used if these two do not suffice.[226] We are told that signs were used with the people, and that they sufficed.[227] We are not told whether the third sign had been needed. One is left to wonder whether the organization of the community, including its rituals and governance, suffice to "guarantee" revelation for those many generations thereafter when no signs are available.

Still, Moses has one more objection: "Oh Lord, I am not a man of words, neither heretofore, nor since Thou hast spoken unto Thy servant; for I am slow of speech, and of a slow tongue."[228] To this a reply is made by the God of Creation: "Who hath made man's mouth? Or who maketh a man dumb, or deaf, or seeing, or blind? Is it not I the Lord? Now therefore go, and I will be with thy mouth, and teach thee what thou shalt speak."[229] But Moses presumes to insist upon this objection further, asking God to send someone else.[230] At this, we are told, "the anger of the Lord was kindled against Moses," but this does not keep Him from designating Aaron, Moses' brother, as someone who can be used by Moses as his spokesman "unto the people."[231]

The third sign available to Moses, in order to persuade his people, is one that was not demonstrated during the Burning Bush encounter: the turning of water into blood.[232] This, it will be remembered, is the *first* of the ten plagues inflicted later upon the Egyptians.[233] The last thing that the Lord says to Moses before he returns to Egypt is that he would eventually have to say to Pharaoh: "Thus saith the Lord: 'Israel is My first-born. And I have said unto thee, "Let My son go, so that he may serve Me"; and thou hast refused to let him go. Behold, I will slay thy son, thy first-born.'"[234] And this, it will also be remembered, is the *last* of the ten plagues inflicted upon the Egyptians.[235]

Thus, the first and last plagues are anticipated during the Burning Bush encounter: the first has water turning into blood, the last has blood turning, in effect, into water (that is, blood loses its power, which is one way that death can be understood).[236]

VI

After the Burning Bush encounter, Pharaoh had to be confronted. Moses, as we have seen, had been supplied with Aaron as his assistant and with signs in order to deal both with the Israelites and with Pharaoh.

The initial demands made of Pharaoh led to even harsher tasks imposed immediately by the Egyptians upon the Israelites. Moses heard recriminations from his people—just as he would hear them again and again in his career thereafter.[237]

Nothing is ever said, by Moses or by the Israelites or by the author of the *Book of Exodus*, to suggest that too much is being done *to* the plagues-ridden Egyptians.[238] This may reflect the harsh treatment that the Israelites had endured—and may reflect as well the resulting hostility among the Israelites toward the Egyptians which made Pharaoh so fearful of the Israelites. The population figures recorded in *Exodus* suggest that there may have been as many as three million Israelites in Egypt.[239]

The power of God is exhibited again and again in Egypt. Why did He not, from the outset, so act as to move Pharaoh to capitulate immediately? A digression, provided in the *Exodus* story, is revealing here: After the ninth plague, there are instructions given by God to Moses for the Passover remembrances in perpetuity—and then the tenth (and final) plague can come.[240] Some modern editors would like to place this digression after the tenth plague, but that would probably be a mistake. The digression suggests that all this is being done, in such dramatic detail (with the ten plagues anticipating, if only in number, the Ten Commandments that would be provided at Mount Sinai)—all this is being done, we are shown, primarily for the sake of the Israelites.[241]

Certainly, these events have made a much greater impression upon the Israelites than upon the Egyptians. It is known, for example, that "we possess virtually no extra-biblical references to the events recorded in [*Exodus*], either in Egypt or elsewhere."[242] The rest of the world cannot be expected to understand what "really happened" with the Israelites in Egypt, as may be seen in the account provided by a Greek geographer, Strabo, who said (two thousand years ago): "An Egyptian priest named Moses, who possessed a portion of Lower Egypt, being dissatisfied with the established institutions there, left it and came to Judea with a large body of people who worshiped the Most High."[243]

VII

We have seen that Moses' four objections to his mission fit together. The same can be said of the ten plagues visited upon the Egyptians: the plague of blood, the plague of frogs, the plague of gnats, the plague of flies, the plague on livestock, the plague of boils, the plague of hail, the plague of locusts, the plague of darkness, and the plague on the firstborn.[244] I have already noticed the relation between water and blood in the first and last plague, framing thereby the entire series.

A number of accounts, some more detailed than others, provide plausible orderings of the plagues, with some orderings (such as Philo's) being thousands of years old. Indeed, it would be surprising if there should not be a principle of order that can be worked out for the material presented, just as there is, for example, in the ways that the sons of Jacob are listed in various circumstances in the Bible.[245] A principle of order for the plagues should be expected, therefore, whether the plagues came from God, from nature, or entirely from a poet.[246]

Perhaps more remarkable than some principle of order for the ten plagues is the insight needed (on the part of God, Moses, or someone else) to anticipate or at least to make use of the plagues. It might even be said that the divine activity recorded here is a reflection of that recorded in the Creation story of *Genesis*, with the infliction of that darkness and death in which the plagues culminate reversing the creation of light and life so critical "in the beginning."[247]

Also remarkable are the responses of Pharaoh to the series of catastrophes recorded in *Exodus*. What does *he* think is causing all this? Why does he not accept the Mosaic view of things and become a believer? Or is it that he recognized that Egypt is always suffering afflictions—and that the Egyptians have their own way of accounting for (and dealing with) them? We should notice that the *Exodus* account of troubles in Egypt may stretch over many months, if not years. We should also notice there is no suggestion, in the account in *Genesis* of the seven-year famine which Joseph dealt with, that Egypt was being punished on *that* occasion for any transgressions. These things just happen, the Egyptians may have come to believe—and yet Egypt somehow keeps going.[248]

VIII

I return briefly to the four objections made by Moses upon being called by God to his mission. Each of them is dealt with in turn by God, with no show of "emotion" on His part. But "anger" *is* said to have been exhibited by God when Moses persists in his fourth objection, that of his being "slow of speech." God's original answer to that objection had drawn upon His capacity as Creator (which He draws upon also in the course of the Ten Commandments, when the keeping of the Sabbath is prescribed).[249]

Moses' unwelcome persistence here takes the form of his asking God to send someone else.[250] This, in turn, leads to God's designation of Aaron as Moses' spokesman.[251] We can do little more than wonder here whether Aaron had been part of God's original plan or whether the designation came only because of Moses' inability to trust God completely.[252]

We do see, further on, that Aaron has both strengths and weaknesses, something that is evident when he gives in to the Israelites' demand for the Golden Calf.[253] We can do no more than notice now that the priesthood stemming from Aaron may always have had flaws built into it, just as kingship, not part of God's preferred plan either, was to have.[254]

IX

We must leave these speculations for the moment. We must return, instead, to the memorable exodus from Egypt. At last the Israelites are allowed to leave, after four hundred and thirty years (which are said to extend over four generations after Jacob and his family came to Egypt).[255]

The Israelites have a final confrontation with the Egyptians—at the Sea of Reeds. No warning is given to the Egyptians this time, although this drowning of the Egyptian host (with its six hundred war chariots) is in effect an eleventh plague, or at least an expansion of the tenth plague. After the sea closes in on the Egyptians their bodies litter the shore.[256]

This can remind the reader of Pharaoh's order, some eighty years before, that every son born of the Israelites was to be "cast into the river."[257] This connection is reinforced by the re-emergence here of Miriam to take part in the ensuing celebration:

> And Miriam the prophetess, the sister of Aaron, took timbrel in her hand, and all the women went out after her with timbrels and with dances. And Miriam sang unto them: "Sing ye to the Lord, for He is highly exalted: The horse and his rider hath He thrown into the sea."[258]

This, too, takes the reader back fourscore years, for it had been the resourceful Miriam who had known what needed to be done along the shore of another body of water in another fateful moment in the history of the people of Israel.[259]

These similarities between the opening and closing scenes of the career of Moses in Egypt encourage us to persist in our belief that there is a thoughtful ordering of events by the organizer of this account. The thinker as artist is very much in evidence here as elsewhere in the Bible. Things somehow hang together, the artist suggests. Chance and irrationality do not rule the world, however mysterious *I AM* and the Burning Bush should always be.[260]

Chapter Eight

Moses at Sinai[261]

And God spoke all these words saying: "I am the Lord thy God, who brought thee out of the land of Egypt, out of the house of bondage. Thou shalt have no other gods before Me. Thou shalt not make unto thee a graven image, nor any manner of likeness, or any thing that is in heaven above, or that is in the earth beneath, or that is in the water under the earth; thou shalt not bow down unto them, nor serve them; for I the Lord thy God am a jealous God, visiting the iniquity of the fathers upon the children unto the third and fourth generations of them that hate Me; and showing mercy unto the thousandth generation of them that love Me and keep My commandments."

Moses[262]

I

The episode of the Israelites, Moses, and the Golden Calf, reported in the *Book of Exodus*, is approached in this fashion in the *Encyclopedia Judaica*:

> *Golden Calf* [*Exodus* 32:4, 1 *Kings* 12:28], the golden image made by Aaron at the behest of the Israelites and venerated near Mount Sinai. . . . *Exodus* 32 relates that the Israelites, anxious about Moses' prolonged absence [on Mount Sinai], demanded that Aaron provide a god to lead them. Complying, Aaron collected the golden ornaments of the people and fashioned the gold into the shape of a calf or a small bull. Aaron probably intended the calf to represent the vacant throne of God, like the cherubim in the Tabernacle, but the image was immediately hailed by the people as a representation of the God who had brought Israel out of Egypt. Aaron then built an altar, and on the following day sacrifices were offered and the people feasted and danced and played.[263]

The encyclopedist continues his description with how God and then Moses responded to these carryings-on:

> Thereupon the Lord told Moses of the apostasy of the "stiff-necked people," whom He proposed to destroy. Moses, however, interceded on behalf of the Israelites and persuaded the Lord to renounce His intended punishment. Carrying the Tablets of the Covenant down from Mount Sinai, Moses saw the people dancing around the Golden Calf. In great anger Moses smashed the Tablets, melted down the image of the calf, pulverized the precious metal, and scattered the powdered gold over the available source of water, thus making the people drink it (verse 20); and there is doubtless a causal nexus between this and the plague that is reported in verse 35.[264]

I will return presently to the *Encyclopedia Judaica* account of this episode. But before continuing we should notice that there was nothing miraculous about what happened in the Israelite camp either while Moses was gone or after his return, whatever may be thought about what may have happened between God and Moses on Mount Sinai before, during, and after the Golden Calf episode in the camp. The sort of things that went on in the camp can happen any day and may be routinely witnessed by people everywhere. Both exuberant idol worship and vigorous reaction to it may even be called natural.

II

Students today, including even sophisticated adults raised under an older dispensation, have a quite limited knowledge of Moses' career. (This includes those who are Jews.) Recollections are particularly dim about the Golden Calf episode. But then, for most people today (even among Jews), cavorting around something like the Calf (which can take the form of, say, infatuations with celebrities) is not troublesome, so long as one does not formally "convert" to another faith.

Our contemporaries find it shocking, therefore, to learn what Moses did after destroying the Calf and pulverizing its gold. Our encyclopedist concludes his account with this report:

> *Exodus* 32 relates that Moses then upbraided Aaron for having "brought great guilt" upon the people. The parallel account in *Deuteronomy* 9:20 relates that but for Moses' supplication on behalf of Aaron the Lord would have destroyed Aaron. Stern punishment was, however, meted out to the calf-worshipers, 3,000 of whom were slain by the Levites who had responded to Moses' call for volunteers. Henceforth, the Levites were consecrated to the service of the Lord. Despite Moses' prayer for divine forgiveness, the Lord threatened that on the day

> of His visitation punishment would overtake the people. Soon afterward a plague broke out among the Israelites. . . . In addition the Lord announced that He would no longer abide amid this "stiff-necked people." The Israelites mourned the departure of the Divine presence and stripped themselves of their ornaments (*Exodus* 33:1–6).[265]

Relatively few these days remember that Moses directed the killing of three thousand people on this occasion. We can be reminded of one lesson of the *Oresteia*, a lesson proclaimed by Aeschylus' Athena even as she reined in the implacable Furies—the teaching that there is a need for tough sanctions in a well-ordered human society.[266]

It is bloody business, indeed, after Moses' return.[267] Moses and his cohorts are not at all deterred here by the prohibition against murder in the Ten Commandments. The slaughter of the three thousand was, it seems to have been understood, *not* the kind of killing that is forbidden.

The rule against idolatry is confirmed both by the slaughter of the three thousand and by the plague that followed. Other misconduct thereafter among the Israelites resulted in severe consequences as well, with even larger numbers perishing through disease, wars, and captivity.[268] But perhaps no other offense by the Israelites ever elicited so immediate and hence so dramatic a response as did the worship of the Golden Calf.

III

Something of the seriousness of idolatry may also be seen in what Moses had to contend with in talking with God. God offered to replace Abraham with Moses, after wiping out this people.[269] Of course, the descendants of Moses would still have been descendants of Abraham but, it seems, Abraham would not have been regarded as their decisive progenitor (just as Abraham's father does not "count").

Moses rejected the offer that he become, in effect, the new Abraham. Should this be regarded as a temptation of Moses to commit a kind of idolatry?[270] This, evidently, was not Moses' way: he may not have had, among other things, the purity of Abraham. Abraham appeared willing to sacrifice Isaac, but Moses was not willing to sacrifice Isaac's descendants.[271] Besides, Moses may have sensed that the Egyptian experience had been useful for his people, however much that experience still had to be refined. So critical is Egypt in the memory of Jews down to our day that it figures prominently in their greatest feast of the year, the Passover celebration. (It is also remembered in the Ten Commandments.) Thus, it would not have been enough to have revived the purity and even the fervor of Abraham. Various political arts, honed by centuries of challenges and hardships endured in captivity and elsewhere, are also needed in order to shape a people for a very long future in which all kinds of circumstances will have to be faced.

IV

The prohibition of idolatry is shown by the Golden Calf episode to be vital to the definition of this people. Related to this prohibition is the sanctity of the Lord's name and of His Sabbath. The other rules set forth in the Ten Commandments may be found elsewhere among civilized peoples. It was the Divinity, and this people's relations to It, that sustained and guided this people in a distinctive way. God and this people somehow "establish" each other.

Maimonides argues that the negation of the corporeality of God is essential for the insistence that God is *one*. To accept any corporeality in the understanding or the representation of God is to deny, in effect, the unity of God.[272] The resort to the Golden Calf represents a turning away from the faith that would have seen the Israelites awaiting Moses' return, no matter how troubling their circumstances. "Next to the fall of man," we are told by the *Jewish Encyclopedia*, "the worship of the Golden Calf is, in rabbinical theology, regarded as the sin fraught with the direst consequences to the people of Israel."[273] Thus, an ancient rabbi observed, "There is not a misfortune that Israel has suffered which is not partly a retribution for the sin of the Calf."[274]

The fateful offense with the Golden Calf occurs immediately after the Ten Commandments had become available, at least to Moses. It seems to have been the first public violation of one of the commandments. Compounding the offense are the questionable things done in the course of the forbidden worship. Thus, some of the language of the account in *Exodus* has been taken to mean that a sexual orgy was in process when Moses returned. A poem by the great Jewish-German poet, Heinrich Heine, suggests the ecstasy to which the Israelites abandoned themselves:

The Golden Calf

Flutes and fiddles call to revel
All the dancers of the devil,
Jacob's daughters circle reeling
Round the Golden Calf in doom—
Boom, boom, boom—
Drumbeats rolling, laughter pealing!

Clasping hands with thrills unworded,
White thighs flashing, robes high-girded,
Highborn maids of noblest feeling

Whirl unstayed and unsurceased
Round the beast—
Drumbeats rolling, laughter pealing!

Aaron joins the mad surrender,
Even he, the faith's defender,
And he dances, wildly wheeling
In his solemn priestly coat,
Like a goat—
Drumbeats rolling, laughter pealing![275]

One must wonder whether the people of Israel would have acted as reported here if they had really believed that the Lord, rather than Moses, had brought them out of Egypt.[276] The Lord, too, spoke on this occasion of Moses' having brought the people out of Egypt.[277] Is this an aspect of His turning away from them? Or did He mock thereby what the people were saying about Moses? The possibility of any change on His part is puzzling, as is any indication that the Lord had learned things about this people that He had not known before. Perhaps His most astonishing statement here to Moses is this: "Now therefore let Me alone, that My wrath may wax hot against them . . ."[278] This might even be taken by some to recognize, or at least to suggest, that the Lord, in His relations with this people, had been fashioned by Moses somewhat as the Calf had been fashioned by Aaron. Perhaps at the root of the difficulty here is a critical deficiency in knowledge on the part of the people. If they *had* known and truly believed that it was God who had done "everything," would not they have acted differently?

V

Moses did not want himself to become a substitute for, or even an image of, God. The people treated him as godlike in various ways. We have already noticed that they could speak of *him* as having brought them out of Egypt. The greatest idolatry may be to have a man regarded as God. After all, Maimonides has taught, no man has ever truly believed that the form he fashions from matter had once created and now governs the world.[279] Even so, the people were not altogether wrong to treat Moses as godlike, in that he *was* specially attuned to the Divine Mind.[280]

Moses is godlike also in that he becomes angry when he in turn *sees* the idolatry of the Israelites. Earlier, God had been angry when *He* saw what was going on in the camp.[281] Moses had not *seen* before; he had "merely" *heard*, albeit from God. (Long after Moses, and down to our day, the people would not see but would only hear marvelous things—for example, about Moses.)

Moses became so indignant that he broke the tablets written by God Himself.[282] Was this somewhat like the worship with, if not of, the Calf? That is, did Moses thereby express his passion through material things or through physical acts, just as the people were doing? We can well wonder whether Moses should have done this. Yet, it can be said, all this was somehow to the good, in the sense that the second time Moses descended from Mount Sinai with tablets his face was said to shine with his holiness. Once again we see that trying experiences can produce a heightening of the spirit.[283]

VI

The Israelites, in resorting to forbidden imitations, had imitated others: the Egyptians, perhaps also the Canaanites, whom they might have recalled from earlier encounters. In short, these Israelites are here the imitators of imitators.

On exhibit here, then, are the fundamental alternatives that the Hebrew Bible considers available to human beings. There are the Israelites (*the* People), on the one hand, and everyone else, on the other hand. It has been argued that some of the Egyptians who left Egypt with the Israelites took the lead in agitating for the Golden Calf. An Egyptian proclivity within the souls of the Israelites contributed perhaps to this debacle, especially since considerable use had long been made in Egypt of animal forms for gods. Some of the Israelites had protested before this that they should have been left in Egypt, a land of milk and honey, the very land that God in the Ten Commandments called "the house of bondage."[284]

That some Israelites were determined to embrace Egyptianism is suggested by the tradition that Hur, a nephew of Aaron, was killed when he tried to stop the people from lapsing into idolatry.[285] This, it has been said, persuaded Aaron that he had to go along with the would-be idolaters. Certainly, Aaron does not resist them—perhaps he, too, wondered what had become of Moses (who was considered overdue in his return)—but Aaron does make them pay for their desires, requiring them to contribute their gold ornaments.[286] Also, Aaron tried to convert the use of the "god" (or "gods") he makes to the service of the "feast of the Lord."[287]

Moses would not have been thus imposed upon by the people. But, then, they would not have required this exercise if Moses had been there. The Calf seems, that is, to have replaced Moses. It did not, strictly speaking, replace God.[288]

Maimonides devotes much of his *Guide* to insisting upon the incorporeality of God.[289] How *im*pure may a people be and still be somehow faithful?[290] That is, what rhetorical accommodations must there be made to the limitations of the people at large, including accommodations that take the form of intimations about divine interventions in human affairs?[291] The dramatization of the particular prophet involved in such transactions is hard to avoid. What does this suggest about the evidence for, and hence the status of, revelation?

VII

Aaron, too, was a kind of prophet, fashioning as he did an object for a worship service and directing how it would be used. We are reminded by this episode that there always were for the Israelites, as for their predecessors, problems with respect to the status of craftsmanship. Is not the reliance upon crafts for the relief of man's estate implicit in the idolatry issue, with human beings seeking thus to take command of their destiny?[292]

We can return to Aeschylus, however briefly, by noticing that the hero of his *Prometheus Bound* is philanthropic, striving to protect the human race from annihilation by the supreme deity. The Prometheus of the ancient Greeks is, in this respect, somewhat like the Moses of chapter 32 of Exodus.[293]

Prometheus acts in the service of the human race by being a patron of the crafts among men.[294] Moses, on the other hand, serves human beings (particularly the Israelites) by rooting out the pernicious effects of craftsmanship among them. This difference, put in modern terms, bears upon the status of rationalism for the welfare of human beings. At the foundation of the difference between the approach of Moses and that of Prometheus may be, at least in part, a difference of opinion with respect to the status of what we (but *not* the authors of the Hebrew Bible) know as *nature*.[295]

On what basis can we choose between these two approaches? Is this a question that is itself intrinsically non-Mosaic in character? In these matters, it seems Moses, for all of his political skills, is very much in the tradition of Abraham. That is, Moses relies in extreme cases upon the voice of God ("Thus saith the Lord . . .") to guide him in the performance of those deeds of singular ferocity necessary for a useful display of the most remarkable faith.[296]

Even so, we presume to notice that there is no indication from the narrator that God gave any directions to Moses for the slaughter of the three thousand.[297] Instead, are there not indications enough that God intended to do His own slaughtering—and of even more than the memorable three thousand?[298] Perhaps Moses resorted to a preemptive strike of sorts, hoping thereby to head off even harsher measures by God Himself. If this is what Moses intended, we also presume to notice, it did not work to spare the Israelites from a deadly pestilence. Or should we say, in defense of Moses, that those who died by his swords clearly (and hence usefully) suffered for their idolatry, while the multitudes who died by God's plagues and by other such afflictions on this and other occasions could be considered "merely" to have paid their debt to nature?[299] Here, as elsewhere, God's purposes and actions may be harder to be sure about than the actions and purposes of human leaders who act in the name of the Lord.

Chapter Nine

The Ten Commandments[300]

> I go the way of all the earth; be thou [Solomon] strong therefore, and show thyself a man; and keep the charge of the Lord thy God, to walk in His ways, to keep His statutes, and His commandments, and His ordinances, and His testimonies, according to that which is written in the law of Moses, that thou mayest prosper in all that thou doest.
>
> David[301]

I

An authoritative account of the delivery of the Ten Utterances (which we know as the Ten Commandments) is provided by Moses himself when, some forty years later, he recalls for the people of Israel what had happened on that great day at *the* Mountain (which had been referred to in the *Exodus* account as Sinai and which is referred to, here in the *Deuteronomy* version, as Horeb):

> The Lord our God made a covenant with us in Horeb. The Lord made not this covenant with our fathers, but with us, even us, who are all of us here alive this day. The Lord spoke with you face to face in the mount out of the midst of the fire—I stood between the Lord and you at that time, to declare unto you the word of the Lord; for ye were afraid because of the fire, and went not up into the mount.[302]

Moses then recalls for them what was said by God on that great day, setting forth the Ten Commandments in the kind of detail (but not quite the same detail) as in the *Exodus* version.[303]

This recitation of the Ten Commandments is followed by further recollection of that time by Moses:

> These words the Lord spoke unto all your assembly in the mount out of the midst of the fire, of the cloud, and of the thick darkness, with a great voice, and it went on no more. And He wrote them upon two tables of stone, and gave them unto me. And it came to pass, when ye heard the voice out of the midst of the darkness, while the mountain did burn with fire, that ye came near unto me, even all the heads of your tribes, and your elders; and ye said: "Behold, the Lord our God hath shown us His glory and His greatness, and we have heard His voice out of the midst of the fire; we have seen this day that God doth speak with man, and he liveth. Now therefore why should we die? For this great fire will consume us; if we hear the voice of the Lord our God any more, then we shall die. For who is there of all flesh, that hath heard the voice of the living God speaking out of the midst of the fire, as we have, and lived? Go thou near, and hear all that the Lord out God may say; and thou shalt speak unto us all that the Lord our God may speak unto thee; and we will hear it, and do it." And the Lord heard the voice of your words, when ye spoke unto me; and the Lord said unto me: "I have heard the voice of the words of this people, which they have spoken unto thee; they have well said all that they have spoken. Oh that they had such a heart as this always, to fear Me, and keep all My commandments, that it might be well with them, and with their children for ever! Go say to them: 'Return ye to your tents.' But as for thee, stand thou here by Me, and I will speak unto thee all the commandments, and the statutes, and the ordinances, which thou shalt teach them, that they may do them in the land which I give them to possess it."[304]

We need not concern ourselves, for the moment at least, with how this *Deuteronomy* account of what happened at the Mountain compares with the account in *Exodus*. We are not told in the Bible itself, as distinguished from traditions about the Bible, who wrote the account in *Exodus*. Here in *Deuteronomy* we are told that Moses himself, as he prepared to end his career, recapitulated the giving of the Ten Commandments some forty years before. The differences in the wording of the Ten Commandments in the two accounts, about which I will say more later, can perhaps be taken as reflecting the experiences of the people of Israel over the intervening generations. Lapses of memory could be suggested, except that the commandments themselves were said to be available on stone. This suggests the possibility that the core of the commandments, as inscribed by God Himself on stone (after their oral delivery at the mountain), was somewhat shorter or less embellished than the spoken version. This should remind us of the importance of the oral tradition in Judaism.[305]

In any event, the *Deuteronomy* account of the great occasion is one that Moses himself evidently wanted to leave with his people. We have long believed in the preeminent statesmanship of Moses, something that even the free-thinking Machiavelli has testified to in eloquent terms.[306] That statesmanship is reflected in Moses' awareness that the circumstances of the delivery of the Ten Commandments are vital both to how they were originally received and to how they would be remembered and regarded.[307]

All this is said by biblical scholars to have happened between 1290 and 1225 B.C.E., which is to say more than three thousand years ago. Many of those scholars, evidently discounting Moses' authorship of the Torah, place the actual writing of the books of *Exodus* and *Deuteronomy* at least five centuries after the date of the events described therein.[308] It seems to be generally agreed that much of what is reported in the Torah is set "at Sinai and its surrounding area, called 'the wilderness of Sinai.'"[309] Thus, it is said,

> Everything that transpires from the beginning of chapter 19 [of *Exodus*] through the rest of *Exodus*, all of *Leviticus* and *Numbers* up through 10:10 will be connected with this area: the theophany, the laws and priestly rules, the great rebellion with the building of the Golden Calf, and the planning and construction of the Tabernacle. Sinai is the locus for much of the Torah.[310]

Descriptions of what is taken to be "the wilderness of Sinai" testify to its awesomeness: I am reminded of what I myself have seen at and heard about Delphi.[311]

Before we turn to the Ten Commandments proper, and to how to begin to read them, let us have one more account, this one from the pen of Martin Buber, which describes what is said to have taken place after the Ten Commandments were delivered by God to the entire people of Israel:

> The story of the tables as told in the book of *Exodus* consists of a series of tremendous scenes, which have always aroused the fervent emotions of believing hearts. Moses summoned to the summit of the mountain in order to receive the tables which YHVH Himself has written for the instruction of the children of Israel [*Exodus* 24:12]; Moses ascending into God's cloud and remaining there for forty days and forty nights [*Exodus* 24:18]; Moses receiving from God the "Tables of the Testimony" written by His finger [*Exodus* 31:18]; Moses on the way down from the mountain becoming aware of the "unbridled" people, and in flaming fury flinging the tables away from his hands, so that they smash below on the mountain-side [*Exodus* 32:19]; Moses, at the command of [the Lord], hewing two fresh tables from the stone "like the first," in order that God may write upon them again and again ascending the mountain with them [*Exodus* 34:1, 4]; Moses with the tables in his hand receiving from the mouth of the God who "passes him by" the revelation of God's qualities [*Exodus* 34:5–7]; Moses again standing forty days and forty nights on the mountain without food and drink and writing on the tables "the words of the covenant, the ten words"; he

> and not YHVH, although YHVH had promised him to do this Himself, and hence, from the viewpoint and for the purpose of the redactor, who considered that the two passages were mutually reconcilable, functioning as the writing finger of YHVH [*Exodus* 34:28]; and Moses going down with the new tables, the skin of his face radiant from his contact with God, and he himself unaware of it. [*Exodus* 34:29][312]

Martin Buber then adds an observation that it is useful to notice as suggestive of a common modern approach to these matters: "If we wish to keep before us a sequence of events possible in our human world, we must renounce all such tremendous scenes."[313] Such observations remind us that there may indeed be special problems (with special solutions?) in reading the special kind of book that the Bible is.

II

Not only is the Bible a special kind of book, but the text of the Ten Commandments is even more special, in that it is traditionally believed "to be the first word the Lord ever spoke to a whole people, the first and last time He was ever to do so."[314] Thus, not only do we have in the Ten Commandments perhaps the oldest, or first, text in the Western world—it was said to be reduced to writing shortly after it was delivered orally—but we have here a text which is understood to have been prepared by the most accomplished Author, by someone infinitely more accomplished than even Moses. It should be assumed, therefore, to be the text most susceptible of careful reading. The reader is intended, or at least induced, to ask again and again: "What could God have been thinking of here?"

Consider the following observations by Leo Strauss about how the Bible itself should be read, observations that apply, it would seem, with even greater force to the Ten Commandments as a text prepared by God "personally" for the people of Israel:

> I have been asked to speak here about *Genesis*—or rather about the beginning of *Genesis*. The context of a series of lectures on the "Works of the Mind" raises immediately a very grave question. Works of the mind are works of the human mind. Is the Bible a work of the human mind? Is it not the work of God? The work of God, of the divine mind? The latter view was generally accepted in former ages. We have to reflect on this alternative approach to the Bible because this alternative is decisive as to the way in which we will read the Bible. If the Bible is a work of the human mind, it has to be read like any other book—like Homer, like Plato, like Shakespeare—with respect but also with willingness to argue with the author, to disagree with him, to criticize him. If the Bible is the

> work of God, it has to be read in an entirely different spirit than the way in which we must read the human books. The Bible has to be read in a spirit of pious submission, of reverent hearing. According to this view, only a believing and pious man can understand the Bible—the substance of the Bible. According to the view which prevails today, the unbeliever, provided he is a man of the necessary experience or sensitivity, can understand the Bible as well as the believer. This difference between the two approaches can be described as follows. In the past, the Bible was universally read as the document of revelation. Today it is frequently read as one great document of the human mind among many such documents. Revelation is a miracle. This means, therefore, that before we even open the Bible we must have made up our minds as to whether we believe in the possibility of miracles. Obviously we read the account of the burning bush or the Red Sea deliverance in an entirely different way in correspondence with the way in which we have decided previously regarding the possibility of miracles.[315]

Thus, Mr. Strauss advised us several decades ago, it may well make a difference what we take for granted as we proceed to read the Ten Commandments—what we now take for granted not only about the terms used and the institutions referred to in the Bible but even more about the workings of the divine in human affairs.

Among the things we take for granted is, of course, the name "The Ten Commandments." In several Torah passages, we are told, the Hebrew term used to refer to this text means literally "a decade of words."[316] The text is more aptly known as the Ten Words or the Ten Utterances—and this makes particularly appropriate the word "Decalogue" (or, ten sayings), which was first applied to this text "by a Greek Church Father, Clement of Alexandria, about 200 C.E."[317] Even so, most people, including Jewish scholars learned in Hebrew, continue to refer to the text as the Ten Commandments.

We have already noticed that there are differences between the *Exodus* and *Deuteronomy* texts. It is convenient for us to work primarily with *Exodus*, for the time being. In *Exodus*, the text of the Ten Commandments is found virtually at the midpoint of the book.[318] There are less than two hundred words in the Ten Commandments, distributed among thirteen sentences in the accepted Jewish versions.[319] The ordering of the subjects dealt with remains fairly constant among the various versions we have. There are two principal exceptions: "in the so-called Nash papyrus, from the second or first century B.C.E., the prohibition of adultery precedes that of murder;" and "in the Samaritan Pentateuch, the Ten Commandments [we have] are compressed into nine to make room for a commandment concerning" a mountain important to the Samaritans.[320]

All this is aside from an even more radical variation, which I need do no more than touch upon here. There have been, at least in recent centuries, those who have argued that the Decalogue referred to in the Bible is not the text we are familiar with, but rather a set of prescriptions concerned primarily with rituals vital to cultic concerns, of which the Sabbath commandment may be illustrative.[321] Although some prominent scholars have been associated with this "theory," it is not one that should concern us on this occasion since we are interested primarily in the text that has been so influential in the West for two thousand years.

Even so, we should notice that that text has inspired significant differences of opinion as to how precisely it is to be divided into ten items, a division which both various biblical references and a long tradition require. Much depends upon what is taken to be the First Commandment. The prevailing Jewish opinion identifies the first as simply, "I am the Lord thy God who brought thee out of the land of Egypt, out of the house of bondage." We are told by scholars, however, that

> such ancient writers as Philo and Josephus, as well as the new Jewish Publication Society translation, the Greek Church Fathers, and most Protestant churches (except the Lutherans), consider the first commandment to be: "I am the Lord thy God, who brought thee out of the land of Egypt, out of the house of bondage. Thou shalt have no other gods before Me."[322]

For such scholars the explicit prohibition thereafter of idolatry forms the Second Commandment. We are also told: "Another division, going back to Augustine, is used in the Roman Catholic and Lutheran churches."[323] This follows the written text of Torah scrolls and includes the prohibition of idolatry in the First Commandment and thereafter divides the coveting prohibition into two commandments.

How the text *is* divided into the required ten items may depend somewhat upon how it is understood. Thus, one can be guided in one's division by one's opinion as to what God's plan is, what His principle of order is. My own opinion in these matters is that longstanding traditions should provide one's point of departure—and so I will be working from the traditional Jewish ordering of the commandments. It has been noticed: "In Jewish tradition the first five commandments were believed to have been inscribed on one tablet, and the remaining five on the other. This division recommended itself because the first five speak of God and the last five do not mention His name."[324] With this observation, we not only begin to discern a principle of order within the text but we are reminded, as with studying the Constitution of the United States, that virtually every observation or insight one may now have has been anticipated, in some form, by someone else over the centuries.[325] The most one can hope to do is to rearrange the more significant of the available observations according to a pattern appropriate to one's general view of things, which view one can hope is respectful of that of the Author of the Ten Commandments.

Let us consider, then, the Ten Commandments one by one as well as all together, those authoritative directives which can be considered central to the biblical enterprise for several millennia now.

III

The First Commandment is: "I am the Lord thy God who brought thee out of the land of Egypt, out of the house of bondage."[326]

If the text is understood as ten *statements*, rather than as ten *commandments*, it is easier to regard this sentence, standing alone, as the first item in the Decalogue. Egypt is always held up to the Israelites as *the* alternative to what they now have. This text begins as something of a declaration of independence—but a declaration of dependence as well, which takes the form of the Israelites' covenant with God entered into on this occasion.[327] All that will be said and done here is in the context of their recent liberation. Since you are liberated, God seems to say, you will need these rules (or discipline) in order to be truly free, to be fully yourselves. Shortly before, God had sent a message to this people (through Moses): "Now therefore, if ye will hearken unto My voice indeed, and keep My covenant, then ye shall be Mine own treasured from among all peoples; for all the earth is Mine, and ye shall be unto to Me a kingdom of priests, and a holy nation."[328]

We notice that God is *not* presented in the First Commandment as Creator, but rather as Liberator. (Creation is drawn upon in the Fourth Commandment, about the Sabbath, and perhaps implicitly both in the Second Commandment, against idolatry, and in the Sixth Commandment, against murder.) The emphasis, at least at the outset, upon liberation may point up the political-legal character of this array of statements and of the covenant entered into. Even so, to say, "I am the Lord thy God . . ." is perhaps to remind them, "I am He in Whose image you have been made by Me."

The exclusivity of this divinity may be implied; it is not yet made explicit. I mention in passing that the divine is referred to in several ways in the course of the Ten Commandments: *Elohim* is used, as is the Tetragrammaton.[329] Much more needs to be said about this, which I am not competent to do—except to suggest that it is made clear that whatever the names used for the divine, *this* Divinity is to be thought of as comprehensive.

What it means, it can be noticed, is that "This is their God" follows thereafter, especially in the Second, Third, and Fourth Commandments, but perhaps in all the rest of the commandments as well. Does worship follow from such an identification and association? The form that worship takes can very well depend upon detailed rules, upon established practices, indeed upon a community. The First Commandment leaves all this to be developed; it is enough to set forth the premise, or first principle, from which all else follows for *this* people. The Oneness of this God seems to be indicated. Perhaps it can even be shown that that Oneness is reflected as well in each of the commandments that follow.

IV

The Second Commandment is:

> Thou shalt have no other gods before Me. Thou shalt not make unto thee a graven image, nor any manner of likeness, of any thing that is in heaven above, or that is in the earth beneath, or that is in the water under the earth; thou shalt not bow down unto them, nor serve them; for I the Lord thy God am a jealous God, visiting the iniquity of the fathers upon the children unto the third and fourth generations of them that hate Me; and showing mercy unto the thousandth generation of them that love Me and keep My commandments.[330]

Not only is the exclusivity of this God insisted upon, but what this means is also spelled out in some detail, like a lawyer's anticipation of all the devices to which an unreliable opponent might resort. It is not clear from this text what, if any, recognition is given here to the other so-called gods. Do they have *any* substance, at least for other peoples? Or is it that the people of Israel are the only (or first) full people, in that they alone have a genuine divinity to take their bearings by?[331]

Creation, not liberation, seems to be drawn upon in the Second Commandment. Not only are the creative urges of the Israelites to be suppressed, but also the creative accomplishments of God are echoed in the references to heaven, earth, and waters (those elements which, it is likely, are so tempting for mankind to make much of and which people all around the Israelites did make much of in their worship). These three elements are returned to in the Fourth Commandment with respect to the Sabbath, where the fact of the Creation is made explicit and becomes critical.

Images are decisively rejected as objects of worship. Perhaps they are not to be resorted to even in an effort to celebrate God Himself. An image of this God easily turns into images of other gods, especially among the uninformed and the susceptible. Idolatry, we have noticed, seems to have been a constant concern of the prophets of Israel—and the form that dangerous idolatry can take depends upon circumstances. As we have been reminded, even while

Moses was communing with God, his people turned to idolatry with the Golden Calf—and this not long after they had been witnesses to the most marvelous manifestations of God. Not inconsequential here is the influence of the aesthetic element in the human soul. Even the love of beauty can lead one astray. Consider how such marvels as the da Vinci *Mona Lisa* and the Michelangelo *Pieta* can be practically venerated.[332]

Any representation of the human form may be a problem, for that can verge on idol worship. That is, no image of God is permitted. Only God is to make images of God, and this He has already done—and done in the only way permitted on earth—in the making of man. And so man can be reminded on more than one occasion that he is indeed made in the image of God.[333]

But care must vigilantly be taken not to allow this to mean that God, too, has physical qualities. It is this care, it will be remembered, to which Maimonides devotes so many of the opening chapters of *The Guide of the Perplexed*.[334] The difficulty for Maimonides is, of course, that there are in the Bible many passages suggesting that God has physical attributes.[335] The Maimonides position has to be insisted upon, for example, in interpreting such passages as that in *Deuteronomy* where the giving of the Ten Commandments is recalled: "And the Lord spoke unto you out of the midst of the fire; ye heard the voice of words, but ye saw no form, only a voice."[336] Yet, it must at once be added, it is difficult to tell a great story, in which God acts upon and with men, without so speaking of Him as to associate passions and hence physical attributes with Him.[337]

Leo Strauss has suggested that the second account in *Genesis* of Creation is intended, at least in part, to deal with difficulties left by the first account there of Creation, which has man created in the image of God. To say man was created in the image of God is to suggest that he is, or should be, in a way like God. And so Mr. Strauss can say:

> Was he not, therefore, congenitally tempted to transgress any prohibitions, any limitations? Was this likeness to God not a constant temptation to be literally like Him? To dispose of this difficulty the second account of creation distributes accents differently than the first account had done. Man is now said to be, not created in the image of God, but dust from the earth.[338]

I have suggested that there is a reciprocal effect to be concerned about here. If man is regarded as created in the image of God, then human beings may be tempted to return the compliment, so to speak, by creating God in *their* image. And if man is also seen as made from dust, it becomes almost natural to see God too as the product, or as an expression, of material causes. This can become a new form of idolatry, with divine causation understood in terms of the laws of physics and chemistry. We can thus be reminded that atheism is rarely, if ever, the problem anticipated in the Bible, but rather idolatry in one form or another. At the root of idolatry may be the all-too-human desire to be able to take charge of one's destiny, even to the extent of making and otherwise directing the gods one "worships." So powerful, and so deadly, is the lure of idolatry that it can be suggested by a thoughtful student of Maimonides that "the Law has, so to speak, no other purpose than to destroy idolatry."[339]

How critical idolatry can be is reflected in what is said in the Second Commandment about the long-term implications of idolatry. Anyone who errs here can do irreparable harm to his children and grandchildren, perhaps even to his great-grandchildren. Is not this a not uncommon extension of the consequences of one's actions?[340] Furthermore, the generations referred to in the Second Commandment are those that one can hope to see for oneself. Thus, one can witness the deterioration that one may be responsible for. On the other hand, proper submission to the God of Israel can lead to thousands of years of goodness, and hence well-being, for a *people*. I emphasize "people" here since, after a number of generations, one is no longer talking about a family but rather about the people that develops out of a family.

V

The Third Commandment is: "Thou shalt not take the name of the Lord thy God in vain; for the Lord will not hold him guiltless that taketh His name in vain."[341]

It may be that recourse to magic is being forbidden here, at least in part.[342] In a sense, this commandment continues the limitation in the Second Commandment upon images: an improper use of *words* about God is addressed in the Third Commandment. God is not to be exploited; He is not to be used.[343] God is the master, not the servant, of man, whereas the reckless name-user attempts to take from God something which is His own.[344]

But notice the profound concession implied by this commandment. Not only does it seem to be conceded that God's name is available for proper use by man, but also, perhaps even more important, it seems to be recognized that the Israelites may know or eventually have access to God's names, perhaps even to the most important name of God.[345]

This commandment warns that "the Lord will not hold him guiltless that taketh His name in vain." We now notice that the two commandments before this one also include something more than the bare statement or command—and, when we look ahead, we notice that the same can be said of the next two commandments as well. Thus, we can now add another set of affinities among the first five commandments, which are the only ones that mention God: they are also the only ones that provide an elaboration in each case upon the command itself. Still another pattern may be noticed: the first commandment is short, the second is quite long, the third is short, the fourth is quite long, and the fifth is short. (Thereafter, there is a series of very short statements up to the last commandment, which so expands as to be a little longer than the shorter ones among the first five.) This alternation of short and long among the first five commandments, as well as the marked shift in the second five, suggest an Author who has a plan in mind.[346]

VI

The Fourth Commandment is:

> Remember the sabbath day, to keep it holy. Six days shalt thou labour, and do all thy work, but the seventh day is a sabbath unto the Lord thy God, in it thou shalt not do any manner of work, thou, nor thy son, nor thy daughter, nor thy man-servant, nor thy maid-servant, nor thy cattle, nor thy stranger that is within thy gates; for in six days the Lord made heaven and earth, the sea, and all that is in them, and rested on the seventh day; wherefore the Lord blessed the sabbath day, and hallowed it.[347]

One contemporary scholar has described this commandment in this way:

> The fourth commandment is the longest and most elaborate, the first that is explicitly positive, and the only one that is concerned with a positive religious institution. Respecting circumcision, for example, the festivals, prayers, or a house of worship, the Decalogue says nothing. Instead, it devotes nearly a third of its space to order the observance of a day of rest.[348]

In its detailed elaboration (or with considerable work), again perhaps with a view to anticipating various evasions, the Fourth Commandment is like the Second. Both of them can be said to deal with images: the Second, explicitly, with the supposed images of the divine that men are prone to resort to; the Fourth, with the Sabbath as an image of what God Himself had done in the Creation.[349]

Sabbath observance is not created by the Decalogue, for it seems to have been already in force. Consider, for example, the earlier prohibition upon gathering manna on the Sabbath.[350] The Sabbath is confirmed or taken for granted at various other places in the Bible after the Ten Commandments.[351] In the *Deuteronomy* version of the Fourth Commandment, the people are enjoined, "*Observe* the sabbath day, to keep it holy," whereas in *Exodus* it had been said, "*Remember* the sabbath day, to keep it holy."[352] The "remember" of *Exodus* is used in *Deuteronomy* where it is explained why the Sabbath should be observed: "And remember that thou wast a slave in the land of Egypt, and the Lord thy God brought thee out thence by a mighty hand and by an outstretched arm; therefore the Lord thy God commanded thee to keep the sabbath day."[353] It can be suggested by scholars that by the time Moses returned to the Ten Commandments in *Deuteronomy* (some forty years later), the recollection of their liberation from Egypt (by then irrevocably established?) may have meant more to the people than what they had heard about the Creation.[354] Moses' own willingness, and ability, to modify his accounts both of the commandments and of the people's response to them—his adaptation of these accounts to changing circumstances—should suggest to us what is essential to all this, as well as what may properly be filtered through the mind of the narrator. In our own reflections upon such things, we might well take Moses' example as our model as our own circumstances change.

It is easy to overlook the assumption, implicit in this commandment, that the people are expected to be working when they are not relieved by the Sabbath or by other observances.[355] Also indicated is the extent of the normal, or complete, household, which includes children, slaves, and animals. What should be made of the fact that one's wife is not mentioned (whereas the daughter is mentioned here and the mother in the Fifth Commandment)? Is not one's wife implied in the "thou" being addressed (just as Eve was part of Adam)? Or is it perhaps recognized that some household work, connected with the care of the family, must continue on the Sabbath, especially since the Sabbath does seem to be regarded not as a day of fasting but rather as a day of celebration? Should the Sabbath observance be taken as a reminder of the first three commandments? It *is* the Sabbath of the God who brought them out of Egypt, Who will not brook any graven or sculptured image or any other thing for worship, and Whose name should not be misused. Three numbers have emerged in the commandments as critical to God: *one*, of course, but also *six* (the days *He* worked), and *seven* (the day *He* rested). Similarly, the people of Israel came to a halt before Sinai after, it seems, six weeks of constant movement. Seven could come to be regarded by the people of Israel, and by students of the Bible, as an indication of perfection (and hence of rest or permanancy?).[356] The importance of seven is reinforced by the listing here of seven who are to be governed by this Sabbath observance: "thou . . . thy son . . . thy daughter . . . thy man-servant . . . thy maid-servant . . . thy cattle, thy stranger that is within thy gates."[357] The extension to the stranger of this deliverance from everyday work—a kind of weekly liberation from Egypt or bondage—suggests that the goodness of the Law, or of this way of life, need not be limited to the people of Israel. Is it also suggested that the seventh day is a stranger to, in being most unlike, the other six days?

VII

The Fifth Commandment is: "Honour thy father and thy mother, that thy days may be long upon the land which the Lord thy God giveth thee."[358]

The regard for parents found in the Fifth Commandment reminds us of the importance of the Creation, which is memorialized in the Fourth Commandment.[359] Those who honor their parents can expect to endure long on the land. An immediate benefit is thus held out for the respectful child. In the Second Commandment, on the other hand, what is immediately threatened is the visitation of the consequences of idolatry upon the idolaters' children. This reminds us of something noticed by Aristotle, that parents naturally care more for their children than children care for their parents. Thus, idolatrous parents are told (in the Second Commandment) of the harm that can come to their children, whereas children are offered something good for themselves (in the Fifth Commandment) if they treat their parents properly.

What are we to understand to be the connections between honoring one's parents and enduring long upon the land to be given them by the Lord? (This is similar to a question we considered with respect to the Second Commandment.) If parents are not honored, there is not apt to be an established community and hence any permanent place.[360] "Parents," it can be said, extend to elders, perhaps generally to those properly in authority. What does "honor" mean? To recognize them *as* parents, as people of special status? Perhaps one honors one's parents most, or most naturally (as *we* might say), when one is respectful of their teachings and of them as teachers (as, for example, Jacob was respected by his children?). An enduring community follows upon honoring parents since parents are likely to be the principal source of the tradition, or teaching, with respect to God and to His commandments about the divine found in the first four commandments. Consider, for example, these instructions from Moses in *Deuteronomy*:

> Hear, O Israel: The Lord our God, the Lord is One. And thou shalt love the Lord thy God with all thy heart, and with all thy soul, and with all thy might. And these words, which I command thee this day, shall be upon thy heart, and thou shalt teach them diligently unto thy children.[361]

The God who elevates parents with the Fifth Commandment is in turn elevated by parents who teach their children thoroughly. In a sense, indeed, parents can be salutary images of God: they are a child's immediate divinity (that is, authority). If one does not honor one's parents, whom one can see and whose care for one has long been obvious, how is one likely to honor, or to worship, a divinity whom one can never see? Thus, as Rabbi Samson Hirsch put it, "[T]he knowledge and acknowledgment of [the basic facts in the history of the Jewish people] depends solely on tradition, and tradition depends solely on the faithful transmission by parents to children, and on the willing acceptance by children from the hands of their parents."[362] It is in God's interest, so to speak, that pious parents be honored by their children—for this means that children will then be more apt to honor, if not even to worship, what their parents worship. It is this, central to the biblical enterprise, that can make the typical conversion among us, as distinguished from steady (even "atheistic") non-observance, a sadly dubious experiment.

In any event, the relations between parents and child can serve as a transition from the relations between God and man dealt with in the first four commandments to the relations between man and man dealt with in the last five commandments—a transition from the commandments respecting piety to the commandments respecting the moral virtues of a social character. The first five commandments can be violated by a man living apart from other human beings. Even then, for example, one may recall properly and hence honor one's parents. The second five commandments, on the other hand, can be kept or violated, practically speaking, only by a man living with other human beings. The Sixth Commandment, to which we now turn, can serve as a transition from the provisions in the first five commandments to those in the remaining commandments.

VIII

The Sixth Commandment is: "Thou shalt not murder."[363]

Just as with the insistence upon Sabbath observance, so with the prohibition upon murder and the following commandments, there is no innovation here. These latter commandments are restatements of established rules perhaps useful to collect in these circumstances. So well established among human beings are the prohibitions against murder and the like that they do not depend upon the God of Israel or, indeed, upon any revelation.[364] All peoples come, one way or another, to recognize the necessity of such prohibitions. But are they not more likely to be respected wherever God is worshiped properly? Even so, there is no need to provide explanations of or justifications for these prohibitions, unlike what had to be done for the first five items in the Decalogue.[365]

Of course, there are questions about meanings. For example, not all killing is ruled out, as may be seen in the capital punishment to be visited upon those who commit various offenses. In addition, war may be called for, as well as acts of self-defense. Here, as elsewhere, a system of definitions and laws is taken for granted. In a sense, the *status quo* is to be preferred, and the powers of government (as well as of God, of course) are presupposed.[366]

William Blackstone has called murder "the highest crime against the law of nature."[367] Murder, it can be said, anticipates all the offenses that follow, which deal with various forms of unauthorized destruction that can be disruptive of community life. From the Sixth Commandment through the Tenth, there is progressively less physical contact between persons in the offense being regulated, moving from violent contact to illicit pleasurable contact, to the taking of another's property (without necessarily touching that person), to the distant contact of improper testimony, and finally to contact in thought only. The degree of contact dealt with in the last five commandments is directly related, it would seem, to the seriousness of the offense. Thus, the Fifth and the Sixth Commandments serve as transitions from the first four to the last four commandments. The family is confirmed, if not made sacred, by the Fifth Commandment, and it is the family upon which the things protected in the subsequent commandments very much depend: human life, marriage, and property. (We have noticed that the people of Israel is itself family-based, regarding itself as the seed of Abraham.) The sacredness of human life can be said to be recognized in the Sixth Commandment, that life which was created in the image of God.

These suggestions about the patterns to be found in the ordering of the commandments are offered in support of the proposition that there is considerable merit to the traditional Jewish arrangement of the Decalogue. I venture, with this in view, to make a further set of suggestions about the relations of the first five commandments to the last five. I begin with the Sixth Commandment by observing that it may be intimately related to the First Commandment. (These two commandments would be opposite each other, if one considers them set forth as five to a tablet.) The Sixth Commandment recalls the First Commandment by saying, in effect, "The God who is your God, in whose image you are made, and who troubled to save you does not want you destroying anyone He has made and saved. Man is to preserve man, just as God has preserved man." Thus, the Sixth Commandment is illuminated by the First. But also, perhaps it should be said, those who are apt to take the Sixth Commandment more seriously than they do the First Commandment (which is probably true of many people today)—such people are being asked to take the First Commandment more seriously than they otherwise might because of their very regard for the Sixth. That is, there may be a reciprocal effect here, as with the relations, we will see, between the Second and the Seventh Commandments, between the Third and the Eighth Commandments, between the Fourth and the Ninth Commandments, and between the Fifth and the Tenth Commandments.

There is another good reason for making the prohibition of murder the *Sixth* Commandment. Does not that point to the sanctity, or goodness, of the world made by God in six days, a whole which is not to be wantonly disturbed? But if the prohibition of murder is appropriately the *Sixth* Commandment, what can be said about the appropriateness of the *Seventh* Commandment?

IX

The Seventh Commandment is: "Thou shalt not commit adultery."[368]

What adultery is also depends upon the laws of the community, including those laws that identify partners as spouses. All kinds of special questions (if not even rationalizations) can arise here, such as whether it is possible to commit adultery in a country other than one's own (that is, in a place where the laws are quite different), or whether it is adultery if no conception of children is possible or anticipated, or if one's spouse provokes, depends upon, or otherwise encourages the liaison.

The specialness of adultery as an offense may be suggested by the fact that it *is* the seventh of the commandments. This can be considered the Sabbath of the commandments in the Decalogue. That is, a kind of rest, if not even perfection, is prescribed.[369] One is required to "stay put," thereby placing limits upon those sexual activities that are not only proper but are depended upon if not even encouraged, by the community, with its obligation to multiply.[370] The Sabbath, too, limits activities otherwise permissible, and perhaps even necessary, to do. Respect for these limitations, whether with respect to labor or with respect to sexuality, can make ordinary, licit activities (whether in one's work or with one's spouse) more satisfying than they might otherwise be.[371]

The specialness of adultery as an offense may be further suggested by the fact that sexuality outside of a marriage can sometimes seem genuinely attractive. Consider, for example, what modern novels attempt to do with it. Consider, also, the relation between David and Bathsheba, which, for all its impropriety, did eventually produce Solomon. Still, sexuality does pose something of a problem in the Bible, as may be seen in the preparations for a special Sinai experience, which include the people of Israel abstaining from sexual relations.[372]

What, then, about the reciprocal relations I have suggested between the Second and the Seventh Commandments? The Second Commandment, as we have seen, makes much of generations; and adultery interferes with the orderly arrangement of generations. For example, adultery can make it difficult for one to honor one's parents, since one may not be able to identify one's father.[373] Does the Second Commandment prohibit the people of Israel from committing spiritual adultery by substituting other gods for their proper God, the God with Whom they are permanently mated, just as marriage keeps a man and a woman together as they should be?

X

The Eighth Commandment is: "Thou shalt not steal."[374]

Theft, too, depends upon the laws of the community. We are reminded that property is important and that the available tangible resources in a community are generally allocated. We can see elsewhere in the Bible that a complicated system of property is taken for granted. But however important property is, it is not as important as life: ordinary property crimes are never capital offenses in the Bible, whereas murder and adultery can be.[375] We can confirm the order of these commandments by observing that property presupposes family, and family presupposes life.

Life on earth, the Hebrew Bible seems to assume, is by and large good. It is further assumed that having property, or a land, *is* a good thing. Respect for property again reminds us of what God has done, for do not the more significant property allocations depend ultimately upon God? Thus, in the Fifth Commandment, the people of Israel are told of "the land which the Lord thy God giveth thee."[376] God's ultimate authority over property is seen elsewhere as well, as in *Deuteronomy* where the people of Israel are told by Moses:

> And it shall be when, the Lord thy God shall bring thee into the land which He swore unto thy fathers, to Abraham, to Isaac, and to Jacob, to give thee—great and goodly cities, which thou didst not build, and houses full of all good things, which thou didst not fill, and cisterns hewn out, which thou didst not hew, vineyards and olive-trees, which thou didst not plant, and thou shalt eat and be satisfied—then beware lest thou forget the Lord, who brought thee forth out of the land of Egypt, out of the house of bondage.[377]

What, then, about the reciprocal relations I have suggested between the Third and Eighth Commandments? The Third Commandment, it will be remembered, makes much of the unauthorized use of God's name. Such an improper appropriation of the name of God can be regarded as a kind of theft, just as theft can be regarded as a failure to respect the naming of owners, or material allocations, that have been made pursuant to God's guidance.

XI

The Ninth Commandment is: "Thou shalt not bear false witness against thy neighbor."[378]

The injunction against false witnessing presupposes a community. Perhaps it can also be taken to imply the need to testify to the truth when properly called upon, especially with respect to the kind of offenses addressed in the Sixth, Seventh, and Eighth Commandments. Would there also be offenses related to the first five commandments? We would be apt to say that *those* may be more appropriately dealt with in the "court of conscience"—but we do recall what was done by Moses and his allies to the Golden Calf idolaters.[379]

What, then, about the reciprocal relations between the Fourth and Ninth Commandments? The false witnessing most to be concerned about, it can be said, is any testimony which unjustly convicts one of murder or of adultery or of theft or which can otherwise lead to deprivations of life or spouse or property. Thus, violation of the Ninth Commandment subverts the application of the Sixth, Seventh, and Eighth Commandments. Similarly, violation of the Fourth Commandment subverts respect for the First, Second, and Third Commandments. That is, to profane the Sabbath is in effect to bear false witness against God and His commandments with respect to the proper relation between God and man.

It can be said, therefore, that false witnessing, like Sabbath-breaking, is an "external" subversion of law. The laws about murder, adultery and theft can be usefully distinguished here from the laws about disbelief, idolatry, and the vain use of God's name.

XII

The Tenth Commandment is: "Thou shalt not covet your neighbour's house: thou shalt not covet thy neighbor's wife, nor his man-servant, nor his maid-servant, nor his ox, nor his ass, nor any thing that is thy neighbour's."[380]

The neighbor's house is mentioned first, set off from the others, perhaps to suggest that the list which follows consists of illustrations of what a household may include for the purpose of this commandment.[381] In the *Deuteronomy* version of the Decalogue, the neighbor's wife replaces the neighbor's house as perhaps the more inclusive term.[382] Had something happened during the forty years since Egypt, or was something about to happen (with the Promised Land so imminent), that called for this substitution?[383] Had a house seemed, in the wilderness, the ultimate in what one could yearn for? Now that the people of Israel are about to move into a more settled life, can the temporal sovereignty (if not the intrinsic superiority) of the marital relationship reassert itself?[384]

What, then, about the reciprocal relations between the Fifth and Tenth Commandments? These two commandments may depend, perhaps more than all the others, upon one's thoughts. They may both deal with the deep habituation upon which genuine conformity to the other commandments depends: honoring of parents means that the teachings of parents about the divine are more likely to be respected; suppression of coveting means that the prohibitions of murder, adultery, and theft are more likely to be respected. Or, put otherwise, disrespect for parents (even if only in one's thoughts) is an "internal" or "private" subversion of the law, just as is coveting.[385] Or, put still another way, just as the Fifth Commandment can be seen as the culmination of the four commandments preceding it, so can the Tenth Commandment be seen as the culmination of the four commandments preceding *it*. In both cases, the shaping of the soul is vital, perhaps in order to make particularly destructive opinions virtually unthinkable.

Thus, we have seen, one of the tablets (each with five commandments inscribed on it) is an image of the other. This suggests how instructive, and otherwise important, images can be—but it can suggest as well how one may become so intrigued by images and imaging as to lose sight of the pious singlemindedness and the moral fervor to which the Decalogue is obviously dedicated.[386]

XIII

Several questions are left which can be no more than touched upon here.

It has long been wondered precisely what the assembled people of Israel are supposed to have heard on the occasion of the delivery of the Decalogue? Only the First Commandment, with all the rest implied? Or the First and the Second Commandments, since they alone have God speaking in the first person? (Are these two special also in that they, alone of the first five, can be reasoned to somewhat by mankind?) And did what the people "heard" come to them in the form of words or in some other way? There has been much discussion about all this that, even more than much of what I have already presumed to say, depends upon a thorough knowledge not only of the Bible and the early rabbinic and other literature, but also of the Hebrew language, which I can lay no claim to at all.

One can also wonder why there are precisely *ten* commandments. Why not twelve, which is a number made very much of throughout the Bible, or thirteen, which can also have a special standing? Of course, ten is also made much of in the Bible, as is seven. The plagues in Egypt, at least according to the traditional count, readily come to mind.[387] Perhaps more important than the total numbers are the patterns which may be discerned in the arrangement of the commandments, patterns which suggest the thinking that went into the development of the Decalogue. Additional patterns can be suggested, for it is also possible to see affinities between the First and the Tenth Commandments, between the Second and the Ninth, between the Third and the Eighth, and so on. Thus, for example, the First and the Tenth are very much concerned with what one might desire. But then, should not one expect the master speech by God to be remarkably patterned, just as are the phenomena described by our laws of physics? Are we not invited to see what is there?

Also to be approached in the proper spirit is the question of what is *not* there to be seen. Thus, there is something of a mystery in the tradition as to what has become of the stone tablets prepared by Moses and God, which were treasured so long by the people of Israel. How is a believer to regard their disappearance? Perhaps he should regard it the way he should regard the fact that it is not known where Moses' grave is or even which mountain was known as Sinai/Horeb.[388] It may be salutary that such material things (including the Temple itself?) should be hidden from view, lest (as we have seen) they be treated as objects or images which form the basis for idolatry. Perhaps also much the same should be said by the believer about various of the problems we have touched upon here, including the difficulty of determining precisely how the Decalogue is to be divided and the difficulty of accounting for the discrepancies between the texts we do happen to have. If one is obliged to compare and to think about differences, may one be less likely to regard any particular "document" as itself holy, if not even as a fetish? In this sense, then, inquiry and reflection can be said to contribute to, or at least to respect, piety.

This happy compatibility of reason with revelation may even be suggested in the recognition by the people of Israel that they could hear "the voice of the living God speaking out of the midst of the fire" and yet live.[389] It may be suggested as well in the counsel we have recalled by the elderly Moses to his people:

> Behold, I have taught you statutes and ordinances, even as the Lord my God commanded me, that ye should do so in the midst of the land whither ye go in to possess it. Observe therefore and do them; for this is your wisdom and your understanding in the sight of [other] peoples, that, when they hear all these statutes, shall say: "Surely this great nation is a wise and understanding people."[390]

Notice again what is implied here about the significance of reason in human affairs. Also notice again that it is anticipated that other peoples will, on the basis only of *hearing* about "all these statutes," recognize the Israelites as "a great nation [of] wise and understanding people." Such recognition by others, it seems, would not depend either upon an experience of miracles or upon stories of miracles. Rather, the Mosaic laws alone, properly understood—that is, as they, once available, can be understood by the aid of natural reason alone—testify to the wisdom and discernment of the people of Israel. It is that wisdom which we have taken for granted on this occasion as we have begun to think about the Ten Commandments.

Chapter Ten

David[391]

When David offered himself to Saul to fight Goliath the Philistine challenger, Saul, in order to give him courage, armed him with his own arms, which, as soon as David had them on, he rejected, saying that he could not be of as good worth with them as by himself, and that he therefore wished to fight the enemy with his sling and with his knife. In fine, the arms of others either fall off your back, weigh you down, or constrict you.

Niccolò Machiavelli[392]

I

There has begun in Israel a fifteen-month-long celebration of what is said to be the three thousandth anniversary of the establishment of Jerusalem as the capital of ancient Israel. The original elevation of Jerusalem had been made by David, who had been king for seven years in Hebron and who would rule all Israel thereafter for thirty-three years.[393]

The specialness of David, which is apparent to almost everyone familiar with these matters, is reflected in the following observations by a contemporary literary critic:

> The large cycle of stories about David, which is surely one of the most stunning imaginative achievements of ancient literature, provides an instructive central instance of the intertwining of history and fiction. This narrative, though it may have certain folkloric embellishments (such as David's victory over Goliath), is based on firm historical facts, as modern research has tended to confirm: there

> really was a David who fought a civil war against the house of Saul, achieved undisputed sovereignty over the twelve tribes, conquered Jerusalem, founded a dynasty, created a small empire, and was succeeded by his son Solomon. Beyond these broad outlines, it is quite possible that many of the narrated details about David, including matters bearing on the complications of his conjugal life and his relations with his children, may have been reported on good authority.[394]

The "complications of [David's] conjugal life" just referred to have been assessed in this fashion by an encyclopedist:

> A shadow is cast over David's life and work by his adultery with [Bathsheba] and his murder of her husband, [Uriah the Hittite] (2 *Samuel* 11:1–27). Although David confessed his sin (2 *Samuel* 12:14), his bad example unleashed the worst passions within his family. [His son] Ammon's rape of his half-sister Tamar led to his assassination by [his half-brother] Absalom (2 *Samuel* 13:1–33), followed by the latter's flight, revolt, and death (2 *Samuel* 13:34–18:33). Intrigues of disastrous consequences were carried on for the succession to the throne, which was ultimately gained by Solomon (1 *Kings* 1:1–53). David died c. 961 B.C. after a reign of 40 years.[395]

Even so, this Christian encyclopedist went on to assess the significance of David's reign thus:

> David was "a man after God's own heart" (1 *Samuel* 13:14; *Acts* 13:22). This judgment does not imply that David was sinless, but refers to his docile and sincere heart. . . . Although David was without doubt a great king, later writers idealized him considerably, holding him up as the model for subsequent kings (1 *Kings* 14:8) and especially on the type of the coming Messiah. . . . The Prophets see the Messianic King as a descendant of David (*Isaiah* 11:1, 10; *Jeremiah* 30:9; *Ezekiel* 37:24). A unanimous tradition praises David also as poet and musician (2 *Samuel* 1:19–27; 3:33–34; 22:1–51; 23:1–7; *Sirach* 47:9), and numerous Psalms have been attributed to him.[396]

Also prominent in the tradition is the reciprocity between David and Jerusalem: Jerusalem is important because of David, but David is special because of Jerusalem. The specialness of Jerusalem is recognized in the traditional Passover salutation: "Next year in Jerusalem."[397] The specialness of David may be seen in his providing the image of the Messiah, so much so that Jesus' legitimacy and mission are keyed for Christians to David.

Thus, David was not only "a man after God's own heart"; he was also, and remains, a man after the hearts of Jews and Christians.

II

On the other hand, there is the David glimpsed in a poem by Heinrich Heine:

King David

Smiling still a despot dies,
For he knows, on his demise,
New hands wield the tyrant's power—
It is not yet freedom's hour.

Like the horse or ox, poor folk
Still stay harnessed to the yoke,
And that neck is broken faster
That's not bowed before the master.

On his deathbed, David told
His son Solomon: "Behold,
You must rid me, in all candor,
Of this Joab, my commander.

"Captain Joab's brave and tough
But he's irked me long enough,
Yet, however I detest him,
I have never dared arrest him.

"You, my son, are wise, devout,
Pious—and your arm is stout;
You should have no trouble sending
Joab to a sticky ending."[398]

There are problems with this translation, as there are with the other published translations I have seen of this poem. But key features of David's deathbed assignments to Solomon are evident in all of them. There is nothing sentimental or "philosophic" or obviously pious about *this* dying old man (even though, in the biblical account of the scene, he opens his final statement with a recommendation to his son of the rules laid down by Moses).[399]

Heine, who was in this as in other respects very much under the influence of the European Enlightenment, expresses modern reservations about David by casting his deathbed commands as primarily an expression of personal animosity. Heine does not seem to make any allowance for the political reasons for David's directions with respect to Joab and others—or, at least, for

Solomon's deference to his dying father's wishes. (In the way that Solomon proceeds there is a strategic sense worthy of Rebekah.) Nor is allowance made either for the character of Joab or for the threat he may pose to the long-term stability of the House of David.[400]

We have descended, that is, from the biblical characterization of David as "a man after God's own heart" to a gifted poet's characterization of him as a vengeful despot or tyrant. How *should* David be regarded by us?

III

David first comes to view, so far as most remember him, as the "folkloric" hero who, as little more than a boy, stood up to and brought down Goliath. (Compare the youthful Moses' smiting the Egyptian.) The encounter with Goliath is legendary in its tone, so much so as to arouse challenges from modern scholars as to its historicity.[401] This encounter has become the prototype for contests between the giant and the seemingly puny.[402] The notoriety of this episode is such that a desperate Tom Sawyer, when pressed in a Sunday School exercise to name Jesus' first two disciples, comes up with the names of David and Goliath.[403]

However folkloric the encounter with Goliath may be, it is not simply magical or miraculous in its details. David, as he prepares to fight with his own sling, carefully selects five stones from a stream.[404] There may not be anything special about the number. And, it seems, David is prepared in case he misses with his first effort.

Not just any effort will do. David has to work with what he, as a shepherd, has used in the field. Machiavelli, in *The Prince*, after reporting that David rejected Saul's arms for his duel with Goliath, draws (as we have seen) the following lesson: "In fine, the arms of others either fall off your back, weigh you down, or constrict you."[405] Machiavelli, however, may not be fully correct here, in that David did have to use Goliath's sword to finish off this Philistine.

Nothing much seems to follow from this encounter. It is almost as if this was a tale that the editor had to keep because it was so popular. This may add to the folkloric impression. But later on, when David's flight from Saul is presented in what is generally considered realistic detail, Goliath's sword proves to be available to David in the sanctuary where it had been kept for years.[406]

IV

David is attractive from the outset, both physically and morally.[407] He is somewhat naive and intrepid in his dealings with Goliath and then with others. He thereafter appears as indispensable to Saul, both as a companion gifted in song and as an effective man of war.[408] Saul's melancholy—a kind of recurrent depression, it seems—affects his capacity to govern; it evidently responds to musical therapy.[409]

The overall impression we get of David, at least initially, is that of youthfulness, courage, ingenuity, enthusiasm, and gallantry. We would also consider him as very fortunate, or as blessed by God, in his early career. He is eager to please both Saul and the people.

At first he succeeds, even becoming what we would consider an "overachiever."[410] But he cannot retain the affection of *both* Saul and the people: the more he impresses the people, the less he is liked by a Saul who cannot always control his passions.[411]

David's youthful ingenuity has to be transformed into shrewdness and his courage into resiliency if he is to survive and prosper, even while he remains respectful of the Lord's anointed. This may be seen, for example, in his ordering the execution of the servant who had perhaps killed Saul.[412] David knows when to run and where, taking advantage of the discontented of the land. He can end up, while Saul is alive, as king at Hebron, ruling over a part of what had become a divided Israel.[413]

V

David is, even in his early adversities, a bright and shining (if not even cheerful) figure. But a darker side of David becomes apparent when he becomes king of all Israel after the death of Saul. Rule can be said to show the man.

When David comes to rule he can be ruthless in turn—but more effectively so than the erratic Saul had been. David's gallant encounter with Goliath recedes from view; his determination not to strike Saul may be seen as grounded in policy.

David's encounter with Bathsheba seems to become vital to his entire career.[414] It affects, as we have been told, not only the succession to the throne but also David's relations with his children and with others. His relations with women are interesting—as with Abigail, a quite sensible woman, and as with Michal, the daughter of Saul who may be the only woman in the Bible who is said to love her man.[415]

But the story of Bathsheba becomes the decisive one. Once David sees her, he "must" have her. But even the king cannot risk being identified as an adulterer, it seems, which makes David vulnerable and then desperate when Bathsheba informs him that she is pregnant. David's first response is one that does not threaten Uriah's life. Rather, Uriah (upon being called home to

Jerusalem from the front) is to be given an opportunity to visit enough with his wife to make it seem plausible later that he is the father of her child.[416] But Uriah, perhaps out of a sense of duty (or of "identification" with his men at the front), stays away from her.[417] David, who is not naturally cruel, "must" then resort to a more cold-blooded approach, providing (through the agency of the tough Joab) for putting Uriah immediately at risk in battle, where he is killed. This permits David to salvage the situation by marrying Bathsheba.[418]

We have seen this way of dealing with Uriah referred to by an encyclopedist as "murder," but it is not simply that. Someone, it could be said, may have had to be put in danger—and there may be questions of *justice* about the selection of Uriah on this occasion. The measure used against Uriah by David is similar to the measure used earlier by Saul against David.[419] Only David is more effective than others in his stratagems, whether compared with what Saul had tried earlier or with what Absalom tried to do later.[420]

Besides, an apologist for David might ask, if the Lord had wanted to save Uriah, could not He have easily done so? This suggests another question that may be more within our competence to deal with: Is anything shown to be wrong with Uriah that he should have suffered the fate he did?[421] Is Uriah meant to be shown as principled? One serious flaw that may well be his, however, is that he did marry Bathsheba, a woman who should not have been expected to be satisfied with anything but the best (or, at least, the seeming best).

Is Bathsheba much more in charge than she seems? One might even wonder how many baths she had had to take on her rooftop before David noticed her. However that may have been, one suspects that Solomon's surpassing wisdom is not without genetic support.[422] Bathsheba's astuteness comes to view during the succession crisis, out of which her gifted son Solomon emerges as the next king of Israel.

Bathsheba evidently found in David a worthy partner. We may well wonder how early in his career did the tough singlemindedness of David assert itself.[423] Bernini's marvelous statue of the youthful David poised to strike Goliath, coolly sizing him up, suggests that David was someone to be reckoned with even at that stage of his career.[424]

VI

The responses by God to David's career can seem ambiguous. Various of his deeds are obviously condemned. But the overall effect remains that David *is* someone who enjoyed God's favor overall.

The Lord's displeasure is evident in Nathan's remonstrance with David after the taking of Bathsheba. (Even though Nathan comes forward as God's agent, he must proceed with care, so presenting the matter that David is moved to condemn himself before Nathan dares to do so.) But there is nothing "personal" in Nathan's intervention. Evidently, he comes to know and to respect Bathsheba, at least enough to side with her and her son Solomon during the succession crisis.[425]

One long-term effect of David's sin, it seems, is that he (as a bloodstained man) is not allowed to build the Temple. A short-term effect is the death of the child that had come out of the adultery. (David is shown as most practical in his prayers and fasting when this son is stricken.) But, it should be noticed, one salutary effect of the death of this child (who might well have been Bathsheba's candidate for the succession if he had lived) is that it leaves no doubt (to the community at large) as to whose son the successor is.[426]

VII

We have noticed the suggestion that David's "bad example unleashed the worst passions within his family."[427] Are not David's sexual mores, including the ruthlessness we have also noticed, reflected in what happens thereafter within David's own family? David's conduct does seem to affect the moral tone of the community.[428]

It can seem almost "natural," therefore, that one of David's sons would kill his half-brother because of his rape of the killer's full sister. This eventually plays out in the rebellion of Absalom, which first puts David at considerable risk, and then, upon the death of Absalom, drives him to lamentation.[429]

Those intimately associated with David can suffer. All but one of the priests who gave him refuge, when he fled from Saul, end up being slaughtered by Saul. David had not been candid with them when he took advantage of their hospitality.[430]

Despite all this, David's career still shines down to this day, so much so that a parliamentary crisis could be provoked in Israel when its foreign minister recently called David's morals into question.[431] David is more truly king than Saul ever was. Saul, we can see from the biblical account, was probably chosen for the wrong reasons by Samuel.[432] That mistake was not made again—a reliance upon appearance, or height, alone—when the time came for Samuel to anoint the proper son of Jesse.[433]

David is appealing, at least in part, because he is so "human." Is not God likely to share the more thoughtful judgment we may have about David? Various developments in David's career may be seen as "natural," yet as compatible with divine governance. One consequence of this is that when the explicitly *natural* comes in with the Greeks, it can be accommodated with biblical thought to a considerable extent, as may be seen in the work of Moses Maimonides and of Thomas Aquinas. The status of miracles, as well as of prophecy, remains a problem in any such accommodation.

VIII

Miracles, as ordinarily understood, do not seem to be much in evidence in the development of David's career, whatever may be expected of that latter-day David, the Messiah. Consider, for example, the limited effectiveness of the maiden introduced into the chills-ridden David's deathbed.[434]

If David can be understood in "natural" terms, what effect has this had upon what Westernized Jews, by and large, have believed ever since about divine intervention in everyday affairs? They do not seem to have the same openness to the conventionally miraculous, not only in later biblical times but also down to our day, that there can still be found among Christians.

Related to the status of the miraculous is the status of the prophetic. How, for example, did Nathan learn what he said at various times? Is what he says usually that which a prudent observer can work out for himself? Certainly, there are various ways of knowing things. Vestiges of an earlier notion of prophecy may perhaps be seen in the career of Samuel, who had been so important in the career of Saul. Particularly intriguing is the report that when Samuel, as a boy, began to hear from God, he repeatedly mistook His summons to be something coming from a man in the next room.[435]

Both the miraculous and the prophetic, as commonly understood, entail or represent interventions by God in human affairs. Such interventions seem to be made more of in the careers of Abraham, Jacob, and Moses than in the career of David. David evidently did not expect or report the kind of divine interventions seen in, say, Moses' career.[436]

In some ways, then, David is decidedly modern. Perhaps this, if not also the grace of God, helps account for his continuing appeal.

IX

The specialness of David extends to his association with the psalms. Scholars differ as to how many, if any, of the psalms he composed. But they are generally willing to recognize him as a musician of note. Also, aside from the psalms, there are poetic passages from him, in *Samuel* (such as the lament for Absalom or for Saul and Jonathan), which are regarded as consistent with his character and talents. He had early come to view, we recall, as someone who could soothe with his lyre and songs the desperate soul of Saul. Also, he can be regarded as someone with whom it is at least plausible to associate the psalms.[437]

As psalmist, or poet, David can be considered to have the same "calling" as the prophet. Thus, David as psalmist or poet is somewhat like an author of the Bible. This may have helped move the biblical authors so to see themselves in David that they were inspired to present him in the most appealing form.

This permits David to be recognized as very much a man of faith, whatever his shortcomings. Those who, recognizing such shortcomings, make too much of them run the risk of blinding themselves to his merits and thereby crippling themselves ever after. We return to Michal, the wife of David, for her response to the way that David brought the ark to Jerusalem three thousand years ago. The scene is laid thus:

> And David went and brought up the ark of God from the house of Obed-edom into the city of David with joy. And it was so, that when they that bore the ark of the Lord had gone six paces, he sacrificed an ox and a fatling. And David danced before the Lord with all his might; and David was girded with a linen ephod. So David and all the house of Israel brought up the ark of the Lord with shouting, and with the sound of the horn.[438]

We are then told:

> And it was so, as the ark of the Lord came into the city of David, that Michal the daughter of Saul looked out at the window, and saw king David leaping and dancing before the Lord; and she despised him in her heart.[439]

David continued with the ceremonies and celebrations devoted to the installation of the ark. When he finished, he went home, at which point we pick up the story again:

> Then David returned to bless his household. And Michal the daughter of Saul came out to meet David, and said: "How did the king of Israel get him honour today, who uncovered himself today in the eyes of the handmaids of his servants, as one of the vain fellows shamelessly uncovereth himself?"[440]

We can see, in David's reply to Michal (who is, in this context, not "the wife of David" but rather "the daughter of Saul") something that is prophetic in both tone and terms:

> And David said unto Michal, "Before the Lord, who chose me above thy father, and above all his house, to appoint me prince over the people of the Lord, over

> Israel, before the Lord will I make merry. And I will be yet more vile than thus, and will be base in mine own sights, and with the handmaids whom thou hast spoken of, with them will I get me honour."[441]

And, indeed, David has gotten honor with the handmaids everafter, and with many if not most others of the people of Israel besides, despite (or is it partly because of?) the way he carried on. (One can be reminded here of a recent president of the United States.) No doubt, those of a censorious temperament and refined tastes might be tempted to endorse Michal's rebuke of David. But the last word here—not from David but rather from the narrator—about this woman may sober the critic: "And Michal the daughter of Saul had no child unto the day of her death."[442]

This suggests that refined tastes cannot suffice, that they must be subordinated to (if not re-educated for the sake of) the common good, a common good that depends to some extent upon an institutionalized (if not even a lively) piety, something that David is displayed as having promoted along with his zest for life.

Chapter Eleven

Solomon[443]

"What's de harem?"

"The place where [a king] keeps his wives. Don't you know about the harem? Solomon had one; he had about a million wives."

"Why, yes, dat's so; I—I'd done forgot it. A harem's a bo'd'n-house, I reck'n. Mos' likely dey had rackety times in de nussery. En I reck'n de wives quarrels considerable; en dat 'crease de racket. Yit dey say Sollermun de wises' man dat ever live'. I doan' take no stock in dat. Bekase why: would a wise man want to live in de mids' er sich a blimblammin' all de time? . . ."

"Well, but he *was* the wisest man, anyway; because the widow she told me so, her own self."

"I doan' k'yer what de widder say, he *warn't* no wise man, nuther. He had some er de dad-fetchedes' ways I ever see. Does you know 'bout dat chile dat he 'uz gwyne to chop in two?"

Jim and Huck[444]

I

Unusual, if not desperate, measures were resorted to as David, the already legendary second king of Israel, neared his end, after some forty years on the throne. This is the way that the *Book of Kings* opens:

> Now king David was old and stricken in years; and they covered him with clothes, but he could get no heat. Wherefore his servants said unto him, "Let there be sought for my lord the king a young virgin; and let her stand before the

> king, and be a companion unto him, and let her lie in thy bosom, that my lord the king may get heat." So they sought for a fair damsel throughout all the borders of Israel, and found Abishag a Shunammite, and brought her to the king. And the damsel was very fair, she became a companion unto the king, and ministered to him: but the king knew her not.[445]

This Shunammite was the last woman that David "acquired." This was done, it seems, upon the suggestion of David's servants. Nothing is said about whether such a lovely maiden would want to be used in this way. Nor is anything said about whether it was good for her, or otherwise proper, to use her thus in this desperate effort. One can be reminded of Samuel's warning to the Israelites, generations earlier, about the impositions that kingship would bring with it. We are given an inkling of the self-centeredness of royalty, sometimes a civic-minded self-centeredness, when we observe the security precautions insisted upon for American presidents.

II

The experiment with the Shunammite woman failed. Evidently this became known, at least to those close to the king. The response of David's oldest surviving son is then reported:

> Now Adonijah the son of Haggith exalted himself, saying, "I will be king"; and he prepared him chariots and horsemen, and fifty men to run before him. And his father had not grieved him all his life [by] saying, "Why hast thou done so?" and he was also a very goodly [handsome] man; and he was born after Absalom. And he conferred with Joab the son of Zeruiah, and with Abiathar the priest: and they following Adonijah helped him. But Zadok, the priest, and Benaiah the son of Jehoiada, and Nathan the prophet, and Shimei, and Rei, and the mighty men that belonged to David, were not with Adonijah. And Adonijah slew sheep and oxen and fatlings by the stone of Zoheleth, which is by Enrogel, and he called all his brethren the king's sons, and all the men of Judah the king's servants. But Nathan the prophet, and Benaiah, and the mighty men, and Solomon his brother, he called not.[446]

Adonijah can be described by commentators down to our day as good-looking and spoiled. For one thing, as our narrator indicates, his father had never done much to restrain him. So he made his move—if not to replace his father, at least to be in a position to succeed him when he died. He was supported in this move by two influential men: Joab, the distinguished general, and Abiathar, the priest.

Did Adonijah, whose name echoes that of the Lord, move too soon? He seems to have believed that he had succeeded in this exercise—and so he celebrated. The support he had *was* significant, but even more significant perhaps (the narrator hints) may have been the support he did *not* have: various "mighty men that belonged to David" were not with him. Did his failure to invite Solomon to his "inaugural ball" recognize that he had in this half-brother a serious rival?

Nothing is said here of David's Shunammite woman. She later proves critical to the fate of Adonijah.

III

Nathan the prophet then makes *his* move, not by going directly to the king (as he had done many years before when David had taken Bathsheba for himself from Uriah the Hittite). Rather, he speaks first to Bathsheba:

> Then Nathan spoke unto Bathsheba the mother of Solomon, saying, "Hast thou not heard that Adonijah the son of Haggith doth reign, and David our lord knoweth it not? Now therefore come, let me, I pray thee, give thee counsel, that thou mayest save thine own life, and the life of thy son Solomon. Go and get thee in unto king David, and say unto him, 'Didst not thou, my lord, O king, swear unto thy handmaid, saying, "Assuredly Solomon thy son shall reign after me, and he shall sit upon my throne?" Why then doth Adonijah reign?' Behold, while thou yet talkest there with the king, I also will come in after thee, and confirm thy words."[447]

What, precisely, had David once promised Bathsheba about Solomon? Does she have to be reminded of, if not coached in, what had been promised? Nathan assures her that he will back up her demand upon David, but only after he has warned Bathsheba that her life and that of her son would be in danger if Adonijah succeeded to the throne of David.

Bathsheba concludes her speech thereafter to David with an insistence upon her vulnerability and that of her son. She, after reminding David of his promise about Solomon, challenges the king: "And now, behold, Adonijah reigneth; and thou, my lord the king, knoweth it not."[448]

Nathan then comes to David, being announced as "the prophet." His own emphasis is upon what Adonijah is doing, even as he wonders whether David had authorized him to act thus.[449] It is curious that Nathan is not reported to have said explicitly to David what he had said to Bathsheba, that the king had promised the succession to Solomon. He seems to have preferred to have Bathsheba be the one to say "publicly" that David had promised this. Perhaps it was even said by David, or could be believed by David to have been said, in a moment of passion with his favorite woman.

We *can* speculate why Nathan preferred Solomon. Was it because Nathan had been ignored just now by Adonijah and his clique? Was such exclusion because of the preference that Nathan had already exhibited for Solomon? Had Nathan been impressed by Solomon, if not also by Bathsheba (even though she had been, years before, an "adversary" of sorts that he had had to deal with firmly)? David had capitulated to Nathan on that occasion, and perhaps Bathsheba with him. Nathan does not say why he prefers Solomon. No guidance from the Lord is reported by him in this matter. It is possible, of course, that Nathan is moved more by Adonijah's liabilities than by Solomon's merits.

Be that as it may, David is moved to swear and say to Bathsheba after she and Nathan had spoken to him:

> As the Lord liveth, who hath redeemed my soul out of all adversity, verily as I swore unto thee by the Lord, the God of Israel, saying, "Assuredly Solomon thy son shall reign after me, and he shall sit upon my throne in my stead"; verily so will I do this day.[450]

The grateful Bathsheba responds, "Let my lord king David live forever."[451]

David then forcefully reasserts himself as king, one last time, calling to him "the mighty men that belonged [to him]." Solomon is to be invested at once with the trappings of royalty. David's action here culminates in this set of directives:

> "And let Zadok the priest and Nathan the prophet anoint him there king over Israel: and blow ye with the horn, and say: 'Long live king Solomon.' Then ye shall come up after him, that he shall come and sit upon my throne; for he shall be king in my stead: and I have appointed him to be prince over Israel and over Judah."[452]

IV

Once Solomon is anointed and publicly acclaimed as king, there is this report: "And all the people came up after him, and the people piped with pipes, and rejoiced with great joy, so that the earth rent with the sound of them."[453]

Among those who hear this jubilation are the party celebrating Adonijah's "victory": "And Adonijah and all the guests that were with him heard it as they had made an end of eating. And when Joab heard the sound of the trumpet, he said, 'Wherefore is this noise of the city being in an uproar?'"[454]

The answer to Joab's question is then given to the party by a messenger they trust. The news that David had had Solomon seated on the throne of the kingdom brought an immediate end to their festivities. David had acted so dramatically, and so decisively, that there seemed to have been no doubt about who would be (indeed, who was already?) king of "Israel and Judah":

> And all the guests of Adonijah were afraid, and rose up, and went every man his way. And Adonijah feared because of Solomon, and he arose, and went, and caught hold on the horns of the altar. And it was told Solomon, saying, "Behold, Adonijah feareth king Solomon: for, lo, he hath caught hold on the horns of the altar, saying, 'Let king Solomon swear unto me first of all that he will not slay his servant with the sword.'" And Solomon said, "If he will show himself a worthy man, there shall not a hair of him fall to the earth: but if wickedness shall be found in him, he shall die." So king Solomon sent, and they brought him down from the altar. And he came and prostrated himself before king Solomon; and Solomon said unto him, "Go to thy house."[455]

Solomon accepts Adonijah's capitulation and commands him to behave himself. But he no doubt recalled the presumptuousness of another older half-brother of his, Absalom. It remained to be seen whether this would be a permanent reconciliation between these half-brothers, especially since their father was still alive. Adonijah's fate seemed to depend upon how he acted thereafter.

V

David, as his death approaches, makes a final speech to Solomon, instructing him in how he should act as king. Nothing is said about how Solomon should deal with Adonijah, however; he is directed to deal with other Israelites of note.

But first David counsels Solomon about the way he should conduct himself not as a king but as an Israelite, which in turn should affect his career as king and the fate of a still-united Israel:

> Now the days of David drew nigh that he should die; and he charged Solomon his son, saying, "I go the way of all the earth: be thou strong therefore, and show thyself a man; and keep the charge of the Lord thy God, to walk in His ways, to keep His statutes, and His commandments, and His ordinances, and His testimonies, according to that which is written in the law of Moses, that thou mayest prosper in all that thou doest, and whithersoever thou turnest thyself; that the Lord may establish His word which He spoke concerning me, saying, 'If thy

children take heed to their way, to walk before Me in truth with all their heart and with all their soul, there shall not fail thee,' said He, 'a man on the throne of Israel.'"[456]

Then the dying king gets "down to business," so to speak, with specific instructions about three men. Here we seem to get to what may now be at the core of his being. It is that which Heinrich Heine presented so grimly in his *King David* poem.[457] First, there is a man who had just sided with Adonijah, but who is more vulnerable (in David's reckoning) for what he had done long before:

> Moreover thou knowest also what Joab the son of Zeruiah did to me, even what he did to the two captains of the hosts of Israel, unto Abner the son of Ner and unto Amasa the son of Jether, whom he slew, and shed the blood of war in peace, and put the blood of war upon his girdle that was about his loins, and in his shoes that were on his feet. Do therefore according to thy wisdom, and let not his hoar head go down to the grave in peace.[458]

The dying king then moves from fierceness to gentleness, following up the condemnation of Joab for offenses against him by gratitude for favors received: "But show kindness unto the sons of Barzillai the Gileadite, and let them be of those that eat at thy table: for so they drew nigh unto me when I fled from Absalom thy brother."[459]

This is brief, permitting the king to "catch his breath" as he then disposes of another longstanding grievance, dealing this time with a man who had *not* sided just now with Adonijah:

> And, behold, there is with thee Shimei the son of Gera, the Benjamite of Bahurim, who cursed me with a grievous curse in the day when I went to Mahanaim: but he came down to meet me at the Jordan, and I swore to him by the Lord, saying, "I will not put thee to death with the sword." Now therefore hold him not guiltless, for thou art a wise man, and thou wilt know what thou oughtest to do unto him, and thou shalt bring his hoar head to the grave with blood.[460]

David had been told earlier that the Lord considered him too bloodstained to build the Temple. Yet David, with his "enemies list," asks Solomon to do for him the killing he had not been able to do himself for one reason or another. Even so, it seems, Solomon will not be considered personally bloodstained because of what he might now do pursuant to his father's dying charge. One of the "charms" of these biblical stories is that the blemishes of heroes may not be concealed.

VI

The old king is finally gone and the new king can now fully take his place: "And Solomon sat upon the throne of David his father; and his kingdom was established firmly."[461] We then see what it took for the kingdom to be "established firmly."

The first move in this consolidation, it turns out, was by Adonijah, a man who had a knack for misjudging his circumstances. Here is how he prepares and delivers his own death warrant for the new king to "sign":

> Then Adonijah the son of Haggith came to Bathsheba the mother of Solomon. And she said: "Comest thou peaceably?" And he said, "Peaceably." He said moreover, "I have somewhat to say unto thee." And she said, "Say on." And he said, "Thou knowest that the kingdom was mine, and that all Israel set their faces on me, that I should reign: howbeit the kingdom is turned about, and is become my brother's: for it was his from the Lord. And now I ask one petition of thee, deny me not." And she said unto him, "Say on." And he said, "Speak, I pray thee, unto Solomon the king—for he will not say thee nay—that he give me Abishag the Shunammite to wife." And Bathsheba said, "Well; I will speak for thee unto the king."[462]

What did Bathsheba think of this? That is, how shrewd *was* she—and how well did she know her son? These questions affect how one reads her announcement to her son: "I ask one small petition of thee; deny me not."[463] Although Solomon then says he will not deny her, he explodes when he learns what she does ask for:

> And king Solomon answered and said unto his mother, "And why dost thou ask Abishag the Shunammite for Adonijah? Ask for him the kingdom also; for he is mine elder brother; even for him, and for Abiathar the priest, and for Joab the son of Zeruiah." Then king Solomon swore by the Lord, saying, "God do so to me, and more also, if Adonijah have not spoken this word against his own life. Now therefore, as the Lord liveth, who hath established me, and set me on the throne of David my father, and who hath made me a house, as he promised, surely Adonijah shall be put to death this day."[464]

Only one of the three men disparaged here by Solomon, Joab, had been on David's "enemies list." They seem to be linked here by Solomon because they had been involved in Adonijah's attempt to secure the throne for himself before David died. We are then told: "And king Solomon sent by the hand of Benaiah the son of Jehoiada; and he fell upon [Adonijah], so that he died."[465] Nothing is recorded here of any effort by Bathsheba to dissuade Solomon from the deadly course of action he was now pursuing following her intervention supposedly on behalf of Adonijah.

VII

Next, the troublesome priest, Abiathar, must be dealt with. His person was evidently inviolate; but he could be removed from office and banished:

> And unto Abiathar the priest said the king, "Get thee to Anathoth, unto thine own fields; for thou art deserving of death: but I will not at this time put thee to death, because thou didst bear the ark of the Lord God before David my father, and because thou wast afflicted in all wherein my father was afflicted." So Solomon thrust out Abiathar from being priest unto the Lord; that the word of the Lord might be fulfilled, which he spoke concerning the house of Eli in Shiloh.[466]

Zadok, a priest who had been loyal to Solomon's cause, was put by him in place of Abiathar.[467]

Joab is next—and he knows it: "And the tidings came to Joab; for Joab had turned after [that is, had supported] Adonijah, though he turned not after [supported] Absalom [many years before]."[468] In fact, Joab had personally killed the rebellious Absalom, but David had not mentioned that, but rather the killing by Joab of Abner and Amasa, which Solomon recalls in his condemnation of Joab, "two men more righteous and better than [Joab]."[469] Nor does Solomon mention that it had been Joab who had been used by David to get rid of Uriah the Hittite, thereby freeing his mother Bathsheba to marry David his father.

A desperate Joab sought refuge at the altar in the "Tent of the Lord."[470] He is called forth by his executioner, but he answers, "Nay, but I will die here."[471] Solomon, when he hears this, says in effect that Joab has condemned himself out of his own mouth, instructing the executioner: "Do as he hath said, and fall upon him, and bury him; that thou mayest take away the blood, which Joab shed without cause, from me and from my father's house."[472] Benaiah, the executioner first of Adonijah and then of Joab (and the man who had been commissioned by David to supervise Solomon's coronation), assumes thereafter the post that Joab had held with the army.[473]

VIII

Solomon can now turn to his remaining target, this one identified by David. Shimei, we have been told, would have been killed by David himself, but for an oath the king had sworn. (David's inability to move against Joab may have been due primarily to his relative weakness politically at the time that Joab offended him. Besides, Joab *was* his sister's son. A new king, David seems to have believed, can be in a stronger position than his much-battered predecessor.)

But Solomon has no political grievance against Shimei. For all we know, Shimei may even have supported Solomon in the struggle with Adonijah. Solomon gives Shimei an opportunity to avert his fate:

> And the king sent and called for Shimei, and said unto him, "Build thee a house in Jerusalem, and dwell there, and go not forth thence any whither. For on the day thou goest out, and passest over the brook Kidron, know thou for certain that thou shalt surely die: thy blood shall be upon thine own head." And Shimei said unto the king, "The saying is good: as my lord the king hath said, so will thy servant do." And Shimei dwelt in Jerusalem many days.[474]

Had Solomon expected that Shimei would not be able to discipline himself in the way necessary to preserve his life?

There did come a day, three years later, that Shimei left Jerusalem to recover runaway slaves.[475] Although he returned immediately thereafter to Jerusalem, his failure to abide by the precise arrangement prescribed by Solomon proved his undoing. There is perhaps something arbitrary-sounding about this matter, but it does have echoes of the fateful Garden of Eden test:

> And the king sent and called for Shimei, and said unto him, "Did I not make thee to swear by the Lord, and forewarned thee, saying, 'Know for a certain, that on the day thou goest out, and walkest abroad any whither, that thou shalt surely die?' And thou saidst unto me, 'The saying is good; I have heard it.' Why then hast thou not kept the oath of the Lord, and the commandment that I have charged thee with?"[476]

The runaway slaves, it seems, proved as tempting to Shimei as the forbidden fruit had been to Eve and Adam and as Abishag the Shunammite had been to Adonijah.

The same executioner is ordered by Solomon to do way with Shimei. The "three years" referred to during which Shimei complied with the terms of his confinement to Jerusalem reminds us that the narrator is first taking care of the succession problems in his account of the career of King Solomon, however much else the king did during those opening years.

After these four men—Adonijah, Abiathar, Joab, and Shimei—are disposed of, the narrator can say again what he had, in effect, said earlier: "And the kingdom was established in the hand of Solomon."[477]

IX

Once Solomon had taken care of Adonijah, along with all of the men his father had spoken of in his last charge, the reader can be reminded of the opening part of that charge: the injunctions with respect to piety. Solomon had been instructed to walk in the ways of the Lord.

Much of what follows the disposal of Joab and the others reports on how Solomon conformed to the divine mandate. It is pleasing to the Lord that Solomon requests wisdom, something he is believed to exhibit in his famous adjudication thereafter of the dispute about the baby.[478]

But before this passage—just after Joab and the others are done with (and the kingdom is firmly "established in the hand of Solomon")—there is an announcement that anticipates the problems there would be with Solomon's glorious reign:

> And Solomon became allied to Pharaoh king of Egypt by marriage, and took Pharaoh's daughter, and brought her into the city of David, until he had made an end of building his own house, and the house of the Lord, and the wall of Jerusalem round about.[479]

This was the first of many foreign (and "political"?) marriages Solomon was to contract. And, not unnaturally (we can say), the more he loved his wives, the more likely it would be that he would tolerate, if not even join in, their foreign religious practices. We can also see here an anticipation of the years of building programs with which Solomon was to burden his people.[480]

By the time Solomon finished his long reign, the soundness of the regime had been compromised, so much so that the kingdom was once again divided thereafter into Israel and Judah.[481] The reader must wonder whether the narrator had appreciated the extent to which the reputed wisdom of Solomon was repudiated by the way he conducted himself. Certainly, it is hard to believe that a man with a "thousand wives" could be less spoiled than the reckless Adonijah, in his yearning for Abishag the Shunammite, had been. Adonijah could be seen, in that endeavor, to have tried to take his father's place. But it could be said of him, as it had been said of David, "but [he] knew her not." It could also be said that Adonijah did not usefully know Solomon either.

Chapter Twelve

Isaiah[482]

> We . . . have read in our sacred books that even the sun itself stood still, when that holy man Joshua asked this boon from the Lord God, until the battle in which he was engaged came to a victorious end; and that it turned back in its course, to signify by this prodigy, as an adjunct to God's promise, the addition of fifteen years to the life of King Hezekiah. But when the pagans believe in the reality of such miracles as those, which were granted to the merits of the saints, they ascribe them to magic arts.
>
> St. Augustine[483]

I

David Ben-Gurion, a latter-day prophet of sorts, is reported to have said: "He who does not believe in miracles, is no realist."[484] How realistic—that is, how sensible—is this observation? How does it bear upon our understanding of Isaiah, a prophet of Israel who lived and prophesied in Jerusalem from about 740 to about 700 B.C.E.? How does all this bear, as well, upon our understanding of prophecy?

There may be, I must confess at the outset of this return to the inquiry initiated in the opening chapters of this book, something presumptuous about my effort here, especially since I will be discussing a work which evidently derives much of its power and hence influence from the beauty of a language which I do not read. *Isaiah* is, furthermore, a work which assumes that the reader knows—knows in his very bones, so to speak—much that I for one simply do not know about what went on among the Israelites and their neighbors before, during, and even long after the time that Isaiah lived. It can all be rather confusing, especially when complicated by the recognition that there *are* various ways that prophecies are said to come to mankind.

We begin to try to grasp all this, however, by noticing that the *Isaiah* text opens with these words:

> The vision of Isaiah the son of Amoz, which he saw concerning Judah and Jerusalem, in the days of Uzziah, Jotham, Ahaz, and Hezekiah, kings of Judah.[485]

That which we would call a political cast seems to be given here to what is to follow. The times and troubles of these four kings are dealt with in the first half of the work. The second half of the work can be seen as dealing with the long-term repercussions and consequences of what these four kings and the people of Israel had and had not done.

I have noticed the political cast, or tenor, of this work, at least in its outset. This is further suggested by the character of the opening and closing observations of the work. It opens with the Lord recognizing the rebelliousness of the people of Israel, a "sinful nation."[486] It closes with the Lord predicting that men will look upon the carcasses of those who have rebelled against Him.[487] Thus, rebelliousness and its consequences are very much part of the relation between God and His people. It is a rebelliousness that runs counter to the explicit rules and the pervasive righteousness and sovereignty of the Lord, especially in His provision for *this* people.

The Lord's provisions extend, of course, to anticipations of a Messianic age, that time in which the political and social ordering implicit in the way that has been prescribed will come to full realization. Thus, at the heart of *Isaiah* is a somewhat Messianic message.[488] It can be said, therefore, that low things (growing out of rebelliousness) frame the central message, at the core of which is an account of the good and bad things that the Lord provides.[489]

II

Isaiah is often regarded as a turning point in the development of Jewish thought, marking (it is said) a transition toward a more "spiritual" Israel, indeed toward a way of thinking about God which is more "universal." But, it should be noticed, it is still the God of Abraham, Isaac, and Jacob—and one must wonder whether anyone subsequent to Abraham should ever be considered more "spiritual" than Abraham himself.

Among the "spiritual" elements in *Isaiah* is the passage about the "Suffering Servant."[490] An eminent Jewish scholar of our day has reported:

> The theological idea contained in the ["Suffering Servant"] poem found no acceptance in subsequent Judaism; the "Suffering Servant" is a stray poem, which in some unaccountable way came to be included in the *Book of Isaiah*. But its importance to Christianity as well as its unequaled pathos commands our attention.[491]

A pious Christian could well agree with what this Jewish scholar has said, but adding that the way this poem came to be included in *Isaiah* may indeed seem "unaccountable" because its inclusion was, after all, the result of a special providence. The pious Christian might even suggest that this poem can be seen as a divine anticipation of Christianity, a Christianity that mainstream Judaism could not accept.

This sort of response reminds us of the considerable use made of *Isaiah* both in the Greek Bible and by Christians as a source for Christological references in the Hebrew Bible. Of course, Jewish scholars insist that there is nothing in *Isaiah* either predicting or anticipating Christianity.[492] A proper understanding of the history of the people of Israel, and of their literature and language, we are cautioned, would make it apparent that the so-called Christological references are simply mistaken readings and misguided interpretations by Christians. But I suspect that it will take more than scholarship, as ordinarily presented, to persuade Christians (especially after centuries of "conditioning") *not* to see something Christological in such passages as this from the "Suffering Servant" poem in *Isaiah*:

> He was despised, and forsaken of men,
> A man of pains, and acquainted with disease,
> And as one from whom men hide their face:
> He was despised, and we esteemed him not.
> Surely our diseases he did bear, and our pains he carried;
> Whereas we did esteem him stricken,
> Smitten of God and afflicted.
> But he was wounded because of our transgressions,
> He was crushed because of our iniquities:
> The chastisement of our welfare was upon him,
> And with his stripes we were healed.[493]

Besides, the pious Christian is encouraged by the Jewish tradition itself to consider *Isaiah* as looking centuries ahead. Not only is much made of a Messiah, but also there is within the book an account of events (connected with the Persian king, Cyrus) which come more than a century after the career of the historical Isaiah. Up until the late eighteenth century, and to this day among the more orthodox Jews, it seems all of what we know as *Isaiah* was generally regarded as the work of one author. If a prophet can be understood to have predicted with precision (and even by name) the advent of a Persian king a century later, why not the advent of Jesus and his doings five centuries later? Once predictive powers are established, the length of time spanned should not be a problem (whatever one may think about the significance and use of a detailed anticipation of a Persian king for Isaiah's immediate audience).[494]

III

Isaiah is traditionally regarded as one book, even though contemporary scholars tend to divide it between two, if not even among three or four, authors. It sometimes seems that scholars are much more interested in determining just how the work should be divided up among authors than they are interested in deciding whether what is being said is sound, assuming that it *is* substantially the work of one author.

How sound *Isaiah* is depends, in part, upon the soundness of the books, primarily *Genesis* and *Exodus*, which seem to be taken for granted as known by the addressees of Isaiah. Thus, there are references to the story of Sodom and Gomorrah,[495] Israel in Egypt,[496] the fall of "the son of the morning,"[497] the house of David,[498] the redemption of Abraham,[499] Adam,[500] the parting of the Reed Sea,[501] and Noah and the waters.[502]

By and large, *Isaiah* is not itself a story, or at least not as obvious and as interesting a story or series of stories as those found in *Genesis*, *Exodus*, or, say, *Jonah*.[503] Still, *Isaiah* does not stand or fall on the basis of its story or its predictive exploits, but rather on the basis of its poetry, poetry which is so compelling that it is used again and again elsewhere—not only in the Greek Bible but also down to our time in such works of art as Handel's *Messiah*.[504]

Predictive exploits in a text are rarely if ever conclusively presented. They are virtually impossible, if not even simply impossible, to establish or to demonstrate. For one thing, it is difficult to establish, on the basis of the usual single version that comes down to us of a text, whether the prediction made and fulfilled took place before the event predicted, or whether it was retroactively contrived to seem prospective.[505]

It is, of course, fairly easy to be able to "predict" retroactively—to say later that a prediction had been made earlier. But it should be far from easy so to present a story as to persuade others that a before-the-facts prediction had indeed been made—and this is so, whether or not there had been such a prediction. One depends upon the poetic art to be able to present such things effectively.[506]

Furthermore, an account, however persuasive, of effective prediction need not be very interesting—or truly memorable. After all, we do not make much of our weathermen, however much we may rely upon them for their forecasts. One is not asked by one's children, for instance, to tell them still another weather forecast. By and large, it can be said, prediction really matters—it is of enduring interest and significance—only when it is in the service of descriptions of how momentous things work, including descriptions of the consequences of this or that kind of character.

Consider, once again, the prophecy given to Sophocles' Oedipus, and earlier to his father and mother, about their future relations.[507] We are prepared to believe that such prophecies were given, or at least that these three people believed them to have been given. But the truly interesting question is not whether such prophecies were given but rather what is being said thereby about the world—about cause and effect, and about how one should respond when confronted by intimidating challenges.

Insofar as one is concerned with what "actually" happened (by way of prediction, responses thereto, etc.), one is dealing more with *history* than with *poetry*. Even if one predicts an event correctly, there remains the question of what the *cause* truly was of what happened. Poetry is often, if not usually, better than history at describing that.[508] Poetry, like philosophy, deals more with causes, although it does work through particulars, for the most part—particular people, particular stories. Poetry makes more believable and apparently more significant whatever is said to have happened. Do we not regard the Odysseus of Homer and the Oedipus of Sophocles to be as "real," and subject to much the same kind of character study, as we do the Pericles of Thucydides and, say, the fifteenth president of the United States?

IV

It is implied in what I have said that there is a considerable affinity between prophecy and poetry. Both can be seen as attempts, by the use of persuasive language, to guide human action.

The prophet, at one time or another, can bring forth the Torah, the Sabbath, and various rituals, demanding respect for these and for other guides and institutions. Sacrifices are played down by Isaiah, evidently because he regarded them as having become ends in themselves, their original purposes having been obscured. What is the relation, one must wonder, between ritual and morality? Is a deep morality to be seen in one's willingness and ability to conform to ritual prescriptions—to subject ordinary self-interest and personal gratification to the discipline of a divine calling?

To say that rituals are played down in *Isaiah* is not to say that they are totally repudiated. They *are* critical, especially if performed with clean hearts and sound minds. Idolatry, which some of the rituals are designed to counter, continues to be forbidden by Isaiah; he insists, as well, upon Sabbath observances.[509] The great strength of Isaiah lies, in large part, in the force of his condemnations and in the way he presents his bills of particulars. It is evident that he stands for something grand and enduring and sovereign, both in what he condemns and in what he advocates. It should also be evident that prophecy, at least in his case, is (as it has been suggested) "the political name for political science."[510]

Prophecy may be seen, then, as a particularly effective way of providing guidance to a community at large with respect to how it should conduct itself in matters both trivial and great. It is guidance depended upon to develop respect in people for rules that they, for the most part, enforce for themselves.

V

Underlying the rules provided by prophecy, and making respect for those rules more serious and hence enduring, is an attempt to say what the world is like. This attempt includes an indication of what God is and how He works.

It may well be that men are open to attempts to say what God is. There may be in the human being a natural desire for the divine, something exhibited again and again in various circumstances, so much so as to suggest something which is virtually universal.[511]

Biblical prophecy seems to assume that the world is one. Thus, for example, catastrophes (especially political catastrophes) are understood to have moral causes. A Messianic age is anticipated, as in *Isaiah*, even when the account is bounded by reminders of human failings. It is because of the standards implicit in Messianic expectations that we can see most clearly the extent and significance of our failings. On the other hand, we are familiar with a view of things that is dominated by skepticism with regard to the supernatural. Such skepticism not only discounts any talk about the miraculous but also considers irrelevant, or at least unfruitful, any inquiry into the character of the divine.

Not all stories about the divine have the same status. We see in Plato's *Republic*, for example, that Socrates would purge various of the received accounts about the gods, recognizing in them features which are simply impossible to attribute to the divine. In Plato's *Apology*, Socrates recognizes as an attribute of the divine that it "cannot lie."[512] Similar critiques may be seen in *Isaiah*—as, for example, when the prophet ridicules idol worship by wondering how anyone can take seriously as a god something that he has made with his own hands.[513]

Of course, graven images may *stand* for something high. The wise men among the Israelites must have recognized how graven images *could* be understood.[514] But even in standing for something higher, the graven image must be explained by the use of words. So, why not remove one of the steps and go to the words immediately? Or are we to understand that graven images are merely materials aids, just as are rituals and ceremonies? But rituals and ceremonies are apt to be seen as restraints, as practices that confine the material, whereas the inclination of most men is to regard graven images "materialistically." Certainly, that which Moses brought back off Mount Sinai, even though set forth on tablets of stone, was incomparably higher and certainly more durable than that Golden Calf fashioned in his absence.[515]

Of course, also, words can mislead, partly because of the bodily attributes of God that they suggest. But it is difficult to avoid the use of such attributes, especially if the prophet (like the poet) is to talk about particular manifestations and interventions of the divine. Even so, if one also says again and again, as the Jews do in perhaps their greatest prayer, that "the Lord is One," that does tend to limit the imagination and doings of men. That prayer, or affirmation, continually reminds human beings that most of what is commonly said, or is said for everyday purposes, about the divine may be in need of rigorous correction.

Thus, although Isaiah may fashion a divinity out of his words, the implications of some of the words he uses point to something superior to him and his doings, something which *is* and which endures independently of the words of mankind, however useful words may be in helping human beings grasp what is there.

The question remains: What is it that determines which revelation (what account of the divine) one is to accept? What kind of argument or support for a revelation is provided by the way of life it advances? Does a very high level of exhortation and guidance with respect to a way of life suggest superiority in the doctrines involved? This may be a circular argument, but need that be a conclusive objection to it? Does such an objection bring to bear upon the question a set of standards that are somehow independent of, if not irrelevant to, the revelation itself?

Certainly, accounts of successful predictions, spectacular miracles, and such events cannot be conclusive in determining what is superior. For one thing, such accounts usually come to human beings through others; only a very small proportion of mankind, or even of a people, has ever seen such things for itself. It *is* believed that all of Israel once witnessed various wonderful things during the course of the Exodus.[516] But is it not critical that all of Israel from a certain time on came to believe (because of *one* man's account) that all of Israel had once witnessed various wonderful things (just as the story of the Creation itself comes ultimately only from one pen, perhaps even "merely" the pen of an editor)?

Besides, we are also told that the wonders witnessed by all of Israel were not so conclusive in their effects as to keep many Israelites from falling away from Moses' own immediate leadership. What does this suggest about the significance and enduring consequences of the miracles described in *Exodus*? What does this, in turn, suggest about miracles in general?

Or is it that we are not to think about the divine and about revelation in this manner? And yet, we should remember the kinds of arguments that Isaiah himself made against idolatry. It is absurd, he said, to take a log, use one part of it for fire and use another part of it to fashion an idol which one would then worship as a god.[517] To argue thus is, implicitly, to concede, and perhaps to expect, if not even to hope, that one's own religious opinions would be subjected to rational analysis.

VI

What should be made, then, of the kind of examination of revelation that we have seen in modern times? Consider again, for example, how Machiavelli speaks of Moses. Four great founders are spoken of, including Moses. But, it is recognized by Machiavelli, the greatness of Moses is dismissed by some as due only to God's intervention.[518] Still, it should become evident that the other three (Romulus, Theseus, and Cyrus) are the equals of Moses—which suggests, at the least, that Reason and Revelation can come out the same "in practice."

Another way of putting this is to say once again that the effective prophet is, at the core, a prudent man.[519] The truly gifted man is someone who understands what is going on. He can fit together in an authoritative and persuasive manner the large and the small, the near and the far, the morality of human beings and the fate of nations.

If one sees the effective prophet as a prudent man, then one has implicitly dealt with perhaps the most critical problem that thoughtful people have with respect to revelation, the problem of what seems to be said therein about the corporeality of God. Is not corporeality implied in the assumption of divine intervention (or particular providence)? If one does not see God as "really" (that is, physically) intervening in the affairs of the world,[520] does not this suggest that all religious rules, including those presented as the direct commands of God, are to be recognized as the work of human reason, including that reason manifested in imagination and rhetoric? This may be still another way of saying that the prophet is a prudent man, someone who takes account of the circumstances, including the traditions and limitations, of his people.

Isaiah as a prophet seems to hold out this "ideal," that no child should ever again die an infant, no old man fail to live out his life, and so forth.[521] The "ideal" is not put in terms of a heavenly reward. It is something that is seen as following from the life of virtue, including that virtue seen in the right ordering of the regime to be expected in the Messianic age.[522]

Isaiah himself, we should remember, is not the highest form of prophet. That status seems to be reserved (at least in traditional Judaism) for Moses, and Moses alone, someone who did *not* rely primarily upon dreams or visions but rather upon waking deliberation.[523] Moses and perhaps Abraham before him, it can be said, laid down the principles that the other prophets in the Bible drew upon and attempted to implement in their varying circumstances.

Isaiah, it has long been recognized, is particularly skillful in the use of metaphor, especially in the early part of the book. Also long recognized, we have noticed, has been the magnificence of his poetry: his language can be described as "breathtaking."

One must wonder how Isaiah differs in principle then from, say, the Shakespeare of *The Tempest*, the Dante of the *Divine Comedy*, and the Bunyan of *The Pilgrim's Progress*. That is, how is *divine revelation* to be distinguished from *poetic inspiration*?

VII

Isaiah, we should remember, is not a miracle-worker. Neither apparent miracles nor remarkable predictions are the hallmark of the greatest prophets in the Hebrew Bible, but rather deep insight and a powerful moral force.[524] For about the former—the miracles and predictions—there is always the problem of the reliability of the reports, but about the latter—the insight and moral force—there is the evidence in the very words themselves.

Various things reported by Isaiah could be regarded as miraculous, such as the way countries rise and fall or the way a large army can be wiped out overnight—but these are not unambiguous instances, of course, and can be explained by other causes. Perhaps the only "conventional" miracle in *Isaiah* is the retardation of the shadow of the sun, in connection with the illness and the saving from death of King Hezekiah, an account which is not far from the center of the book.[525] A more extended account of this episode, with some interesting features, may be seen elsewhere in the Hebrew Bible.[526] This suggests that Isaiah himself may not have been the ultimate source for this story.

One must wonder, therefore, whether Isaiah vouches for it all himself, even though he is reported to have been personally involved in the episode. One must also wonder what Isaiah intended to be meant by the fact that he took only a part of this story as reported earlier? Does he thereby suggest that stories about miracles must be adapted to the circumstances? One must wonder as well whether such an account of a miracle is substantially still another instance of the use of corporeality to say something, for people of limited imaginations, about the sovereignty of God.[527]

In any event, there is in *Isaiah* little concern about "proving" various assertions. The stories are told—this may be true throughout the Bible—as if there should be no serious question about their reliability. One falls into sin not because of one's faith or opinions but, it seems, because of the desires to which one gives in. At least, this is true of the people of Israel, as distinguished perhaps from the idolaters who do suffer from ignorance of the true way.[528]

It should also be noticed that whatever testing *of* Isaiah there may be by means of predictions, that is substantially confined to Isaiah's contemporaries. His early readers, with one massive exception to which I will soon return, were limited to an account of predictions he had made which had already been fulfilled. His later readers, including us, have (if of a skeptical turn of mind) no practicable way of testing to learn whether in fact he had predicted something that had come true. What is critical to us now are the set of principles, the lessons, and the guide that Isaiah provides us.

But, then, can we not say that verbal inspiration of a very high order may itself be miraculous, providing in itself proof of something divine?[529] In this sense all prophets are poets. Whether all—that is, all genuine—poets are in turn prophets is a question we must leave for another occasion.

VIII

Do we have in Isaiah *one* prophet-poet or two or more? This question, too, bears upon the problem of the nature of prophecy, particularly its uses of predictions.

Modern critics often assign the first thirty-nine chapters of *Isaiah* to the original prophet, the one who told of the reigns of four kings, concluding with Hezekiah. Then, in the fortieth chapter, there begins the comforting of Israel, a comforting following upon the grim warnings found in the preceding chapters.

The comforting includes, as I have indicated, anticipations of the rescue of a people exiled because of its sins—a rescue brought about by King Cyrus long after the life of the historic Isaiah. Since most modern scholars implicitly, and sometimes explicitly, regard such long-term prediction as impossible, *Isaiah* from chapter 40 on, is assigned to other hands than those of the author of the first thirty-nine chapters.

But for us, I have suggested, it is *all* ancient history—both the predicting and the fulfilling of predictions. And so it was for whatever man who put together the book we now have, whether it was Isaiah himself or some editor many years later. For even Isaiah, if "truly" predicting, was looking back, so to speak, from the perspective of what was to happen after Cyrus.

The full story of Isaiah, we are given to understand by this arrangement, requires both the catastrophic warnings and the exalted comforting. The two parts must go together. Whoever put the parts together seems to have said that there is implied in, or following from, the first part that which may be seen in the second part.

Can we be sure that we understand the first part well enough to be able to say that the second part does *not* belong with it? If we insist upon separating the two parts, do we not pay more deference to history than to poetry,[530] even as we repudiate the history of two thousand years of substantial opinion that the parts do belong together?

In short, what understanding of the whole is reflected in the fact that *Isaiah* has "always" been put together as it is?[531]

IX

Let us now gather together some of the things we have noticed, still another time, about prophecy.

We return still another time to the Oedipus story, if only briefly. We do not doubt that Oedipus' most traumatic experiences with his parents (as related by Sophocles and others) have happened again and again among human beings. Nor do we doubt that we may sometimes even somehow desire such things to happen. In any event, most if not *all* good stories have "happened" before, in one sense or another.

But, it will be said, there *was* a prophecy in Oedipus' case. What does "prophecy" mean in such cases? That there is an awareness of earlier, or improper, desires? That one is reminded that certain bad things do happen to one sometimes even unawares? Certainly, the prophecy in Sophocles' *Oedipus Tyrannus* reflects what a man might want—that is, to get rid of his overbearing father in order to possess his mother (or whatever his mother has or represents). A prophecy, then, may do little more than remind us of old truths or causal relations or deep-rooted concerns.

Now, to return to *Isaiah* once again. When one looks at a man's or a country's situation, and when one sees (that is, by thinking about it) that *this* conduct has been followed by *those* consequences (whether prosperity or disasters), surely one can (if one has insight) point out the connections between conduct and consequences. This may be done in order to help people to understand what happened and in order to induce them to act well in the future. The great gift is to see the connections, to explain why they are there, and to present them graphically. How much is added by being able to "predict" (that is, by being able to say in advance) what precisely is going to happen because of such conduct? Is that necessary only for those who cannot or will not understand what is being said about cause and effect? Reports of previous predictions, of a people's refusal to respond, and of the consequences thereof can serve to shape a people in the future, even without additional specific predictions.

Thus, it can be said, the man who predicts may add surprisingly little to what the observer does who subjects it all to proper study after the fact. (I say "surprisingly little," because successful prediction does *seem* to add a great deal.) From our point of view it is the connection (or an account of cause and effect) that matters, the standards invoked, the lessons taught—and we get these things whether the account is before the "fact" or after the "fact." By the time *most* readers of *Isaiah* have gotten the account, and have seen its significance, it is *all* after the fact (in the sense that they, Isaiah-like, have seen the prediction and its consequences). What makes the story *live* is not the assertion therein of a successful prediction—there are all kinds of rather uninteresting stories available about *that*—but rather the understanding reflected therein about the world and about human beings in it, to say nothing about the Divine.

The conventionally miraculous, in any event, is rare—and really not very useful, especially since there *is* usually a considerable problem of evidence left by such an account. The most useful part of an account of the miraculous, therefore, may be that it can induce us to notice and hence to take somewhat more seriously what is being taught, not about the miraculous but about how things *are* and about how human beings should act—and what difference it makes how they do act.

Besides, it can also be said, the miraculous is hard to recognize for what it is, to say nothing of accounting for it. I return to the observation with which I began this discussion of *Isaiah*: "He who does not believe in miracles, is no realist." This suggests that the true realist can see the miraculous all around him, however rare it may be.[532] Perhaps it is best seen in the highest workings of the human spirit, whether in poetry, or in philosophy, or in prophecy (including a noble politics).

This observation, I have mentioned, is from David Ben-Gurion, one of the founders of modern Israel. I happened upon the quotation in a speech by a foreign politician visiting the White House in 1964, a politician who added, "Although I cannot embrace this point of view, I understand it."[533] When we notice that this politician was a German chancellor, and that he should have drawn upon and should have spoken as respectfully as he did of a Jew, that should suggest that there may indeed have been something sound to Ben-Gurion's "point of view." For who would have dared to prophesy in, say, 1944, that not two decades would pass before a German chancellor would speak thus of a Jewish leader and in public? Is there not something more miraculous (and yet readily verifiable) in this than in the various contested stories that are incidental to the enduring teachings of Isaiah?

Chapter Thirteen

Job[534]

> And worse I may be yet. The worst is not
> So long as we say, "This is the worst."
>
> Edgar[535]

I

Job teaches us, cautions us, and elevates us. This book is a priceless aid to us, having contributed significantly to our shaping and education.[536]

I lay down common ground for our discussion of Job by drawing upon passages from an encyclopedia article about this book in which we are informed at the outset:

> The Biblical *Book of Job*, called in Hebrew *Iyyov*, is classed among the Writings (Ketuvim) of the Hebrew Bible and among the Poetic Books of the Old Testament. Its hero, Job, is ordinarily presented as a model of patience (see *James* 5:11), although he is presented in the Biblical poem as a rebel.[537]

We are then introduced to the story of Job, a Syrian or Edomite (that is, evidently not an Israelite), a story referred to as "The Folk Tale and the Poem":

> Interpreters have long observed profound discrepancies of style, language, and ideas between the prose prologue and epilogue on the one hand (*Job* 1:1–2:13, 42: 7–17) and the poetic discussion on the other (*Job* 3:1–42: 6). The hero of the folk tale is a seminomadic sheik, pious, virtuous, and prosperous, suddenly stricken with the loss of his children, his health, and his wealth. To Job, his wife, and his three friends (Eliphaz, Bildad, and Zophar), this uncommon misfortune

> is inexplicable, but the audience is permitted to learn, through a vista into the heavenly council, that Job is being tested, with the acquiescence of God whom Job calls Yahweh), by the prosecuting attorney of the celestial court, called "the *satan*" (not a proper name), one of "the sons of Elohim [a name for God]." Job refuses to curse the deity for his unfair treatment. After the visit of the three friends, "who had not spoken the truth about [God]" (*Job* 42:7), the hero receives again his health and his wealth along with a new set of sons and daughters. Like the Hebrew patriarchs, this model foreigner dies at an advanced age. . . . The prose prologue and epilogue are separated by a complex sequence of poems, two soliloquies, the discourses of the three friends with the hero's rebuttals, a hymn, an oath of innocence, the speeches of a younger friend (Elihu), and, finally, God's intervention with a long series of questions spoken from the whirlwind, with Job's responses.[538]

Further on, we are instructed by the encyclopedist about the "Literary Genre and Oriental Parables" suggested by *Job*:

> Taken in its final composite form as a unit, the book defies literary classification. It combines parabolic narrative, lament, hymn, diatribe, proverb, judiciary procedure, sapiential discussion, theophany, prophetic vision, and introspective meditation. The dialogue genre became well known in Greece, but its Hellenic form differed markedly from the Jobian exchanges. In Plato's philosophic dialogues, conversation moves back and forth with lively interruptions and quick repartee, whereas in *Job*, each character speaks at length. The discourses of the friends, the hero, and God present strophic structures and stately developments appropriate for chanting in a cultic environment. The hero's short answers to Yahweh's questioning constitute an exception on account of their climactic impact (*Job* 40:1–5, 42:1–6). In form and general themes, the Jobian poem is closely similar to the wisdom writings of Mesopotamia, the Akkadian *Poem of the Righteous Sufferer* (fourteenth century B.C.E.) and the *Acrostic Dialogue on Theodicy* (ninth century B.C.E.). It even recalls the Egyptian *Dialogue of the Man Weary of Life and His Soul*. The poet of *Job* may have borrowed the genre, but his ideas were strikingly original.[539]

Finally, in our borrowings from an encyclopedia article on *Job*, there are these suggestions about interpretations of Job in the Christian tradition and by twentieth-century secularists:

> The chief Greek version of Job (in the Septuagint) paraphrases, softens, and considerably shortens the Hebrew original. In spite of the clear teaching of the poem, [the] rabbis and church fathers have presented Job as a paragon of humble endurance under stress. The frescoes of the Roman catacombs picture him as a prototype of Jesus. The *Moralia* of Gregory I (sixth century) represents him as a paradigm of piety. The Middle Ages were hardly acquainted with the Bib-

> lical book but read widely an apocryphal *Testament of Job* that is filled with fanciful adventures and portrays the hero as a king of Egypt. After the Crusades, Job became the favorite protector of lepers. In the sixteenth century, "Monsignor Job" was the intercessor for syphilitics. In Flanders, he appeared on many altars as the patron saint of musical guilds. Contemporary secularism hails him as a type of defiance in a meaningless universe. Jewish and Christian thinkers salute him as a theological fighter and a nonconformist seeker of truth.[540]

I do *not* draw here upon encyclopedia accounts about *Job* in the *Jewish* traditions since that is what I will be considering in my own remarks.

It should be added, in these preliminary observations, that the Voice from the Whirlwind *never* reports to Job what had happened between God and the Satan. Or, as a Christian reference book puts it: "This version does not reveal the why of the particular sufferings of Job or of any other believer, but it does present the servants of God with a framework for hope."[541] *Job* is one of that select body of exceptional works of the spirit that can contribute to our efforts to recognize the most important questions about human existence, questions that are intrinsic to what we are born with and into.

One such question is that which Job in effect asks of God: "Why me?" One proper answer to that question is that which can be said to be given in this story: "Why should you be different from everyone else?"

II

It is instructive to ask whether the *Book of Job* is as important as many have long believed it to be.

Job himself is identified by the author at the outset of this book as "whole-hearted and upright, and one that feared God, and shunned evil."[542] The author's assessment is ratified by what God is reported to have said to the Satan: "Hast thou considered My servant Job, that there is none like him in the earth, a whole-hearted and an upright man, one that feareth God, and shunneth evil?"[543]

Job's world did not have, as a vital part of its own "canon," the *Book of Job* nor, so far as we can tell, anything like it. Thus, *we* are provided guides that Job did not have. We have not only his story but also countless commentaries upon that story. Things are much more sophisticated for us—in some ways better, in some ways worse.

On what basis, we may well wonder (and wonder also about the author's silence about this)—on what basis did Job take the positions he did and conduct himself as he did (for example, with respect to sacrifices)?[544] In short, who *was* Job's Job?

Similar questions could be asked about such figures as the Achilles of Homer's *Iliad* and the Odysseus of his *Odyssey*. By the time of the *Odyssey*, stories about the exploits of the *Iliad* are said (in the *Odyssey*) to be circulating in the Mediterranean world.[545] Consider, also, how the second part of *Don Quixote* includes references to the circulation in Spain of the reports of the adventures of the memorable knight that had been published by Cervantes some years before in the first part of his novel.[546]

Do such characters implicitly shape the texts that they populate, almost as if the characters preceded the texts? At the same time, the texts can seem to provide guidance to their own characters with respect to both thought and action.

Even so, are we not bound to be decisively different from the people in the texts that help shape us? Consider, for example, our sympathy for the Socrates of Plato's *Apology*, even though we may not be any more cultured and sensible than the Athenians who condemned him. In a sense, it can be said, we can never encounter the Socrates that the Athenians did.[547]

But, it can be argued, the more thoughtful characters in texts may be able themselves to figure out from their careers what *we* learn from those careers. One obstacle that Job faces here, however, is (if his story is taken literally) that he does not learn all that we do about what is happening to him and why.

III

We have already noticed that we are not told how it is that Job knows, or believes himself to know, what is routinely required from him by God.[548] Specificity about sacrifices *is* a case in point. Why should taking perfectly good animals and killing them "please," confirm, or satisfy the appetites of any divinity? The killing of such animals, the number to be killed, when, and how can (it seems) hardly be figured out. Some kind of divine guidance, real or apparent, seems to be needed here, unless one relies primarily upon what happens to be the local practice.

Similarly, we may ask, how did the friends of Job learn what they drew upon and said about God's interests and God's will? Perhaps we can see reflected here whatever truth there may be to an observation recorded by Herodotus: ". . . I think that all men know equally about the gods."[549] Perhaps, also, there are more sources of revelation assumed by the Bible than we usually notice.

Whatever may be the condition of most of us, Job has at times been considered by Jewish commentators to have been as pious as Abraham, relying as Abraham did upon a remarkable intuition. About Abraham, too, we might ask: "Who was Abraham's Abraham?"[550]

Whether *Job* was originally written in Hebrew (or by Israelites), it is significant that the people of Israel took the book to themselves and were able thereby to ensure the preservation of a great poetic work. Its universalism evidently seemed to the Israelites to be consistent with the specificities of the Mosaic message.[551]

There are, it has been pointed out again and again, many ironies and complications in the dozen or so speeches recorded in *Job*. Is not the reader intended to ponder them for a long time, and in such a way as to be moved by such things differently from Job? After all, as I have noticed, the context for these things for the reader *is* quite different from that which Job had for them.

In more ways than one, Job could not have known what he was missing.[552]

IV

Consider how much different Job's circumstances and sentiments would have been throughout the story if he had known what we as readers are told at the outset about the immediate cause of his troubles. Certainly, things would have been radically different if Job and his friends had known of God's high praise "in public" of Job. This praise confirmed the high opinion that Job had, or at least *should* have had, of himself.[553]

Job's friends believe that Job's troubles make sense, but they may have been right for the wrong reason, deducing the wrong causes from the effects they do observe. Job himself can wonder whether he is afflicted *because* of his piety.[554] Does he ever learn how sound his ironic intuition is here?

Does it matter that we know things that Job does not know—or that *he* does not know these things? Perhaps, we may be meant to suspect, the whole can never be known by us: there is no place for the human being to stand from which the whole can be regarded. We *are* given more of a view of things than Job is—but on what do we stand (that is, what is taken for granted and hence not examined) for our viewing?

In considering what we have been privileged to acquire after Job, three words of caution are in order. The first should help us appreciate *Job*: "Literature spreads suffering around."[555]

The second word of caution is appropriate in considering old texts fashioned in circumstances quite different from ours. This consists of a report I recently happened upon about a mid-nineteenth-century parrot on a South Seas island, a parrot with so long a lifespan that it could no longer be understood because it spoke the language of an extinct tribe.[556]

The third word of caution, appropriate for those of us who may be moved to act impulsively upon the instructions we believe we have heard from those in authority, is something I once heard on an airliner loudspeaker: "Any passenger sitting in an exit row should be sure to look outside the window before opening his door in any emergency." For one thing, I suppose, the passenger should check to make sure that the plane has indeed been set down before anything is attempted with a door. One can well wonder what incident had led to this warning.

Critical doors can open up for us all to the beginnings of things—but they can also open the way to disaster if used prematurely or in the wrong way. I have suggested that a sound intuition can help us establish our beginnings. Does Job show us the limitations that even so pious a man as Job can suffer from because he cannot grasp properly the beginnings of his troubles? Should he have been able to figure out that something special was going on?[557] Certainly, it was once argued (but not perhaps in Hebrew), a truly or fully virtuous man knows not only what virtue requires but also whether he personally complies with such requirements and what follows from such compliance.[558]

Dare we go further by suggesting that we may be instructed by *Job* what to look for as the true beginnings of such things as the story about Adam, Eve, and the Serpent provided us in the third chapter of *Genesis*?[559]

V

Scholars have pointed out that various things said by Job and his wife and also by Job and his friends echo things said by God and the Satan.[560] Job's friends, who in a sense make the Satan's arguments, doubt Job's virtue. Indeed, we must be prepared to consider, would the Satan (who is *not* the Devil of Christianity) have treated Job as he did if he had believed that Job was truly virtuous? That is, does not the Satan somehow seek the good? And, we can also ask, is the Satan himself enlightened and hence made better by this encounter?

All this suggests that the exchanges between God and the Satan may be intrinsic to what *we* (but *not* the Bible) can call "the nature of things." We can sense and even know such exchanges without conventional revelations, just as perhaps the author, or poet, of *Job* may have. Should Job also have been able to figure out how things truly were?[561]

Or is it essential, if not even natural, that Job *not* know what is going on *in particular*? This may bear upon what virtue is like and what follows from it. Job does not always seem to understand why and how virtue should be desired primarily for its own sake, regardless of consequences from time to time.[562] Should not *we* be better able to accept virtue for its own sake once we learn about Job's experiences and about his, perhaps necessary, ignorance of his circumstances?

Does the Satan, or an external and less principled willfulness, interfere with the natural workings of the virtues? Chance (a term that seems to depend upon some awareness of *nature*) can also interfere with such workings, but rarely so thoroughly or so singlemindedly as is seen in *Job*. Left to themselves, would not things usually work out better than they do in this story (before its epilogue), with the virtues usually "paying off" more or less?

A proper grasp of *nature* (a term that *is* foreign to the Hebrew Bible [and to most of the Greek Bible, as well]) encourages us to see *Job* in still another way. Does not this story deal with the human problem of mortality? After all, no matter how virtuous and careful one may be, things are apt to begin deteriorating in and around one sooner or later. Thus, one's family and friends have troubles; one grows old, feeble, and probably ill. Is not this kind of not-uncommon deterioration accelerated and hence dramatized in the case of Job? That is, is not what the Satan visited upon Job pretty much intrinsic to "the human condition," with even the best eventually collapsing, usually with some suffering? Thus, that which happened to Job so dramatically happens to all or almost all human beings eventually—the obliteration for each of them of everything which they hold dear and which they may have earned and deserve.

Another way of putting all this is to suggest that without an adequate grasp of the idea of *nature*, the perennial question "Why evil?" becomes more troublesome. In these circumstances, people can easily come to believe that a malevolent will governs, or at least intermittently disrupts, human affairs. Socrates, on the other hand, might ask Job: "What else did you expect—and why?"

VI

Socrates argues, again and again, that the virtues are intrinsically rewarding to their practitioner. Socrates presents them as worth having for their own sake. But neither Job nor his chronicler seems to understand that virtue should ultimately be regarded as its own reward. To expect consistent worldly rewards for virtue is, I have suggested, to make too much of *will* and too little of *chance* in the general workings of things—and this may be what comes from an inability to observe adequately the workings of nature. In short, neither Job nor his chronicler is a philosopher.[563] It should not be surprising, therefore, that Job in his adversities does not display the serenity that Socrates can. His constant sacrificing, like that of Plato's Cephalus, should be compared with the dying Socrates' single cock for Aesclepius.[564]

Do not the virtues, partly because of their design, promote good things by and large?[565] Do not the virtues naturally tend in their everyday consequences toward a healthier, safer, more pleasant, and more interesting (as well as a more self-respecting) life? The skillful poet can reinforce this tendency by the teachings he provides those whom he can engage. Thus, an Egyptian priest proclaimed, several millennia ago: "It is Horus when he riseth up with a double head, whereof the one beareth right and truth and the other wickedness. He bestoweth wickedness upon him that worketh wickedness and right and truth upon him that followeth righteousness and truth . . ."[566] We do not require continuing allegiance to Horus and other Egyptian deities in order to recognize the sensibleness of this suggestion that goodness promotes the good and that badness promotes the bad.

VII

I now touch upon a few more questions suggested by *Job*. Is Job personally better off because of all that happened to him? Does he need *all* that happened to him in order to have any part of it? Are the dreadful things that happened to Job necessary for the spectacular revelation he was finally privileged to have? Do his sufferings point up the complexity of things? Does it matter to us whether Job ever existed as we exist?

Among the good things that happened to Job is that he has become helpful to others who have learned about his life. Would *he* have considered *that* a good thing? Did he, assuming that he did exist, ever recognize that his career could become an instructive story?

Preeminent among the things that happened to Job is that God came to him, evidently for the first time, at least in so dramatic a form. Why had not God come to Job earlier and said: "There is going to be a test"? Or should Job, if truly thoughtful, have already known that into every life some tests must fall?

How *is* God's coming to a human being to be understood? Is it somehow inherent in things in some circumstances? Is this kind of divine revelation available to every pious man or woman, especially if one is both afflicted and thoughtful?

Some interpret *Job* as calling for further revelation, pointing indeed to the Christian revelation. But the book itself need not be read as implying that more revelation is needed for *anyone's* personal salvation, except in the sense that the reader may be in a position to learn more about the workings of divinity than even Job was.[567]

However all this may be, we do have in this book an account of how God came to Job and, it seems, to one of his friends as well (who is rebuked by God).[568] In this and other ways, Job is a privileged character. The democratization of life in the United States is reflected in a fact reported by ABC Television News: 36 percent of Americans report that God has spoken to them.[569] Everyone of us, it now seems, is able, if not entitled, to hear personally from God—and one-third of us already have. Such statistics encourage us to wonder further both about what being spoken to by God means and about what form God's speaking to Job is supposed to have taken.[570] A whirlwind, we can surmise, is an unsettling sort of experience out of which almost anything may come.

Is God "compelled" to come to Job by the Satan's efforts? Are both God and this kind of Satan always active in human affairs, perhaps even necessarily so? That is, does either the Satan or God do anything, or appear in any way, to Job that could not "naturally" happen in its essentials anywhere? We *are* obliged to wonder whether the things depicted in *Job* happen all the time, however inspired and hence rare the most sublime poetic depiction of such things may be. There may not be, strictly speaking, anything miraculous in any of the good and bad things that happen to Job, perhaps not even the Voice heard by him out of the Whirlwind.

A significantly different depiction of Job's career would be from the point of view of Job's wife. She may suffer even more than he does, not only because *she* had borne the children who were suddenly lost but also because she does not happen to have his faith, his patience, or his reputation. However harshly Job speaks to her, it should be noticed, God does not rebuke her in the ways He does both Job and the friend(s) of Job. Does the naming in the epilogue of Job's three restored daughters, but not of his sons, serve as a kind of recognition of (if not even solace to) Job's wife? *She* is not named, but her daughters are.[571] This story, told from the point of view of Job's wife, could well be included in a collection of an account by Eve about what really happened in the Garden, an account by Sarah about what her God-driven husband once tried to do to *her* only son, and an account by Bathsheba about what Nathan and perhaps David did do (in the name of God) to her first-born son.

Did any of these strong-willed husbands—Job or Abraham or David—ever understand what their women went through for their sake, so to speak? If they did not, can they truly be said ever to have fully known themselves, however privileged they may have been in the service of God?

That Job can prosper as much as he does after God's sustained verbal assault upon him suggests how generous God's standards can be in judging human beings. God, despite what He says directly to Job, does seem to concede from the outset of this story that the lives and virtues of puny human beings can be significant.[572]

Is, then, the principal limitation of Job that he does not recognize the implications of the virtues that God always sees in him? Should everything that happens to Job—including what is said to him by God as well as by his wife and his friends—should all this have been anticipated and perhaps understood by Job throughout his testing? If so, then Job's Job is always available to the more thoughtful, perhaps even without any sustained personal afflictions.

Chapter Fourteen

Jesus[573]

> And Abraham prayed unto God; and God healed Abimelech, and his wife, and his maid-servants; and they bore children. For the Lord had fast closed up all the wombs of the house of Abimelech, because of Sarah Abraham's wife.
>
> Moses[574]

I

Today, February 22, is the traditional date for the celebration of the birth of George Washington. It is fitting that a founding document of a great religion, the *Gospel of John*, should be discussed on a Founder's birthday, thereby implicitly reaffirming for us the order in the universe.

The other three gospels are critical also. *Matthew*, for example, is more important than *John* for establishing the connection of what we know as Christianity with what we know as Judaism (its prophecies anticipating a Messiah and redemption). *Matthew* can be thought of as having been written by a Jew for Jews. *John*, on the other hand, can be thought of as explaining Jesus, his doings and sayings, to the Greeks and hence to the world—to those who knew relatively little about the Jews but who knew something about philosophy.

It is difficult for the patriot, whether political or religious, to go behind or beneath a founding document critical to his way of life.[575] Perhaps one can most safely begin to examine the presuppositions of a founding document by considering how it, or at least an aspect of it, is organized. Such an inquiry can suggest the understanding of things implicit in the document. Consider, for example, how the Constitution of the United States appears when it is recognized that it is indeed carefully crafted and skillfully put together. The same can be said about the Ten Commandments.[576] When one recognizes this, one approaches a text with greater respect and hence with greater care. A livelier attention is apt to be devoted to the mind evident behind and in it.

John, with its celebrated invocation of *Logos*, is perhaps emphatically a constitutional document in that a constitution can be thought of as the deliberate effort to order the things of this world according to the Word—that is, according to reason. In this respect, this gospel can be seen as reshaping the traditional Hebrew teaching in the spirit of Greekness.

II

It is, I have observed, difficult to go behind a founding document, to bring to light the act of faith (and perhaps the chance developments) involved in its establishment. The author of such a book as *John* is usually trying to influence people to "believe in" something, more than simply to examine and to understand something.

The typical lay reader cannot reasonably hope in his reading of a text such as *John* to have recourse to the available evidence with respect to the stories told or to analyze the language and origins of the text. Particularly difficult is any effort to arrive, in the modern world, at a judicious appraisal of the miracles in the Bible.[577] I propose to gather here some thoughts about the miracles in *John*, to see what can be said about them and thereby to offer suggestions about how one may begin to think about such a book in times such as ours.

I propose, that is, to examine an aspect of what *is* said about the miracles and thereby to consider the implications of what is said. To evaluate the evidence *for* the miracles is *not* something I intend to do—that is "history," with the overwhelming problems that even ordinary historical writing pose for serious understanding. Rather, I propose to see what the account of miracles in this gospel suggests about how the author of *John* understands what he is doing.[578]

III

By proceeding thus, one can talk about the "rational element" in the story, about that which makes sense and hence *is* subject to general discussion. One could consider in the process what is presupposed about men and communities, what is presupposed about God, and what is presupposed about the relations of God and man. Even if one regards such a book as primarily a work of spiritualized rhetoric, one can consider how it accomplishes what it sets out to do as well as what indeed it sets out to do.

These questions, which I can do no more than touch upon here, can be elaborated as follows (using our, not the author's, term—*human nature*): What is the author's (or the Christian) view of human nature? What is it about human nature that leads to man's predicament? What is it about human nature that is reflected in the means available for his salvation? What is it about human nature that is reflected in the story of Jesus? What is it about human nature that is reflected in the way the story is framed, in what is appealed to?

It is particularly appropriate that our inquiry should be directed as it is to the "rational element" since John is celebrated as the gospel which does take its departure from the *Logos*. *Logos*, we are given to understand at the outset of *John*, is critical from (if not also critical for) the very beginning of things.[579]

I believe it prudent to assume that the intended reader of *John* was not counted upon to have much more than this particular gospel available to him *in writing*. The author seems to assume that the reader (or listener) has heard of Jesus and his life, and perhaps may even "believe in him" as the Son of God and as the only way to salvation, whatever that may mean. He may also assume that his reader already knows of, and is prepared to "believe in," if he does not already "believe in," the miracles associated with Jesus. And, I will argue, the author undertakes to organize those miracles so as to validate (or, at least, to reinforce) his story, that is to say, *the* Story. I anticipate what I have to say by observing that it seems that the author organizes or marshals his miracles in such a way as to reinforce the notion that *Logos* does govern the universe, and especially the relations among human beings and between God and man.

One other effect of what I have to say here should be to suggest things about the relation of *Logos* and history, about the Greek effort to make sense of what would otherwise be an essentially meaningless chronicle.

I turn now to *John* and its miracles.

IV

This book, we are told, is quite late among the gospels, perhaps the last of them. Its language and assumptions are said to indicate the lateness of its final composition.

A number of miracles associated with Jesus are obviously available to the author. John refers to numerous healings, evidently miraculous in character, which he does not pause to describe.[580] He selects for *somewhat extended presentation* only half a dozen out of the many accounts of miracles he could probably have drawn upon.

What then is the author's principle of selection or—perhaps this is decisive in the selection—what is the principle of his arrangement of the miracles that he dwells upon? This arrangement, I have suggested, reflects an opinion that the universe is *Logos*-minded, that it is rational, that it makes sense. The author of *John* can be taken to say: "I don't intend to *prove* that the miracles were genuine. Indeed, it would be foolish of me to try to do so, considering the very character of miracles. But if you are disposed to believe in the miracles of Jesus, you should pay attention to the ones I have selected for your instruction."

To list the miracles—to be moved to list them with a view to determining the principle of order implicit therein—is to be well on the way to an understanding of them, including a recognition of the purpose they serve in this story. To *think* of listing them in this fashion is already to assume something critical; it is already to be "logical," to rely upon *Logos*.

There were, I have noticed, a number of miracles upon which the author could probably have drawn to describe. But, I have also noticed, he strictly limits himself. The changing of water to wine is referred to by the author as the "beginning of signs." The second miracle described is also numbered (as "the second sign") by the narrator.[581] Are we not thus instructed that we should (and that we can) do our own numbering thereafter? Numbering, it should be further noticed, is essential to *Logos*, at least as we know it in the Western world.

The half-dozen miracles of Jesus described at length by the narrator in *John* are to be distinguished, it seems to me, from the "frame" in which these miracles appear—that is to say, the very Incarnation of God as man (the birth of Jesus) and the Resurrection of the crucified Jesus. Those two can be thought of as "super-miracles." The set of half-dozen described (not merely referred to) miracles and the set of two super-miracles may be dependent upon each other.

Here, then, are the pre-Resurrection miracles by Jesus which are described *in some detail* by the narrator in *John*:

1. Turning water into wine;[582]
2. Healing of the nobleman's son;[583]
3. Healing the infirm man at Bethesda;[584]
4. Multiplying loaves and fishes;[585]
5. Walking on water;[586]
6. Healing the blind man;[587]
7. Raising the dead Lazarus.[588]

Except for the Resurrection, I believe that is all. No other miracles are described *at length* after chapter 11 and before the Resurrection. (The gospel continues thereafter for another ten chapters.)

What I am examining, therefore, is a series of events described in the first half of *John*. I do not propose to say much about the second half of the book, except insofar as what I say about the first half—or, more precisely, about the miracles in the first half—sheds light upon what is taught in the second half, that half in which there are more sermons and of course the account of the arrest, trial, execution, and resurrection of Jesus.[589]

V

I now make some suggestions about the principle of order in the author's selection of the miracles described at some length. I do not propose to mention everything I happen to have noticed about this, but only enough to suggest matters for further inquiry.

First, and perhaps foremost in its significance for the human being open to *Logos*, is the remarkable symmetry of the arrangement in *John*. Consider the first and last of our seven miracles: the changing of water to wine and the raising of Lazarus.[590] "Dead" water is transformed into "living water"—just as Lazarus' corpse is reanimated. Is the resurrected Lazarus better than he was before he died, just as the wine provided by Jesus is said to be the best at the wedding party in Cana? Does a better life await a man after having been revived by Jesus? I also notice that these two miracles, the first and the last, are done primarily at the behest of women: the first upon the suggestion of Jesus' mother, the last in response to Lazarus' sisters.

Consider, in turn, the second and the next-to-last miracles: the healing of the nobleman's son and the healing of the blind man.[591] In both of those cases, Jesus works at a distance. That is, the absent child is healed at the hour Jesus says he is healed; the blind man will be healed when he washes off, at another place, the mud that Jesus has put on his eyes. Both of these healings, I notice, are performed at the behest of men: an anxious father, in the first case; the inquiring disciples, in effect, in the second case (as well as, presumptively, the blind man himself).

We move even further from the first and last miracles by turning to the third miracles, counting from the beginning and from the end—that of the healing of the infirm man at Bethesda and that of Jesus walking upon the water.[592] Both of these miracles involve acts of walking: one by the helpless man upon land, the other by Jesus upon the water. Both walkings are water-related: the infirm man was not able to walk (as he desired for his cure) from the land *to* the miraculous pool at Bethesda; Jesus was able to walk to his disciples in the boat and thus to bring them all *to* land. Both of these miracles involve the stirring of water by the wind. Is not God responsible for the effect of the stirring of the water at Bethesda (the curative effect)? But we also see that Jesus can control the effects of storm-tossed water.

We now have left only one miracle in this list, that of the loaves and fishes.[593] I mention a small point first, that just as the land-water relation is critical in the miracles on either side of this central miracle, so the food which is bountifully multiplied comes from both the land and the water. It is universal in its scope, or more nearly so than the others. This miracle is also unique in the extent of its beneficiaries. There are far more people here, it would seem, than at the Cana wedding party. In some ways, this miracle is the least miraculous of all: it *can* be understood "merely" as a drawing upon the previously hidden resources of the multitude around Jesus. It is not said that the five loaves and two fishes were themselves actually changed into a bountiful supply, even though this is spoken of as a remarkable *sign*. Is this intended to cast light upon "what really happened" as well with the other miracles? Does Jesus somehow help people to draw upon personal resources, thereby bringing out the best in human nature?

However that may be, the multiplication of the loaves and fishes is something around which the account of miracles in *John* turns. Are not the three miracles following this multiplication more impressive, less open to doubt as anything but genuine miracles (if they happened), than the three preceding it? Thus, the raising of the dead is more critical than converting water to wine. (After all, water can be mixed with the remnants of wine, or jars can be substituted.) Thus, the curing of a longstanding blindness is more critical than the curing of a just-sick child (children do have remarkable recuperative powers). And thus, walking upon water (if not even calming a storm) is more critical than curing a bedridden man. (The power of suggestion is obviously more likely to affect the infirm than the sea.) Is there something about the miracle of the loaves and fishes that permits thereafter the "escalation" of the miracles? Are people (including, it seems, the disciples) prepared after that miracle for grander things?[594]

VI

I trust I have said enough to make a prima facie case for the argument that there is a careful orchestration in *John* of the miracles described in detail therein. Such care should give us pause to think, just as should the kind of data collected by, say, Charles Darwin about the natural articulation of the parts of animals and about the relation of those parts to the environment and activities of such animals. One can think about *John* the sort of thing one should think when one sees in any work of art, if not also in nature, signs of thought in arrangements. A high order of sophistication is indicated in this gospel, and in a place where one does not expect it—that is, in a place where much is made of faith in miracles. A disciplined use of miracles does seem to be evident.

This is not to suggest that the typical reader of the gospels is asked to think. Rather, as we have noticed, he is asked to believe, or he is reinforced in his belief. If thinking happens to promote belief, well and good; if it does not, then it should be set aside. We as students of these matters, however, need not settle for that. Serious questions about, and an understanding of, a gospel teaching emerge only when one has a reliable notion of what is going on. Was such an understanding intended, if only for a few readers, by the artist responsible for *John*? This is another way of asking how thoughtful that author may really have been.[595]

VII

The concluding passage in the *Gospel of John* can be taken to suggest still another miracle of note:

> Peter, seeing [John], saith to Jesus, "Lord, and what shall this man do?" Jesus saith unto him, "If I will that he tarry till I come, what is that to thee? Follow thou me."[596]

But *this* suggestion of a miracle is immediately followed by a disclaimer:

> Then went this saying abroad among the brethren, that this disciple should not die, yet Jesus said not unto him, "He shall not die," but, "If I will that he tarry till I come [again], what is that to thee?"[597]

The emphasis then shifts, in the very last words of this gospel, from miracles (both actual and contemplated) to other deeds of Jesus:

> And there are also many other things which Jesus did, the which, if they should be written every one, I suppose that even the world itself could not contain the books that should be written. Amen.[598]

There is a shift here from what has been done to what is *said* about what has been done. It is appropriate that a Gospel that opened with a celebration of *Logos* should close with a recognition that *Logos* could fill up the world. (The word here translated as *books* is, aside from *Amen*, the last one in the Greek text.) To say that the world could be filled with books may be still another way of saying that *Logos* is everywhere and eternal.

Chapter Fifteen

The Lord's Prayer[599]

When David saw that his servants whispered together, David perceived that the child [for whose life he had besought God and fasted] was dead. . . . Then David arose from the earth, and washed, and anointed himself, and changed his apparel; and he came into the house of the Lord, and worshipped [and thereafter] he did eat. Then said his servants unto him: "What thing is this that thou hast done? Thou didst fast and weep for the child, while it was alive; but when the child was dead, thou didst rise and eat bread." And he said: "While the child was yet alive, I fasted and wept; for I said: 'Who knoweth whether the Lord will not be gracious to me, that the child may live?' But now he is dead, wherefore should I fast? Can I bring him back again? I shall go to him, but he will not return to me." And David comforted Bathsheba his wife, and went in unto her, and lay with her; and she bore a son, and called his name Solomon.

Samuel[600]

I

I cannot hope to say anything about the Lord's Prayer that is truly new and at the same time sound. The world is filled up, it can seem, with comments upon that prayer, probably the most familiar *Logos* of Christendom.

Not only is the Lord's Prayer, prescribed by Jesus, very much a part of the Christian liturgy, as it has been for almost two millennia, but its influence extends far beyond its obvious manifestations. For example, Abraham Lincoln's Gettysburg Address resembles the Lord's Prayer, as both the address and the prayer draw upon *Exodus* in critical respects. The Gettysburg Address begins (as does the Lord's Prayer) with an invocation of the paternal and concludes (as does the prayer's doxology) with a view of the everafter.[601]

The Lord's Prayer (known by many as the "Our Father") is of general interest in part because of its author. It has been observed by Albert Schweitzer: "There is no historical task which so reveals a man's true self as the writing of a Life of Jesus."[602] It has also been observed by Hans Kung: "You cannot read one passage of the New Testament without being challenged. Take the 'Our Father': there is a challenge in every phrase. But the challenge is not expressed in terms of a mystery. It is never said that you must believe, that there is a whole dogmatic system."[603] It is more the challenge (and perhaps some mystery) posed by the Lord's Prayer that we respond to here, recognizing as we do so that we cannot avoid the risks implied in any effort to examine, however indirectly, the life of Jesus.

So much has been said about the Lord's Prayer, as about any recognized "classic," that one cannot hope to exhaust, or even substantially to sample, "the literature." Consequently, one is obliged to think for oneself. One way of thinking for oneself, as one considers how to begin to read the Lord's Prayer, is to organize what is said in the prayer, to see how it is put together. This is something that most readers, of most things, neglect to do in their efforts to work out what a text means.

II

It is difficult for Christians to know what the Lord's Prayer means since there is the perhaps insuperable prior problem of determining what it says. The typical Christian, in reciting the Lord's Prayer, relies upon a translation. This fact he may know—and not be much troubled by. What he is not likely to know is that the translation he uses works from a Greek text which is itself a translation from an ancient Middle Eastern language, probably Aramaic.[604] There may well be nuances in the original that are different from the Greek as well as from the English. Thus, the English salutation *Our Father* may be more solemn, less intimate, than the Aramaic *Abba*, if that *is* what the original said.[605]

Jesus provided the Lord's Prayer about 30 C.E. Several generations passed before there had crystallized the various gospels we have in the New Testament which are regarded as the most authoritative account of what Jesus said and did during his ministry. With the Lord's Prayer there are special complications, since there are two versions of the prayer, the shorter one found in *Luke* (from perhaps around 90 C.E.) and the longer one found in *Matthew* (from perhaps around 120 C.E.).[606] The two versions are different enough, it has been suggested, to indicate that each must stem from a separate liturgical tradition in the early church. (Among the differences is that the version in *Matthew* has seven petitions, whereas that in *Luke* has only five.)[607]

In *Matthew*, it has been pointed out, the prayer is given as a pattern to be followed ("After this manner . . . pray ye . . ."),[608] whereas in *Luke*, it is an actual prayer to be repeated ("When ye pray, say . . .").[609] Hence it has been asked:

> Are we to conclude that Jesus taught the prayer on two occasions? If so, why did he teach two different versions? If, on the other hand, we conclude that he is more likely to have taught only one form of the prayer, we are still left with the problem of deciding which is the original, or even whether either of them is.[610]

It seems to be generally held by scholars that the version in *Luke* most closely represents, in the number of its petitions, the form of the prayer spoken by Jesus.[611] On the other hand, it has been argued, the fact that the *Matthew* form is the one adopted in the liturgy in the early church probably shows that it is the more primitive. Luke, it is also observed, has the habit of abridging.[612]

The form familiar to most English-speaking Christians is that found in *Matthew*, but with a doxology appended to it.[613] It is that version which I am primarily interested in examining here, partly in order to suggest how one might usefully think about the sacred texts of a people. It should at once be added that one may not be called upon, as a pious human being, to understand that doctrine in which one has a faith which merits salvation. St. Augustine could speak of the superiority over the philosopher, with respect to the most important things, of the illiterate peasant woman who rested her faith in Jesus Christ.[614] I, for one, would not presume to instruct, or even to question, such a woman. But I can wonder what is being said, explicitly, by the prayer developed for her and others by those in authority.

III

One problem is how far back that authority extends. It goes back to Jesus, of course, but does it go even further back? That is, how *Jewish* is the Lord's Prayer?

An old Jewish friend of mine, who has served as a member of the governing board of his congregation, learned only recently, upon my asking for his impressions of the prayer, that it was not an "official" Jewish prayer. He had been taught it in "Sunday School," more than forty years ago; he had always considered it part of one of the psalms. A much younger Jew has told me that it was understood in his quite liberal family that one did *not*, as a loyal Jew, recite the Lord's Prayer.[615] Even so, the typical Jew in this country would probably take the stance toward Jesus that the free-thinking Thomas Paine did two centuries ago, making it clear, despite his reservations about organized Christianity, that no disrespect was meant to the character of someone who could be described as "a virtuous and an amiable man."[616]

We hear these days more and more reminders that Jesus was a Jew, not a Christian.[617] This is part of a fairly recent development described as "the re-Judaizing of Christianity."[618] Thus, the "Jewish background" of the Lord's Prayer "is seen in its echo of the language of synagogue litanies; in its opening ascription of praise; and in its naming of God as Father."[619] Certainly, *Matthew* has long been regarded as the most Jewish of the Gospels, which is reflected (it is said) in such things as the author's preference for the term "kingdom of Heaven."[620]

It has been argued that the very fact that there appear in the Gospels two versions of both the text of the Lord's Prayer and the circumstances of its transmission—this fact suggests that Jesus was not giving his followers a fixed prayer formula such as other Jews had.[621] Another Christian commentator suggests:

> Most of the phrases of the prayer are to be found in Jewish sources but its simple brevity and the deliberate exclusion of the spirit of Jewish nationalism (markedly present, e.g., in the great Jewish prayer, the *Tephillah* or *Shemoneh Esre*) prove that though the body may be Jewish, the soul is Christian.[622]

Such distinctions can be made, as we have seen, in distinguishing generally between Judaism and Christianity.

In any event, there are many scholars who can insist that the Lord's Prayer *is*, for the most part, a thoroughly Jewish prayer.[623] The doxology, added to the *Matthew* version quite early, is something that is "normal in Judaism [with which] to conclude prayers."[624] It is also pointed out that Jesus contrasts the Lord's Prayer not with Jewish prayer but with pagan prayer, which is dismissed by him as "babbling."[625] Also Jewish in mode is the early injunction in the Church that Christians recite the prayer three times a day.[626]

But to say that considerable Jewish influence may be seen in the Lord's Prayer is not to suggest that Jesus did not reshape the Jewish heritage that he passed on to his followers. The status both of the law and of the community was affected. In some ways, things were made easier (as various daily restrictions were lifted); in other ways, things were made harder (as more demands were made upon one's imagination). Certainly, considerable differences followed from Jesus' intervention, not the least of which was that a Jewish sect would soon be dominated (even in the language of its own scriptures) by Gentiles. This meant, among other things, a way of life in which much was made of the awesome responsibilities of "the individual" in making critical choices on his own, substantially (or in principle) independent both of family and of community.[627]

IV

We can turn now to the Lord's Prayer itself, pausing before doing so to notice a problem with its very name. Many among us, I have noticed, are accustomed to calling it the "Our Father" (or, if one prefers the Latin version, *Pater Noster*, or, if one prefers the Greek version, *Pater Emon*). What one calls it usually depends upon where or how one was brought up.

It can be argued, of course, that neither "Lord's Prayer" nor "Our Father" (in whatever language) is the proper name, but rather "The Disciples' Prayer." For it is said to have been given by Jesus to his disciples for their use. In one version of the story, it is given in response to the disciples' request that they be given a prayer just as the disciples of John the Baptist had been given a prayer.[628] This can be seen, by the way, as still another Jewish feature of the prayer—it is the sort of thing that a master did for his disciples.[629] I have seen nowhere any indication of precisely what John had provided his disciples. This reminds us of how much depends in such matters upon the record developed and transmitted by an organized community, however much "individuality" or "personal choice" is featured by a doctrine.

It did not seem to matter to the early Christian community what the immediate context was of the prayer that it adopted for its liturgy. Most Christians over the ages probably have not known precisely where the Lord's Prayer came from, or even that there are two versions available (with several variations of each). Rather, the prayer seems to stand alone—and it is to that prayer, as most Christian churches have used it, that we now turn.

V

Commentators can again and again be struck by the intimacy and immediacy of Jesus' invocation of God as Father, not only in the Lord's Prayer but also throughout the Gospels. Thus, one commentator can say about the opening of the Lord's Prayer: "The tenderness and trust of the whole prayer are revealed in the bold word 'Father.' The phrase '*our* Father' draws our Lord's followers together as children of one family."[630] Another commentator can report:

> It has been pointed out that the way God is addressed in Jesus' teaching simply as "Father," in the Lord's Prayer and elsewhere, is unique in Jewish literature in

> its directness and intimacy, and that many of the sayings and traditions of his activity imply an assumption of authority and independence of human traditions which is without parallel in Judaism. All this suggests that, whether or not Jesus used himself any of the titles of honor (such as Messiah) which the church later adopted to describe him, he did assume that he was destined to play an unprecedented role in God's dealings with the world, a role which it was the later function of the church's faith to describe.[631]

The significance of Jesus' use of "Father" (as understood by the authorities consulted recently by a popular writer) is reported in this fashion:

> What chiefly seems to distinguish Jesus from other Jewish charismatics is the intensity of what has been called his Abba experience, an experience that perhaps lies at the heart of his sense of authority. *Abba* is an Aramaic word for a male parent—the word a son would use (the connotation is "father dear," but the word's simplicity and ease of pronunciation suggests the speech of a child) rather than a word that might be used by a historian, an exegete, or a social-welfare agency. Jesus refers to God as "Abba" repeatedly in the Gospels. *Abba* is not a word that first-century Jews commonly used in prayer or supplication. The word is not unique to Jesus, but it is employed by him in a unique fashion, and if there is any word in the New Testament that one can be absolutely certain that Jesus used, used frequently, and used with a particular meaning, it is this one.[632]

Still, although we cannot be certain that it *is* "Abba" that the Greek text translates as "Our Father," the observation I have just quoted does tell us something important about what Jesus came to stand for.

It might be added that particularly *un*Jewish was what Jesus said and did about the earthly (or natural) family as a result of his considerable and intimate emphasis upon the divine father. He could call men to follow him, in the name of the Father, despite what their family allegiances seemed to call for.[633] He himself could ask on one occasion: "Who is my mother? Who are my brethren?"[634] And he could counsel: "And call no man your father upon the earth: for one is your Father, which is in heaven."[635]

On another occasion, Jesus was obliged to argue that there would be no marriages in heaven. That is, the widow described to him who had married several husbands in turn would not be the wife of (or subordinated to?) any of them in the hereafter.[636] But if no marriages, then no parent-and-child relations either, it would seem. There is indeed something revolutionary about the "kingdom of Heaven" envisioned by Jesus.

The first set of three petitions found in the Lord's Prayer speaks of the kingdom coming. It is not clear to us what this means. It may not have been clear to Jesus' audiences either. At the least, it would seem to mean an end to the way things are now on earth. This would follow whether the anticipated event is the earthly reordering of the Messianic "First Coming" of the Jews or the earthly "last days" of the Christian "Second Coming."[637]

The early Christians soon came to recognize that the promised "Second Coming" might well be delayed.[638] And the "kingdom come" language could eventually be understood among them as "May the Holy Spirit come upon us and cleanse us."[639] Even so, the anticipation of the kingdom (there are dozens of references to this in the *Gospel of Matthew* alone) could not help but call into question long-established, even natural, family and social relations.[640]

Particularly intriguing here is that Jesus' authority rests in part, at least initially, upon his being able to trace his lineage back to David. Such family and tribal identifications and concerns (evident, for example, in the opening chapter of *Matthew*) seem to become obsolete, however, once Jesus fully asserts himself. Thus, the mundane and temporal were to be used as the disposable platform from which the quest for the cosmic and eternal was to be launched.

VI

The primacy of divine, and hence eternal, things is indicated in the way the Lord's Prayer is organized. The first three petitions recognize God's prerogatives or interests. The next four (or three, depending on how one counts)—the next four petitions recognize human needs. A proper servicing of human needs depends, it seems, upon the due recognition of the divine. Thus, the ordering of the petitions indicates the proper relation between the high and the low. Is it assumed that men do not know how to conduct themselves except by reference to the guidance provided by the very being, as well as by the commandments, of God? It is God's name which is to be hallowed, not man's. It is God who matters, and man only by reflection, with the first three petitions expressing in different ways a due recognition of the sovereignty of the divine.

God is seen as concerned (or, at least, as authoritative) with respect to both the heavenly and the earthly realms. God is brought down to earth, so to speak—or is man raised up to heaven? Either way, the connecting of the two realms does make human life appear more meaningful than it might otherwise appear. Or, as it is put elsewhere in *Matthew*, "Seek ye first the kingdom of God, and his righteousness; and all these things shall be added unto you."[641] The healing miracles by Jesus indicate all this in another way. It is assumed throughout the Gospels that physical disability is intimately related to moral disability (or sin): to forgive a man's sins is to heal his affliction.[642]

The petitions for human needs move from the personal and daily to the social and thereafter to the spiritual and eternal. They begin with the provision for bread, which is the bodily equivalent of that hallowing of God's name with which the first set of petitions begins.

The divine provides a standard of perfection by which the mode of satisfying the needs of men should be determined. It is taken for granted in the Lord's Prayer that human beings know what they are, and are not, supposed to do. Guidance has long been provided by such pronouncements as the Ten Commandments.

The sequence of the seven petitions can be seen, therefore, in this fashion. The first three are related primarily to the proper worship of God, with the third one ("thy will be done") explaining or bringing about the preceding two—it is God's will which determines what His name means and when (or how) His kingdom is to come (and what that in turn means). These are the divine things and the realm of heaven, concluding with God coming down to earth.

Earth is the realm where man is, that creature whose mortality is reflected in the need for repeated or daily replenishment. It is that mortality, and the natural desires to minister to it, that account for the vulnerability of man.

That vulnerability may be seen in the final three petitions that are related primarily to the proper conduct of man. It is human vulnerability that accounts for trespasses, which makes a man susceptible to temptation, and which leaves him a victim of the evil one. We have thus moved (in the voraciousness of the evil one) to the other extreme from the recognition of the divine with which the prayer had opened.

Another way of putting all this is to say that we move from the divine and the cosmic in the first three (positive) petitions to the human and the mundane in the last three (negative) petitions. Somehow or other, it seems, the transition between the cosmic concerns and the mundane concerns (which may be sensed as one repeats the prayer day after day) is provided by how the securing of daily sustenance is regarded. Both sound worship and proper conduct are keyed to how man regards his mortality and hence his efforts to minister to that mortality. (Is there not in the arrangement of the Lord's Prayer an echo of the arrangement in the Ten Commandments?)

VII

In both the *Matthew* and the *Luke* versions of the Lord's Prayer, the concern about daily sustenance is the central petition (the fourth out of seven in one, the third out of five in the other). Everything in the prayer, it can be said, turns around this petition.

The first temptation of Jesus in the wilderness, it will be remembered, found Satan suggesting that Jesus, in his hunger, convert stones into bread.[643] Elsewhere in *Matthew* there are various references to bread, both in itself and as metaphor.[644] It will also be remembered that thc Grand Inquisitor in the celebrated episode in Fyodor Dostoyevsky's *The Brothers Karamazov* explains to "Jesus" that the Church had mercifully exploited the need for mankind to have bread provided it.[645]

At the very center of the Greek text in Matthew from which the early church fashioned the Lord's Prayer for liturgical use is the term *ton epiousion*.[646] English translators usually render *epiousion* as "daily" or as "for the morrow." But there is considerable uncertainty about this, especially since it seems that there is no use of that word in any other surviving Greek text from that period, or from an earlier period, or from several centuries thereafter. By the second century the typical Christian who recited that prayer (in Greek) may have had little if any reliable notion of what that word meant—and the same is true today. The difficulty with this word is suggested by the lengths to which some translators have gone in order to make something more significant than "daily" out of it. St. Jerome rendered the line, "Give us this day our supersubstantial bread," attempting thereby to connect this petition with the Eucharist.[647]

But the challenge of this term may lie in the immediacy that it reinforces, however redundant or tautological it may seem.[648] Why should both "daily" and "this day" be asked for? Is there not a recognition here that if one gives oneself up to God completely one's immediate concerns will be always (and hence immediately) taken care of?[649] The version in *Luke* of this petition suggests that early Christians did see this as a petition for daily, or constant, sustenance.

Something of this concern may be seen as well in the Jewish compilation, "The Eighteen Benedictions," where one of its central benedictions (No. IX) is the most "materialistic." It reads:

> Bless this year unto us, O Lord our God, together with every kind of the produce thereof, for our welfare; give a blessing upon the face of the earth. O satisfy us with thy goodness, and bless our year like other good years. Blessed are thou, O Lord, who blesses the years.[650]

In various ways, nevertheless, this petition in the Lord's Prayer is special. It is, for example, the only one in which the object of the verb (*the bread*) comes before the verb (*give*). It should read in English: "Our daily bread give us this day." What one considers necessary for subsistence, the prayer indicates, depends upon one's view of, and relation to, the divine. The term *ton epiousion* urges the Christian to respect the essential dailyness of his mundane concerns, seeing them however in the light of the divine and dedicating even them to the divine service.

Christianity, we all know, looks beyond daily concerns to the eternal, even as the daily is somehow provided for. Besides, the eternal, for man, depends upon what happens here on earth. There is for the human soul no existence prior to that here; the mundane is for him the condition for the eternal.[651] The emphasis upon the daily in this prayer is, by placing it completely in God's hand, a kind of purification of it. Is there an attempt thereby to recognize, and yet to go beyond, the traditional Jewish emphasis upon the importance of life here, and of the temporal kingdom of the Messiah?

Be that as it may, there does remain something mysterious about this central petition of the Prayer with its ambiguous central term (*ton epiousion*). Somehow or other there is a turning here around bread which is both more and less than bread, as the Christian is instructed not to concern himself about his sustenance even as he is assured of an enduring sustenance (of *ousia* piled upon *ousia*?). This mysterious movement may not be unrelated to the central mystery of Christianity, evident in the insistence upon one who can be both "true God and true man."[652]

Did the decisive author of the Lord's Prayer, in the form that would be important for liturgical use, recognize and indeed prefer the mystery of its central term? That is, did the framers of the Prayer for church use notice what we have noticed about it? Did they indicate by the choices they made that there should indeed be something mysterious at the core of this communion with God, thereby pointing up what it means to have and to be guided by faith?

VIII

We have considered the ways in which the Lord's Prayer draws upon, even as it modifies, the predominant Jewish approach to the matters with which it deals. That aspect of modification that takes the form of playing down, if not even denying, the place in human life both of family and of community would have posed a problem also for the ancient Greeks. Certainly, this is not the kind of prayer that an Aristotle would have devised, or endorsed, for his truly virtuous man.

Not only is one's people (or one's tribe) subordinated in the Lord's Prayer to one's personal relation with God, but also a political (and hence politic) approach to things is discouraged. Elsewhere Jesus could announce: "I will utter things which have been kept secret from the foundation of the world."[653]

This is what comes, it seems, from recognizing a much greater *active* sovereign than the city or the political order.[654]

All this is aside from the question of whether the Lord's Prayer is a personal prayer, however much it is recited by congregations. What does it say about the natural order of things, which political life depends upon and responds to, when it is taken for granted, as the prayer seems to do, that nature does not suffice, that God must be looked to even for one's ordinary material concerns?

Another way of putting these matters is to remind ourselves of the Aristotelian advocacy of the confident self-sufficiency which the truly virtuous man can hope to secure (especially if the circumstances do not happen to be too much against him).[655] Christianity, on the other hand, can regard pride as the first and greatest of sins to be purged.[656] The ultimate, if not even the constant, dependence of man upon God is insisted upon. This is evident in the Lord's Prayer. However much resemblance there may be between the virtues discussed by Aristotle and those urged by the Scriptures, there remain vital differences between them which reflect different opinions about the possibility of the substantial self-sufficiency of the truly virtuous man, a self-sufficiency which can permit him to be truly happy here on earth, a happiness which does not depend upon, nor expect, any life beyond the grave.[657]

Even the disciples, the salt of the earth, are taught to pray in this fashion. The best, too, are fundamentally dependent upon God. They, too, are radically in need of help, unlike Aristotle's fully virtuous man, who is aware of what is called for and who routinely does it. Still another way of putting these matters is to say that everything for the Christian is the Lord's, including the prayer (properly then the "*Lord's* Prayer") which registers and reinforces the ultimate dependence of man upon God.

IX

Aristotelian self-sufficiency does mean that the self, or one's own human soul, is made much of. The Christian, on the other hand, is urged to leave his self behind—and yet the individual is to be recognized and ministered to beyond the grave.[658] The concern about temptations assumes that the will of man is never fully, or reliably, shaped—that he is always somewhat prone to sin.[659]

This goes back, it seems, to the original, or intrinsic, sinfulness of man. Tertullian regarded the Lord's Prayer as "a brief form of the whole gospel."[660] The Gospels generally testify to the ultimate helplessness of man without divine intervention, without the divine sacrifice that alone expiates the inevitable sins of mankind. Thus, the ministry, or career, of Jesus is devoted to the development of conditions and to the offer of an opportunity that permit the forgiveness of mankind.

The need of man for forgiveness is pointed up by the fact that the petition for forgiveness is the only one of the seven petitions in the prayer which calls for action on the part of the human being: one seeks forgiveness, just as one forgives others.[661] This reciprocity is emphasized again immediately after the prayer and elsewhere in the Gospels.[662] It is as if man cannot secure the divine forgiveness he so desperately needs unless and until he manifests both in his thought and in his own practice the forgiveness towards others that he seeks for himself. Only if he himself loves others can he become lovable. This is another form of the Golden Rule relied upon in the Gospels.[663]

Just as the Lord's Prayer may be seen as a brief form of the whole Gospel, so can Jesus' identification of the two greatest commandments be seen as a brief form of the Lord's Prayer. These are the commandments to love the Lord and to love one's neighbor as one's self.[664] Do not these two commandments, cast in the form of love, mirror the two sets of petitions in the Lord's Prayer? It is love that permits the forgiveness that man needs to experience both as a forgiver and as a forgiven.

It is love, it seems, which permits man to rise, with the help of God, above the temptations to which he is constantly subject. It is not for him a question of *knowing* what is right but rather of *willing* what is right—and it is difficult, without God's constant help, to keep one's will on course. The difference between Aristotle and Jesus in this respect is reflected in the different responses to the prospect of power; "Ruling will show the man," an ancient Greek could observe, with some hope, whereas the Christian Lord Acton could only lament, "Power tends to corrupt; absolute power corrupts absolutely."[665] Does not this juxtaposition reflect quite different opinions about the nature of the soul, about its passions, and about its prospects?

X

The mysterious relation between the divine and the human, between this world and the next, which may be seen in the Lord's Prayer may be seen as well in the very fact that there *are* temptations which one can ask to be spared.

What does it mean to ask that one not be tempted? What does that suggest about the ultimate source of various famous temptations recorded in the Scriptures—such as those of Adam and Eve in the Garden of Eden, of Cain, of Abraham with respect to the sacrifice of Isaac, of Job, and of Jesus in the wilderness?[666]

The Lord's Prayer opens with an affirmation of God's power and closes with a recognition of the Evil One's power. Whatever the omnipotence of God may mean, it is in a sense suspended here on earth in that much depends upon man's choices. There is something necessary and hence good, that is, about the existence of evil, or at least about the existence of the potential for evil choices. "If God had deprived the world of all those things which prove an occasion for sin," it has been argued, "the universe would have been imperfect."[667] Human beings incapable of sin would also be incapable of praiseworthy choice and hence of virtue.[668]

Thus, one must acknowledge the perfection of God, and then figure out from that why the world is, and has to be, the way it obviously is. We can again see, with this observation, how the two halves of the Lord's Prayer are related to one another, turning as they do around that routine "incarnation" found in that daily bread which is so prosaic and yet so exalted.

XI

Three sets of questions remain for us to notice, but not to try to answer, before I bring to a close this introduction to the Lord's Prayer.

Our first set of questions should help us compare the Lord's Prayer with authoritative statements both preceding and following it—statements such as the Ten Commandments and the Nicene Creed.[669] Both of these statements are more elaborate than the Lord's Prayer. What is the effect for any people whose declaration of faith is substantially guided by something like the Lord's Prayer?

It is of profound significance for us, in the modern world, that any ancient saying should be regarded as authoritative among us. Also of significance is precisely which of the ancient sayings available to us should be regarded as most authoritative, or most accessible, and what we do with it or because of it.[670]

It is not insignificant that the Lord's Prayer is about as elaborate as "theology" is allowed to become for most American Christians at this time. Is one consequence of this to encourage people, so long as they *are* Christians, to make much of their "personal relation" with Jesus—and, if so, with what effects? Similarly, we can wonder what it means that the emphasis should shift from ten commandments to primarily one, that we "forgive our debtors." Does it matter why such forgiveness is practiced?[671]

XII

The second set of questions remaining for us to notice, but not to try to answer here, has to do with what we think, or believe, about the Incarnation, about the Resurrection, and about Jesus' foreknowledge (whether prophetic or poetic) with respect to all things. These questions bear upon what Jesus can be understood to have known about what would become of his prayer and upon how we are to understand what he intended and what has happened. These questions occurred, of course, to Jesus' contemporaries, as may be seen in the astonishment of people upon hearing Jesus teach not as their teachers did but rather with the authority of one of the great prophets.[672]

The difficulty of dealing with these, and such, questions is suggested by one scholar's observation: "It is not too wide of the mark to sum up the Jewish-Christian debate in the early church by saying that for the church the resurrection of Jesus was the justification for claiming that he fulfilled Scripture, while for the Jews his crucifixion proved that he did not."[673]

XIII

The third set of questions remaining for us to notice has to do with what *prayer* itself means. These questions, which too could well have required all our effort here, should perhaps have been considered prior to our discussion on this occasion—unless we can say that our inquiry here might help us figure out what prayer does mean by considering at length perhaps the most famous prayer of all time, at least in the Western world.

What is the significance of the massive fact that something as well known as the Lord's Prayer should be so little thought about by the Christian community at large? Does this suggest something about the nature of prayer, or at least about how it is likely to be used? A prescribed prayer may seem anomalous, especially for those who believe a prayer should be uttered with a view to one's immediate circumstances—and this would seem to call for more spontaneity (and hence a sincerity keyed to relevance?).

A prescribed prayer may still have the purpose of training a people, at least by reminding them of, and disciplining them in, what those of a common faith have "always" believed. A prescribed prayer may also be a form of communing with one another. This is not unrelated to the opinion by one theologian that prayer takes the place of sexual love in heaven.[674] However this may be, we can appreciate the suggestion of Thomas Hobbes: "To pray to another, for aid of any kind, is *to* HONOUR; because [this is] a sign we have an opinion he has power to help; and the more difficult the aid [sought for] is, the more is the Honour."[675]

A proper consideration of questions about prayer itself would have to take into account what divine aid is to be sought for and to be expected. The answers here depend upon considerations of what "God" means and of what the proper as well as the possible relations may be between God and man, including how, if at all, God intervenes to change what would otherwise have happened "in the Course of human Events."[676] To what extent is prayer an instance of God helping those who help themselves? Does one truly help oneself by praying in a way that requires and reflects a sound understanding of one's circumstances and of what is properly to be sought and done?

One purpose of prayer, it can be said, is to help us develop and maintain sound opinions about the most important things. We can see in some commentaries upon prayers, or upon any sacred texts, the thoughtfulness or at least the articulated piety that long-received doctrines can promote, however many questions one's preliminary inquiry may leave unanswered. Thus prayerfulness, along with sustained reflection upon the long-established prayers of a people, can stimulate and even guide reasoning about such matters as the relation of the low to the high, indeed to the most high.

Chapter Sixteen

The Nicene Creed[677]

> But before we start, let me say a few words about myself. I stand in some awe of your authority, Balbus, and of the plea which you made to me at the end of your discourse that I should remember that I am Cotta and a [Roman] priest. By this you meant, I take it, that I ought to defend the beliefs which we have inherited from our ancestors about the immortal gods, with all their attendant ceremonies and sacred rituals. And I shall always defend them, as I have defended them in the past. Nobody, be he learned or unlearned, shall ever argue me out of the views which I have received from my forebears about the worship of the gods. When it is a question of religious observance, I follow such religious authorities as Titus Coruncianus, Publius Scipio and Publius Scaevola, and not [such Stoics as] Zeno or Cleanthes or Chrysippus. . . . So now you know, Balbus, the views of Cotta the priest. You must now explain to me some of your own views. I believe what our ancestors have taught us, though they give no reasons. But from you, as a philosopher, I have a right to ask for a rational explanation of religious faith.
>
> Gaius Cotta[678]

I

The teachings of the Bible as developed for twenty centuries by the Christian Church may be usefully examined by noticing several differences between Eastern Orthodoxy and Roman Catholicism, which go back a millennium. The year 1054 is often given as the critical one for the break between the two Sees, the Roman and the Constantinopolitan. There had been by then many divergences—divergences that became so determined, it is sometimes said, that the fifteenth-century Byzantines preferred the sultan to the pope—and, it is also said, this contributed to the imposition of Turkish rule over the Greeks for several centuries.[679]

These divergences between Rome and Constantinople manifested themselves in, or were produced by, various differences that are with us to this day. Most obvious, perhaps, is with respect to the role of the pope (the Bishop of Rome) in church governance. This is related to differing opinions about the role of Peter among the disciples. (No doubt, political differences between Rome and Constantinople contributed to the ecclesiastical struggle—but the ecclesiastical differences continued long after the two underlying political empires had come to an end.) Questions about the standing of the Bishop of Rome are related to different opinions about the status of the priest, perhaps about the celibacy of priests, about the greater use in the Orthodox Church of lay theologians, and about other matters of this character. This definition of authority, reflecting as it does the issue of how the church is to be administered, is seen in still another form, in the different approaches of Roman Catholicism and Eastern Orthodoxy as to how saints are discovered and proclaimed. The Roman Catholics have elaborate procedures and standards with respect to canonization; the Orthodox seem to rely upon the general sense of the community, somehow or other arrived at. Suggestive of the different approaches to these matters—that is, the standing of the pope, the status of priests, the recognition of saints—is that the greatest church building of the Roman Catholics should have been known as St. Peter's, while the greatest church of the Eastern Orthodox should have been known as Aghia Sophia (Holy Wisdom).

II

What lies behind such differences? Critical to these differences are doctrinal differences. Doctrinal differences, I have suggested, are sometimes the causes, sometimes the effects, of other differences. But, I have also suggested, such differences can (whatever their origins) take on a life of their own—especially as a people is induced and obliged to defend its own.

A devout Greek Orthodox priest, who left his parish in this country to transfer to the jurisdiction of the Russian Synod, protested: "We're rapidly becoming a Church that is Roman Catholic in administration, Greek Orthodox in ritual, and Protestant in dogma."[680] Such a criticism, if sound, would mean that what remains Orthodox in the Eastern Orthodox Church is the ritual, the most obvious manifestation of the faith. But if dogma should indeed be changed, can ritual be far behind?

If one is to talk properly about the meaning of the Orthodox Church, one must consider what the meaning of the church is simply. Creeds serve to affirm that meaning. We, as Americans, are familiar with the significance and effect of a creed among us. We recognize ourselves to be rooted, as the *American* people, in an authoritative creed and to be guided by an authoritative constitution. We can see, for instance, how Abraham Lincoln used one element in that creed (the dedication in the Declaration of Independence to the equality of all human beings) as the foundation of his policy. What we, as Americans, are *not* familiar with is a creed—and here I refer, of course, to the Nicene Creed—that goes back almost seventeen centuries, a creed determined and promulgated by a united Christendom.[681]

A people such as the Greeks, the descendants of the Byzantines, sense that a long time *has* influenced various developments and shaped peoples. (Thus, it took the Byzantine empire four hundred years to fall, once it went into decline.) The Orthodox churchgoer, for example, gets used very early in life to the church's "air of antiquity, its apparent changelessness."[682] This goes against the grain, so to speak, of the American openness, even zeal, for novelty. Also going against the American grain is the *apparent* monarchical organization of the Orthodox Church and the obligation and willingness of the Orthodox to say: "I will accept and understand Holy Scripture in accordance with the interpretation which was and is held by the Holy Orthodox Church of the East, our Mother."[683]

A creed, we sense, can be significant for defining a people. We are now in the third century under the American creed; we are now in the seventeenth century of *the* Orthodox creed. There were, of course, "incipient" Americans or "incipient" Christians (in the modern sense) before the proclamation of their respective creeds—but the creeds decisively confirmed vital doctrines in each instance, consolidating much that had developed theretofore and helping to determine the direction of future developments.

III

Thus, the Nicene Creed was critical to Christianity as it developed. It was also critical, as we shall see, to the great separation of Eastern Orthodoxy from Western Christendom. This separation anticipated, although it was different from, the separation between Roman Catholics and Protestants centuries later in Western Christendom.

Certainly, the creed is special for the Eastern Orthodox Church, as it is to the Roman Catholic Church. The worshiper recites it every Sunday during the service. (The Lord's Prayer is also recited—but that comes out of the Bible itself, whereas the creed, although rooted in Scripture, was settled upon by the church after several centuries of development and debate.) Such a creed is, for most Americans, something of a problem, not only for the reasons I have suggested but also because the tendency of the typical American Christian (of a Protestant inclination) *is* to "relate" directly to Jesus, and a somewhat simplified Jesus at that.[684]

Of course, the Orthodox Church claims universality; it is not, it insists, exotic or oriental; rather, it stands for simple Christianity—and that is set forth in the creed. It is difficult for most Americans to appreciate that simplicity, however, when confronted with the trappings of the Orthodox church service. One can expect Americans raised in the Orthodox faith to have reservations themselves, after two or three generations in this country, about those trappings—and no doubt these reservations will make themselves felt in the decades ahead, if they have not already.

However this may be, the Nicene Creed is special for the Greeks. It is for them different from what it is even for the other Orthodox congregations, including the Slavic peoples with whom the Greeks have been so long associated (for good and for ill). After all, the creed *is* written in Greek. It is, in a sense, the creed of the Greeks, just as the New Testament (and hence Christianity itself) is theirs. Thus, one must wonder, do not the Greeks have Christianity in their bones? Is it more abstract, less rooted in ordinary life and its language, for most peoples of the West (and especially among the Protestants) than it is for the Greeks?[685]

To say this about the Greekness of Christianity is for the Greeks not only a matter of pride; it is even more a matter of deep responsibility. There is, of course, also the Jewish element in Christianity—and it is significant that the Jews and the Greeks are in so many ways similar. But notice how even the Hebrew Bible is regarded by the Greeks: the Orthodox Church, I understand, once considered the early Greek translation of the Old Testament (the Septuagint), whenever it differs from the Hebrew Bible, to be superior—that is, the Septuagint was considered divinely inspired, while the Hebrew Bible (it was argued) has suffered corruption since it was originally divinely inspired.[686]

Thus, it can be said that Christianity, as it comes down to the West, is massively Greek (despite the considerable influence that was exercised by Christianity in a Latin form). I refer to Christianity as we have it, since the Aramaic of Jesus and his companions is largely lost. Thus, the Greeks are the only Western people, up to the re-emergence of Israel in our day, to be able as a nation to understand *somewhat* the original language of their ancient faith. (Before the re-emergence of Israel, many Jewish men and some Jewish women could thus use Hebrew in their religious life.)

IV

How much of their ancient faith, "their" creed, *do* the Greeks understand? Many Greeks, when they recite, or hear recited, the Nicene Creed, do have the impression that they understand it; it *sounds* like something that makes sense to them. Also, for them, and perhaps for them alone, it is poetic; the beauty, or power, of it is lost in all the English translations I have seen.

Yet, for modern Greeks, it is to a considerable extent incomprehensible. They, for the most part, do not think about what they truly believe, what is implied by what they recite.

What, then, does the seventeen-hundred-year-old Nicene Creed say? In English, it goes something like this:

> I believe in one God, the Father Almighty, Maker of Heaven and Earth and of all things visible and invisible.
>
> And in one Lord Jesus Christ, the only-begotten Son of God, begotten of His Father before all Ages. Light of Light, Very God of Very God, begotten not made, consubstantial with the Father, through Whom all things were made,
>
> Who for us men and for our salvation came down from Heaven, and was incarnate by the Holy Spirit and of the Virgin Mary, and became Man.
>
> And He was crucified for us under Pontius Pilate, and suffered and was buried.
>
> And the third day He rose again, in accordance with the Scriptures.
>
> And He ascended into Heaven, and sitteth on the right hand of the Father.
>
> And He shall come again with glory to judge both the quick and the dead; Whose Kingdom shall have no end.
>
> And in the Holy Spirit, the Lord, the Giver of Life, Who proceedeth from the Father, Who with the Father and the Son together is worshiped and glorified; Who spoke by the Prophets.
>
> In One, Holy, Catholic and Apostolic Church.
>
> I acknowledge One Baptism for the remission of sins.
>
> I look for the Resurrection of the dead.
>
> And the life of the ages to come. Amen.[687]

Much can be said about this. Indeed, much has been said about it. (The creed is like the Ten Commandments and the Lord's Prayer in this respect.) This means, among other things, that any short statement about it will likely be a distortion; it also means that it is highly unlikely that anything I might say about it, short or long, will have in it anything original. But perhaps I can usefully touch on a few points, if only to suggest how one might proceed, what questions are raised by any serious consideration, and why one should carefully examine the creed.

That which we call the Nicene Creed was evidently developed in two stages. The first Ecumenical Synod met in Niceae in 325, the second met in Constantinople in 381.[688] Thereafter the creed was established in the form that the Orthodox Church has relied upon ever since. Of the circumstances that led to the Nicene Council and the subsequent formulation of the creed, an English scholar has given this account (variations of which can be found in many other accounts):

> One day in the year 318 or 319 a discourse was delivered by Alexander, Bishop of Alexandria, on the great mystery of the Trinity in Unity. Exception was taken to its teachings by one of the Alexandrian clergy named Arius, on the ground that it tended to obliterate the distinction of the Three Persons in the Godhead, and therein savoured of Sabellianism [an earlier heresy]. Arius proceeded to disseminate his own views, which exaggerated those elements which he conceived to be implied in the Sonship of the Second Person, until he arrived at the point where Sonship was replaced by creatureship, and the co-eternal and co-essential Deity of the Word was surrendered.
>
> After repeated failures to reclaim Arius to orthodoxy, Alexander was obliged to excommunicate him. [Arius'] party, however, grew in numbers, and a large council was held at Alexandria in 321 which investigated the Arian teaching and condemned it. Meanwhile Arius had found partisans in Nicomedia and in Palestine, whither he had gone after leaving Egypt. Thence he wrote to Alexander and also popularized his views both in prose and in verse ("Thalia"). Alexander issued an encyclical letter, but the heresy continued to spread in the East. The Emperor Constantine, who naturally underrated the dogmatic importance of the dispute, attempted to allay the trouble by addressing a letter to Arius and Alexander, in which he described the controversy as arising out of foolish speculation on an insignificant matter.[689]

But the emperor learned that his political efforts, and attempts at negotiation, did not suffice. There were fundamental issues at stake about the very nature of things that, it seems, had to be argued out and settled. And this, it also seems, is what the councils of 325 and 381 did. Among the points settled was that the Son is "Very God of Very God, begotten not made, consubstantial [*homoousions*] with the Father."[690] Thus the Arian Heresy, which tended to dilute the divinity of Christ, was authoritatively repudiated by the united bishops of Christendom (East and West).[691]

These developments, it should be noticed, took place a good five centuries before the events that led to the separation of the universal church into its Eastern and Western parts. It should also be noticed that since the crises that brought forth Protestantism were centuries after the division into Eastern and Western churches, the Reformation passed by the Orthodox Church. In a sense, the Reformation was not needed in the Orthodox Church, certainly not to the extent that the Reformation was an insistence upon national self-determination in religious matters.[692]

V

The Reformation must wait. Let us consider the Nicene Creed itself (aside from the circumstances which led to its formulation). That is, let us consider what it in effect says to the many millions who have affirmed it long after they had forgotten, if they ever knew, the circumstances of its formulation.

Those who gathered in the great councils which formulated the Nicene Creed agreed not only upon the "nature" of the divine but also upon something which is in some ways even more difficult to determine: precisely what had happened in the life of Jesus some four centuries before. (This would be comparable to our being able to agree today upon what happened during one particular weekend to, say, a Pole in Eastern Europe who was momentarily notorious locally at the time of Columbus.)

At the very heart of the creed—if one works from a count of the words in the Greek text—are the statements about the crucifixion, burial, and resurrection of Jesus.[693] This event is central to everything: those three days, we are given to understand, are the days around which the movements of ages turn. This lends considerable support to the importance placed by Christendom upon Easter.

In what sense is the Resurrection to be taken? Is it allegorical? Or is it physical and, as we say, "actual"? The Orthodox Church does seem to consider Jesus' death to have been physical, just as we all die, and the Resurrection to have been in those terms also. St. Paul is drawn upon in support of this interpretation:

> And if Christ be not risen, then is our preaching vain, and your faith is also vain. Yea, and we are found false witnesses of God; because we have testified of God that he raised up Christ: whom he raised not up, if so be that the dead rise not. For if the dead rise not, then is not Christ raised: and if Christ be not raised, your faith is vain; ye are yet in your sins.[694]

Does this account of a unique physical resurrection "make sense" today? (I say "unique," because the Hebrew Bible does not seem to make much of any clear resurrections. And such stories as that of Lazarus in the Greek Bible can be considered more ambiguous, if only because Jesus' companions made far less of *it* than they did of Jesus' resurrection. Besides, we are told, they did not expect Jesus' revival, which suggests that they considered what happened to Lazarus a different kind of thing—if only because Lazarus had died a natural death rather than having been killed.) Did a physical resurrection ever make sense? Is it believable?[695]

Notice the role of the community (the church) in defining, promulgating and establishing this doctrine. Not only did the creed come from church councils, but the creed itself also implicitly ratifies the role of the church in matters of faith.

The Creed includes three great contradictions or paradoxes: one is that God should take on human form; another is that a virgin should produce a child while remaining a virgin; still another is that a man like us in critical respects should be killed and once again thereafter live on earth.[696] It had long been known that it is difficult—some thinkers have said it is impossible—for the divine to take on human form.[697] And yet, it was also known that it is difficult for "the man in the street [as well as] for the philosophers of common sense . . . to imagine the immortal gods except in human form." Thus, it would once have been argued, the Incarnation is even harder to accept philosophically than the Resurrection: that is, it would have been said, the Incarnation is simply inconceivable, whereas the Resurrection is merely highly improbable. Still, what Incarnation means *can* be subject to "interpretation"—which makes the Resurrection the critical question, for practical purposes. And so it can be said that everything does turn upon *the* Resurrection: if *that* could happen, virtually anything can happen. It is not surprising then that St. Paul should give the Resurrection the emphasis he did and that the Nicene Creed should literally turn around it.

Perhaps the most remarkable thing about the Nicene Creed is the most obvious, something which because of its radical obviousness easily escapes notice: it *is* a creed. No proof or evidence is offered; rather, a belief is no more than stated. An attempt is made to state it as clearly as possible in the circumstances (which circumstances include the necessity of securing the assent of the assembled bishops). In a sense, it can be said, they do not say they *know* these things; they do say (and ask Christians ever after to say with them) that they *believe* these things. Is it not implied that a certain kind of belief is better, because deeper in its inspiration, than mere knowing based on ordinary evidence, argument, and demonstration?

The creed may come down essentially to the statement: "We are among those who are, based on the testimony of those who went before us, willing to say that *this* is so." It is, in a decisive respect, a pledge of allegiance. Does the creed mean that the faithful Orthodox—indeed, the right-believing Christian—is rooted in wondrous things, *not* in wondering and hence inquiry?[698]

VI

A few more comments on the creed should be useful for our immediate inquiry. Of the 174 words in the creed, 110 (many more than half) are about Jesus directly. It is there that one may find the distinctive Christian doctrine. What is said in the creed about God the Father could have been said, for the most part, by some Jews independent of Christianity. Perhaps the same is true of the statements about the Holy Spirit (except as it relates to the Son). What is said in the creed about the church and about baptism depends upon the doctrines set forth there about Jesus.

Thus, the biography, so to speak, of Jesus is critical: his story is decisive, at least for the Christian, as to the relation of God and Man. Very little is said in the creed about man directly or about nature. It seems implied that man and his nature are known—and are known to be such that, without Jesus, salvation is unlikely if not simply impossible. *With* Jesus, with his unnatural yet somehow natural life and death and re-life (that is, resurrection), something so unnatural as eternal life can be held out.

The biography, or history, of Jesus is vital to this affirmation. It is not simply an abstract statement about the divine. It is also much more particular or concrete than the critical Jewish affirmation: "Hear, O Israel, the Lord our God, the Lord is One."[699] God, as such, has no "history"; He is always, and is always unchanging. This may be as far as we can be led by reason. But a God without history is, we would say, "hard to relate to."[700]

We notice as well that little if anything is said in the creed about Jesus' teaching (or God's, or the Holy Spirit's). There is no indication of a moral code, or of standards of right and wrong (aside from the fact of belief). It is not even said that Jesus died without sin, or that man is overwhelmed by sin. Sin itself is not mentioned, nor is virtue. Nor is anything said explicitly about justice (it is reflected in the anticipated judging) or about love (it is reflected in Jesus' sacrifice). More is made explicitly of glory—the glory of the Father, of Jesus the Son, and of the Holy Spirit.

This creed, then, is not like the Ten Commandments. Rather, as I have suggested, it is more like a pledge of allegiance. And once the allegiance is settled, much follows, including the preaching and practices of the authoritative church with its teachings about morality and other matters, including of course the Ten Commandments.

What is critical to the faith, I have also suggested, is what is said about Jesus, with his death and resurrection somehow at the heart of it all. And yet, the decisive schism between East and West (in the eleventh century) came over something said about the Holy Spirit in this creed. Even so, that *too* was about Jesus, about the status of Jesus in the divine scheme of things. Was he, or was he not, to be considered virtually like God, even though he had had the various earthly manifestations and experiences insisted upon?

I refer to the notorious *filioque* controversy, which concerned itself with the addition to the creed of the term *filioque* (in the Latin text), meaning "and the Son"—the addition of this term by the Western part of the church. That

Western addition has the statement about the Holy Spirit reading: "And in the Holy Spirit, the Lord, the Giver of Life, Who proceedeth from the Father *and from the Son*, Who with the Father and Son, etc." Thus, whereas the East (or what we now know as the Orthodox Church) has the Holy Spirit (or Holy Ghost) proceeding from the Father alone, the West (which is almost all the rest of pre-Reformation Christendom) has a double procession of the Holy Spirit—that is, both from the Father *and from the Son*.

This difference was at the core of the controversy between Eastern Orthodox and Roman Catholic, even though the article of faith about the Holy Spirit is not at the core of the creed itself. Is this because that which *is* at the core of the creed is likely, because of the principal issue before the councils, to have been thought through and hence disposed of, while a peripheral affirmation (about, for example, the Holy Spirit) is apt to leave loose ends?[701]

It can be argued, of course, that the Eastern Church made as much as it did of the *filioque* addition by the West primarily in order to have a pretext for declaring itself independent of the growing Rome-based power. But whether or not one settles for this explanation, one should at least be aware of the implications of the different formulations. Is it not true that in the Eastern (or original) formulation of the creed (which, it will be remembered, was intended to counter the Arian dilution of the divinity of Jesus), the Father remains somehow special? Clearly, there is something about the Father (aside from some kind of priority) that is different from (and superior to?) the Son. Both are worshiped and glorified, but only the Father is the source of the Spirit (just as He had been, in a perhaps different way, the source of the Son). Without the *filioque* addition (which the Western church seems to have added in an effort to counteract subsequent heretical developments *in the West*), each of the three principal statements about the Trinity distinguishes the Father from the other two Persons of the Trinity.[702]

Does this singling out of the Father remind the Christian of what the philosophical tradition had said about the oneness and uniqueness of God? It is almost as if it is thereby recognized that there had been something to what the Arians had contended for after all, even if they had gone too far. It has been suggested that the Arians reflected Jewish monotheistic inclinations. Certainly, the Jewish converts to Christianity can be understood to have been the most fervent guardians of monotheism among the Christians.[703]

In any event, the addition of the *filioque* seemed to some Orthodox to lead to ditheism, a doctrine of two supreme gods.[704] Perhaps the Greeks were particularly alert by this time to the "natural" inclinations of people in the ancient world toward polytheism, toward the pagan reliance upon and use of a multitude of gods.[705]

A related question is just what the Holy Spirit is, what its purpose is. Does it necessarily provide the bridge between the Father (who is invisible, unchanging) and the enfleshed Son (who is quite visible, changing)? Is this a way of indicating a moderate course between sinking into polytheism, on the one hand, and denying any Incarnation, on the other?[706] In any event, it does seem that there is not such a special status for the Holy Spirit in the Hebrew Bible. This reminds us that little, if anything, is said about Old Testament doings in the creed, except perhaps in the reference to the prophets.[707]

Of the many questions inspired by the *filioque* controversy, three are of particular interest to us. One is what the creed implied about the question that the addition of *filioque* purported to answer. Another is what, in effect, Scripture authorized. The third question is whether the Western Church had any authority, on its own, to change a long-established pronouncement of a universal council. This brings us back, of course, to the problem of papal authority—and points up, in still another way, the relation of doctrinal questions to questions of constitutional arrangements. The Orthodox Church has always made much of the argument that, whatever the doctrinal merits of the Western addition to the creed, the Western Church simply had no jurisdiction and hence no authority to act as it did.[708]

And, the Orthodox Church had been inclined to ask, if the Roman Catholic Church can act thus even toward a long-established pronouncement of a universal council, how can it be trusted with the broad power claimed by it for the pope with respect either to doctrinal questions or to church governance?[709]

VII

The *filioque* controversy (between the Orthodox and the Western Church) may be related to another great controversy, but one within the church before its division—that is, the Iconoclastic Controversy of the eighth and ninth centuries, which was so important in the East. That controversy developed when an attempt was made to remove all icons from the churches.[710]

Protestant churches and even Roman Catholic churches, we know, need not have icons. But is it possible to have today a permanent Orthodox place of worship that is stripped of icons? Icons are everywhere, including in the homes of the pious. Much has been written about the icons and about the great iconoclastic struggle. Anyone familiar with Orthodoxy can understand why icons can be called "the eyes of the world."[711]

I need not say much more about the icons here. It is enough for my inquiry to notice that there was in that struggle an anticipation of sorts of the later *filioque* struggle between East and West. That is, the "Judaic" elements in the church wanted the icons destroyed as idolatrous, invoking for that purpose the Second Commandment. They were resisted by the "Hellenistic" elements in the church, which are to be distinguished from the philosophical elements that are probably closer on this issue to the Judaic elements.[712] The Hellenistic elements, with their memories of the great art of pagan antiquity, fought for the icons, and they won.[713]

Are not what I, following the lead of others, call the Hellenistic elements seen in the insistence of the Nicene Creed (indeed, of Christianity itself) upon the history of Jesus, if not in the Incarnation? Thus, the defenders of icons could argue that "God took on flesh, and therefore can be depicted."[714] It is added:

> When the second commandment was given, God did not appear in the flesh. But when Jesus appeared and became Incarnate then it was right thereafter to depict him. So orthodoxy began making icons of Jesus Christ against those heretics of the Fifth and Sixth Centuries (Monophysites, Docetists, and others) who said that the divine nature of Christ had absorbed the human nature and there remained only one, the divine, which could not be depicted. Or, again, that Christ was a mere phantom who never lived in reality. Against these, the Church began to make the Holy Icons of Jesus and His Mother and friends, the Saints.[715]

Notice that the critical heresies of the fifth and sixth centuries, practically denying the human nature of Jesus, go to the opposite extreme from the Arian heresy of the fourth century, which had practically denied the divine nature of Jesus.

The icons have gone so far as to depict in human form not only the Son but the Father as well. Thus, some acceptable icons of the Holy Trinity, in attempting to depict the three Divine Persons, present God the Father as an old man, the Son as an infant, and the Holy Spirit as a dove.[716]

How *is* the use of icons to be understood? Does a complete "human" experience, on the everyday level, require both the Hellenistic and the Judaic elements in any attempt to grasp the divine? We can be again reminded of what has been said about this, from the perspective of the philosophical tradition, that it is difficult for most people "to imagine the immortal gods except in human form."[717] Does nature lead human beings to give due weight to both the Judaic and the Hellenistic elements? If art *is* to have a place in the religious life of the community, then must there not be a deliberate (but disciplined) use of the Hellenistic elements? It is important to remember that the *look* of things—of concrete, material things, even—is somehow related to how things truly are, to the "abstract" *ideas* themselves.[718]

Did the restorers of icons go too far in turn? The determined Orthodox position with respect to the *filioque* addition can perhaps be understood as a revival of the Judaic element which had eventually been restrained if not even suppressed in the Iconoclastic Controversy.[719] That element, which may be seen in Islam as well, encourages limits, austerity, and indeed a curb on idolatry and polytheism.[720] Perhaps, it can be added, Roman Catholics could "afford" the *filioque* addition to the creed because they did not have the emphasis (and hence the considerable reliance) upon icons that the Eastern Church did.

Consider, in any event, the response of Mother Alexandra, abbess of the Orthodox Monastery of the Transfiguration in Pennsylvania, to the question, "What can the Eastern Church learn from the Western Church?" Her answer: "The importance of having a better knowledge of the Bible."[721] She had also been asked, "What can the Western Church learn from the Eastern Church?" And her reply to that question was: "Western Christians always have wanted to dot the i's. Eastern Christians have never done this. We are less legalistic."[722] On the other hand, it can be added, there may have been considerable "legalism" in the insistence by the Orthodox Church that the *filioque* addition to the creed was clearly bad because it was unauthorized.

Does the long-run vitality of Orthodoxy, and not only in the United States, lie in a sensible reunion with Roman Catholicism? Is it possible to reunite, or is "reunion" an inappropriate term, inasmuch as both have changed considerably in the millennium since the schism? The Orthodox *have* become even more "ethnic" since 1054. But what is assimilation doing to ethnicity in this country and perhaps in Europe also? On the other hand, Roman Catholics *have* even gone so far as to declare the Bishop of Rome infallible in key matters. But this was little more than a century ago, and perhaps can be reinterpreted to the satisfaction of all parties involved in a new, elevated union?[723]

What is shared by Eastern Orthodox and traditional Roman Catholicism, as against the respectable Protestantism toward which most Americans are still inclined, is suggested by the response of one of James Joyce's characters, a young Irish poet who has lost his Roman Catholic faith—a response to the question whether he would become a Protestant. His response is one that could be made as well both by the troubled Orthodox Christian and by the thoughtful Jew, especially when moved by a sense of honor:

> I said that I had lost the faith, but not that I had lost selfrespect. What kind of liberation would that be to forsake an absurdity which is logical and coherent and to embrace one which is illogical and incoherent?[724]

That sense of honor may be evident as well in the determined defense by the Byzantines of the precise language of the Nicene Creed.[725]

I have done no more than touch upon various of the assumptions and implications of the creed with respect to everyday life, with respect to nature, and with respect to community. What is to be believed, for example, about eternal damnation? Is that implied by the judging that is anticipated? These are questions to be left for another occasion, as are questions about the effects of their language upon the Greeks, including the effects of services (even the significance of services, where virtually no one may be present but the priest).

A key question for this occasion remains: How do the creed and its implications fit in with modern life?

It is important to remember that the moderns are correct as to the importance of that philosophy rooted in the classics (it is recognized there that man seeks to know), but they are wrong as to the frequency of genuine philosophical dedication among us. This means that the moderns do not truly understand philosophy, or its vulnerability, or the vulnerability of communities because of the misuse of "philosophy."[726]

Why is this? Enlightenment is not the same as philosophy. The classical position is apt to be reduced by many to Socrates' example as the martyr to free inquiry. To see Socrates only as a martyr to uninhibited inquiry fits in with the American emphasis upon personal as well as political liberty: All is subject to relentless examination, without concern for the stability of the community.[727] But we should be aware that this *is* a problem; some things must be presupposed (including particular, perhaps not fully examined, opinions) if there is to be a community. The Enlightenment tends to deny that there is any significant tension between philosophy and the common good.[728]

Yet these are not problems for Orthodoxy alone. Perhaps, then, the most important question that remains here is whether that which the Nicene Creed affirms is indeed true. The authors of the creed do *not* seem to consider this an open question—or a question that one can (or should?) investigate. But this may be the most important question. To what extent is the truth of the creed ratified by its success and the endurance of the church, both East and West? Can truth be revealed or confirmed through such events? If so, this could suggest that the Christian Church itself is an Incarnation, if not also an icon, of the doctrines distilled by the Nicene Creed from the Bible.

Chapter Seventeen

On the Yearning for Personal Immortality[729]

> For the living know that they shall die; but the dead know not any thing, neither have they any more a reward; for the memory of them is forgotten.
>
> Solomon[730]

I

Christianity, in questioning the happiness available on earth, has intensified whatever yearning human beings may naturally have for personal immortality. Neither traditional Judaism nor classical philosophy ever challenged openly, to the extent Christianity has, the significance of an earth-bound human existence. It should be instructive to consider further, however briefly, a few of the many questions about "the human condition" left by our preliminary inquiries in this series of readings of the Bible.

What should we in the West now say is the meaning of life on earth? What *is* it all about, anyway? Such are the questions that are affected by one's recognition of the chance factors that can very much affect who and how one is.

Consider how "the human condition" is described at the outset of the last story about Sherlock Holmes and Dr. Watson published by A. Conan Doyle:

> Sherlock Holmes was in a melancholy and philosophic mood that morning. His alert practical nature was subject to such reactions.
>
> "Did you see him?" he asked [Dr. Watson].
>
> "You mean the old fellow who has just gone out?"
>
> "Precisely."
>
> "Yes, I met him at the door."

"What do you think of him?"

"A pathetic, futile, broken creature."

"Exactly, Watson. Pathetic and futile. But is not all life pathetic and futile? Is not his story a microcosm of the whole? We reach. We grasp. And what is left in our hands at the end? A shadow. Or worse than a shadow—misery."

"Is he one of your clients?"

"*Well, I suppose I may call him so.* He has been sent on by [Scotland] Yard. Just as medical men occasionally send their incurables to a quack. They argue that they can do nothing more, and that whatever happens the patient can be no worse than he is."[731]

People do wonder, especially when "in a melancholy and philosophic mood," what all this does mean and whether it is worthwhile. Especially is this so as they become aware of their limitations, observing (as almost all of us are likely to do eventually) their powers ebbing and their fortunes fluctuating. A particularly traumatic form of such awareness may be seen in what is reported to have happened to the sheltered prince who has become famous as *the* Buddha:

One day, while out driving with his charioteer, [Gautama] saw "an aged man as bent as a roof gable, decrepit, leaning on a staff, tottering as he walked, afflicted and long past his prime." The charioteer, questioned by the prince as to what had happened to the man, explained that he was old and that all men were subject to old age if they lived long enough. The prince, greatly perturbed by this sight, went back to the palace and became absorbed in thought. Another day, again driving with his charioteer, he saw "a sick man, suffering and very ill, fallen and weltering in his own excreta, being lifted up by some. . . ." Because [Gautama] was perturbed, the charioteer explained, as before, that this was a sick man and that all men are subject to sickness. On a third occasion the prince saw a dead body and again the charioteer provided the explanation. Finally, [Gautama] saw "a shaven-headed man, a wanderer who has gone forth, wearing the yellow robe [of a monk]." Impressed with the man's peaceful and serene demeanor, the prince decided to leave home and go out into the world to discover the reason for such a display of serenity in the midst of misery.[732]

II

Our problem, then, is to determine what our lives *are* like and what can be made of them, especially our lives on earth. I will assume familiarity with four readings collected for a conference recently on "the quest for meaning": Thomas Aquinas's discussion of happiness in the *Summa*,[733] Plato's *Apology of Socrates*,[734] the Bible's *Ecclesiastes*,[735] and Leo Tolstoy's somewhat Christianized *Master and Man*.[736] Related discussions by Aristotle and Augustine will also be drawn upon, as will the *Book of Job*.[737]

We turn, first, to the challenge posed in the discussion of happiness by Thomas Aquinas, where he inquires into whether a human being can be truly happy on earth. That which St. Thomas says here had been anticipated by St. Augustine and others centuries earlier. The argument they make seems to be deeply ingrained in Christianity. Consider how Thomas begins:

> ARTICLE 3. Whether One Can Be Happy in This Life?
>
> [We proceed thus to the Third Article:] It would seem that Happiness can be had in this life. . . .
>
> On the contrary, it is written (*Job* 14: 1): "Man born of a woman, living for a short time, is filled with many miseries." But Happiness excludes misery. Therefore man cannot be happy in this life.
>
> I answer that, A certain participation of Happiness can be had in this life, but perfect and true Happiness cannot be had in this life. This may be seen from a twofold consideration.
>
> First, from the general notion of happiness. For since happiness is a "perfect and sufficient good," it excludes every evil, and fulfills every desire. But in this life every evil cannot be excluded. For this present life is subject to many unavoidable evils: to ignorance on the part of the intellect, to disordered affection on the part of the appetite, and to many penalties on the part of the body, as Augustine sets forth in the *The City of God*. Likewise neither can the desire for good be satiated in this life. For man naturally desires that the good which he has be abiding. Now the goods of the present life pass away, since life itself passes away, which we naturally desire to have, and would wish to hold abidingly, for man naturally shrinks from death. Therefore, it is impossible to have true Happiness in this life.
>
> Secondly, from a consideration of that in which Happiness specially consists, namely, the vision of the Divine Essence, which man cannot obtain in this life, as was shown in the First Part (Q.XII, A.2) [of the *Summa*]. Hence it is evident that none can attain true and perfect Happiness in this life.[738]

Thomas's discussion in the *Summa* includes these suggestions about the status here of nature:

> ARTICLE 5. Whether Man Can Attain Happiness by His Natural Powers?
>
> [We proceed thus to the Fifth Article:] It would seem that man can attain Happiness by his natural powers. . . .
>
> On the contrary, Man is naturally the principle of his action by his intellect and will. But final Happiness prepared for the saints surpasses the intellect and will of man; for the Apostle [Paul] says (1 *Corinthians* 2:9): "Eye hath not seen, nor ear heard, neither hath it entered into the heart of man, what things God hath

> prepared for them that love Him." Therefore man cannot attain Happiness by his natural powers.
>
> I answer that, Imperfect happiness that can be had in this life can be acquired by man by his natural powers, in the same way as virtue, in whose operation it consists: on this point we shall speak further on (Q. LXIII). But man's perfect Happiness, as stated above (Q. III, A.8), consists in the vision of the Divine Essence. Now the vision of God's Essence surpasses the nature not only of man, but also of every creature, as was shown in the [First Part (Q.XII, A.4)]. For the natural knowledge of every creature is in keeping with the mode of [its] substance; thus it is said of the intelligence (*De Causis* . . .) that "it knows things that are above it, and things that are below it, according to the mode of its substance." But every knowledge that is according to the mode of created substance, falls short of the vision of the Divine Essence, which infinitely surpasses all created substance. Consequently neither man, nor any creature, can attain final Happiness by his natural powers.[739]

Full or true happiness depends, it seems, upon eternal standards. It also depends upon conditions and opportunities available only after death. The *Book of Job* may seem to support the proposition that human life here on earth is full of misery—and, we know, this can be said even about the life of an eminently upright man such as Job.[740]

The teachings of Augustine and Thomas seem to be anticipated also by *Ecclesiastes* with its questioning of the very possibility of earthly happiness. Those teachings may seem to be confirmed by the Tolstoy short story, *Master and Man*: the surviving peasant (Nikita=victorious?) is accustomed to looking beyond the grave for something far better than what he has here.[741]

Does this attitude tend to make life here better than it would otherwise be, if only in that it helps people endure the inevitable afflictions of the flesh? Or does this attitude encourage people to put up with more misery than is necessary?[742]

It has been argued, in any event, that human beings yearn for much more than seems to be humanly (that is, naturally) available.

III

Compare Aristotle's approach to these matters. Aristotle and Thomas Aquinas are connected in several ways. For one thing, Thomas evidently regards Aristotle as *the* philosopher. The best commentary on Aristotle's great treatise on ethics is still that prepared by Thomas.[743]

Human happiness, here on earth, is grounded for Aristotle in virtue. Virtue may not be enough to ensure one's happiness, but it is essential—and it is the most difficult element to secure. It helps in this endeavor to have as well a modest amount of property, decent health, and good fortune (or, at least, not very bad fortune).[744]

One gets the impression from Aristotle—and from his greatest predecessors, Socrates, Plato, and Xenophon—that a rather full, and satisfying, happiness *can* be enjoyed by human beings on earth. Augustine, however, might wonder whether these four pagans lived in a fool's paradise—for he believes himself privileged to know vital things about the nature of human life that even the most enlightened pagans could not have known, things that display earthly happiness in its true light.[745]

Among the things Augustine and Thomas believe is that a reliable way to eternal salvation is now revealed to human beings. This obliges us to wonder how the traditional virtues are affected when they are seen from the perspective of eternal salvation.[746]

IV

Consider now how Socrates approaches the problem of personal immortality immediately after he is sentenced to death. What awaits him, he suggests, is either complete oblivion (a dreamless sleep) or more opportunities to pursue in Hades the kind of life of inquiry that he had always pursued on earth.[747]

We can assess each of these alternatives somewhat on the basis of our own experiences. Do we not all know how nice a sound, apparently dreamless sleep can be? We can also know how satisfying a fruitful inquiry can be. But, we may well wonder, is it possible to have a bodiless existence during which genuine inquiry occurs? Can there be significant mental or psychic experiences without bodies? And does the satisfaction of a "dreamless" sleep depend upon our continued existence and awareness, if not upon our awakening eventually?

Such are some of the questions that are left when we are limited to everyday experiences and natural capacities. It does seem that thinkers such as Aristotle, Socrates, and Plato considered themselves to be without reliable access to detailed divine revelation either with respect to ethics (or how one should live) or with respect to happiness (including eternal salvation). There did not seem to be for them any substantial sacred sources, whatever intimations they may have had, with respect either to morality or to the eventual fate of the human soul.

For them, therefore, virtue and happiness depended substantially, if not even exclusively, upon the materials and guidance provided by nature. They seemed to believe that considerable, perhaps "enough," satisfaction is available to the human being who conducts himself sensibly in this life.

The divinity that philosophers such as Aristotle refer to seems to be *observable* (or *knowable*) without the aid of revelation.[748] The nature of man is such as to permit, if not even to urge, human beings to grasp the nature of things, including the ordering of the universe.

V

The challenges to philosophy here by the revealed religions in the West must be faced up to, challenges to what is a substantial if not even an exclusive reliance (by philosophers) upon nature for guidance of both action and the understanding.

Christianity speaks of *a fallen nature*. This is related to the notion of *original sin*. Judaism, even earlier, could speak of the things of this world without referring at all to *nature*, that nature which evidently first came to full light in the Greek world. Theological depreciations of nature are compounded by what has happened in modernity with its dedication to the *conquest of nature*. One way or another, nature is depreciated, if not even shunted aside.[749]

Much more is made, both in ancient religious belief and in modern social science, of *the will*.[750] This has roots perhaps in the importance, in the Bible, of *faith*. If nature and that human judgment which is rooted in nature are thus lowered in rank, it "naturally" follows that we can hear asked again and again the demoralizing question: "Who is to say what is right (or true or beautiful)?"[751]

A key question here is: What is the nature of nature? Does nature provide guidance as to how one should live? In short, what kind of a world *is* it anyway?[752]

Socrates and those of like mind did not recognize, it seems, that nature was inadequate: they did not recognize that it is fallen or that it is substantially unknowable or that it is not enough for any human being to be guided by—and hence that vital help must come from "outside" (that is, from revelation). This help is needed if critical things are to be pointed out. Once pointed out, however, they may become apparent to all, believers and nonbelievers alike.[753]

We return to another key question: What does true happiness depend upon? It depends upon far fewer and far other things, Socrates argued, than most people believe it does. Happiness, he said, certainly does not depend upon bodily pleasure or wealth or power, perhaps not even upon a long life. Certainly, Socrates was critical of those people who make much of self-preservation, as if they can somehow manage to avoid death forever.

The Socratic position seems to be, instead, that the richest and deepest experiences of the human soul are available during the lives we *do* know—that is, during the normal lifespan available to us here on earth. It may even be understood that human life without death would be less interesting, and otherwise less attractive, than that life can be when well-ordered during one's allotted time. Or, as I have suggested elsewhere, the "immortal" gods of the Greeks may not truly live.

VI

It seems evident to Augustine and perhaps also to Thomas Aquinas, if not to modernity generally, that we do have (or, at least, are at times aware of) intense *yearnings* that the ancients evidently did not recognize or at least did not defer to as much as we do. These are yearnings for something significantly different from and significantly more than what is naturally available to us. There is, then, a sense of deprivation or incompleteness in mortality-conscious human beings that cannot be naturally ministered to.[754]

Such unrequited, and naturally unrequitable, yearnings promote sadness, a sense of a lack if not even of a loss. Life itself may be recognized to be good, so far as it goes, but something more is pointed to, of which the best of any human life on earth can be no more than a tantalizing sample.

All this is linked to the desire for immortality. Socrates did argue on occasion for the immortality of the soul. But what did he assume or point to when he did so? "Only" to the immortality of *soul* (or of *soulness*), it seems to me. The immortality of individual souls, of the personal self, is rarely made much of by him, except perhaps when some form of reincarnation is conjured up for the sake of an argument (as in Plato's *Meno* and in the last book of Plato's *Republic*).[755]

Critical to the modern condition, on the other hand, is an emphasis upon the status of individuality. The yearning for immortality with which we are now familiar may be intimately related to an enhanced sense of self. A primitive form of the sense of self may be seen in the desire for self-preservation. This desire is natural enough, but how it is understood, directed, or catered to may vary from time to time. We can be reminded of this upon comparing the resources, psychic as well as material, devoted to health care in various times and places.[756]

The variations observable with respect to such matters induce us to wonder whether the kind of intense yearning for immortal bliss that Augustine and his successors make so much of has been, at least in part, artificially created. Are the intense feelings that we in the West have about a one-time-through existence on earth and about personal immortality any more natural than the intense feelings that many in the East seem to have about reincarnation *and about the merit of eventual personal annihilation*?[757] To what extent are such feelings socially or culturally conditioned? Neither the intensity nor the prevalence of particular feelings, however "natural" they may seem in one place or another, suffices to validate them.

To notice both the variety of opinions about such matters and the role here of conditioning does not mean that none of the contending positions can be correct. But all too often the evidence available leaves the thoughtful observer unpersuaded, however much others around him may be moved.

The evidence in these matters may not be permanently convincing even for those who do happen to be moved. The power of such evidence tends to wear out, or so it can seem. Modernity, with its great respect for individuality, has seen the yearning for permanent happiness diverted from spiritual to secular forms. But whatever the forms and substances experimented with in order to satisfy such yearnings, frustration and anxiety have become common phenomena in modernity—and this, all too often, has provoked not only melancholy or malaise, but also intermittent outbursts of rage.[758]

It would be salutary to recognize that few, if any, of us are as special as we like to believe, so special that it makes sense that we should personally endure forever. Beliefs in our specialness may only reveal that we do not truly know ourselves.

VII

Again, it can be instructive to compare our sometimes-desperate yearnings with the composure exhibited by the sixty-nine-year-old Socrates despite the prospect of complete personal annihilation (that is, disappearance?) following upon his impending execution. We have noticed that he likens such personal oblivion to a dreamless sleep. We have wondered, however, whether the satisfaction of such sleep depends somehow upon some awareness of continued personal existence, not only in a wakened state, but even during sleep as well.

Socrates could have further pointed out that "we" have, unless the Eastern reincarnationists happen to be correct, "experienced" before our births, as much as "we" may "experience" after our deaths, vast reaches of time during which we did not exist. What is troubling about *that* personally, whatever the effects may be on the survivors who happen to be deprived (for awhile) of continued association with us?

Someone might observe, however, that our pre-birth deprivation should not have troubled us as much as a post-death deprivation might, since one does not truly exist until one is personally conceived and thus brought to life. Or did we exist then as much as we can exist hereafter once we no longer have bodies to serve as "containers" and instruments for our souls? At the very least, it *is* a great mystery how the soul, once it happens to come into being, could continue after death to exist (to observe, to learn, to know, to feel pleasures and pains, perhaps even to choose) without a body.[759]

How does the prospect of complete personal oblivion that Socrates anticipates bear upon the significance of earthly life? Should we be encouraged to move from a preoccupation with personal interests to a dedication to something universal—or at least to a dedication to something of a very long tenure on earth which does not depend upon an individual body and hence upon the lifespan one happens to have? Something more enduring does seem to be offered by one's family, by one's people or country, and (in a few cases, but in a different way) by philosophy. Whatever the soundness of these offers, each of them may be critically limited by one's personal circumstances.[760]

In short, the very best may not always be available to everyone. Socrates may be willing to accept this conclusion, but not someone who is attracted to the offer of eternal personal salvation made on some occasions to human beings, an offer that is drawn upon by Augustine, Thomas Aquinas, and perhaps Tolstoy.

VIII

What should be made of and done with, on the one hand, the reliance upon criticisms of the solidly natural approach of a Socrates and, on the other hand, the assurances about eternal life that the sacred teachings of revelation (depending on where and when we are) may happen to provide us? We need not concern ourselves, at least for the time being, about the varying (if not even contradictory) assurances that revelations or purported revelations seem to provide.

The kind of personal immortality that we in the West are accustomed to hearing about seems to imply an essential changelessness. We have been taught that whatever an individual will forever be is already there, if only incipiently as in a spiritual embryo, at the moment of his death. By then we have made all the decisive choices that count, choices that do seem to depend upon both the bodies and the lives we have had. Do we not all sense that the time available for such choices should be limited? That is, may we not wsense that the finest human things would be neither produced nor treasured if mortality did not provide restraints and necessities?[761]

If one's immortal life is regarded as changeless, it can appear to be a life during which nothing happens. *Is that truly living*? If things do happen to us after death, then the immortal soul would always be subject to change or, at least, its circumstances can change—and this means that things are sometimes better, sometimes worse, even after death. We have noticed that one alternative anticipated by Socrates, on the brink of death, is a career of further inquiry in Hades. This means that he would continue to learn and hence to change in important ways after death. If this *is* an alternative to be taken seriously, it suggests that there may not be significant differences between such an after-death existence and the long stretches of a well-ordered life on earth during which one need not be constantly conscious of one's mortality.

Still, Augustine and Thomas Aquinas insist that only the immortal soul has access to that supreme knowledge which the most thoughtful seek: the vision of God. Socrates might wonder to what extent, or in what ways, both the desire for and the possibility of knowing God depend upon what we learn from and in nature about eternal things and about the nature of knowing. Reasoning, philosophy, and morality do come only to rational beings, so far as we know—and these happen more or less naturally for beings of our capacities and in our circumstances. Is not morality, as generally understood, intimately linked to an awareness of mortality?

IX

To the extent that there is in us a powerful natural yearning for eternal things, if not for personal immortality, should there not be a way provided in nature for satisfying that yearning? An Augustine might suggest that this is evidence for the immortality of the soul and perhaps as well for the validity of some claims of divine revelation. Others might suspect that these yearnings for an enduring existence find satisfaction either in the political order or in participation in the millennia-old philosophical enterprise. Still others might suggest that such yearnings, especially if artificially stimulated, naturally move people to resort to, if not even to invent and develop, divine revelations.

This sort of thing may be reflected in what poets do and say. The human imagination exhibited by poets can remind us of what is expected from prophets. The poets who talk about human things may, again like prophets, necessarily draw upon some notion of the good. Whatever the truly divine does—that divine to which prophets we are familiar with minister—it has reasons: it is not simply arbitrary. Must there not be some sense to the way that the divine orders and assesses human passions, thoughts, and actions?[762]

Both poets and prophets do seem to depend upon inspiration.[763] Should we not recognize, therefore, that revelation is natural to human beings? Certainly, it is natural that human beings (especially the more intelligent and conscientious among them) be able to receive, to treasure, and to use whatever revelation there may be. Is it not also natural for human beings to develop the incipient revelation available to them? What, for example, are we to understand to have been the form in which Moses received the detailed directives that he recorded in page after page of the Torah under "The Lord said"? What did Moses "actually" receive, by hearing or otherwise?

Socrates was able to assess the most celebrated revelations of the Greeks, the old stories about the gods. He could speak with confidence about what can and cannot *be* with respect to the divine.[764] If one can reliably assess purported revelations in this fashion, is one also equipped to discover (if not even to create) revelations? Whatever traces of the divine there are in the world could be, in principle, detected by the astute observer, just as Sherlock Holmes could detect signs of "a great malignant brain" in the affairs of London:

> "From the point of view of the criminal expert," said Mr. Sherlock Holmes, "London has become a singularly uninteresting city since the death of the late lamented Professor Moriarty."
>
> "I can hardly think that you would find many decent citizens to agree with you," [Dr. Watson] answered.
>
> "Well, well, I must not be selfish," said he, with a smile, as he pushed back his chair from the breakfast-table. "The community is certainly the gainer, and no one the loser, save the poor out-of-work specialist, whose occupation has gone. With that man in the field one's morning paper presented infinite possibilities. Often it was only the smallest trace, Watson, the faintest indication, and yet it was enough to tell me that the great malignant brain was there, as the gentlest tremors of the edges of the web remind one of the foul spider which lurks in the centre. Petty thefts, wanton assaults, purposeless outrage—to the man who held the clue all could be worked into one connected whole. To the scientific student of the higher criminal world, no capital in Europe offered the advantages which London then possessed. But now—" He shrugged his shoulders in humorous deprecation of the state of things which he had himself done so much to produce.[765]

Compelling notions of the good, and hence of the eternal, are somehow drawn upon by the inspired speaker and responded to by his audience. One thing that our most gifted teachers are counted upon to do is to see through or past the appearances of things (including appearances of the good) to the real things, to the enduring things. We should notice, for example, that the miserable "client" of Sherlock Holmes introduced in section I of this chapter turns out to be even more miserable than he had seemed, in that he is really a crafty (if not insane) murderer.[766]

Is it not natural for revelation, and not only that "revelation" which is prompted by nature, to help us question whatever may happen to be routinely available to us? That is, it may be natural to test in various ways the everyday appearances of things in order to discern and to understand what in the universe is truly good and enduring, if not even divine.[767]

Appendix A

Reason and Revelation: On Leo Strauss*

> Keep therefore and do [these statutes and judgments]; for this is your wisdom and your understanding in the sight of the nations, which shall hear all these statutes, and say, Surely this great nation is a wise and understanding people.
>
> Moses

I

Leo Strauss, who was an ardent Zionist in his youth, retained a lifelong interest in Jewish things. His least controversial major achievements were as a scholar working with Jewish texts.

Professor Strauss's Jewishness was a significant factor to be taken into account in any effort to understand what he said and meant even as a student of political philosophy. I ventured to say something about this in my 1974 tribute to him [reprinted in Anastaplo, *The Artist as Thinker*, 249 (1983)] which includes the text of the talk he made at a 1961 funeral, a passionate talk which indicates as much as anything the intensity of what Judaism meant to him.

These observations bear upon an argument of sorts I have had for some years now with various other students of Mr. Strauss. Old and dear friends of mine have objected when I notice in print what has long seemed obvious to me about the importance of Judaism for him. They seem to believe that something troublesome is being suggested thereby about the character of his philosophical pursuits. (See appendix E of this book. See also Anastaplo, "Leo Strauss at the University of Chicago," in Kenneth L. Deutsch and John A. Murley, eds., *Leo Strauss, the Straussians, and the American Regime* (1999).)

II

A valuable 1983 paper by Ernest Fortin can be read as offering support for my position. He helps explain why I have made the observations I have, if not also why I have elicited the adverse responses I have. Professor Fortin notices "the absence of any thematic treatment of Christianity anywhere in Strauss's writings or of any extended commentary by Strauss on the works of an unmistakably Christian author." (See Ernest L. Fortin, *Classical Christianity and the Political Order* [Lanham, Md.: Rowman & Littlefield (1996)], II, 287.) On the other hand, we recall the many fine commentaries by Mr. Strauss on Jewish texts, including the work he did on *Genesis*, on Maimonides, and on Halevi. Compare the considerably greater interest shown in Christian things by Jacob Klein, Mr. Strauss's longtime friend and colleague.

What Mr. Fortin says, and says in a particularly useful fashion, about the lack of a political program in original Christianity may help explain why Mr. Strauss did not devote himself to Christian texts: Mr. Strauss did consider *political* philosophy as the most reliable way into philosophy itself, in these times at least if not always. Perhaps, as well, he saw Christianity as a major source of innumerable woes for Jews over the centuries. He did not want to appear to compromise in any way, by his interests and pursuits, the integrity of his deeply-felt Jewish allegiance.

There seems to have been as well the judgment on Mr. Strauss's part that the miracles required for faith in Christianity are significantly different from those required for the Judaic faith. Indeed, he could see the Maimonidian version of Judaism as requiring no, or virtually no, reliance upon miracles, aside from how the Creation itself is to be understood.

III

Not only did Mr. Strauss avoid Christian texts for any major study, he also avoided making explicit the kinds of reservations I have just speculated about. He did not consider it prudent to spell out in public whatever reservations he may have had about Christianity.

For one thing, he recognized and many times said that there is, at least in the United States, common ground shared by political philosophy and Christianity, especially the Roman Catholic Church, in the struggle against modern relativism and vulgar hedonism. Besides, Mr. Strauss always was in these matters a very cautious man: he was always aware, that is, of his minority status as a Jew and even more as a student of political philosophy, an awareness which very much contributed to his sensitivity to the possibility of esotericism.

Certainly, he did not want to jeopardize the always-precarious position of Judaism by making much in public of any reservations he may have had about Christianity. Nor did he want to make philosophy even more vulnerable than it ordinarily is in the face of accusations of irreligion, if not even of atheism. Such accusations may not seem to matter as much these days as they once did, but times do change. Contemporary casualness about these matters may be misleading.

Furthermore, Mr. Strauss could see that any reservations expressed openly about Christianity would serve, in our circumstances, to call all revelation into question. He did not want to do pious Jews a disservice in this respect. Lest it be thought, however, that it would be a disservice for us now to speak somewhat frankly about the things he preferred to treat in a more guarded fashion, it should be remembered that he himself routinely uncovered many more, and more deeply hidden, things than I for one am capable of doing. Whether what I have to say contributes to an understanding of the "limitations," and hence of the remarkable range, of this, perhaps the greatest philosophical teacher of our time, remains to be seen.

IV

The proper relation between political philosophy and revelation in the thought of Mr. Strauss is stated in a most useful manner by Mr. Fortin when he notices the openness of philosophy, on principle, to the possibility of arguments and evidence that may prove decisive against it.

Mr. Fortin's observations here are nicely anticipated by a comment made, by another of Mr. Strauss's students, at a St. John's College memorial service for him in 1973 (Laurence Berns, "Leo Strauss, 1899–1973," *The College*, St. John's College, April 1974, 5):

> The most impressive alternative to philosophy in the life of Leo Strauss is summed up by the name of a city, Jerusalem, the holy city. What if the one thing most needful is not philosophic wisdom, but righteousness? This notion of the one thing most needful, Mr. Strauss argued, is not defensible if the world is not the creation of the just and loving God, the holy God. Neither philosophy nor revealed religion, he argued, can refute one another, for, among other reasons, they disagree about the very principles or criteria of proof. Leo Strauss was a Jew, a Jewish scholar, and if I know anything about the meaning of the word, he was a philosopher, but he insisted that strictly speaking there is no such thing as Jewish philosophy. This mutual irrefutability and tension between philosophy and Biblical revelation appeared to him to be the secret of the vitality of Western Civilization.

One may wonder whether the closing remark in this comment, about the secret of the vitality of Western civilization, has to be made, for its full force, from a perspective, whether or not Straussian, superior to both philosophy and biblical revelation. One may wonder as well what the perspective is from which Father Fortin spoke in advising his fellow theologians to take "Leo Strauss's pioneering work" more seriously. Particularly challenging for anyone trying to place Father Fortin himself is the following sentence in his paper about the vulnerability of early Christianity: "The new religion would have gone the way of the radical sects of late antiquity had it not succeeded in demonstrating its adaptability to the needs of civil society."

The deep differences between two ways of life—the way grounded in the Bible and the way grounded in philosophy—are suggested upon comparing characteristic responses to reported sayings of God, the responses by their respective "founding fathers." Socrates was moved, by a remarkable saying of the Delphic oracle seeming to commend him personally, to inquire into the meaning of what that oracle had said. He had spent much of his life, he said, *testing* that saying. Abraham, on the other hand, immediately proceeded in response to a dreadful saying by God to take the steps necessary for the sacrifice of the son upon whom so much seemed to depend. There was evidently no inquiry or testing at all on *his* part on that occasion.

V

To recognize an unbridgeable gulf between philosophy and revelation—a gulf which Abraham's unquestioning obedience dramatically points up—is not to say that anything goes as revelation. For one thing, philosophy can question various claims of revelation, and has on occasion done so with propriety. Consider, for example, Socrates' insistence in Plato's *Republic* that some of the generally accepted stories about the gods simply could not be true. One can see in Scripture itself the use of reason to test supposed revelations: Gideon's experiments with respect to the dew on the fleece come to mind, as does the ridicule in *Isaiah* of any worship of a god that one has fashioned for oneself out of a log. (See *Judges* 6: 36–40, *Isaiah* 44: 9–20. See also the text accompanying note 50 of appendix F in this book.)

A further testing of revelation may be seen in the proposition (as in the work of Thomas Aquinas) that there are even things denied to God Himself, such as being able to make something not to have ever been which has once been. One can imagine as well what the Socrates of Plato's *Euthyphro*, who questions in the name of piety what a son is about to do to his perhaps guilty father, would have said to a father about to sacrifice his obviously innocent son.

VI

A philosophical critique of the claims of revelation is, then, sometimes possible. It is something of which the pious man must recognize the occasional legitimacy. In this way, philosophy and revelation collaborate.

They collaborate as well when revealed religion makes use of philosophy, something that Mr. Fortin so ably describes Christianity to have done. It was thus, he explains, that Christianity could supply—one may even say, was inspired to supply—its grievous lack of guidance for political action. (Similarly, one could say, philosophy has used religion in support of its moral and political programs: the many cannot be expected to accept consistently and for the right reason the prescriptions of philosophy.)

Philosophy can be useful as well in helping revealed religion avoid being trapped by irrelevant scientific developments, as for example with respect to astronomy or to evolution. In addition, philosophy can help theologians hold in check the Dionysian element in their religion: charismatic movements are restrained, and fundamentalist interpretations are corrected. Presumably, the return to classical thought prepared for by Mr. Strauss, and endorsed for theologians by Father Fortin, would have the effect of helping to keep religion sober. Do some Christians sense, however, that such reliance may place an inhibition on the purest form of religion? Do they suspect, indeed, that any Classical thought thus made available to them is apt to *use* religion rather than to be a handmaiden to it, however political philosophy may allow itself to be described?

VII

Any well-established religion, it should be expected, *is* apt to have had exerted upon it over the centuries the sobering influence of nature. And, as Mr. Fortin points out, recourse to political philosophy made Christianity politically responsible in this world. In being thus useful, it should be noticed, political philosophy may pose more of a threat to Christianity than it does to Judaism. Has not Judaism always been more concerned with the things of this world, and hence with worldly wisdom? (See, for another discussion of this matter, appendix F in this book.)

For this reason, and aside from the question of the place in one's view of things of miracles and of the intervention of God in human affairs, the risk from associating with Classical political philosophy may be greater for Christianity than it is for Judaism. Judaism has always exhibited a greater respect than Christianity for family duties and for political association and its consequences, matters that political philosophy too has traditionally been concerned about. Has not Judaism also had, even if in a concealed way, a greater respect than Christianity for that grasp of nature so vital to political philosophy? In any event, Mr. Strauss himself always made much of the wisdom incorporated in the Mosaic law, as seen in his fondness for *Deuteronomy* 4:6.

Strictly speaking, then, it is *Christian* theology that has both more to learn from Classical political philosophy and more to risk from its revival. The Christian reluctance that Mr. Fortin reports is not without plausible causes, aside from the tendency of theologians today to be decisively moderns. On the other land, the Straussian approach to political philosophy is something the pious Jew can more easily live with, if not even welcome.

Still, it is hard to believe that Socrates would have responded as Mr. Strauss did to the largely impenetrable Mosaic code. Even the detailed legal code in Plato's *Laws*, laid down by a Socrates-like character, is largely accounted for and justified on that occasion. It is also hard to believe that Mr. Strauss, had he not been a Jew, would have been as inclined as he was to make as much as he obviously did of Judaism, however much any of us in the West should want to acknowledge and make use of the teachings about righteousness and mercy impressed on us by Scripture.

To speak as I have ventured to speak here about Mr. Strauss is not only to suggest that he concerned himself considerably (some, but not I, would say, unduly) with certain matters only because he was a Jew, but it is also to suggest that there may have been opinions he held, as a student of political philosophy, that he would not have held *or perhaps would not have held quite the way he did*, if he himself had not happened to have been a Jew. His Judaism, with its wise righteousness, encouraged him to ignore to the extent that he did the lures of modernity, even as it taught him how to read with great care.

One is obliged to wonder, of course, what our contemporary opinions might be which the pagan political philosopher might not have held, or might not have held the same way, opinions rooted in Scripture and in elaborations upon Scripture. These opinions may be found among us not only as a result of direct Jewish influence but perhaps even more as a result of Christianity, which is perhaps the most influential consequence in the modern world of Judaism.

I have suggested where the biblical influence might manifest itself in Mr. Strauss's thought. Some might also discern that influence in what Mr. Strauss has had to say, and how, about one's own, about the naturalness of desperate efforts to preserve one's self, and consequently about the considerable importance of the doctrine of esotericism (for which there is more than one motive). But I must leave further conjectures about biblical influences to others, to those who know far better than do I both the work of Leo Strauss and the two great traditions to which he so brilliantly and so imaginatively looked for guidance, the one rooted in the Bible, the other nurtured by political philosophy.

NOTE

*This paper was prepared for a Claremont Institute for the Study of Statesmanship Panel, Annual Convention, American Political Science Association, Chicago, September 1, 1983. The epigraph for this paper is taken from *Deuteronomy* 4:6, a text drawn on several times in this volume.

The application of Leo Strauss's teaching to contemporary affairs by supposed "Straussians" has aroused considerable controversy in recent years. I had occasion to speak to this issue in the following letter to the editor of June 9, 2003, which has been reproduced in John A. Murley, ed., *Leo Strauss and His Legacy: A Bibliography* (Lanham, Md.: Lexington Books, 2005), 854:

> Leo Strauss's daughter has reported that she does not recognize her father in the recent news stories about him as the mastermind behind the neo-conservative ideologues who are said to control American foreign policy today. [See her *New York Times* article of June 7, 2003, p. A29.] Some of us, who were Mr. Strauss's students at the University of Chicago, also fail to see him as the reactionary guru that some would evidently like him to be. I recall, for example, what he said to me after I lost my Illinois Bar Admission "loyalty-oath" case in the United States Supreme Court. [366 U.S. 82(1961)] That is, his two-sentence letter to me, of June 22, 1961, was hardly that of a right-wing ideologue: "This is only to pay you my respects for your brave and just action. If the American Bench and Bar have any sense of shame they must come on their knees to apologize to you." I suspect that Leo Strauss, upon confronting those Administration adventurists who now claim to find in his teachings support for their presumptuous imperialism, would recall (as he often did) the Dutch grandmother's advice: "You will be surprised, my son, to learn with how little wisdom this world of ours is governed."

Joseph Cropsey, who had been a colleague of Leo Strauss at the University of Chicago, said, upon being asked recently about Mr. Strauss's "influence on current events" (*Dialogo*: The University of Chicago, Fall 2007, 3):

> In public policy, I must say that I would have trouble discerning it. I know that there have been journalists who have criticized Paul Wolfowitz, for example, who was my student in two courses. But he was not primarily a student of Leo Strauss. His main interest was international relations, and I think Albert Wohlsetter was the main influence on his dissertation. I have a lot of trouble understanding how anyone can attribute to Strauss the desire to attack Iraq in order to spread democracy. Of course Strauss favored democracy. Strauss owed his life and his careers, his success, and everything to this country. The idea that he would be in favor of going to war all over the place in order to spread democracy—I mean, somebody who thought as carefully as Strauss would have been able to think about the situation in Iraq and might very well have had second thoughts about it.

Appendix B

Reason and Revelation: On Odysseus and Polyphemos*

The earth is untroubled
And purely designed;
Its beauty is doubled
By a noble mind. . . .

In the mind of the wicked
The earth is not good;
The trees are naked,
And the seas are blood.

Close your eyes, bind them
With a white kerchief;
Cover them, blind them
With a broad green leaf.

Or turn them sunward
To dazzle them blind,
But never look downward
Through a wicked mind.

Elinor Wylie

I

I accidentally discovered yesterday afternoon that some in this audience tonight expect me to make some "trenchant and provocative" remarks about the Polyphemos story in Book IX of Homer's *Odyssey*. Unfortunately, I had to devote the time available to me yesterday afternoon to the lecture I gave last night about the Clinton presidency. Also, unfortunately, I have had to devote myself, until noon today, to the seminar on Book X of the *Iliad* that I conducted this morning. [The Clinton presidency lecture is available in the *Public Interest Law Reporter*, July 1998. It followed a discussion of that presidency which is available in the April 1998 issue of the same journal.]

Fortunately, I myself learned so much from the discussion of the lecture last night and from the *Iliad* seminar this morning that I can look forward to your responses this evening to the not-so-trenchant remarks I did manage to prepare for you this afternoon. I suggest, by this prologue, that it may be particularly fitting, seeing that I am dealing with a master of improvisation in Odysseus, that I have been obliged to improvise as much as I have in preparing my lecture for this evening.

I am gratified to be regarded, in a memorandum announcing this lecture, as "a long-time University of Dallas friend." I find rewarding—and hence friendly—the amount of productive work somehow required of me whenever I visit your most challenging campus.

The question of the relation of *revelation* to *reason* has always challenged the thinking human being. It is a question that can be illuminated for us by examining a few details in the Homeric story of Odysseus and Polyphemos.

The mutual irrefutability of reason and revelation has been noticed. Few, if any, would assert that argument by itself (that is, reason or philosophy) can establish or validate revelation, however useful reason may be in ridding us of various purported revelations that are highly questionable.

Poetry (that is, art) seems more important than philosophy for the establishment of revelation. Certainly, poetry, with its dependence upon inspiration, resembles revelation in critical respects. It is inspiration, not reasoning, that elicits a revelation, making it seem reliable and relevant. (This is not to deny that reason—and reason of a very high order, as may be seen in the work of Thomas Aquinas—can and should be used to good effect in the service of revelation.)

The promotion of a sense of reliability may be seen in how stories "work." Stories, including those special stories incorporating revelations, can seem to take on lives of their own. Consider, for example, this episode of a week ago today. We had left a performance, at the Chicago Cultural Center, of George Bernard Shaw's *Mrs. Warren's Profession*. That play virtually ends with an intense conversation between Mrs. Warren and her daughter, a spirited daughter who insists upon liberating herself from her independent yet possessive mother. It happened, as we walked to our train, that we fell in with "Mrs. Warren" for a few minutes. I asked her, after complimenting her on her stirring performance, "Do you think you will ever see her again?" Our actress had no difficulty with this and subsequent questions as she described how the encounter between her and her "daughter" struck her, how there had not been any "bonding" between them (because of the separation required by Mrs. Warren's profession), etc. No, she concluded, they would never meet again. In short, the story was very much alive for her, as for us, extending years backward and forward from the two hours she had just spent on the stage.

II

Another story that is very much alive is the account given by Odysseus to the Phaecians about his encounter with Polyphemos. Odysseus does seem to us to live in that story, whatever questions we may have (and perhaps are intended by Homer, if not by Odysseus, to have) about what "really happened."

That Odysseus should want to tell this story to the Phaecians is understandable. He knows, for example, that the Phaecians have suffered much at the hands of the Cyclops. They are reminded in effect not only of this, but also of how much the gods cherish hospitality, including the generous bestowal of guest-presents. Odysseus, as a favorite of Athena, is shown to be eager to receive gifts from his hosts.

So eager in this respect was Odysseus that he ran risks in Polyphemos' cave that his men had warned him against. He can even admit that he should have listened to them. His uncharacteristic (if not unbelievable) rashness seems to be compensated for, however, by the glory of his achievement on that occasion, something that can be expected to impress the Phaecians.

Besides, he reports, his Cyclopean adversary had had a prophecy about Odysseus blinding him. Rash or not, it seems to be said, this encounter between Odysseus and the Cyclops was somehow necessary.

The recollection by the just-blinded Polyphemos of his fateful prophecy and his response to it includes these observations (IX, 506–17):

> Ah now, a prophecy spoken of old is come to completion. . . . [It was] told me how all this that has happened now must someday be accomplished, and how I must lose the sight of my eye at the hands of Odysseus. But always I was on the lookout for a man handsome and tall, with great endowment of strength on him, to come here; but now the end of it is that a little man, niddering, feeble, has taken away the sight of my eye, first making me helpless with wine.

Had the prophecy lulled the Cyclops instead of putting him on alert? This reminds us of the limits of prophecy, even as it shows us how accurate it can be.

Had there indeed been such a prophecy? Odysseus can now tell the Phaecians that the Cyclops had reported a prophecy about the blinding reported by Odysseus. Does not this tend to make Odysseus seem quite important, as somehow part of a divine scheme? The cosmic meaningfulness of the life of one or more of the participants in this drama is thereby suggested.

III

But however important Odysseus may be, he does need the help of others. Polyphemos had spoken of being blinded by *Odysseus*, which can mean that the men who assisted him, like the sharpened beam he used, were his instruments. In fact, it is the help of still others—in this case, the Phaecians—that he seeks in order to be able to go home in proper shape.

Even so, Odysseus at this stage of his career has become a *Nobody*: he is essentially on his own, no matter what instruments (human, divine, or inanimate) he must employ in order to accomplish what he (if not also the gods) may have in view. It is only after Odysseus deals with Polyphemos, and what he represents, that he can be announced with full identification among the Cyclops, however much of a *Nobody* he will remain until he *can* get home.

Perhaps the Phaecians are being told that they, too, will become *Somebody*—as part of the epic celebrating the accomplishments of the homecoming Achaean heroes—once they have helped Odysseus go home. (One can be reminded of how the published account in the first volume reporting Don Quixote's adventures is known and incorporated in Cervantes's second volume.)

IV

Something further should be noticed about the men who help Odysseus deal with the Cyclops. The selection of those men is reported at the center of Odysseus' account of the encounter with Polyphemos. Here is how it is put (IX, 331–34):

> Next I told the rest of the men to cast lots, to find out which of them must endure with me to take up the great beam and spin it in Cyclops' eye when sweet sleep had come over him. Those men drew it whom I myself would have wanted chosen.

Odysseus points out here that the lots (or fate or the gods) coincide with the choice of Odysseus. Perhaps, we can venture to believe, this is the way prophecy usually if not always works also. That is, there is more than one way to a result, especially in a well-ordered world. Put another way, there is more than one path to the truth, or to the appropriate action.

Thus, it can be suggested, many prophecies or reports of divine interventions may serve to dramatize and reinforce, it not even to legitimate for some, the conclusions that a properly balanced reason can develop—or can "rationalize."

Also, prophecies and the like tend to "personalize" an account, whereas "a properly balanced reason" tends to be a *Nobody*. That is, nothing essential distinguishes one proficient reasoner from another.

V

But, as we all know, a geometry text (which is one form "a properly balanced reason" can take) does not make for exciting reading for most people, no matter how ingenious one may be in applying mathematical forms in either the construction or the analysis of works of art. So we do not want Odysseus to take leave of the Cyclops as a *Nobody*. (Compare, however, the appearance of Odysseus in Book 10 of Plato's *Republic*, where he is said to seek a private life for his next incarnation.)

Odysseus, it will be remembered, identifies himself to the Cyclops (at what he believes to be a safe distance) as "Odysseus, sacker of cities. Laertes is his father, and he makes his home in Ithaca." (IX, 504–5) This full identification includes not only his name and his "trade" ("sacker of cities") but also his parentage and his community.

Polyphemos, in his prayer to his father Poseidon, draws upon this identification in line 531 of Book IX. I find intriguing A. T. Murray's note in the Loeb Classical Library edition of the *Odyssey*, which informs us that this line is omitted in most manuscripts. (I do not recall ever having noticed that note before today.) That is, the version of Polyphemos' identification of Odysseus to Poseidon may well omit his enemy's parentage and his community.

Whoever added line 531 may not have appreciated what Homer may have been doing here. Polyphemos, even though he is addressing his father, is so much on his own—so much of an "individualist"—that neither parentage (and family) nor community matters to him. He had, early on in his conversation with Odysseus, reported (IX, 375–77): "The Cyclopes do not concern themselves over Zeus of the aeges [the god of hospitality], nor any of the blessed gods, since we are far better than they." But Polyphemos is spoken of as living apart from the other Cyclopes (IX, 188); and the others recognize that "there is no avoiding any sickness sent by great Zeus." (IX, 411) (Polyphemos, living alone in his cave, seems at an earlier state of development than that described in Book I of Aristotle's *Politics*, that life in households which the other Cyclopes, albeit in caves also, do seem to have. Life in communities, which makes possible the citizenship described in Book III of the *Politics*, seems to be beyond them. Perhaps life in caves precludes that. Or is it that caves must be settled for until the skills develop which permit the building of houses?)

VI

Odysseus tells the Phaecians that Poseidon heard the Cyclops' prayer. How does he know *that*?

He also tells the Phaecians that Zeus had not been "moved by [Odysseus'] offerings." How *does* he know such things?

Perhaps he knows such things in the way that Homer does, partly from consequences. Indeed, it can sometimes seem, Odysseus is Homeric in critical respects: certainly, he too is a great storyteller, not only reporting how the gods respond to human intercessions, but also using poetic gifts in telling his stories. The Homeric talent is very much in evidence, for example, when Odysseus describes how the eye of the Cyclops was pierced. (I do not recall that stories told by other characters in the *Iliad* or the *Odyssey* have the distinctive Homeric uses of similes and the like.)

Such considerations should make us wonder whether Homer wanted the more thoughtful members of his audiences to wonder whether Odysseus had "actually had" any of the adventures with which he captivated the Phaecians. Among these adventures is his visit to Hades, which Homer may want us to recognize to be as reliable an account as are Homer's accounts of his own visits, in effect, to the gods on Olympus.

VII

Homer may provide us as well material useful for the assessment of prophecies. Polyphemos, in his prayer to Poseidon, could be heard to say, even at the very great distance Odysseus is (IX, 530–35):

> [G]rant that Odysseus . . . may never reach home; but if it is decided that he shall see his own people, and come home to his strong-founded house and to his own country, let him come late, in bad shape, with the loss of all his companions, in someone else's ship, and find troubles in his household.

This prayer is, in effect, also a prophecy as to what is going to happen to Odysseus, and as such it is testimony to how accurate prophecies *can* be.

Here again, however, an attempt may usefully be made to subject a purported revelation to the discipline of reason. One question that often comes up when a remarkable prophecy is before us is: "When was this prophecy originally uttered?" (Some of you will recall that this is the kind of question that can be posed with respect to the latter part of the *Book of Isaiah*.)

Here, the prophecy is reported as having been made before the events described. There seems to be something, that is, to Polyphemos' powers of divination. Unfortunately for the cause of divination, however, almost all of the events described in the Polyphemos prayer had taken place by the time Odysseus speaks to the Phaecians. The critical event that remains is that he should return to his own country "in someone's else's ship." Are not the Phaecians being told, in effect, that *they* are destined to do the one remaining thing that is fated to be done to Odysseus before he can deal with his problems at home, problems that can be expected because of his absence of two decades? (It is the encounter with the Cyclops that Odysseus, upon confronting the suitors in his palace, remembers as having been theretofore his most threatening challenge. [XX, 30])

The reasonable, indeed salutary, uses of revelation seem to be suggested by a remarkably intelligent poet very much aware both of what he is doing and of what he seems to be doing. This is a poet who, it would be prudent to assume (pending further study of our text), is at least as ingenious and as hard to pin down (in a cave or anywhere else) as both his most inventive character and the wise goddess who is said to inspire him.

NOTE

*This talk was given at the Institute of Philosophic Studies, University of Dallas, February 28, 1998. This school is Roman Catholic in its orientation. The epigraph is taken from Elinor Wylie, "Dark Mirror." See *Collected Poems of Elinor Wylie* (New York: Alfred A. Knopf, 1932), 286.

See, on Homer, John A. Murley, ed., *Leo Strauss and His Legacy: A Bibliography* (Lanham, Md.: Lexington Books, 2005), 894. (This is a quite useful bibliography.)

Appendix C

On the Status of the Political Order*

> Philosopher-kings, and communities governed by philosopher-kings, were however the theme . . . of Platonic politics. And divine laws, which prescribe not merely actions but opinions about the divine things as well, were the theme of Plato's *Laws* in particular. It is therefore not surprising that, according to Avicenna, the philosophic discipline which deals with prophecy is political philosophy or political science, and the standard work on prophecy is Plato's *Laws*. For the specific function of the prophet, as Averroes says, or of the greatest of prophets, as Maimonides suggests, is legislation of the highest type.
>
> Leo Strauss

I

Both of the papers I am commenting on today recognize the importance, if not even the primacy, of the political order in human endeavors. (This is appropriate for papers prepared for a political science association convention.) In both papers, it can be said, the political order is relied upon for proper development and effective preservation of the moral virtues.

In one of the papers, issue is taken with Alasdair MacIntyre, who, although somewhat historicist, nevertheless sees the virtues as more or less independent of the political order. The modern state, we are told, can even be dismissed by Professor MacIntyre as something not worth dying for.

In the other paper, support is offered to Dante Alighieri who challenges those churchmen who consider the ecclesiastical establishment, or at least the way of life it promotes, as superior on earth to the state (or the political order). The Dante challenge is particularly directed, we are told, against the insistence by ambitious churchmen upon the exercise by them of any paramount political control.

II

The author of our anti-MacIntyre paper deliberately speaks from the perspective, at least in part, of traditional Judaism. This ancient faith encourages a noteworthy sensitivity to righteousness and a deep-rooted sympathy for community-mindedness. The political order is reinforced thereby in the anti-MacIntyre paper, perhaps with a suggestion that the most exalted of political organizations is an inspired form of theocratic state. (Reservations are expressed, in the course of that paper, about the possibility of divine incarnation, something that may be relevant also to the controversy in which Dante is shown, in the second paper, to be engaged.)

The author of our pro-Dante paper seems to defend the great Florentine's understanding of Roman Catholicism as a temporal power. That understanding includes, in the affairs of this world, a subordination of priests and bishops to the political order. Philosophy is seen as allied to the political, and as such is preferred to poetry (however fine the poetry with which Dante champions both philosophy and the political order). Also preferred is a discouragement of the theocratic state.

III

But does either of these perceptive papers recognize sufficiently something higher than what the political order, or rather the moral/political order, offers? This is aside from whatever is believed, either by Judaism or by Christianity, about the earthly regime to be established by the coming (whether the First Coming or the Second) of the Messiah.

That is, what (until, if not also after, the Messiah comes) is the status of the contemplative life, or the life of philosophy? That way of life does seem to be regarded as the highest by Aristotle, the authority most critical to the philosophical reflections of both of the authors (Alasdair MacIntyre and Dante Alighieri) discussed in our two papers.

IV

There is a sense in which both of the positions criticized in these papers (Mr. MacIntyre's and the churchmen's) recognize the status of something higher than the political order. We may even be reminded by these papers of the substantial affinity between prophecy (as commonly understood) and poetry, both of which are very much beholden to inspiration.

The best (related, in the MacIntyre view, to the moral virtues) can exist independent of substantial reliance upon the political. In fact, it sometimes seems to be argued by him that one may be a better human being only if one is *not* caught up by political concerns. This kind of opinion seems central to the "world view" of the contemporary intellectual, however much it is regretted when it takes such a form as, say, voter apathy.

The best (related, in the churchmen's view, to personal immortality) is not limited to life on earth, and so the political order is likely to be depreciated. In fact, life on earth can be said by them to be a hindrance to the full development of the human soul. This kind of opinion can arouse the spirit of martyrdom, which is often distressing in a healthy community.

However mistaken both Professor MacIntyre and the churchmen may be either in what they regard as truly highest or in how the best may be reliably attained, their reservations about the political order remind us of something that Plato and Thomas Aquinas have taught us, that it is hard (if not impossible) for an intelligent human being to be completely wrong in any serious disputation.

V

Be that as it may, neither Mr. MacIntyre nor Dante's churchmen can be considered simply correct to place as much emphasis as they are said to do upon the individual. The man devoted to the contemplative life rises above his personal circumstances and individual concerns. In this respect, even if in no other, this man is somewhat like the political man.

Even so, however important the community and its virtues may be, the community as well as the moral virtues to which the community may be dedicated, must take second place for the man devoted to the life of contemplation. This leaves open for him the ultimate status both of Judaism and Christianity. (I emphasize the male in what I say here, deferring thereby to the old-fashioned opinion that the female is more naturally inclined than is the male to be devoted to the family rather than either to political life or to the life of contemplation.)

VI

The contemplative life, especially as it is extolled by Plato and Aristotle, may be divine at its core. At least, the nature of the divine—what it is and is not, what it does and does not do—is a proper subject for serious contemplation. *Being* itself is thereby subject to intense examination.

This kind of dedication to the divine is to be distinguished from the piety vital to both Judaism and Christianity, whether in the form of righteousness with a view to complete submission to God, or in the form of the moral and theological virtues with a view to securing eternal salvation. In these matters it may be salutary to distinguish the godly (that is, an unqualified worship of God by the pious) from the godlike (that is, an informed contemplation of the cosmos by the philosophic). (Such contemplation may be significantly different from the contemplation evidently celebrated in Dante's *Paradiso*.)

VII

Does not a lifelong devotion to the highest, or the godlike, tend to undermine dedication to the community and its political order? Socrates, for example, can be said to leave something to be desired as the model of a patriotic citizen. At times, in fact, he even seems to suggest that there is something more important than that morality upon which poetry depends and to which politics should be dedicated.

Indeed, may not the political order, whether or not theocratic, depend considerably upon received opinions, if not even upon chance (or, if one prefers, upon Providence)? Much is naturally made by human beings of what happens to be their own. On the other hand, the most enlightened statesman may be guided, in his educational and related policies, by the recognition that the community (in its inevitable pursuit of happiness) somehow yearns for that fulfillment (if not even for that transcendence) of the human found here and there, however rarely, in the contemplative life.

NOTE

*This talk, along with the remarks "On Being and One's Own" (appendix D), was given at the Annual Convention of the Midwest Political Science Association, The Palmer House, Chicago, April 24, 1998. It was in response to papers by Michael S. Kochin ("Narrative, Myth, and Character: Aristotle on Human Wholeness") and Joseph Macfarland ("Dante's Practical Resolution of the Eternal Quarrel of Philosophy and Poetry"). These papers were part of a panel, "Philosophy and Poetry." (Papers were also presented by Katherine Philippakis and Warner R. Winborne, which were commented upon by Norma Thompson.) The epigraph for this talk is taken from Leo Strauss, *Jewish Philosophy and the Crisis of Modernity*, Kenneth Hart Green, ed. (Albany: State University of New York Press, 1997), 419–20. See appendix E.

Appendix D

On Being and One's Own*

> I remind you of [an] essay which is still worthy of being read by everyone who is interested in [these matters], an essay by Ahad Ha'am which he called "In External Freedom and Internal Slavery," and in which he compared the situation of the Jews in the Russian ghetto to the chief rabbi of France, who was also the head of the Sanhedrin—you know, an institution founded by Napoleon himself. The chief rabbi was highly respectable, with badges and all. . . . And then Ahad Ha'am showed him, on the basis of what this man said—this chief rabbi—that he was a slave, not a free man. Externally, he was free: he could vote, and do many other things, acquire property, whatever kind he liked. But in his heart he was a slave. Whereas the poorest Polish Jew (if he did not happen to be an individual with a particularly lousy character, which can happen in any community) was externally a man without rights and in this sense a slave, but he was not a slave in his heart. And that is of crucial importance in this matter.
>
> Leo Strauss

I have argued in the formal remarks prepared for this panel that poetry is naturally allied to politics, more so at least than philosophy is likely to be. One form that poetry can take, which is apt to be challenged by conventional politics, is prophetic revelation, so much so that the political order can even become theocratic. Yet there may be poetry, or art, that is primarily a form of exploration, not a form of communication. That is, the investigation one conducts, in order to understand if not to come to terms with "the cosmos," may find one's speculations and discoveries taking the form of artistic formulations.

A determined pursuit of understanding, and with it a grasp of the whole, can be socially disruptive, even deeply disturbing (however acceptable what is discovered may eventually be, once it is recognized, translated into familiar terms, and skillfully placed on exhibit). This is evident in any extended encounter with a "driven" genius. Perhaps Henry Darger (1892–1973), who lived most of his life here in Chicago, was such a man, someone who was hard to understand and, it seems, also hard to be comfortable with on a day-to-day basis. His was an austere life, barely sustained by the meager wages he earned at the modest tasks he could be depended upon to perform. Perhaps his only reliable "recreation" was to attend mass several times a day in his parish church.

His housing was also modest. It happened that his room of many years was shown to my wife and me, some two decades ago, by his former landlord. Nathan Lerner (1913–1997), someone I first met when he enrolled in one of my University of Chicago adult education classes, inherited Henry Darger as a tenant when he bought the building next door to his own. The Darger room was shown to us shortly after Mr. Lerner's eccentric tenant died, which was long before he came to be noticed by a few critics. It was a small, cluttered, even stuffed room. My wife recalls the incongruity of a large trunk dominating the room, providing in effect its only adornment. It was hard to imagine how anyone could ever display to himself in that room whatever of size he was working on, those things (of which we have come to know) stored perhaps in that impressive trunk.

Henry Darger (a kind of Van Gogh of epic narrative) was very fortunate in his landlord, an accomplished photographer who kept the rent low (and who even lowered it at one point) and who left his tenant pretty much alone to pursue his peculiar, even secretive, ways unmolested. We, too, are fortunate in that this landlord salvaged so much of what had been left behind by his tenant, in circumstances where other landlords might have quickly disposed of it all as trash. It can even be considered providential, considering the subject of our panel, that a generous sample of that work (which remains generally unnoticed) is now on display at the Chicago Cultural Center, only a few blocks north of where we are. We can be reminded thus of the odd forms that a not-unhappy life can take, even as we have illuminated for us in a quite instructive way our topic of the relation of philosophy to poetry and politics. We can also be reminded of how much it *is* possible for someone of determination to achieve despite quite limited material resources.

At the core of the Darger work, which can be regarded as what is now known as Outsider Art, are the mammoth stories typed by him on a very old typewriter (also on display at the Cultural Center), stories which feature a family of little girls resolutely confronting an ugly and violent universe. A Miltonic struggle thus dominates a darkened version of the world of Lewis Carroll. These massive manuscripts are, in their physical appearance, rather grim monuments to a lifelong obsessive effort by their disturbed and disturbing author. Also on display are some of the collaged drawings (which can be as large as one yard by four yards in size), done on paper with watercolors. They evidently illustrate episodes in these still unpublished stories (which can run to fifteen thousand pages), episodes in which pre-adolescent girls are featured in their adventures in a fantasy world in which goodness (in the form of innocence) seems to triumph more often than not. These well-composed drawings, by a man with no known training in art, are surprisingly light, colorful, and fresh, even cheerful here and there, with sexuality rigorously "sublimated." (See, on Henry Darger, the critiques available in *The New York Times*, January 12, 1997, sec. 2, 43; *The New York Times*, January 24, 1997, sec. C, 27; *The New Orleans Times-Picayune*, January 31, 1997, L19; *The Economist*, February 8, 1997, 92; *Time*, February 24, 1997, 71; *The Nation*, March 10, 1997, 33; *The San Francisco Chronicle*, September 20, 1997, E1; *The San Francisco Examiner*, September 26, 1997, C-8; *Art in America*, January 1998, 72; *The Chicago Tribune*, April 10, 1998, 60; *The Chicago Sun-Times*, April 19, 1998, Show, 19; *The Hyde Park Herald* (Chicago), April 29, 1998, 11; *The Chicago Tribune*, May 1, 1998, 70; *New Art Examiner*, June 1998, 36, 47 ("Since the discovery upon his death of his astonishing output, Darger has been the subject of intense speculation. *In the unique position of having apparently never mentioned his project to a soul*, with no family or friends to lend insight into his activities, Darger has become the ideal blank screen upon which to project theories about the nature of his work." [Emphasis added]). See also Anastaplo, "Samplings," 27 *Political Science Reviewer* 416 (1998) (Virginia Woolf section). See as well Anastaplo, "Law & Literature and the Bible," 775n.)

All this represented, on the part of Henry Darger, who is said to have been diagnosed as schizophrenic, a radical effort to organize and somehow come to terms with what had long threatened to be for him a chaotic universe, so much so that he would find himself both following weather reports religiously and quarreling vigorously with God. In the somewhat Dionysian effort through his work to keep ominous forces at bay he was more like a philosopher than like a poet, not least in that his effort was determinedly private, with evidently no desire for or expectation of either display or recognition.

That is, what he produced need not be regarded in the way that poetry or art generally is, which tends to be more social and hence more political than philosophy is likely to be. (I was particularly struck, after I first saw the Darger exhibit two days ago, by the contrast between his grubby but somewhat "real" room and the splendid but somewhat antiseptic recently-renovated quarters, "with badges and all," of the Chicago Symphony

Orchestra which we visited the same evening.) This perhaps tormented soul attempted in his work to establish, if not to find, order in the cosmos at large, not just here on earth. This testifies to the possibilities of self-sufficiency in the life of the mind, however much that life may have to depend upon an erotic (if not even a perverse) element—and however much it may occupy itself more with constant struggle than with either beginnings or ends. (See appendix F, below.) In one's philosophic inquiry into the nature of being, that is, one may ultimately have to be essentially on one's own, however useful and important one's teachers, colleagues, and students can be. The grave risks here are obvious; less obvious is that wonderful communion with the highest, if not with the eternal, which can result from the most successful human endeavors. Both the risks and the communion are suggested by that challenging work by Henry Darger to which we are fortunate to have access. Our natural uncertainty about how to regard all this is suggested by the apt title bestowed upon the exhibit now at the Chicago Cultural Center: "The Unreality of Being."

NOTE

*This talk was given at the Annual Convention of the Midwest Political Science Association, The Palmer House, Chicago, April 24, 1998. It served as an addendum to the talk, "On the Status of the Political Order." (See appendix C.) The epigraph for this talk is taken from Leo Strauss, *Jewish Philosophy and the Crisis of Modernity*, Kenneth Hart Green, ed. (Albany: State University of New York Press, 1997), 341. (See appendix E.) See, on the sensitivity exhibited upon the use today of the Ahad Ha'am sentiments, George Anastaplo, "A Hellenic Retrospective," *The Greek Star*, May 24, 2007, Chicago, 8 (on a supposed "ethnic slur"). These Hellenic Bar Association of Illinois remarks are to be included in the third collection of Anastaplo responses to September Eleventh, to be found in volume 5 of the *Loyola University Chicago International Law Review*. The first such collection is in volume 29 of the *Oklahoma City University Law Review* (2004) and the second in volume 4 of the *Loyola University Chicago International Law Review* (2006). See the note for appendix J, below.

A Henry Darger exhibit was mounted by the University of Chicago Smart Museum in 2008.

Appendix E

Leo Strauss and Judaism Revisited*

> Oh, that is not true; I mean, that is simply not true. . . . Oh, God! That is, I think, really unfair.
>
> Leo Strauss

My 1974 eulogy of one of my teachers, Leo Strauss (1899–1973), was not well received by some of my former fellow students. One of their complaints [glanced at in appendix A of this book] seems to have been that I made too much of his Jewishness. I had said, for example:

> My limitations, even as the mere reporter I here try to be, should be acknowledged at the outset of these recollections: I was a quarter century Leo Strauss's junior; I was never an intimate of his; and I am neither Jewish nor conventionally conservative, both of which conditions did tend to promote intimacy with him. . . .
>
> It should be evident, when I speak of Mr. Strauss and Judaism, that I do presume to speak of matters which I can glimpse only at a distance, if at all. Even so, as I have indicated, the outsider can recognize that there is something here to be investigated by a competent student. Thus, Mr. Strauss could acknowledge publicly that there was a disproportion between the "primitive feelings" he always retained from his Orthodox upbringing [in Germany] and the "rational judgment" guided in him by philosophy. [Anastaplo, *The Artist as Thinker: From Shakespeare to Joyce* (Athens: Ohio University Press, 1983), 254, 270.]

Now, a generation later, I am intrigued to see Kenneth Hart Green's collection of materials which very much testifies to Mr. Strauss's lifetime interest in, if not even devotion to, Jewish things. Mr. Green is indeed "a competent student" of these matters. (My observations about the significance of Mr.

Strauss's Jewishness are generously noticed by the editor of this carefully annotated collection. (55, 59, 476. But, at 55, my "perhaps above all" becomes simply "above all.") He can refer to my 1974 Strauss eulogy, understandably, as "a provocative article." (476) "What neither [Strauss's disciples nor Strauss's many detractors have], until recently, been quite prepared to countenance is the utter centrality of Judaism, of the 'insoluble Jewish problem' to Leo Strauss's *oeuvre*." (George Steiner, "Inscrutable and Tragic: Leo Strauss's Vision of the Jewish Destiny," *Times Literary Supplement*, November 14, 1998, 4.)

Much more of Mr. Strauss's "Jewish writings" is scheduled to come. Mr. Green opens his preface with these announcements (xi–xii):

> The following is a collection of essays and lectures written by Leo Strauss in the field of modern Jewish thought, which have been gathered together for the first time. It is meant to offer the reader an introduction to the enormous range of Strauss's Jewish interests. In doing so, I have been guided by two intentions: first, to present the best of Strauss's shorter writings on modern Jewish thought; and second, to present a comprehensive view of how Strauss expressed himself as a modern Jewish thinker. . . . I have included only those works of Strauss that were produced in the years following 1945. The reason for excluding all but the later writings is simply that this is merely one of five volumes to appear in a State University of New York Press series, "The Jewish Writings of Leo Strauss" (series editor, K. H. Green). The series will consist of the following volumes: the early German Jewish writings, 1921–32; a new translation of *Philosophy and Law* (1995); Strauss's writings on Moses Mendelssohn; Strauss's writings on Moses Maimonides; and the present work.

Almost all of the score of pieces in this *Jewish Philosophy* collection have been previously published. Those pieces are collected by Mr. Green in seven parts: I—Essays in Modern Jewish Thought; II—Studies of Modern Jewish Thinkers; III—Lectures on Contemporary Jewish Issues; IV—Studies on the Hebrew Bible; V—Comments on Jewish History; VI—Miscellaneous Writings on Jews and Judaism; and VII—Autobiographical Reflections.

My point of departure in this cursory book review is provided by the items in Mr. Green's part III, the two lectures given by Mr. Strauss forty or so years ago at the Hillel Foundation Jewish Student Center at the University of Chicago. Until recently, those two Hillel House lectures, which were delivered by Mr. Strauss from notes, were available only in unpublished transcriptions of tape recordings, which transcriptions evidently were never reviewed by him. The lectures are "Freud on Moses and Monotheism" (1958) and "Why We Remain Jews: Can Jewish Faith and History Still Speak to Us?" (1962). A personal Jewishness is more on the surface in these lectures than it is in almost all other materials Mr. Strauss had published or had anticipated publishing. This is particularly so during the question-period following upon the "Why We Remain Jews" lecture. It is from that question-period, for example, that the epigraph for this book review is taken. (337) Consider a 1961 funeral talk by Mr. Strauss that also revealed what I call a personal Jewishness. (475–76; Anastaplo, *The Artist as Thinker*, 570–71)

One can be reminded here of the materials that may best illuminate the mode of thought of this remarkable scholar, the transcriptions of many of his courses during his two decades (1949–1968) at the University of Chicago. (One can be reminded also of what is said in Plato's *Phaedrus* about the superiority of living speech to unresponsive writing. Mr. Strauss himself once had occasion to speak of a formidable display of doctoral dissertations as "the dead husks of once living thoughts.") Those course transcriptions, too, were never reviewed by Mr. Strauss. But the master teacher may be seen at work there, especially in the extended discussions that would often occupy much of each meeting of his classes. Mr. Green notices that those course transcriptions "do perhaps convey something of his charm, humor, and power as a teacher." (xii)

It is to be regretted that those of us who attended Mr. Strauss's University of Chicago classes have not yet managed to have those transcriptions reviewed for their many errors. He himself recognized that those course transcriptions might be published some day—and he agreed, in several conversations with me, that he should write something that would serve, in effect, as their introduction, explaining particularly the difference between materials prepared for publication and the sort of thing that may be said and done in the classroom. I do not believe he ever wrote that explanation, which would no doubt have included a thoughtful elaboration upon what I have just reported. Perhaps someone as learned, energetic, and careful as Mr. Green could now put the Strauss course transcriptions in proper shape, consulting with the "first generation" Strauss students who happen to be still available. [This project has now been initiated by the Olin Center at the University of Chicago.]

The two Hillel House lectures I have referred to reveal Leo Strauss as a loyal Jew, standing for a manly refusal to abandon one's people, which is consistent with his youthful dedication to political Zionism. (See 505.) The distinctiveness of the Bible is very much in evidence here as elsewhere, as is Mr. Strauss's insistence upon the unique contributions made by Judaism to the development of standards of righteousness, if not also of rationality, in the Western world. (See, for example, *Deuteronomy* 4:6.) Also evident are the passions Mr. Strauss was capable of when caught up in an inquiry into things, whether philosophical or personal, which mattered to him. Such inquiry may be seen throughout this fine collection. But however superior Mr. Strauss may have considered Judaism, in its rootedness in rationality as well as in righteousness, to the other religions of the world, he never seemed to suggest that sensible Gentiles with "religious" inclinations should try to become Jews. Is it then primarily a matter of chance (if not of Providence) who is, and hence who should remain, a Jew? (See, for the bearing of the Aleinu prayer and of Yehuda Halevi's *Kuzari* upon this question, 120–21, 210, 288, 327–28, 352–53, 399–400, 469–70. See, on the Noahide laws for the non-Jew, Hugo Grotius, *On the Law of War and Peace*, I, xvi; *Encyclopedia of Religion & Ethics*, vol. 9, 379–80 (1917); *Encyclopedia Judaica*, vol. 12, 1189–91 (1971); David Novak, *The Image of the Non-Jew in Judaism* (Lewiston, N.Y.: The Edwin Mellen Press, 1983); Elijah Banamozegh, *Israel and Humanity* (New York: Paulist Press, 1994), e.g., 237 ("There are . . . innumerable scriptural texts following the election of Israel which portray God speaking and acting as the God of all mankind, watching over the destinies of every people. . . . [A] radical forsaking by God of virtually the entire human race in order to attach Himself exclusively to a tiny people [as some suppose] is a hypothesis as monstrous as it is improbable.").)

There may be a problem with the term "Jewish Philosophy" used in the title of Mr. Green's collection. One may wonder whether a mode of thought is properly called *philosophy* if it is distinctively Jewish (or, for that matter, if it is distinctively Christian or Buddhist or whatever). Mr. Green seems very much aware of this problem. (See xvi–xvii. See, on "Jewish thought (philosophy)," 496.) Even more intriguing is the question whether one can be fully a Jew, in the traditional sense, if one is truly a philosopher. Mr. Strauss was reluctant to call himself, or anyone else he knew personally, a philosopher. He was obliged to distinguish between the rare philosopher and, for example, the many members of philosophy departments in this country and abroad. Related to this question is the concern about what the failure to be an observant Jew does to one's condition, if not to one's status, as a descendant of Abraham, Isaac, and Jacob. Mr. Strauss recognized this concern during his 1962 "Why We Remain Jews" question-period (344):

> I believe—and I say this without any disrespect to any orthodox Jews—that it is hard for people, for most Jews today, to believe in verbal inspiration (I mean, in verbal inspiration of the Torah), and in the miracles—or most of the miracles—and other things. I know that. My friend Rabbi [Monford] Harris is not here, but I am in deep sympathy with what he means by a "postcritical Judaism." I think that it offers a perfectly legitimate and sensible goal, namely to restate the essence of Jewish faith in a way which is by no means literally identical with, say, Rambam's "Creator of the world," or with something of this kind—I mean, with any traditional statement of principles. That is not the point. But a Judaism

> which is not belief in the "Creator of the world," that has problems running through it.

(The reference here to "Rambam" is to Moses Maimonides (1135–1204). See, on "postcritical Judaism," Mr. Green's preface, xii, xiv–xv. See also 32f, 45, 47–48, 94, 380. See, on Gershom Scholem and the mysticism underlying Jewish rationalism, Hayim G. Perelmuter, *Harvest of a Dialogue* (Hoboken: KTAV Publishing House, 1997), 119f.)

This kind of inquiry has even been taken so far as to erupt from time to time in a controversy, since Leo Strauss's death, as to whether he was an "atheist." This has been alleged recently in a somewhat hostile manner by one scholar. (See Patrick Glynn, *God: The Evidence* (Rocklin, Calif.: Forum, 1997), 12–14, 171–73.) A far friendlier argument, but perhaps to somewhat the same effect, has been made by one of Mr. Strauss's devoted students. (See David Novak, ed., *Leo Strauss and Judaism* (Lanham, Md.: Rowman & Littlefield, 1996), 169–71. In some quarters, Mr. Strauss is even regarded as Nietzschean.) A stout rejoinder to such talk has been provided by still another of his devoted students, and could no doubt be provided by others as well. (See Hilail Gildin, "Déjà Jew All Over Again," *Interpretation*, Fall 1997, 125. Consider also both the spontaneous invocation of the divine in the epigraph for this book review and the juxtaposition previously noticed of "primitive feelings" and "rational judgment.") It *was* observed, during Mr. Strauss's lifetime, that he made many of his students, both Jews and Gentiles, take their religious heritage seriously. (Perhaps some of his secularized Gentile students should have been regarded as Christians in the sense that he was regarded as a Jew?) It could also be observed that he spoke morally (or, as we say, responsibly) about what completes or transcends morality.

Mr. Strauss, in considering what the charge of "atheism" can mean, reminded students of the precepts of natural theology. (See, e.g., K. H. Green, *Jew and Philosopher* (Albany: SUNY Press, 1993), 237–38.) Even more critical here, it seems to me, is what Mr. Strauss had to say, again and again, about the relation of reason to revelation, if not also about the Idea of the Good. Consider how this relation was put by still another devoted student of his:

> The most impressive alternative to philosophy in the life of Leo Strauss is summed up by the name of a city, Jerusalem, the holy city. What if the one thing most needful is not philosophic wisdom, but righteousness? This notion of the one thing most needful, Mr. Strauss argued, is not defensible if the world is not the creation of the just and loving God, the holy God. Neither philosophy nor revealed religion, he argued, can refute one another; for, among other reasons, they disagree about the very principles or criteria of proof. Leo Strauss was a

> Jew, a Jewish scholar, and, if I know anything about the meaning of the word, he was a philosopher; but he insisted that strictly speaking there is no such thing as Jewish philosophy. This mutual irrefutability and tension between philosophy and Biblical revelation appeared to him to be the secret of the vitality of Western Civilization. [Laurence Berns, "Leo Strauss," *The College* (St. John's College), April 1974, 5. See also appendix A of this book, section IV.]

Would not anyone who takes seriously this kind of juxtaposition of biblical revelation and philosophy have to concede that a reasoned atheism is impossible? That is, does not a *reasoned* atheism imply that biblical revelation has, in effect, been refuted, something which Mr. Strauss had good reason to believe could never be done? (See 10–12, 14, 27–28, 32f, 39f, 50–51. See, on atheism, 489. See, on natural theology, 499. See also Virgil, *Aeneid*, I, 8–11, IV, 376–80. See as well Thomas S. Engeman, Book Review, *Journal of Politics*, vol. 57, 875–77 (1995). Compare Christopher A. Colmo, "Alfarabi on the Prudence of the Founders," *Review of Politics*, vol. 60, 721 (1998); Colmo, *Breaking with Athens: Alfarabi as Founder* (Lanham, Md.: Lexington Books, 2005). My own additional discussions of biblical texts, influenced somewhat, I hope, by the Strauss legacy, may be found in collections published by me in volume 22 of the *Loyola University of Chicago Law Journal* and in volumes 20 and 23 of the *Oklahoma City University Law Review*. See, on the Idea of the Good, Anastaplo, *The Thinker as Artist: From Homer to Plato & Aristotle* (Athens: Ohio University Press, 1997), 396. See also Anastaplo, "Law and Literature and the Christian Heritage: Explorations," 40 *Brandeis Law Journal* 191–533 (2001).)

Mr. Strauss has made invaluable contributions in showing what Judaism and Jewish things (including, of course, the Bible, carefully read) contribute to the thought of the West. Gentiles may be more apt to notice than are Jews these days that Christianity can be understood as a remarkable consequence of the combination of Judaism and Greekness (or philosophy). (But see *Acts* 17; *Colossians* 2:8; Thomas Aquinas, *Summa Theologica*, I, 1, A.8, ad.2.) Put another way, Christianity (which has helped both preserve and discipline philosophy across millennia) can be seen as a Jewish sect for Gentiles, albeit a sect suspected, if not considered heretical, by the observant Jew.

These derivations from, and influences of, Judaism can be generally appreciated. What does not seem to be sufficiently appreciated, I venture to add, is how much Judaism (as something to be taken seriously in and by the modern world) relies upon Christianity, illuminated (as well as distorted) as Judaism has come to be, for many of us, by the great tradition of Christian theology and dependent as Judaism now is upon the political influence of that Christendom which once subjected it to many uncharitable trials. (See 13–14.) This is illustrated most dramatically perhaps by the extent to which the formidable patronage of a still-Christian United States has made it possible for the country of Israel ("a tiny people") to emerge and survive. The long-term consequences of Israel for Jews, and for their ability to probe deeply into and to speak frankly about issues which they have had to approach with caution for millennia, can be profound. (See, on esotericism, 492. See, on the "theological-political crisis," 504. Is this crisis more Jewish than Christian to the extent that Christian thinkers are correct in believing that Christian revelation is in principle compatible with the truths of philosophy? (Friedrich Nietzsche evidently regarded Christianity as Platonism for the masses.) See, on Israel, 496. See, on the case for supporting Israel, Anastaplo, *Human Being and Citizen* (Chicago: Swallow Press, 1974), 155–59; Anastaplo, "On Freedom," 17 *Oklahoma City University Law Review* 465, 622–25 (1992). See also Anastaplo, "Our Iraq Follies, and the Perhaps Inevitable Search for Scapegoats," *The Greek Star*, Chicago, August 16, 2007, 8.)

That Mr. Strauss was much more sensitive to the questions I have raised than most of us are ever likely to be is illustrated by his pioneering work in both Maimonides and Machiavelli (who could celebrate the political prowess of Moses). One can see in Mr. Strauss's Hillel House "Freud" lecture his concern about the threats to Judaism and the Mosaic community posed by secularized Jewish intellectuals. He recognized, as we have noticed, the power of Maimonides's going to the roots of the differences between the philosopher and the man of faith. At these roots is, among other things, a divergence in opinion as to whether the world had a beginning in time—that is, whether, instead of being eternal, the world was created by God out of nothing. (Throughout the collection I am reviewing here Mr. Green's references to the considerable literature about Mr. Strauss are very useful. See, on Creation, 491. See also Moses Maimonides, *The Guide of the Perplexed*, II, 13–31 (Shlomo Pines, trans., 1963). [See as well my *Great Ideas Today* article on "Beginnings," also appended in an expanded form to this book.])

These and like matters are usefully considered in this *Jewish Philosophy* collection. Professor Green's instructive introduction closes with the following passage (48):

> Strauss came to maintain that the search for wisdom in the midst of our contemporary crisis seems to require us to return to the original sources of our wisdom. Over and above everything else, this meant in Strauss's mind that we need especially to turn to the Hebrew Bible, the most fundamental Jewish source, in order to consider whether this book contains a unity of forgotten knowledge that had provided us with our first light, and with an unrefuted truth that we can still recover.
>
> Just as Maimonides focused on the Hebrew Bible in order to meet the medieval philosophic challenge and the crisis it provoked, Strauss believed that

> modern Jews should return to studying the Hebrew Bible as one book with one teaching about God, man, and the world. As this suggests, Strauss thought that we are in need of its essential teaching about God, man, and the world. As this suggests, Strauss thought that we are in need of its essential teaching—blurred by tradition and obscured by modern critique—which we must try to grasp afresh. This is because, to Strauss, it is only in the original sources of our wisdom that true wisdom may reside and can best be rediscovered.

It makes sense that the editorial mind evident in these remarks has produced a collection that should be well received not only by Leo Strauss's students.

NOTE

*This is an expanded version of a review, published in the 1998 volume of *The Great Ideas Today*, of Leo Strauss, *Jewish Philosophy and the Crisis of Modernity*, Kenneth Hart Green, ed. (Albany: State University of New York Press, 1997). (See also appendix A.) See as well note 575 of this book. The epigraph is taken from the Green collection, 337 (February 4, 1962). Unless otherwise indicated, the citations in this book review are to the Green collection.

See, for a discussion of Leo Strauss's *Philosophy and Law*, George Anastaplo, "Constitutionalism and the Good," 70 *Tennessee Law Review* 737, 843–51 (2003). At page 843 of that article, "understood" should be "undertook," in my sentence that reads, "Leo Strauss, when he wrote, seventy years ago, his *Philosophy and Law*, undertook to rescue the religiously Orthodox from the centuries-old assault of the Enlighteners, an assault (reinforced by the findings and technology of modern science) which had seriously called into question, among educated men and women in the West, the received opinions of the religiously-minded."

Appendix F

On Beginnings (with Endnotes)*

> You certainly are Romans who claim that your wars are so fortunate because they are just, and pride yourselves not so much on their outcome, in that you gain the victory, as upon their beginnings, because you do not undertake wars without cause.
>
> The Rhodians

INTRODUCTION

Our sampling of accounts of beginnings includes, on this occasion, a poem by Hesiod, a book of the Hebrew Bible, and the work of a contemporary scientist.[1] Before we discuss these beginnings we should consider, however briefly, what usually permits the beginning of a recognition of the very idea of "beginning." The variety in the more or less inspired accounts of beginnings collected in this appendix may suggest what if anything is constant, if not "always," about beginnings.

There may have to be, if only as a practical matter, some change that is visible if there is to be an observation of, or productive speculation about, beginnings. But, on the other hand, for change itself to be noticeable, is not substantial stability required as well?

It also seems that an *end* is implicit in the notion of *beginning*.[2] *End* can refer to something temporal, something at the other extremity of the process that starts with the beginning. *End* can refer as well to the purpose for which something exists or is done. The end of a thing, in both senses of *end*, may thereby be implied in its beginning.[3]

The *beginning* of a thing may assume not only an end or conclusion. It may assume as well something prior to the beginning, something that brought about a beginning or for the sake of which something begins. We venture here upon the theology of our perhaps most influential ancients, both Greek and Judaic.

Language seems to be needed if there is to be the recognition, to say nothing of the examination, of any beginning. Rationality, or at least the potential for rationality, seems to be required for language. That potential, in turn, seems to depend for its proper realization upon a community, or at least upon that minimum of social cohesiveness provided by the family.[4]

Poets draw upon, as well as help shape, the language of a people.[5] Poetry, however much it (like music) charms audiences by its mode of expression, depends upon and serves an opinion about what the world is like. Each of the three works surveyed in this appendix stands somewhat alone, instructive though it may be to notice the light cast by each on the other two as we consider what each suggests about beginnings.

Before we delve into the beginnings and doings of particular poets, we should notice (and not only in anticipation of part 3 of this appendix) the understanding of things advanced by scientists dedicated to the study of nature. The *nature* that is studied—the apprehension of which permits scientific inquiry—may imply perpetuity.[6]

That is, a reliance upon nature could mean that there is no temporal beginning to some of the things of the world. Why may not matter, if not also the universe itself, be regarded as are, say, numbers and geometrical relations? That is, there *are* things always available (for scientists and others) to be discovered, separated out, and studied, if not even to be manipulated and otherwise used.[7]

Does *nature* also suggest *purpose* or *meaning*? Some argue that nature can guide us in how we should act. We can, it is said, be helped by nature to make sense of things not only by what we study, but also by how we are shaped by the way we conduct ourselves.[8]

The poet is usually to be distinguished from the scientist in these matters. We can see here an opposition similar to, if not quite the same as, that identified by Moses Maimonides as existing between the philosophers and those faithful to the Law of Moses, an irreconcilable opposition which rests, it seems, on an opinion as to whether the world had a beginning in time by having been brought into existence out of nothing by God.[9] In these matters, the poets tend to be the allies of the faithful, especially those poets who undertake to describe the bearing of the divine upon human affairs. With these observations we are prepared to turn to Hesiod, a poet who, like the authors of the Hebrew Bible, never uses any word that should be translated as *nature*.[10]

PART 1—HESIOD'S *THEOGONY*

> The noble voice of Calliope, whom Hesiod called chiefest of the Muses, has sounded steadily since Homer. It has not sounded all of the time, but whenever it has sounded it has given strength to those through whom it spoke. It is the source of great poetry—of great story. [Mark Van Doren][11]

I

Although little is known about Hesiod, we may know more about his personal life—as a resident of that part of Greece known as the Boeotia to which his father had immigrated from Asia Minor—than we do about any other author of his time. An encyclopedist records the following additional information:

> *Hesiod* (Greek, Hesiodos; fl. c. 730–700 B.C.E.), one of the earliest recorded Greek poets. The earlier of his two surviving poems, *Theogony*, is of interest to students of Greek religion as an attempt to catalog the gods in the form of a genealogy, starting with the beginning of the world [this may not be quite so] and describing the power struggles that led to Zeus' kingship among the gods. . . .
>
> Hesiod's other poem, *Works and Days*, is a compendium of moral and practical advice. Here Zeus is prominent as the all-seeing god of righteousness who rewards honesty and industry and punishes injustice.
>
> Also attributed to Hesiod was a poem that actually dated only from the sixth century B.C.E., the *Catalog of Women*, which dealt with heroic genealogies issuing from unions between gods and mortal women. It enjoyed a status similar to that of the *Theogony*, but it survives only in fragments.[12]

A much earlier introduction to Hesiod is provided us by Herodotus in fifth-century Greece. He says in his *History*:

> Whence each of [the gods to whom the Greeks sacrifice] came into existence, or whether they were forever, and what kind of shape they had were not known until the day before yesterday, if I may use the expression; for I believe that Homer and Hesiod were four hundred years before my time—and no more than that. It is they who gave to the gods the special names for their descent from their ancestors and divided among them their honors, their arts, and their shapes. Those who are spoken of as poets before Homer and Hesiod were, in my opinion, later born.[13]

It should be noticed that Herodotus does not say that Homer and Hesiod invented or even discovered the gods, but only that they offered the Greeks a clear picture of the forms, functions, and relationships of the gods.[14] It should also be noticed that there remains to this day some uncertainty as to who was earlier, Homer or Hesiod. There may be an instructive uncertainty here: in one sense, Homer is prior, but in another, Hesiod is.[15]

It should be noticed as well that there is in Homer no systematic account of the beginning of the gods, to say nothing of the beginning of the universe or of cosmic forces. There is not even much attention paid explicitly by Homer to the beginning of the great war in which the Achaeans and the Trojans find themselves. Rather, there is in Homer's *Iliad* a detailed account of the beginning of a quarrel, between Achilles and Agamemnon, late in a very long war. This leads to a detailed account of one episode in that war, an episode that says much about the overall war, if not also about the world itself.[16]

Why is not Homer concerned about the beginning of things? Is it partly because this does not seem to be a concern of his characters? *They* take the world, including the gods, as *given*. Whether or not the gods are really *given* for Homer personally, he is willing to make them seem so, even as he presents events and results in such a way that few if any of them may require the much-spoken-of gods for them to be understood in human terms. This does not deny that Homer presents events and their consequences in the terms of human beings who are very much open to the gods.[17]

Much of what Homer, or a particularly gifted predecessor, does can be understood to prepare the way for Hesiod: the language is developed, a poetic meter—the hexameter—is established, and the audience is shaped. This can be said even though Hesiod seems more primitive, and hence earlier, than Homer in some respects, especially with his cataloguing of gods and others.[18]

II

We can now look more directly at Hesiod and his beginnings by returning to the account of the *Theogony* by our encyclopedist:

> The cosmogony begins with Chaos ("yawning space"), Earth, [Tartarus,] and Eros (the principle of sexual love—a precondition of genealogical development). The first ruler of the world is Ouranos ("Heaven"). His persistent intercourse with Earth [who had generated him on her own] hinders the birth of his children, the Titans, until Kronos, the youngest, castrates him. Kronos later tries to suppress his own children by swallowing them, but Zeus, the youngest, is saved and makes Kronos regurgitate the others. The younger gods [led by Zeus] defeat the Titans after a ten-year war and consign them to Tartarus, below the earth, so that they no longer play a part in the world's affairs.[19]

Our encyclopedist then adds:

> This saga of successive rulers is evidently related to mythical accounts known from older Hittite and Babylonian sources. Hesiod's genealogy names some three hundred gods. Besides cosmic entities (Night, Sea, Rivers, etc.) and gods of myth and cult, it includes personified abstractions such as Strife, Deceit, Victory, and Death. Several alternative theogonies came into existence in the three centuries after Hesiod, but his remained the most widely read.[20]

Hesiod's account of the origins of the things that he can see and has heard about culminates in the emergence of the supreme and now supposedly unchallengeable rule of Zeus. Here, as elsewhere, the end may help shape the beginning, providing that by which the poet takes his bearings. Gods other than those Hesiod mentions are worshiped elsewhere, such as the Egyptian divinities, but these, whatever Hesiod may have heard or thought about them, are pretty much ignored by him.

Hesiod works, then, with what he observes: the earth beneath, the heaven above (which always keeps its distance), perhaps the under-earth, and those erotic relations among living beings which are so critical for "peopling" the world. Along with these can be observed human beings and "evidences" among the Boeotians, if not among the Greeks at large, of the divine, such as shrines, altars, and stories about the gods, as well as their names. Also to be observed is how things do not stay the same: sometimes considerable effort is needed in order to keep things going; sometimes, however, all the effort immediately available cannot be used effectively to preserve things as they have been. This may suggest that the element of chaos is always near, if not always with, us. Among the vulnerable things, Hesiod could notice, are the gods themselves, as memories and other signs survive of divinities that have been permanently, or at least long, eclipsed.

It can be gathered from Hesiod's account that it was difficult, if not impossible, to celebrate properly any divinities who appeared before Zeus and his colleagues manifested themselves. That is, Zeus is recognized as responsible for the song and perhaps the poetry critical to any celebrations that are likely to depend upon and endure as extended if not comprehensive accounts of the gods.[21] Thus, in order for Hesiod to present his account of the beginnings (or birth) of the gods, he must describe, however briefly, how he himself got *to be*—that is, how *he* began as a singer (or, as we would say, as a poet). Without the inspiration available from the Muses, daughters of Zeus, Hesiod would be like most if not all human beings everywhere, merely a "belly" living as little more than an animal dominated by pleasure, fear, and pain.[22]

Piety, in Hesiod's time, consists then of celebrating the regime of Zeus, which is comprehensive in its ministering to the potential that human beings have for maturation, understanding, and justice.[23]

III

Why does not Hesiod say that the divine is always? Can this be said, with sustainable plausibility, only about a single unchanging god? Hesiod inherits a theology that includes not only Zeus as dominant, but also a history both of other divinities and of how Zeus' current ascendancy was established. Perhaps any divine history that is going to be interesting as a story requires a variety of named gods who rise and fall. Almighty Zeus himself first comes to view in the *Theogony* as Kronion ("son of Knonos"); even he cannot be understood completely on his own.[24]

It has been noticed that the "Succession Myth" forms the backbone of Hesiod's *Theogony*: "It relates how Ouranos was overcome by Kronos, and how Kronos with his Titans was in his turn overcome by Zeus. It is not told as a self-contained piece, but in separate episodes, as each generation of gods arises."[25] An account is given by Hesiod of Ouranos' eighteen children by Earth and of Kronos' six children by Rhea before the poet turns to the struggles of Zeus to establish himself and thereafter to secure himself in his rule.[26]

The overall account begins, as has been said, with Chaos, Earth, Tartarus, and Eros somehow emerging, evidently each of the four separately from the other three, into effective being.[27] Nothing seems to be said by Hesiod about what was prior to these four. Nor does anything seem to be said by him about what caused Chaos, Earth, Tartarus, and Eros to come into being, if that is what they did, or to manifest themselves when and where they did.[28]

There is about Chaos, Earth, Tartarus, and Eros something more durable, if not eternal, than there is about the divinities that come to view, beginning with Ouranos, who is produced by Earth on her own, and followed by the children of Earth and Ouranos, especially Kronos, and followed in turn by the children of Kronos and his sister Rhea, especially Zeus. The sequence begins with Earth's production of Ouranos (Heaven, or Sky). This makes sense, not only in that the earth provides the stage upon which all this action takes place, but also in that what the sky, as distinguished from all the vastness of the universe, is somehow keyed to the dimensions of the earth, with Ouranos completely covering Earth.[29]

Nothing is said about "the place" where all of these beings appear. Does their very appearance, "wherever," establish *the* place?[30] Does Earth emerge to provide a place for gods as well as for human beings? She does produce Ouranos on her own, but not Tartarus and Eros, which emerge after her, perhaps in relation to her. That is, Tartarus' location is defined by Earth's. Eros exerts an influence among beings on or near Earth, including among the Olympian gods. Chaos is always there, it seems, perhaps as an alternative. It is after Chaos, or alongside Chaos, but *not* necessarily *out* of Chaos, that the generations of divinities and human beings manifest themselves.[31]

We are left to wonder what it may be, what it is that is "always," which accounts for the emergence of Chaos and Earth, each of which has the capacity to produce others on its own—those others who will then be able to help engender still others.[32]

IV

The gods, including those who are supreme for a while, do not emerge independently as Earth seems to do (along with Chaos, Tartarus, and Eros). Instead, the gods who are shown as, in turn, supreme (Ouranos, Kronos, and Zeus) are generated by others.[33] We can wonder whether only generated beings can have fates. (Again, we might ask: What if anything is it that is "always" which may be responsible for the fates?) In their susceptibility to fate the generated gods resemble human beings. Ouranos, Kronos, and perhaps Zeus were fated to be overthrown—and each took measures that (in the case of Ouranos and Kronos) might have made their overthrow even more likely.[34]

The vulnerability of these deathless gods—Ouranos, Kronos, if not also Zeus—may be related to their having been generated: that is, each has come out of another; they were, before they manifested themselves, confined in another. Perhaps this makes them susceptible to being confined thereafter by adversaries, most obviously so in the case of Kronos. Kronos and his siblings are confined by their father Ouranos in the womb of their mother Earth; Kronos in turn swallows and thereby confines his children, all but Zeus, in his womblike stomach.[35]

What about the fate of Zeus? He, like Kronos before him, is warned by Earth and Ouranos that a son of his would surpass him. And he, like Ouranos and Kronos before him, takes preventive measures, using in effect the technique relied upon by his grandfather and father, but doing it more effectively. Here is how this is summed up:

> Zeus is now elected king of the gods. He apportions their functions, and undertakes a series of marriages to establish order and security in the new regime. His first wife, Metis, is destined to bear a son stronger than Zeus; but Zeus, instead of waiting to swallow the child, as Kronos had done, swallows Metis, thus halting the cycle of succession. (881–929)[36]

We are left to wonder precisely how the prophecy to Zeus had been put. For instance, did it say that *if* he had a son by Metis, he would be overthrown by him?[37] Hesiod does not address this question; one is left to wonder whether it interested him. We do learn that Metis, when she was swallowed by Zeus, was already with child by him—and this is what leads to Athena being born from the head of Zeus.

Perhaps Zeus, in swallowing Metis (or *Cleverness*?), incorporates prudence within himself, thereby personally becoming something other than what he had been. Perhaps, indeed, Zeus can even be said to have been supplanted in this sense. Does Hesiod understand that the reign of Zeus, perhaps because of his defensive prudence, is dedicated to justice much more than the preceding reigns of Ouranos and Kronos had been?[38]

V

It has been said, as we have seen, that succession struggles among the gods dominate the *Theogony*. Other stories are told, some at considerable length, but the successor struggles provide the core around which the other stories are organized. We see in Homer's *Iliad* how Zeus can "physically" threaten the other Olympian gods effectively.[39]

But Earth cannot be overcome in the way that, say, Ouranos can be. Earth does provide the stage upon or around which all of the named gods act. And it is on Earth that *we* have seen the eclipse of Zeus since the time of Hesiod and Homer. Does this suggest that Zeus never "really" existed? Or is it a fulfillment of the prophecy about any son that Zeus may have by Metis? Did that son somehow get conceived, in one sense or another of *conceived*?

There is here a way of accounting for the prophecy to Zeus which a Christian Hesiod might (in the spirit of St. Augustine) try to do something with. That is, something mysterious can be said to have gone on here, of which the pagans could have had no more than intimations, something consistent perhaps with the deification of the *Logos* recorded in the opening chapter of the *Gospel of John*, a Gospel in which Greek influences are quite evident.[40]

VI

Human beings are secondary in the account laid out in the *Theogony*; there is not evident in that poem the concern with human beings that can be seen elsewhere in inspired texts, such as in the Christian Gospels. The life of human beings is described more in Hesiod's *Works and Days*, with much said there about everyday life.[41] A different succession story may be seen there, with five stages of mortals described.

Five seems to be an inauspicious number for Hesiod, with the fifth stage of mortals on Earth representing quite a decline from the opening golden and silver ages.[42] Perhaps *five* can be seen as well in the development of *Theogony*, which is a kind of "works and days" survey for the gods: these are the stages, in turn, of (1) Chaos, Earth, Tartarus, and Eros; (2) Ouranos and his progeny; (3) Kronos and his progeny, which may have been, in some ways, the best time ever for human beings; (4) Zeus and his divine mates and progeny, as well as the progeny of Zeus and other divinities with mortals; and (5) the career, perhaps yet to come (if not already initiated among us) of Zeus' son by Metis, which would be a departure, if not a decline, from that age of Zeus which Hesiod is commissioned by the Muses to celebrate.[43]

Thus, the correspondences between Hesiod's two great poems may be worth exploring. Further correspondences include the fact that there is in both poems the suggestion that femaleness is an affliction among human beings, if not also among the gods. Still, does not femaleness testify to male incompleteness and hence to the vulnerability of the human species? (Is not the female, more than the male, able to produce offspring alone?) Furthermore, Earth and Rhea are critical to the overthrow of Ouranos and Kronos. The biblical parallels here, going back to the Garden of Eden, can be intriguing.[44]

The correspondences between *Theogony* and *Works and Days* may include indications that the gods are somewhat dependent upon human beings, and not only for sacrifices and worship. When human beings change, especially in the vital opinions they hold, so may the gods change somehow, if not even disappear. Besides, the gods of Hesiod and Homer can be said to have the physical forms, and all too often the passions, of human beings.

We can again be reminded of Maimonides, not least for his insistence that the God of the Bible should never be understood to have either a human form or human attributes.[45] In addition, we have been taught, "The Bible is the document of the greatest effort ever made to deprive all heavenly bodies of all possibility of divine worship."[46] Even so, we should also be reminded, as has been said: "In the poetry of Homer, Hesiod, and Aeschylus, the myths of the gods are a source of order."[47]

VII

We return, as we prepare to close the first part of our inquiry on this occasion, to the questions touched upon at the outset of this appendix, "On Beginnings": Is an end implied by *any* beginning? Is there expected, in the temporal sense, an end to the gods depicted by Hesiod and Homer? And is there, in the sense of the purpose of their existence, an end or aim?

Little, if anything, is suggested in Hesiod about the immortality of human souls, whatever may be understood about those rare mortals, such as Zeus' son, Heracles, who are evidently transformed into immortals. What should be expected of the cosmos that is described in the *Theogony*? Should it be expected to continue forever?

Chaos and Earth, we are told in the *Theogeny*, did come into view, if not into being, evidently on their own. Might they somehow go away eventually, perhaps to return and to leave over and over? Is there, for example, something about Chaos, Earth, and Eros, if not also about the particular gods generated in Hesiod's account—is there something which endures, however hidden from view these beings may be from time to time, just as can be said about the ideas which are perpetually available to be discovered and to shape and nourish reason?[48]

Although Hesiod and Homer do not seem to recognize and address such questions explicitly, they can be said to have helped prepare the ground for the philosophers who would first discover these and like questions to be so much in the very nature of things that they are properly the end of the account which an inspired poet may offer as a beginning.[49]

PART 2—THE BIBLE

> And Gideon said unto God, "If Thou wilt save Israel by my hand, as Thou hast spoken, behold I will put a fleece of wool on the threshing-floor; if there be dew on the fleece only, and it be dry upon all the ground, then shall I know that Thou wilt save Israel by my hand, as Thou hast spoken." And it was so; for he rose up early on the morrow, and pressed the fleece together, and wrung dew out of the fleece, a bowlful of water. And Gideon said unto God, "Let not Thine anger be kindled against me; and I will speak but this once: let me make trial, I pray Thee, but this once more with the fleece; let it now be dry only upon the fleece, and upon all the ground let there be dew." And God did so that night; for it was dry upon the fleece only, but there was dew on all the ground. [Anonymous][50]

We need do no more here than remind the reader of beginnings in the Bible, thereby pointing up aspects of the Hesiodic account in part 1 of this appendix and preparing the ground for the extended scientific account in part 3. Our principal source here is the *Book of Genesis*, both names of which refer to origins or beginnings.[51]

Seven forms of beginnings are either described or anticipated in *Genesis*. First, there is the beginning of the world itself, as set forth in the first chapter of *Genesis*.[52] Then there is the beginning of the human race, with its twofold creation and its indelible experiences in the Garden of Eden.[53] Then there is the beginning of the troubled career of the human race outside of the Garden, starting with the fatal conflict between Cain and Abel and almost ending with the devastating flood attributed to human wickedness.[54]

A new beginning for the human race follows in *Genesis* after the flood, leaving the descendants of Noah subject to the Noahide Law that can be said to continue to govern most of mankind.[55] Then there is the beginning of the people of Israel, the descendants of Abraham, Isaac, and Jacob, who are to have a special relation with God, with profound implications for the rest of the human race.[56] Then there is, still in *Genesis*, an anticipation of the beginning, or liberation from Egypt and Egyptian ways and hence the revitalization of the people of Israel under the leadership of Moses and his successors who promulgate and administer a comprehensive system of laws for the life and well-being of a designated people.[57]

Finally, there is, also as an anticipation in *Genesis*, the beginning of the career of the people of Israel in the Promised Land and thereafter, with exiles and returns, with priests and kings, with triumphs and disasters.[58]

In all seven of these accounts, it seems to be assumed that things cannot be properly understood without some recognition of whatever beginnings they may have had. Each of these accounts has inspired libraries of commentaries, which testifies to both their richness and their elusiveness.

The first two words of the Septuagint, a pre-Christian Greek translation of the Hebrew Bible, are *En arché* ("In the beginning").[59] Christian theology evidently drew upon this *Genesis* account by using the same Greek words to open the *Gospel of John*—but there, instead of the making of the world by God being "in the beginning," the Word—*Logos*, or the divine itself—was "in the beginning."[60]

This reminds us, if reminder we need, that there is no account in *Genesis* of the beginning of the divine: the divine seems to have been regarded as existing "always"—and hence as mysterious. We have seen in the *Theogony*, as we can also see in many other such accounts elsewhere, how the gods came into being, whatever there may have always been "somewhere" or "somehow" before the birth of the named gods described by Hesiod.

I turn now—not without an awareness of my limitations as a layman here—to the way that modern science can approach these matters, that way of accounting for things that combines somehow the emergence of the idea of nature in Classical Greece and the almost instinctive respect for rationality in the Bible.[61]

That is, the world of the Bible—whether the Hebrew Bible or the Greek Bible—is more or less orderly, especially when compared to the worlds of the great non-biblical religions of the human race. Due recognition should be given to the considerable physical stability as well as to the challenging shrewdness evident in the Bible, both of which may be seen in the career of Gideon. Both of these—in the form of an acceptance of the idea of nature, developed among the Greeks, and in the form of a respect for rational discourse, evident in the Bible—are very much taken for granted by modern science, as well as by its predecessors.[62]

PART 3—MODERN SCIENCE

> It can scarcely be denied that at the present time physics and philosophy, two sciences of recognized durability, each handed down in a continuous tradition, are estranged from one another; they oppose one another more or less uncomprehendingly. By the Nineteenth Century a real and hence effective mutual understanding between philosophers and physicists concerning the methods, presuppositions, and meaning of physical research had already become basically impossible; this remained true even when both parties, with great goodwill and great earnestness, tried to reach a clear understanding of these issues. [Jacob Klein][63]

I

There is in modern cosmology far less of an opportunity than in other sciences to have theories guided and validated either by experiments or by how attempted applications "work." There is, instead, an unleashing among cosmologists of an imagination, poetic or rhetorical in some respects, that can be a key to professional success. The layman rarely senses how little the cosmologists have available to go on and how much something akin to fantasy has to be relied upon by them. Although *most* physics today is much more sober, a glance at contemporary cosmology should help the layman, who can be quite uncritical in response to spectacular announcements by scientists, to notice some of the temptations to which *all* of modern science may be subject.[64]

Consider, as a particularly dramatic illustration, a remarkably popular book by an English cosmologist—Stephen Hawking's *A Brief History of Time*.[65] His book comes to us with the authority—or is it the burden?—of more than two years on the *New York Times* bestseller list.

An examination of the Hawking book can be a useful way to investigate a few aspects of the character of modern science and what it is that we seek by our recourse to science. Are we truly wiser (and not only about beginnings), we must wonder, because of books such as this and the investigations and conjectures they report?[66]

A Brief History of Time and its remarkable author have been conveniently described for us by the publisher in words that sometimes echo the author's.

I draw here upon the opening and closing paragraphs of the dust jacket of the book (first published in 1988):

> Stephen W. Hawking has achieved international prominence as one of the great minds of the twentieth century. Now, for the first time, he has written a popular work exploring the outer limits of our knowledge of astrophysics and the nature of time and the universe. The result is a truly enlightening book: a classic introduction to today's most important scientific ideas about the cosmos, and a unique opportunity to experience the intellect of one of the most imaginative, influential thinkers of our age.
>
> From the vantage point of the wheelchair where he has spent the last twenty years trapped by Lou Gehrig's disease, Professor Hawking himself has transformed our view of the universe. His groundbreaking research into black holes offers clues to that elusive moment when the universe was born. Now, in the incisive style which is his trademark, Professor Hawking shows us how mankind's "world picture" evolved from the time of Aristotle through the 1915 breakthrough of Albert Einstein, to the exciting ideas of today's prominent young physicists.
>
> . . . *A Brief History of Time* is a landmark book written for those of us who prefer words to equations. Told by an extraordinary contributor to the ideas of humankind, this is the story of the ultimate quest for knowledge, the ongoing search for the secrets at the heart of time and space.
>
> Stephen W. Hawking is forty-six years old. He was born on the [three hundredth] anniversary of Galileo's death, holds Newton's chair as Lucasian Professor of Mathematics at Cambridge University, and is widely regarded as the most brilliant theoretical physicist since Einstein.[67]

This somewhat extravagant description of book and author by the publisher is accentuated by the eerie picture of the author on the cover.

The contents of the Hawking book are further suggested by the following passage on its dust jacket:

> Was there a beginning of time? Will there be an end? Is the universe infinite? Or does it have boundaries? With these fundamental questions in mind, Hawking reviews the great theories of the cosmos—and all the puzzles, paradoxes and contradictions still unresolved. With great care he explains Galileo's and Newton's discoveries.
>
> Next he takes us step-by-step through Einstein's general theory of relativity (which concerns the extraordinarily vast) and then moves on to the other great theory of our century, quantum mechanics (which concerns the extraordinarily tiny). And last, he explores the worldwide effort to combine the two into a single quantum theory of gravity, the unified theory, which should resolve all the mysteries left unsolved—and he tells why he believes that momentous discovery is not far off.

> Professor Hawking also travels into the exotic realms of deep space, distant galaxies, black holes, quarks, GUTs, particles with "flavors" and "spin," anti-matter, the "arrows of time"—and intrigues us with their unexpected implications. He reveals the unsettling possibilities of time running backward when an expanding universe collapses, a universe with as many as eleven dimensions, a theory of a "no-boundary" universe that may replace the big bang theory and a God who may be increasingly fenced in by new discoveries—who may be the prime mover in the creation of it all.[68]

Many of the things said here by the publisher about the Hawking book are of general interest to us, commenting as they in effect do upon the modern scientific approach. Hawking's special interests and theories are likely to pass in time, but the scientific project continues. We may usefully consider that project by observing various features of it as exhibited in this book.

A prominent feature of the scientific project today is its abandonment—perhaps, from its point of view, its necessary abandonment—of what is generally regarded as common sense. The ancient scientist was much more respectful of that common sense, and this is sometimes seen today to have contributed to his limitations. Modern physical scientists consider themselves fortunate to have been liberated from such restraints.[69]

Still, common sense continues to be relied upon, for much is inherited from our predecessors without our always recognizing it. But since we often do not notice what is indeed inherited, we sometimes make inadequate use of it, if only in our efforts to understand what we are doing.[70] Modern scientists can seem rather amateurish, therefore, in explaining the basis or presuppositions for the wonderful things they do come up with.

Consider how much common sense, as commonly understood, is still with us even in the most exotic scientific activities today. Elementary observing and counting depend upon ordinary experience. Common sense is needed to direct us to the relevant observations, to determine how many observations suffice,[71] and even to assure us that a particular collection of data is from our laboratory assistant, not from, say, our stock broker. Common sense is needed as well in hooking up equipment, in reading dials, in deciding how accurate one has to be, in sorting out aberrations. In addition, common sense has to be drawn upon in what is to be understood as cause and effect and in what is to be understood as a contradiction, if not also in what the significance of contradictions is.[72]

I now put my common-sense point in another form: What is the role of judgment in science? Albert Einstein's old-fashioned reservations about critical modern theories should be taken more seriously than younger scientists today evidently do. God, he insisted, "does not throw dice."[73] If one does *not* have deep common sense and good judgment, can one be reliably "in tune" with nature and the universe? I will have more to say about this further on.

The ancients (because they had generated far less evidence to work with?) *seem* to have been more sober than modern scientists in assessments of the alternatives they confronted. The practical judgment of the ancients was more evident even in theoretical matters. We may be more accustomed than they to a kind of madness in speculative work, from which our proliferating science-fiction literature and fantasy films are derivations.[74] One consequence of the differences between ancients and moderns is that the rate of change, for reigning theories as well as for everyday practice, was much lower for the ancients than it is for us.

The modern propensity for innovation may be seen in the series of novelties conjured up by Hawking in his relatively short career, some of which novelties have already had to be repudiated by him. Another way of putting this reservation is to say that Hawking is astonishingly brilliant, especially as a puzzle-solver, but not truly thoughtful.[75] Still another way of putting all this is to observe that I do not recall another book from a man of his stature with so many questionable comments in it.[76] One does not always have the impression of a mature mind at work here. This may be related to the prominence in these matters, as noticed on the dust jacket and reported in the book, of young physicists. The role here of mathematics may also contribute to the overall effect.[77]

II

It is important to notice the contributions of modern technology, itself dependent upon and permitted by modern science, in developing scientific discoveries.[78] In fact, the character of "discoveries" is likely to be affected by the "character" of the technology relied upon. There may be a self-perpetuating spiral here. Whether such a spiral is up or down remains to be seen.

We should be reminded again and again of how slim the physical evidence is that is usually exploited for the most fanciful cosmological speculations, a practice that can be said to go back to Ptolemy and his colleagues. (The contemporary scientist is apt to observe here that the modern evidence is much better than that which supports either Hesiod or *Genesis*.) We should also be reminded that the fundamental alternatives about the cosmos, including with respect to its extent and its origins, may have been noticed long, long ago. It does not seem to me that Hawking and his associates appreciate what their predecessors routinely faced up to—and in a sophisticated way.

One consequence of the volatility of modern scientific thought is that bizarre things tend to be promoted, which should not be surprising whenever ingenuity and innovation are constantly encouraged and lavishly rewarded. Radical changes can be made, as with respect to Hubble's Constant—changes which require stupendous curtailment or enlargement of the estimated age, extent, or "population" of the universe. These remarkable changes, which *are* consistent with a large body of established mathematical theory, can sometimes seem to be made without blinking an eye.[79]

Hawking does caution against jumping to conclusions; he encourages people to admit their mistakes. But is not much of modern science (or at least those who describe it to the public) peculiarly susceptible to rashness and consequent bad judgment?[80] Again, one wonders whether all this is conducive to the sobriety and thoughtfulness that may be necessary for a sound grasp of fundamental issues in science just as in, say, theology.

Hawking may be most obviously a modern in his inability to grasp what predecessors such as Aristotle said, an inability that reveals his own limitations. Whenever he reaches back—if not even to Isaac Newton, certainly to before Newton—he is apt to be sloppy, if not simply wrong.[81]

Consider, for example, his remarks about why Aristotle believed the earth to be at rest. Aristotle is seen, here as elsewhere, to have been "mystical."[82] There is no recognition of what we have long been told about the parallax with respect to the fixed stars expected to be observed if the earth is really in a great orbit around the sun, and about the significance of the inability of observers of Aristotle's day and for centuries thereafter, with their equipment, to detect such parallax. Much of what is said by Hawking about predecessors such as Aristotle and Ptolemy is trivial stuff, evidently picked up from unreliable "pop" history.[83] Yet various experts seem to have let him get away with this sort of thing, both before and after publication of this book. Why is that? Because they do not know better themselves? Or because they do not believe it matters? I suspect there is something of both explanations here.

It is a sign of bad judgment not to be more careful in these matters, not to check things out, and perhaps most important (as Socrates taught us) not to be aware of how much one does not know. It is this bad judgment that contributes to a mode of scientific endeavor that permits, if it does not actually encourage, all kinds of wild things to be tossed around and regarded as profound efforts. Another way of putting these observations is to suggest that all too many competent scientists today do not appreciate that the best of their ancient predecessors may have been at least as intelligent as they are.

The three biographies appended to Hawking's book confirm that his limitations are not confined to reports on the ancients. In those biographies three of the modern heroes of science, Einstein, Galileo, and Newton, are dealt with.[84] For many readers, the Hawking biographies may be the only extended accounts they will ever have of these men. This is not fair either to these men or to the typical reader. Newton, for example, is dramatized as a sadistic self-seeker.[85]

An intelligent high school student with access to standard reference works could be expected to do better than Hawking (or his research assistant) does here. Such a student might also ask himself what the purpose of such biographies might be, something that is far from clear in this book. The "history" thereby provided is rather flimsy.[86]

What, according to Hawking, are scientists really after? One thing that scientists seem to be after, he indicates, is the Nobel Prize. The reader can be surprised by how often Hawking feels compelled to mention that this or that discovery had earned a Nobel.

Related to this may be the use he makes of chance relations, such as the fact that he was born three hundred years after Galileo died.[87] Similar connections are made with Newton. We can suspect here the spirit of numerology and astrology, perhaps not surprising in an age when so much is made, and not only by pollsters and other gamblers, of numbers.[88]

Even as Hawking connects himself with Galileo and Newton, he shows himself "with it" in comments and illustrations which draw upon passing fancies. In all this, in short, a lack of seriousness may be detected.

I have touched upon various things that contribute to the popular success of the book, a success that may be a tribute as well to the recognized eminence of Hawking as a physicist. The successful mixture here of the high and the low is similar to what we can observe in other surprising bestsellers from recognized scholars. In such cases, the authors have previously shown themselves to be capable of much more competent work.[89]

What *do* readers get from the Hawking book? They are both flattered and reassured. They are led to believe that they now understand things that they did not understand before or, at least, that they have been exposed to some wonderful things.

But I must wonder if much is gotten in the way of a serious understanding of things. There is much in the book which is serious-sounding, but a good deal of that is simply incomprehensible.[90] Indeed, much of the book must be unintelligible for most of its purchasers.[91] Furthermore, the typical reader is likely to be misled as to what the fundamental alternatives are in facing the cosmological questions that are glanced at in the Hawking book, fundamental alternatives that have been developed long ago and far more competently elsewhere.

III

Hawking and his colleagues, I have suggested, do not appreciate how naive they can be. They are certainly intelligent, even gifted, hardworking, and imaginative. Yet, I have also suggested, they all too often lack the kind of productive sobriety that obliges one to take the world seriously and that disciplines flights of fancy. They sometimes seem far from accomplished in their grasp both of how the thoughtful investigate serious matters and of how they promulgate their discoveries and conjectures.

Another way of putting my reservations is to suggest that Hawking and his associates do not know what a real book is like.[92] One who is not practiced in reading carefully is unlikely to write with the greatest care.[93] Is the cosmos of the modern cosmologist as shallow as his book? If it is not, then the modern cosmologist may not be equipped to have a soulful encounter with the cosmos. No doubt, competent scientific work can be done without the utmost seriousness—but are not great souls required for the highest activities?[94]

It may not be possible to read or write with the greatest care if one is imbued with our modern prejudices. One such prejudice is that of the Enlightenment, as illustrated in the concluding paragraph of the Hawking volume. It is there suggested that "if we do discover a complete theory [which concerns both the extraordinarily vast and the extraordinarily tiny], it should in time be understandable in broad principle by everyone, not just a few scientists." Hawking goes on, "Then we shall all, philosophers, scientists, and just ordinary people, be able to take part in the discussion of the question of why it is that we and the universe exist."[95]

Such egalitarian sentiments are found elsewhere in the volume as well. This hope or expectation *is* very much in the Enlightenment tradition, and it may be reflected in the intriguing popularity of this volume. It is not recognized, however, what the limits are as to how many can truly grasp the most serious things. That is, the limits placed here by nature and by circumstances are not taken into account.

Related to this can be the irresponsibility exhibited by all too many intellectuals in how they present what they come to believe. The social, moral, and psychic consequences of ideas are not properly assessed.

We have been told that 85 percent of all the scientists who have ever lived are alive today. Their influence is evident and so are their marvelous works. But since they are usually no more thoughtful than most of their fellow citizens, the dubious consequences of many of their innovations, in their intellectual as well as in their technological manifestations, are also evident.

The immaturity, even the not-infrequent juvenile cast of expression, among contemporary scientists may be sanctioned, if not encouraged, by the insulating effects of the mathematics so critical to modern scientific activity. The spirit here is very much that of games, especially of those sports in which much is made of recordkeeping and of statistics.[96] The childishness evident in contemporary scientific enterprises may well be accompanied by, and depend for success upon, considerable ingenuity and a laudable integrity.

Childishness is not unrelated to the self-centeredness that sometimes seems to be, in principle, at the heart of the scientific method today. Self-centeredness may be seen in the anthropic-principle explanations of the universe as understood by contemporary scientists.[97] It sometimes seems to be believed that things exist only if there is, in principle, a human observer.[98]

Common sense does *not* say what contemporary cosmologists, if not physicists generally, seem to say, "If I *cannot* know it, it does not exist—or, at least, it has no consequences."[99] Nor does such a spirit (which can remind one of Plato's Meno) encourage genuine inquiry, but rather limits us to looking into matters that seem to promise "results."[100] We all know that what appears to be the limits of "knowability" in one generation may be superseded in another—and yet what is "real" is hardly likely to have changed over the years.[101]

Besides, is it true what is often said by cosmologists—that we cannot possibly know *anything* about what happened before the Big Bang? May there not have been, for instance, an extraordinary compacting then of the matter that resulted in the Big Bang? What can be known about *that*, if it did happen? It will not do to say that "events before the Big Bang can have no consequences," for informed conjectures about such events, however difficult they may be to grasp "scientifically" and thus to "verify," can affect the grasp we may have of the whole.[102]

The anthropic-principle explanations taken up by some modern scientists are not of the kind seen in, say, the *Book of Genesis*. Nor do they seem of the kind that sees reason as vital to the universe, as that to which energy can be said to be naturally moving. One implication of the anthropic-principle approach seems to be that if anything had been even a little different in the laws of physics, conditions would be very hard if not simply impossible for human beings as we know them. This might bear upon the status of the ideas in the world.[103]

To argue, as some do, that only the measurable exists so as to be knowable is to make too much of the way—the remarkably productive way—we do happen to approach scientific inquiries today. Hawking recognizes, "In effect, we have redefined the task of science to be the discovery of laws that will enable us to predict events."[104] Various animals effectively "predict" events—and yet they do not seem to understand what is going on.[105]

The earth, we are often reminded, is no longer regarded as at the center of the universe. It sometimes seems, however, that the centrality of the earth has been replaced by the centrality of the scientist, for whatever *he* cannot measure does not exist, at least for practical purposes if not also for human understanding. The predictability made so much of by the scientist does rely considerably upon measuring.[106]

That which can be measured is no doubt important. But if genuine understanding is not truly limited to that, even in scientific endeavors, then for scientists to proceed as they do is to subvert the possibility of human excellence. Reviewers of the Hawking volume do not seem to be aware of the serious epistemological problems left both by what he says and by the way he says it.

I conclude my primary critique of this volume by saying that it is hard for me to believe that we know more because of all this. It does not seem to be generally appreciated, I have argued, how slim the evidence is that Hawking builds upon or how even slimmer is all too many scientists' understanding of what it means *to know*. The approach and spirit of current cosmology may effectively cut us off from the most thoughtful awareness of the fundamental issues posed by the inquiries touched upon here. There may even be something unnatural in making so much of so little in the way that modern cosmologists "have" to do, exciting though it may sometimes be.[107]

IV

What, one may well ask, *does* nature suggest here? Although I will continue to comment upon the Hawking volume, it is only fair, after the criticisms I have presumed to make, to put myself at risk by venturing now some "cosmological" speculations of my own.

Nature, taken by herself, means (to repeat) that there need be neither a beginning nor an end to the universe.[108] This in turn means, as Hawking sometimes seems to recognize, that there need be no beginning of time, however limited the means may be in one set of circumstances or another for noticing or measuring the passage of time. Nature seen in this way is opposed, at least in spirit, to the professional, not necessarily any personal, self-centeredness of modern scientists. Thus, nature and self-centeredness contend for the central position in the human soul, if not in the universe.[109]

A somewhat different, perhaps laudable, kind of self-centeredness may also be seen in the goal set by Hawking, which is "to know why we are here and where we come from."[110] Much is made here and elsewhere of the universe as a place in which human beings do live.[111] But, as both Hesiod and the Bible (as well as philosophy) have taught us, human beings may not be the highest things in the universe, and so to understand the universe primarily in human terms may not give the universe its due.[112]

Nor may it do to frame a study of the universe, or even of physics, as a history of *time*. To put it thus may make far too much of process and of human perceptions, not enough either of substance or of principles. This is not to suggest that it is unnatural for time to be made so much of by human beings who regard themselves as personally vulnerable.

But does not nature also direct us to look for those enduring things by which we can take our bearings as we notice and deal with the transitory? Hawking has in his volume a brief account of the origins of life on earth, with the eventual emergence of mammals.[113] This *seems* to me far easier to grasp than the astronomical, or cosmological, conjectures he and his colleagues offer us, and it was fairly easy to grasp as well (however much it was opposed) when first developed by Charles Darwin and his associates more than a century ago.[114] It also seems to me that this greater ease depends in part upon the fact that nature and a common-sense awareness of things may be closer to the surface of this evolutionary account than they are to the surface of many of the cosmological and other speculations of our physicists.

Is it not easier to believe that life on earth had a beginning, and even that the earth itself had a beginning, than it is to believe that the universe did? Aristotle evidently believed that the human understanding of things depends upon the opinion that the visible universe is eternal—that is, that it is more or less unchanging.[115] Since this evidently is not so, Aristotle seems to be vulnerable. But perhaps a sound intuition was at work in Aristotle, which may be appreciated when we recognize that "visibility" may extend far beyond what he could be immediately aware of in his circumstances.[116]

In some sense, then, things may always have been as they are now, with a variety of forms available for the enduring substance of the universe. The ancients who looked to cycles—ancients such as some of the Platonists and perhaps Lucretius—may also have been sound in their intuition.[117]

V

Hawking talks at times (we have noticed) about a beginning of time with the Big Bang and at other times only about an ascertainable time beginning with the Big Bang. More seems to be made of the former than of the latter, as is reflected in the dust-jacket summary I have quoted. Would not the tenor and force of Hawking's argument change significantly if *the* beginning he makes so much of were simply recognized as merely the *most recent* cataclysmic "beginning," and as such no more than a useful starting point for our inquiries?

If we take the Big Bang seriously, must we not also consider the implications of something that has been called the Big Crunch—that concentration of "all" matter that eventually led to the Big Bang? And why should we believe that we happen to be the beneficiaries of, or "tuned in" to, the only occasion that this sequence came about? Is not this too self-centered or otherwise unimaginative on our part?[118]

If, on the other hand, a cyclical pattern of Big Crunches and Big Bangs is assumed, what follows? Whether there was indeed a beginning of time may be intimately related to whether there is a beginning of space. Here we can be reminded of Lucretius and his tireless spear-thrower, repeatedly pushing back the "frontiers" of the universe.[119]

To argue as I have done just now is to speak from the perspective of human reason—albeit, perhaps, an unsophisticated reason—contemplating nature. We must leave open, at least at this point of our inquiry, the question of whether there is truly a genuine divine revelation—and, if so, which one of the many revelations that have been offered to the human race *it* may be—instructing us about a single beginning of time.[120]

However beginning-less (and hence infinite?) both time and space may be, it is hard, perhaps impossible, to imagine infinite matter. Do our cosmologists try to imagine that? I am not sure. They do seem to talk about infinite density—the Big Crunch concentration of all matter into one "point"—at the "time" of, that is, culminating in, the Big Bang. If their calculations show all matter in the universe compacted to virtually a point—and if they mean this literally—my natural inclination (a kind of untutored defensiveness?) is to suggest that they had better calculate again. Lucretius was particularly insistent upon the good sense of recognizing what cannot be.[121]

We have been investigating, in effect, the nature of science, that great work of the mind that is distinctively Western both in its origins and in its presuppositions. We should not forget that science must, like all reasoning, begin with premises that cannot themselves be demonstrated. Related to this is the fact that Newton, for example, does not define the matter of which he makes so much. No doubt, he could have done so, but the thing(s) in terms of which he might have defined matter would in turn have had to be left undefined. Perhaps he preferred to leave as his principal undefined premises those things that are sufficiently available to us by our natural grasp of the everyday world.[122]

The comprehensive account of the universe that the modern cosmologist aims at, as seen in the loose talk at the end of the Hawking volume about knowing "the mind of God," may be, in principle, impossible to attain. I suspect that it is also impossible to comprehend—that is, to grasp, to describe, or to understand—either the smallest element in the universe or the largest, that is, the universe itself. To try to comprehend them is like trying to demonstrate the premises that one uses. I do not pretend to *know* whether matter is infinitely divisible (whatever that may mean) but I have long wondered whether any ultimate "particle" can be both found and identified as such.[123]

I suspect that we see in the celebrated Uncertainty Principle of Werner Heisenberg a reflection of the impossibility of avoiding a dependence upon premises.[124] The ambition of modern cosmologists makes them less thoughtful than they might otherwise be, for it keeps them from recognizing and perhaps refining the premises they must inevitably depend upon.

VI

Critical to our Hawking volume is a discussion of black holes. One can become particularly aware, upon considering the basis for the imaginative accounts we have had in recent years about black holes, how slim the basis for much scientific speculation has indeed had to be.[125]

Perhaps related to this state of affairs is what is said by modern cosmologists about chaos.[126] It is difficult to see, especially if the stuff of the universe does oscillate between Big Crunch and Big Bang, that any state can be considered truly chaotic. I again ask: Is it not possible, if not even probable, that matter, or at least the idea of matter, has always *been*, and hence has always been susceptible to the same "rules"? Why would the rules ever change, except in accordance with a Rule of Rules, or a Cosmic Constitutionalism?

Chaos may be, therefore, only a way of talking about our unsettling ignorance about any particular state of things. Among the things implicit in each state of things is the eventual emergence not only of life but even of reason. The potential for, if not even an "inclination" toward the emergence of, reasoning is thus always present in the universe.[127]

But to say that reason always *is*, in some form or other, does not mean that reason should be able on its own to understand the whole, including why the whole (including reasoning) exists at all. The eternity of the universe probably cannot be demonstrated. But it does seem to be conceivable, whatever that may mean. And it may be vain, if not even maddening, to wonder, or to insist upon wondering, why things "have" to exist at all. That is, there may be no place to stand upon in answering (or even in asking?) such a question.[128] Again, it is prudent to leave open the possibility of what genuine revelation may be able to teach us, if only now and then or only here and there, about such matters.

Is it not possible that matter has always to be as it is, just as (we might more readily concede) numbers have always to be as they are, and perhaps reason (and not only human reason) as well? To what extent, or in what way, reason depends upon matter is another question better left perhaps for another occasion.[129]

It is possible (I again conjecture) that even the divine, however conceived, might be obliged to accept matter as well as numbers for what they are. One reading of the opening chapter of the *Book of Genesis* finds matter already in existence when the creation described there begins.[130] Also, when the days are being counted during Creation Week, it does not seem that the numbers drawn upon there, culminating in *seven*, are being created as well at the same time.

It may not make sense, therefore, to pursue very far the inquiry of why matter exists. Numbers can be used in describing the operations of matter—but, I again venture to suggest, we should be careful not to assume that the most important things to be known about anything, including matter, come to view only by way of measurements, with or without experiments.

Numbers can give us the appearance of orderliness and even of comprehensiveness, especially as they are projected indefinitely. But an awareness of important aspects of things may be sacrificed in the process. Consider, for example, the limitations of a census-taker in grasping the spirit of a people. Consider, also, this suggestion by Bertrand Russell: "Physics is mathematical not because we know so much about the physical world, but because we know so little: it is only its mathematical properties that we can discover."[131]

VII

One defect to be guarded against, especially by the more clever and talented among us, *is* presumptuousness. Presumptuousness is dependent, in part, upon a failure to appreciate what is assumed or presupposed—or, more generally speaking, upon a failure to recognize what has gone before or is always.

Thoughtfulness is needed for the most serious grasp of things. An awareness of one's limitations can contribute to, even if it does not guarantee, thoughtfulness. Such an awareness is far less likely to be secured if one is presumptuous—if, for example, one has been imbued with scientific doctrines which hold out the prospect of a comprehensive understanding of everything, including the very process and form of that understanding.

Why are people today as interested in cosmology as they evidently are? No doubt, they simply want to know about the grandest things. That is natural enough. Perhaps also they seek material confirmation or reassurance about eternal matters, including as they bear upon the standards by which they live and understand. That, too, is natural enough. But does modern cosmology provide the means to grasp these things? Is there not a limit to what can be learned, even by a select few, about such things in this way?

The appeal for us of Hawking's remarkable fortitude and perseverance in the face of great personal adversity is a reflection of our own awareness of, and respect for, the significance and enduring worth of various virtues. Do we not have from him, here, access to something much more solid, even magnificently so, than the cosmological doctrines spun out of the flimsy data that even the most gifted scientists seem destined to have to settle for—and to replace from time to time?[132]

It is instructive here to be reminded that Socrates said that he had been moved, in the course of his career, from such inquiries as contemplation of the heavens to a concern primarily with human things.[133] It is hardly likely that access to such instruments as electron microscopes and radio telescopes would have induced him to conduct himself otherwise.

To turn to human things, as Socrates says that he did, includes an effort to know oneself. Unless one does know oneself it may be difficult, if not impossible, to know reliably any other thing—for how can one be certain otherwise that one's own psyche does not distort what one believes one sees or how one reasons about such things?

But as one comes to know oneself and hence what it means to know, one may also learn that the whole cannot be truly and fully known by human beings. This may be one reason Socrates can speak of *philo*sophy or *love* of wisdom, not of wisdom itself, as that which characterizes the thoughtful human being.[134]

The evident limitations of even the most thoughtful may encourage many human beings to look to some faith in the divine as a way of providing themselves a meaningful universe. But if one is unsettled by the prospect of a universe without beginning, how does recourse to a God also without beginning truly take care of one's sense of groundlessness?

It may be said that God is unchanging, while matter, and hence the universe, is always changing. There is a sense, however, in which an eternal material universe, however varied its forms, is as unchanging as a divinity which is forever.[135] One may have to look elsewhere, then, for justification of that faith in the divine which has meant so much to so many for so long.

The "mind of God" talk of which much has been made in the Hawking volume and elsewhere can seem the essence of presumptuousness. It may be intended as a kind of piety, of course, however misconceived it may be. The fundamental innocence of such statements today is testified to, in effect, by the lack of reproof for these particular statements from most reviewers of the Hawking volume. Evidently this kind of talk is not taken to mean what it might have once been taken to mean.

The perhaps unbridgeable gulf, and hence the prudence of a truce, between reason and revelation may not be generally appreciated these days, however fundamental that gulf has been for millennia in Western thought.[136] The popular appeal of the Hawking volume may rest in part upon its being perceived as siding, in the name of science, with theology against philosophy, however much Christian theology in the West once considered itself in principle compatible with philosophy, thereby distinguishing itself in still another way from the various "schools" of non-Western thought.

Something of the divine is elicited by the enormous numbers invoked by the modern cosmologist. Thus we can be told, as if we are being offered a revelation that should mean something to us, that a thousand billion stars have already been accounted for.[137] Are not numbers on this scale, whether applied to stars or galaxies or distances or time, simply incomprehensible, if not literally non-sense?

Numbers of this scope do suggest the magnitude of the divine, as traditionally understood. But they may not suggest the awesomeness of the truly holy, partly because they are numbers that are repeatedly being revised, almost (it can sometimes *seem*) at the whim of the cosmologist.[138]

How does the mythology of the modern cosmologists compare with the theology of our ancients, whether Greek or Judaic? We have to understand the old better than we now do in order to be able to answer this question—and, for that understanding, a grasp of what each of these ways of thinking takes to be the *beginning* should be useful, if not even essential. Also useful here can be at least an informed awareness of what the non-Western "schools" of thought have revealed across millennia.

Be that as it may, we can see, in the considerable popular response to the kind of story of the universe told in the Hawking volume, why the Bible can be said to be "the document of the greatest effort ever made to deprive all heavenly bodies of all possibility of divine worship."[139]

Be that too as it may, we must wonder if the old mythology, if mythology it be, is keyed more to human capacities and expectations than is the new. One reliable model in responding to the speculations of modern cosmologists may well be that of Socrates' determinedly sober response to the ambitious speculations of Anaxagoras.[140]

CONCLUSION

Morale among physical scientists can be high, however much their efforts can remind one at times of the high-minded but ill-fated Children's Crusade. The enthusiasm of gifted students is stimulated, in large part, by the considerable talents and obvious dedication of their teachers, by the noble hope that the general understanding as well as the material conditions of mankind will be enhanced, and by the plausible perception that much has already been accomplished because of the technology generated by science. The more thoughtful scientists are not unaware of some of the reservations I have sketched on this occasion about the modern scientific project.[141] Particularly challenging is the question of what it is that the scientist is entitled to believe and to say on the basis of the evidence that happens to be available to *him*.[142]

To what extent should continual examination of the evidence that can be mustered in support of scientific speculation include assessments of the technology to which these speculations have no doubt contributed? We can still see, in various parts of Europe, North Africa, and the Middle East, Roman aqueducts, perhaps often repaired if not rebuilt since antiquity, that carry water as they did thousands of years ago. The technology of the Romans has continued to work long after the natural sciences of their day were superseded, if not even discredited. It is instructive thus to notice that a "theory" may "work"—it may have substantial practical applications—even if not strictly or fully true. Many are the marvels associated with modern science—not least with the technology inspired by and otherwise keyed to modern science—but these marvels should not be taken to validate that science, certainly not to validate it unqualifiedly when it speculates about the beginnings of things. Similar comments can be made about the religious foundations upon which great enterprises have been reared and sustained for centuries, if not even for millennia, all over the world.

A story I once heard at the weekly physics colloquia at the University of Chicago assures us that some scientists are alert to the follies to which unbridled speculation can lead: Two American engineers who had made fortunes developed a passion for archaeology. This led them to purchase villas in Rome where they could excavate to their hearts' content. Their zeal was rewarded. One of the engineers came to the other with exciting news. Excavations on his grounds had turned up some ancient metal strings. This proved, he was pleased to report, that the ancient Romans had invented the telephone as well as the aqueducts for which they were already admired by everybody. The other engineer was inspired by this report to dig further on his own grounds. Eventually, he too had exciting news to report. He had dug all over and had found nothing. "Then why are you so excited?" his friend asked. "Don't you realize what this means?" came the reply. "The Romans must have invented the radio also!" Scientists intend to remind us by such stories about the difficulty, as well as the allure, of discovering the true beginnings, and hence the very nature, of things, even as we keep in mind these propositions:

> Philosophy in the strict and classical sense is quest for the eternal order or for the eternal cause or causes of all things. It presupposes then that there is an eternal and unchangeable order within which History [including the "history" of Big Crunches and Big Bangs?] takes place and which is not in any way affected by History.[143]

ENDNOTES FOR APPENDIX F

*This is an expanded version of an article, "On Beginnings," originally published in the 1998 volume of *The Great Ideas Today*. See also George Anastaplo, *But Not Philosophy: Seven Introductions to Non-Western Thought* (Lanham, Md.: Lexington Books, 2000), 261–301. (See, on the unfortunate demise of *The Great Ideas Today*, Anastaplo, "Law & Literature and the Bible: Explorations," 23 *Oklahoma City University Law Review* 515, 865–66 (1998).) The notes for this "On Beginnings" appendix are provided *here* as endnotes (as distinguished from the notes for this book as a whole that are found at the back of this book). The epigraph for this appendix is taken from Hugo Grotius, *The Law of War and Peace*, II, i, 1 (quoting remarks recorded by Livy from a speech made to the Romans by the Rhodians).

1. Our scientist, a cosmologist discussed in part 3 of this appendix, "On Beginnings," is *not* representative of physical scientists today, whose speculations do tend to be much less spectacular. But his kind of cosmology does fit in nicely with the poetic and the biblical accounts considered in parts 1 and 2 of this appendix. Although contemporary cosmology may not be representative of disciplines such as "ordinary" physics, it does suggest the direction in which science is moving, with speculations about the most minute and immediate things matching, in their inventiveness, speculations about the grandest and most remote things. See the texts accompanying notes 80, 95, and 123, below. (All references to notes in these 143 notes are, *unless otherwise indicated*, to the notes in this "On Beginnings" appendix.)

2. Quintillian, Seneca, and many others have observed that everything ends that has a beginning. See, e.g., *Genesis* 3:19. Consider also the opening line of T. S. Eliot's *East Coker*: "In my beginning is my end." Consider as well the opening lines of his *Burnt Norton*. See, on these poems, George Anastaplo, "Law & Literature and the Moderns: Explorations," 20 *Northern Illinois University Law Review* 251, 539 (2000).

3. Must there be an ultimate "particle"? If not, what (in a particle-theory approach) provides the foundation for such substantial steadiness as we observe and depend upon in the world? So far as we know and perhaps so far as most of us can imagine, however, all material particles can be divided. If there is an ultimate particle, therefore, is it likely to be material? Rather, may it not be somehow immaterial? And, if so, how is the marvelous transition effected between the immaterial and the material? Do we touch here upon that "mystery" of the relation between body and soul? See notes 117 and 143, below. See, on the soul, George Anastaplo, *But Not Philosophy: Seven Introductions to Non-Western Thought* (Lanham, Md.: Lexington Books, 2002), 303. See, on the *ultron*, note 123, below. See also section VIII of appendix K in this book.

4. The languages essential for rationality, as well as for responsible families, seem to depend upon community. This suggests the limits to radical individualism. See the text accompanying note 128, below.

5. See, on Homer as the educator of Greece, George Anastaplo, *The Thinker as Artist: From Homer to Plato & Aristotle* (Athens: Ohio University Press, 1997). See also the text accompanying note 11, below.

6. See the text accompanying note 142, below. See, on nature, Anastaplo, *The Thinker as Artist*, 399. See also the texts accompanying notes 62, 108, and 115, below. I have been told that Leopold Kronesker said, "God created the natural numbers [1, 2, 3, etc.]. Everything else is man's handiwork." Compare the text accompanying note 129, below.

7. See the text accompanying note 142, below.

8. See, e.g., George Anastaplo, "Natural Law or Natural Right?" 38 *Loyola of New Orleans Law Review* 915 (1993); Leon John Roos, "Natural Law and Natural Right in Thomas Aquinas and Aristotle" (University of Chicago doctoral dissertation, 1971). See also Anastaplo, *But Not Philosophy*, 303.

9. See Moses Maimonides, *The Guide of the Perplexed*, II, 15 sq.

10. Homer uses *nature* only once, and that use is curious. See Homer, *The Odyssey*, X, 303. See also the text accompanying note 62, below.

11. Mark Van Doren, *The Noble Voice: A Study of Ten Great Poems* (New York: Holt and Co., 1946), xi. See George Anastaplo, *The Artist as Thinker: From Shakespeare to Joyce* (Athens: Ohio University Press, 1983). See also note 5, above.

12. *The Encyclopedia of Religion* (New York: Macmillan, 1987), vol. 6, 307–8. See the text accompanying note 47, below.

13. Herodotus, *The History*, David Grene, trans. (Chicago: University of Chicago Press, 1987), II, 53.

14. See R. M. Frazer, *The Poems of Hesiod* (Norman: University of Oklahoma Press, 1983), 13.

15. See, for a challenging discussion of Hesiod, Seth Benardete, "The First Crisis in First Philosophy," *Graduate Faculty Philosophy Journal* (New School for Social Research), vol. 18, 237 (1995). The Bernadete challenges here begin with the unfortunate opening line: "Virtually everyone knows that Aristotle sometimes lies." See also note 21, below. See, for (Pythagorean?) reservations about both Homer and Hesiod, Diogenes Laertius, *Lives of Eminent Philosophers* (Cambridge, Mass.: Loeb Classical Library, Harvard University Press, 1925), II, 339 (viii, 21). Compare the "poetic" epigraph for appendix K of this book.

16. Similarly, in Homer's *Odyssey*, the story begins late in the course of Odysseus' effort to return home. By the sixth book, in this twenty-four-book epic, Odysseus reaches the last stop before he gets home. This bears upon whether the Homeric epics were "folk" productions. See Anastaplo, *The Thinker as Artist*, 367f.

17. See, e.g., *ibid.*, 13f. Virgil's *Aeneid* seems critically different in this as in other respects.

18. The Catalogue of Ships, in Book II of Homer's *Iliad* (see Anastaplo, *The Thinker as Artist*, 23, 37–39, 375–77), can be seen as a Boeotian element adopted (and transformed) by Homer. In any event, Homer can be taken to suggest that human beings almost always, if not always, find themselves in the midst of *some* struggle.

19. *Encyclopedia of Religion*, vol. 6, 307–8. Dante, in his *Divine Comedy*, even immobilizes Titan-like beings at the bottom of the Inferno. Elsewhere, as in Homer, Zeus can be referred to as the oldest of the Olympians. Does Zeus, because of his superior power, act and regard himself as the oldest, even though he is sometimes said (in other stories, such as Hesiod's) to be the youngest of the Olympians?

20. *Encyclopedia of Religion*, 308. See, on the Babylonian and Hittite sources, "Mesopotamian Thought: The *Gilgamesh* Epic," in Anastaplo, *But Not Philosophy*, 1.

21. Poets (or prophets, who may sometimes be the same as poets?) had sung of other gods, but not as effectively (that is, not as truly?) as Hesiod can. Thus, as the Muses told Hesiod, the Muses "know how to speak many false things as though they were true." Hesiod, *Theogony* 26. Perhaps this helps account for the dubious stories about the gods that have been challenged. See, e.g., Plato, *Republic*, Books II and III. See also Virgil, *Aeneid*, VI, 893–96. John Milton argues, in his *Areopagitica*, that the truth is much more likely to prevail than is error in a fair contest. See also note 15, above. See, on prophecy, Anastaplo, *But Not Philosophy*, 389–90. See also chapter 2 of this book.

22. See Hesiod, *Theogony* 26f.

23. See the text accompanying note 47, below.

24. See Hesiod, *Theogony* 4. See also "Jupiter" in Pierre Bayle's *Dictionary*.

25. See M. L. West, ed., Hesiod, *Theogony* (Oxford: Clarendon Press, 1966), 18.

26. See *ibid*., 17–18.

27. Eros is critical for the generating to be done later by divine as well as by human couples. Tartarus becomes important later as a place to be used by Zeus to confine permanently his defeated challengers. See Hesiod, *Theogony* 713f. See also Virgil, *Aeneid*, VI.

28. Nor is anything said about any other place but Earth and its environs (which could include where the gods are most of the time). See Aristotle, *Physics*, 225a sq. See also the text accompanying note 143, below.

29. See Hesiod, *Theogony* 126 sq.

30. We recall that the Lord could be referred to, in ancient Hebrew, as "the place."

31. See, on Chaos, the text accompanying note 126, below.

32. We have similar questions about what preceded the Big Bang examined in part 3 of this appendix, "On Beginnings."

33. See Hesiod, *Theogony* 126 sq., 453 sq, 491 sq.

34. They are in this respect like Oedipus, whose (presumptuous?) efforts to avoid his fate may have made that fate come about in the worst possible way. That too, by the way, is a Boeotian story, and one in which, like the story of Ouranos, a son mates with his mother to produce a much-troubled dynasty. See, on Sophocles' Oedipus, George Anastaplo, *On Trial: From Adam & Eve to O.J. Simpson* (Lanham, Md.: Lexington Books, 2004), 444; Anastaplo, *The Thinker as Artist*, 3, 6–8, 119–28, 400.

35. See note 33, above. See also Anastaplo, *But Not Philosophy*, 75–76.

36. West, ed., Hesiod, *Theogony*, 19.

37. Was this the kind of prophecy that Laius, the father of Oedipus, had had?

38. See the text accompanying note 47, below.

39. See, e.g., Homer, *Iliad*, XV, 48 sq.

40. See, on *Logos* and the *Gospel of John*, the text accompanying note 60, below. See also chapter 14 of this book. See, on St. Augustine, George Anastaplo, "Teaching, Nature, and the Moral Virtues," in *The Great Ideas Today*, vol. 1997, 9 (1997); Anastaplo, "Rome, Piety and Law: Explorations," 39 *Loyola University of New Or-*

leans Law Review 2, 83 (1993). Furthermore, it can be wondered whether Athena (the ominous "child of Zeus"?) generated that rationalism which eventually undermined the Olympian divinities.

41. See Stephanie A. Nelson, "An Honest Living: Farming and Ethics in Hesiod's *Works and Days* and Virgil's *Georgics*" (University of Chicago doctoral dissertation, 1992).

42. See, on *five* in Hindu accounts, "Hindu Thought: The *Bhagavad Gita*," in Anastaplo, *But Not Philosophy*, 67.

43. This is perhaps somewhat like Hesiod's fellow Boeotian, Pindar, being commissioned to celebrate the winners of the great athletic games. See Anastaplo, *The Thinker as Artist*, 76. See also Anastaplo, *The American Moralist*, 51f. See, as well, note 40, above.

44. Consider, for example, the decisive career of Rebekah. (See chapter 5 of this book.) Consider also the story about Eros told by "Aristophanes" in Plato's *Symposium*. See Anastaplo, *The Thinker as Artist*, 171.

45. See Maimonides, *The Guide of the Perplexed*, I, i sq. See, on Maimonides, Anastaplo, *The American Moralist*, 58. See also chapter 6 of this book.

46. Leo Strauss, *Jewish Philosophy and the Crisis of Modernity*, Kenneth Hart Green, ed. (Albany: State University of New York Press, 1997), 293. This work is reviewed in appendix E of this book. See also the text accompanying note 139, below. See as well Anastaplo, *But Not Philosophy*, 205, n. 4.

47. Charles Segal, *Dionysian Poetics and Euripides' "Bacchae"* (Princeton, N.J.: Princeton University Press, 1982), 339. See also the texts accompanying notes 12, 38, above.

48. See, on the Doctrine of the Ideas, Anastaplo, *The Thinker as Artist*, 307, 397. See also the texts accompanying notes 103, 127, below.

49. See the text accompanying note 143, below. Parmenides helped open up the West to nature and hence to philosophy. He shows himself, in a Homeric-style poem, introduced to his topics by a goddess. This can remind the reader of Hesiod's initiation by the Muses. See, on Parmenides "as the first extant author deserving to be called a philosopher in a present-day sense of the word," *Parmenides of Elea*, David Gallop, ed. (Toronto: University of Toronto Press, 1984), 3. The evident coextensiveness, for Parmenides, of *thinking* and *being* suggests that "beginning," as distinguished from that which is "always" or eternal, may be for him little more than an illusion, except that the process of change itself may be eternal. See the text accompanying note 116, below. See also note 135, below. See, for a useful introduction to Parmenides and the Platonic dialogue by that name, Albert Keith Whitaker, *Plato's Parmenides* (Newburyport, Mass.: Focus Press, 1996). See also the discussions of Parmenides by Martin Heidegger, Jacob Klein, Karl Reinhardt, Kurt Riezler, and (it is to be hoped) Joseph Cropsey.

50. *Judges* 6:36–40. Compare *Judges* 6:14–24.

51. The traditional Hebrew name for this book is *In the Beginning*. The title *Genesis* is a much later usage from the Greek. The other four books of the Torah are also called traditionally by the word or words that appear first in the text. See the text accompanying note 59, below. See also Robert Sacks, "The Lion and the Ass: A

Commentary on the Book of Genesis," *Interpretation*, vol. 8, 29 (1980). See as well note 40, above.

52. See, e.g., Strauss, *Jewish Philosophy and the Crisis of Modernity*, 359.

53. See, e.g., Anastaplo, *On Trial*, 5.

54. See, e.g., chapter 4 of this book.

55. See, e.g., chapter 13 of this book; Anastaplo, "Lessons for the Student of Law: The Oklahoma Lectures," 20 *Oklahoma City University Law Review* 17, 97 (1995).

56. See, e.g., Anastaplo, *On Trial*, 111; chapters 5 and 6 of this book. See also note 44, above.

57. See chapters 7, 8, and 9 of this book. See, for instructive introductions to the career of Moses, three articles by Jules Gleicher in *Interpretation* (in 1999, 149–81; in 2003, 119–56; in 2004, 119–63).

58. See chapters 10, 11, and 12 of this book. Indeed, it can sometimes seem, much of the Hebrew Bible is written for a people that is somehow always "abroad."

59. *Arch-* is the term evident in such English words as *archetype*, *architect*, and *architectonic*. See note 51, above. Some readers of the Hebrew text have it open, "When God began to create . . ."

60. Should this be understood as God *speaking* or *thinking*? See the text accompanying note 40, above. Goethe has his Faust open a book and begin to speak thus:

> It says: "In the beginning was the *Word*!"
> [*Geschrieben steht: Im Anfang was das Wort!*]
> Already I am stopped. It seems absurd.
> The *Word* does not deserve the highest prize,
> I must translate it otherwise
> If I am well inspired and not blind.
> It says: "In the beginning was the *Mind* [*der Sinn*]!"
> Ponder that first line, wait and see,
> Lest you should write too hastily.
> Is mind the all-creating source?
> It ought to say: "In the beginning there was *Force* [*die Kraft*]!"
> Yet something warns me as I grasp the pen,
> That my translation must be changed again.
> The spirit helps me. Now it is exact.
> I write: "In the beginning was the *Act* [*die Tat*]!"

Johann Wolfgang Goethe, *Faust*, Walter Kaufman, trans. (Garden City, New York: Anchor Books, Doubleday, 1963), 153. Consider, on the natural tendency toward the animation of matter (and hence the power of "Mind"?), appendix K of this book.

61. See, on miracles in the New Testament, chapter 14 of this book. See also Anastaplo, *On Trial*, 155f.

62. See, on Gideon, the text accompanying note 50, above. See also note 133, below. Compare Robert Graves, "Introduction," *Larousse Encyclopedia of Mythology* (London: Paul Hamlyn Limited, 1951), 5:

> Mythology is the study of whatever religious or heroic legends are so foreign to a student's experience that he cannot believe them to be true. Hence the English adjective "mythical," meaning "incredible"; and hence the omission from standard European mythologies, such as this, of all Biblical narratives even when closely paralleled by myths from Persia, Babylonia, Egypt and Greece; and of all hagiological legends.

See Anastaplo, *On Trial*, 71f, 155f. Most of the major religions of the world, when compared to those grounded in the Bible, can seem rather "wild" to us in the West. See notes 20 and 42, above. See, for what the West is accustomed to, Anastaplo, "Law & Literature and the Christian Heritage: Explorations," 40 *Brandeis Law Journal* 191 (2001). An exception, although it may not really be a "religion," is the Confucian way. See, e.g., Anastaplo, *But Not Philosophy*, 99f. See also the text accompanying note 136, below.

63. Jacob Klein, *Lectures and Essays* (Annapolis, Md.: St. John's College Press, 1985), 1. I have found very helpful the comments made by often *quite*-critical readers of part 3 of this appendix, "On Beginnings." Those readers include Laurence Berns of St. John's College, Peter Braunfeld of the University of Illinois, Keith S. Cleveland of Columbia College of Chicago, and Stephen Vanderslice of Louisiana State University, as well as Nikilesh Banerjee, Hellmut Fritzsche, Edward Kibblewhite, Joseph J. O'Gallagher, Robert G. Sachs, and Noel M. Swerdlow of the University of Chicago. See note 109, below.

64. A mature physicist (who is not himself a cosmologist) has told me that one did not hear much if any talk, forty years ago, about the age of the universe; there was little talk then of a "beginning." But, he insists, observational evidence is now available, primarily because of the work earlier of Edwin Hubble, arguing for the steady expansion of the universe, and because of the discovery in the 1960s of the cosmic background radiation, which suggests a beginning of time—that is, the Big Bang. (This "beginning of time," we shall see further on, seems to mean to cosmologists today the beginning of *knowability*. See the text accompanying notes 98–100, below.) It is hard, this physicist can add, to fathom either a finite universe, in time or space, or an infinite universe, in time. See note 80, below. See, on the risks of *imagination*, as noticed by Enrico Fermi, the *Interpretation* book review cited in note 70, below.

As for the prospects of an unending "expansion of the universe" (see note 118, below), consider one implication of the natural animation of matter examined in appendix K of this book: May there even be in matter, because of whatever natural ensoulment there might be, a tendency toward universal "in-gathering"? See as well note 758 of this book.

65. The full title of the Hawking book is *A Brief History of Time: From the Big Bang to Black Holes*. The book was first published by Bantam Books in 1988, and subsequently revised. See note 89 (end), below. See, for recent speculations about these matters, "Papers from a National Academy of Sciences Colloquium on the Age of the Universe, Dark Matter, and Structure Formation," 95 *Proceedings of the National Academy of Sciences U.S.A.* 1 (1995).

66. See note 107, below. See also the text accompanying note 94, below.

67. See, for "A Brief History of *A Brief History*," Stephen Hawking, *Black Holes and Baby Universes and Other Essays* (New York: Bantam Books, 1993), 33f. See also the text accompanying note 87, below.

68. See, on the challenging mission of combining the extraordinarily vast and the extraordinarily tiny, the text accompanying note 95, below. See also note 1, above, and the text accompanying note 123, below.

69. Has our "common sense," if not even our "intuition," been shaped by such grand innovations as Newton's "system of the world"? For example, what we accept as his law of inertia can be said to have defied "common sense"; that is, everyday observation is that things moving on earth do come to a stop unless pushed or pulled further. See also notes 116 and 126, below. Still, consider how current scientific speculations can be regarded:

> Contemporary cosmologists feel free to say anything that pops into their heads. Unhappy examples are everywhere: absurd schemes to model time on the basis of the complex numbers, as in Stephen Hawking's *A Brief History of Time*; bizarre and ugly contraptions for cosmic inflation; universes multiplying beyond the reach of observation; white holes, black holes, worm holes, and naked singularities; theories of every stripe and variety, all of them uncorrected by any criticism beyond the trivial. [David Berlinski, "Was There a Big Bang?" *Commentary*, February 1998, 38.]

But see note 80, below. See also note 131, below.

70. See, e.g., the commentaries in the Joe Sachs translation of Aristotle's *Physics* (New Brunswick: Rutgers University Press, 1995). See also my discussion of this useful edition of the *Physics* in *Interpretation*, vol. 26, 275 (1991).

71. Statistical theory is important here, as is a distinction between discovery and verification. Few, if any, rules govern discovery—one inspired conjecture might suffice—while, on the other hand, fairly strict rules may govern what is accepted as verification. Be that as it may, the contemporary physicist can insist that precise measurement is impossible. See note 143, below.

72. See the text accompanying note 121, below. The Hawking career puts to a severe test the ancient prescription of *mens sana in corpore sano*. Hawking himself has had to compensate for a dreadful disease for which he was in no way responsible. See Hawking, *Black Holes and Baby Universes*, 21–26. It is a disease which has made him, in key respects, very much a creature of modernity—not only in his reliance upon more and more technology for survival and communication but also in his being able to divorce his mental activity to a remarkable degree from bodily activity and hence from the material element. (One can be reminded of René Descartes, one of the founders of modern science, who argued that scientific progress required the investigator to abstract from his body and his circumstances. See George Anastaplo, *The American Moralist* (Athens: Ohio University Press, 1992), 83. See also Anastaplo, "The Forms of Our Knowing: A Somewhat Socratic Introduction," part 2, in Douglas A. Ollivant, ed., *Jacques Maritain and the Many Ways of Knowing*, an American Maritain Association publication (Washington, D.C.: Catholic University of America Press, 2001).) One can wonder whether a radical independence from the body con-

tributes to a spectacular imaginative power, if not to even more such power than is called for by the available facts. See note 122, below. Socrates does seem to argue that if the soul withdraws from the body (that is, dies?), it should, if properly prepared while still alive, be able to think better—but such speculations came from a Socrates who always did have a sound body—and his having such a body may have contributed to the sobriety that can be seen underlying even his most imaginative ventures. However impressive Hawking's intellectual achievements, they are likely to be superseded within decades, given the volatility of modern science, while the remarkable achievements of the spirit that he has exhibited should be celebrated for generations, if not for centuries. See the text accompanying note 132, below. See also note 117, below. Compare Anastaplo, *But Not Philosophy*, 337, n. 36.

73. Consider, for example, this comment by Einstein in a letter to Max Born, December 12, 1926:

> Quantum mechanics is certainly imposing. But an inner voice tells me that it is not yet the real thing. The theory says a lot, but does not really bring us any closer to the secret of the Old One. I, at any rate, am convinced that He does not throw dice. [Ronald W. Clark, *Einstein: The Life and Times* (New York: World Publishing Company, 1971), 340.]

See also *ibid*., 396 ("God is subtle but he is not malicious"). See, on imagination, note 64, above. See, on the Enlightenment and deism, Edward O. Wilson, "Back from Chaos," *The Atlantic Monthly*, March 1998, 52. Compare note 89, below. See as well note 143, below.

74. See Eva T. H. Brann, *The World of the Imagination* (Savage, Md.: Rowman & Littlefield, 1991), 603–31. See also *ibid*., 579–600. See, as well, notes 95 and 140, below. See, for the rigor employed by the very best of the ancients in using fully the relatively little evidence then available about the heavens, Aristotle, *De Caelo*. See also notes 97 and 114, below.

75. The puzzles of modern physicists are largely technological in character and are dictated in various ways by technology, even as solutions tend to expand technology.

76. He starts well enough (on page 1) with the charming story about the tower of turtles, but he is all too often flip thereafter. Consider, for example, what is said about astronauts falling into black holes, about the risks run at a Vatican conference, about such things as *Penthouse* and *Private Eye*, about various of the ancients, and about the biographies of great predecessors. I will return to some of these matters. See also note 69, above.

77. See section III of part 3 of this appendix, "On Beginnings." Hawking is said to rely less on mathematics, even in his professional papers, than most of his colleagues. See Jeremy Bernstein, "Cosmology," *New Yorker*, June 6, 1988, 118.

78. See Hawking, *A Brief History of Time*, 85. The engineering art seems to be a vital part of contemporary physics. See also note 75, above.

79. Consider the implications of such changes while the accompanying technology continues to work. Indeed, much of the technology can be opaque. We sometimes "know" that if we do A and B, our result will "always" be C, without our having the least idea why. See, for puzzlement about the attraction of masses, Anastaplo,

"Lessons for the Student of Law," 157–58. See also the conclusion of this appendix. See as well the text accompanying note 138, below. See, on Hubble's Constant and its elusiveness, Donald Goldsmith, *Einstein's Greatest Blunder? The Cosmological Constant and Other Fudge Factors in the Physics of the Universe* (Cambridge, Mass.: Harvard University Press, 1995), 90f.

80. A particularly dramatic instance was the cold fusion scandal of the late 1980s. But the scientific community itself dealt with *this* apparent aberration decisively. See, e.g., John R. Huizenga, *Cold Fusion: The Scientific Fiasco of the Century* (Rochester: University of Rochester Press, 1992). Consider, also, this report by the eminent scientist (notes 84 and 107, below) who first popularized contemporary cosmology:

> It is conceivable that some of the skeptics will turn out to be right about the big bang theory, but this seems unlikely. [Martin] Rees cautiously gives odds of only 10 to 1 in favor of the big bang, but he quotes Yakov Zeldovitch as saying that the big bang is as certain "as that the Earth goes round the Sun." At least within the past century, no other major theory that became the consensus view of physicists or astronomers—in the way that the big bang theory has—has ever turned out to be simply wrong. Our theories have often turned out to be valid only in a more limited context than we had thought, or valid for reasons that we had not understood. But they are not simply wrong—not in the way, for instance, that the cosmology of Ptolemy or Dante is wrong. Consensus is forced on us by nature itself, not by some orthodox scientific establishment. [Steven Weinberg, "Before the Big Bang," *New York Review of Books*, June 12, 1997, 20.]

See also the text accompanying note 125, below. See, on the "originality" of the moderns, G. M. D. Anastaplo, Book Review, *Isis*, vol. 82, 713 (1991). See also note 122, below. See as well note 131, below.

81. This seems to be due to a combination of carelessness, ignorance, and presumptuousness. See, e.g., Martin Gardner, "The Ultimate Turtle," *New York Review of Books*, June 16, 1998, 17–18. See also note 84, below.

82. See, e.g., Hawking, *A Brief History of Time*, 2. See, on Aristotle's *Physics*, note 70, above.

83. This is evidently done, in part, to bolster the "history" anticipated in the title for the book. See the text accompanying note 86, below.

84. Consider these observations by Jeremy Bernstein ("Cosmology," 120–21):

> As much as I like Hawking's book [*A Brief History of Time*], I would be remiss if I didn't point out an important way in which it might be improved. Hawking has a somewhat impressionistic view of the history of recent science. Very few active scientists—[Steven] Weinberg is an exception, and that is one of the reasons his book [*The First Three Minutes* (note 107, below)] is so good—actually take the trouble to read the papers of their early predecessors. A kind of folklore builds up which bears only a tangential relationship to reality, and when someone with the scientific prestige of Hawking repeats these legends it gives them credibility.

85. See Hawking, *A Brief History of Time*, 181–82. See, for the grandeur of Newton's work, Subrahmanyan Chandrasekhar, *Newton's "Principia" for the Common*

Reader (New York: Oxford University Press, 1995); George Anastaplo, Book Review, *The Great Ideas Today*, vol. 1997, 448 (1997); appendix H, section VIII of this book. See, on Newton as a "lion" for Chandrasekhar, George Anastaplo, "Thursday Afternoons," in *S. Chandrasekhar: The Man Behind the Legend*, Kameshwar C. Wali, ed. (London: Imperial College Press, 1997), 125. See also Anastaplo, "Law & Literature and the Bible," 864–65. See as well note 92, below.

86. See note 83, above. See also the text accompanying note 143, below.

87. See Hawking, *A Brief History of Time*, 116. See also the text accompanying note 67, above.

88. See, e.g., George Anastaplo, *The Constitutionalist: Notes on the First Amendment* (Dallas: Southern Methodist University Press, 1971; reprinted by Lexington Books, 2005), 806–8; Anastaplo, "Thursday Afternoons," 126, n.2.

89. See, e.g., Stephen Hawking, "The Unification of Physics," *The Great Ideas Today*, vol. 1984, 2 (1984). Compare *ibid.*, 4:

> Einstein spent most of the last forty years of his life trying to construct a unified theory of physics. He failed partly because not enough was known about nuclear forces and partly because he could not accept the limits on our ability to predict events, limits which are implied by the quantum mechanical uncertainty principle. He said: "God does not play dice." Yet, all the experimental evidence suggests that God does. In any case, we now know a lot more than Einstein did, and there are grounds for cautious optimism that a complete unified theory is in sight. Were I a gambling man, I would bet even odds that we can find such a theory by the end of this century, if we do not blow ourselves up first.

See note 73, above. See also the text accompanying note 124, below; note 143, below. See, as well, George Anastaplo, "*In re* Allan Bloom: A Respectful Dissent," *The Great Ideas Today*, vol. 1988, 252 (1988); *Essays on "The Closing of the American Mind"*, Robert L. Stone, ed. (Chicago: Chicago Review Press, 1989) (it was at my suggestion that this useful collection was made when it was and published where it was); Anastaplo, "McCarthyism, The Cold War, and Their Aftermath," 43 *South Dakota Law Review* 103, 111–13, and related appendices (1998); Bill Goldstein, "Let Us Now Praise Books Well Sold but Seldom Read," *New York Times*, July 15, 2000, A19. See as well Robert H. Henry, "Anastaplo's Bible as Legal Literature: A Guide to the Perplexed, or a Perplexing Guide," 23 *Oklahoma City University Law Review* 501, 503 (1998).

90. Jeremy Bernstein, himself a scientist with literary accomplishments, considers *A Brief History of Time* "charming and lucid"; "Cosmology," 117. See note 84, above.

91. Compare Hawking, *Black Holes and Baby Universes*, 38.

92. This limitation is reflected in how the typical physics colloquium is presented these days, with an inordinate reliance upon slides and other such visual aids. One exception that I happened to witness during the past decades was a lecture by Subrahmanyan Chandrasekhar, at the weekly physics colloquium at the University of Chicago, which featured his filling of yards of blackboard with mathematical expressions (and all from memory). I was duly impressed, even though a senior physicist muttered to me, as we walked out, "Show-off!" See note 85, above.

93. See Leo Strauss, *Persecution and the Art of Writing* (Glencoe, Ill.: Free Press, 1952).

94. May not great souls be discerned in scientists such as Galileo Galilei, Isaac Newton, Albert Einstein, Erwin Schrödinger, Leo Szilard, Enrico Fermi, Subrahmanyan Chandrasekhar, and perhaps C. F. von Weizsacher, Werner Heisenberg, and Neils Bohr? See note 109, below. See, on Schrödinger, note 131, below. See, as well, on the inclination toward animation (if not even "soulness") that may be somehow inherent in the matter of the universe, appendix K of this book.

95. Hawking, *A Brief History of Time*, 175. Consider the cautions in Anastaplo, "Scientific Integrity, UFOs, and the Spirit of the Law," in "Lessons for the Student of Law," 187. See also the text accompanying note 74, above.

96. An illuminating anticipation of the Hawking volume in this respect is James D. Watson's *The Double Helix* (New York: Atheneum, 1986), in which the contest for winning the Nobel Prize awaiting an authoritative description of the DNA molecule is vividly presented by one of the exuberant winners. See, on sports today, Anastaplo, "Law & Literature and the Bible," 860–61.

97. See Hawking, *A Brief History of Time*, 124–25:

> There are two versions of the anthropic principle, the weak and the strong. The weak anthropic principle states that in a universe that is large or infinite in space and/or time, the conditions necessary for the development of intelligent life will be met only in certain regions that are limited in space and time. The intelligent beings in these regions should therefore not be surprised if they observe that their locality in the universe satisfies the conditions that are necessary for their existence. . . . According to [the strong version of the anthropic principle], there are either many different universes or many different regions of a single universe, each with its own initial configuration and, perhaps, with its own set of laws of science. In most of these universes the conditions would not be right for the development of complicated organisms; only in the few universes that are like ours would intelligent beings develop and ask the question: "Why is the universe the way we see it?" The answer is then simple: If it had been different, we would not be here!

See also John D. Barrow and Frank J. Tipler, *The Anthropic Cosmological Principle* (Oxford: Clarendon Press, 1986); Jacques Demaret and Dominique Lambert, *Le Principe Anthropique: L'Homme est-il le Centre de l' Univers?* (Paris: Armand Colin, 1994); Michael A. Corey, *God and the New Cosmology: The Anthropic Argument* (Lanham, Md.: Rowman & Littlefield, 1993); Bernstein, "Cosmology," 118. See also the texts accompanying notes 103, 111, and 127, below. It should be noticed that Hesiod, if not also the creation story in *Genesis*, can seem rather childish (if not even crippling) to some moderns. See note 74, above.

98. Thus, Hawking can observe (*A Brief History of Time*, 46): "As far as we are concerned, events before the Big Bang can have no consequences." This can seem to be the inverse of that aspect of the Uncertainty Principle, which has the object observed altered by the very act of observing it. See note 124, below. See also note 118, below.

Peter Braunfeld has observed, "Although a few of the best mathematicians I know are modest, many of them are just the opposite. Doing mathematics (or science) can be a lonely risky business, and arrogance can help you to keep at it."

99. See Brann, *The World of the Imagination*, 175. See also note 64, above.

100. Modern scientists sometimes act as if they are bound by the laws of evidence in courts of law. See, on Plato's *Meno*, George Anastaplo, "Teaching, Nature, and the Moral Virtues," 2.

101. Nor do the things that have been discovered stop "existing" when they happen to be forgotten by all living rational beings for a while or even "forever"?

102. See the text accompanying note 118, below.

103. See notes 49 and 97, above. See also note 126, below.

104. Hawking, *A Brief History of Time*, 173. The sentence quoted concludes, "up to the limits set by the uncertainty principle." See note 124, below.

105. Human beings, too, can predict events, or can proceed confidently with the predictions by others, that they do not understand.

106. Compare Plato, *Republic* 602D sq.

107. The most cautious, and hence most reliable, of the popular accounts here still seems to be Steven Weinberg, *The First Three Minutes: A Modern View of the Origin of the Universe* (New York: Basic Books, 1997). See notes 80 and 84, above. The physicists I have consulted for the Hawking part of this appendix speak well of the Weinberg book.

108. See, e.g., Plato, *Timaeus* 27C; Anastaplo, *The Thinker as Artist*, 279; note 70, above. See also the text accompanying note 6, above. (I note, for the record, that it is Plato's *Critias* that is "unfinished." Compare Anastaplo, "Lawyers, First Principles, and Contemporary Challenges: Explorations," 19 *Northern Illinois Law Review* 353, 444 n.236 (1999).)

109. See, on the self, Anastaplo, *Human Being and Citizen*, 87. See also note 94, above. Thus, one of the scientists who read this appendix concluded his comments with the (Cartesian?) observation, "The only true beginning and end is our own individual birth and death."

110. Hawking, *A Brief History of Time*, 13. What would Hawking consider sufficient answers to these questions, and why?

111. See, e.g., *ibid.*, 171. See also note 97, above.

112. See also Plato, *Apology of Socrates*; Aristotle, *Nicomachean Ethics*, Book VI. See also Anastaplo, *Human Being and Citizen*, 8; Anastaplo, *The Thinker as Artist*, 318.

113. See Hawking, *A Brief History of Time*, 120–21.

114. The National Academy of Sciences has recently recommended that evolution should be taught in public schools as "the most important concept in modern biology." See "Scientific Panel Urges Teaching of Evolution," *Chicago Tribune*, April 10, 1998, sec. 1, 13. See also Larry Arnhart, *Darwinian Natural Right* (Albany: State University of New York Press, 1998); Anastaplo, *The Artist as Thinker*, 482. Can the advocates of "creation science" in this country justify settling on any particular story of

Creation among the many that have long been available around the world? See the text accompanying note 120, below. See also Anastaplo, *The American Moralist*, 341–44; note 143, below. Consider, as well, how the evolution theory is drawn upon in the following 1957 poem, "Sally," by Sara Prince Anastaplo:

Hooray, hooray, hooray!
Let the old bands play!
The only talking baby is
In this world to stay!

She screeches, she crows,
She works her mouth and toes,
She arches neck and back,
Full of what she knows.

"Last year, gilled, I floated in the dark.
What was really me, except a hungry spark
Coaxing, 'Become, be-oh-something
For a lark'?

"So this spring
I kick and sing.
Finny sisters mild,
Furry brothers wild,
Bow to my choice,
I am a human child!"

Be all this as it may, cosmologists can say, Darwin is easier to understand because his theory is largely qualitative, so it doesn't presuppose a technical facility with sophisticated mathematics. Besides, he is talking about the everyday world, the very world our common sense was honed to cope with. It is when we want to think about the world of the subatomic or the world of galaxies, or the world of unimaginable densities and forces that common sense deserts us, and mathematics is our only tool, cosmologists would add. Consider here the implications of the observations in appendix K of this book.

115. See Leo Strauss, *Natural Right and History* (Chicago: University of Chicago Press, 1953), 8; Klein, *Lectures and Essays*, 113, 187f. See also the text accompanying note 6, above. Hawking himself seems open to the possibility, if not even to the likelihood, of a universe without a beginning or an end.

116. See note 49, above. See also the text accompanying note 135, below. Does the discovery that light has a velocity play a role here? Thomas Aquinas and others, including *perhaps* Galileo, basing themselves on everyday experience, seem to have considered light's transmission as instantaneous. See Anastaplo, "The Forms of Our Knowing," part 1. See also note 69, above; note 126, below.

117. I have sometimes wondered what sense we can have of, or what "feel" we can have for, the matter that our bodies are composed of—what intuition we can have, if any, of the eternity that that matter has "experienced." See note 72, above; the text accompanying note 129, below. Does this contribute to a sense of personal invulnera-

bility? Consider as well appendix K of this book ("Yearnings for the Divine and the Natural Animation of Matter").

118. Recent conjectures by some cosmologists have the universe expanding indefinitely, thereby making another Big Crunch unlikely, if not even impossible. See, e.g., George Johnson, "Once Upon a Time, There Was a Big Bang Theory," *New York Times*, March 8, 1998, 3 (WK). But even more recent conjectures about the mass of neutrinos can perhaps be taken to suggest otherwise. See, e.g., Simon Singh, "The Proof Is in the Neutrino," *New York Times*, June 16, 1998, A31. Is it not far too early to be confident about any of these conjectures? See the text accompanying note 138, below. Perhaps, indeed, the nature of things may be such as to make it impossible, in practice, for human beings, to arrive at a permanent stopping place. This may be related to the Uncertainty Principle *rediscovered* in our time by Werner Heisenberg. See note 123, below; the text accompanying note 124, below. See also note 98, above. See as well note 64, above.

119. See Lucretius, *On the Nature of Things*, I, 958 sq.

120. See the book review cited in note 46, above. If one grasps a single cycle of Big Crunch and Big Bang, has one (in principle) grasped them all? See also note 114, above, note 126, below. See, as well, appendix K of this book.

121. See Lucretius, *On the Nature of Things*, I, 72 sq. See also *ibid.*, I, 536, V, 55. See, as well, the text accompanying note 72, above.

Still, it should be noticed that cosmologists may extrapolate the universe back to a point only in the sense of a *limit*. As long as the universe is finite, it makes sense to them to speak of the laws of physics. But they might not apply these laws to a genuine point.

122. Laurence Berns has observed, in commenting on this passage, "It may be possible to overrate demonstration (even in mathematics). As Leo Strauss once put it, 'Order and orderliness are very nice, but I prefer illumination.'" See note 72, above.

123. See, on the *ultron* that I posited three decades ago, Anastaplo, *The Artist as Thinker*, 252–53, 355; Anastaplo, "Thursday Afternoons," 127, n. 4. See also notes 3 and 118, above; note 126, below. See as well section VIII of appendix K in this book. *Is* my *ultron* akin to the classical "atom"? See as well the epigraph for appendix K in this book.

It remains to be seen what can be made of recent talk about the minimum *length* that things may have. Are the dimensions of the *ultron* thus conjectured? See, e.g., T. D. Lee, "Physics in Terms of Difference Equations," in J. de Boer, E. Dal, and O. Ulfbeck, eds. *The Lesson of Quantum Theory* (New York: Elsevier Science Publishers, 1986), 181. In any event, there *is* the question put in Plato's *Theaetetus* (203B): "But how can one state the elements of an element?"

124. See, e.g., *The Uncertainty Principle and Foundations of Quantum Mechanics: A Fifty Years' Survey*, William C. Price and Seymour S. Chissick, eds. (London: John Wiley & Sons, 1977). See also Malcolm Sharp, "Crosskey, Anastaplo, and Meiklejohn on the United States Constitution," 20 *University of Chicago Law School Record* 14, 18 n. 52 (1973). See as well notes 98 and 118, above.

125. See, e.g., the Anastaplo book review cited in note 85, above, 450. See also note 80, above. See, on the evidence for black holes, note 131, below.

126. See, on chaos, part 1 of this appendix, "On Beginnings." How is contemporary chaos theory related to the talk one hears from some physicists today about many "universes"? The physicists with whom I have discussed such talk have *not* been receptive to my suggestion that there "must" then be a universe of universes, which "regulates" and accounts for the relations among "universes." This notion is similar both to the notion of "a Rule of Rules" and to the notion of the *ultron* (note 123, above); section VIII of appendix K of this book (unless Chance is deemed sovereign?). See also notes 64, 69, 120, and 123, above; the text accompanying note 135, below.

127. See note 97, above. See also note 48, above. See, as well, appendix K.

128. See the text accompanying note 4, above.

129. See Anastaplo, *The Thinker as Artist*, 178. See also notes 72 and 117, above. See, as well, note 7, above. Of course, most people (including most mathematicians?) would insist that matter and numbers exist in somewhat different ways.

130. See Sacks, "The Lion and the Ass," 32–33. See also Plato, *Timaeus* 30C, 35B.

131. See Anastaplo, *The Artist as Thinker*, 252, note 77, above. See also section VIII of appendix K of this book. I was astonished to hear a Nobel Laureate in physics ask, in the course of one of the physics colloquia at the University of Chicago during the 2000–2001 academic year, whether the experiment just described provided *at last* some evidence that black holes actually exist. Evidently not! Scientists do wonder, from time to time, about what is really going on. See, on "alarming prospects" (and anticipations of the cosmic radiation background discovery and current inflation theory?), Erwin Schrödinger, "The Proper Vibrations of the Expanding Universe," 6 *Physica* 899 (October 1939).

132. See note 72, above. See also Anastaplo, *But Not Philosophy*, 337, n. 36.

133. This redirection of his thought is recalled by Socrates on his last day, as recorded in Plato's *Phaedo*. But had he not been obliged to think through a notion of the whole, however provisional, which allowed or accounted for the rationality, however limited it may be, found in the human things? See the text accompanying note 62, above.

134. See, on what Socrates did know, George Anastaplo, "Freedom of Speech and the First Amendment," 21 *Texas Tech Law Review* 1941, 1945f (1990).

135. Are we not accustomed to expect the laws of nature to work everywhere and always? See the text accompanying note 116, above. See also notes 49 and 126, above. See as well appendix K of this book.

136. See, e.g., Anastaplo, *The Artist as Thinker*, 265–66. See also the text accompanying note 62, above. See as well Anastaplo, *But Not Philosophy*, 99, 345.

137. See Hawking, *A Brief History of Time*, 37. Others can speak, with apparent confidence, of fifty billion *galaxies*, still others of a million million (and even more) galaxies.

138. See the text accompanying note 79, above. See also note 118, above.

139. See the text accompanying note 46, above. See also Klein, *Lectures and Essays*, 109f.

140. See Plato, *Phaedo*, 97B. See also note 62, above. Has some science fiction literature provided a better mythology than the cosmologists in that such literature may

make the cosmos *seem* more accessible for human beings? See the text accompanying note 74, above. See also as a restrained sample of what the tabloid press can do with modern cosmology, "The Great Debate," *Weekly World News*, May 5, 1998, 36f. See also Anastaplo, *But Not Philosophy*, 175. Compare William Burton, "The Beginnings of the End: The Omega Factor," *University of Chicago Magazine*, April 1998, 20f.

141. See, e.g., note 94, above.

142. See, e.g., Hellmut Fritzsche, "Of Things That Are Not," in *Law and Philosophy: The Practice of Theory*, John A. Murley, Robert L. Stone, and William T. Braithwaite, eds. (Athens: Ohio University Press, 1992), 3f. I emphasize "him" here because the University of Chicago Physics Colloquium that I am familiar with continues (as it has for decades) to be heavily dominated by males. It may well be that the female psyche is genetically more prudential in accounting for "how things are," so much so that modern theoretical physics is naturally avoided by women as woefully impractical (however useful its applications often are). Thus, there has not been, during the past half-century, in the movement by women into physics anything like the rush that there has been into such disciplines (once also regarded in this country as "naturally male") as law and medicine. See note 384 for this book. See also note 767 for this book. See as well note 74 for this book.

143. Strauss, *Jewish Philosophy and the Crisis of Modernity*, 471. See note 49, above. The concerns that scientists have about what is and is not established may be seen in the opening paragraphs of a famous paper by Albert Einstein and two colleagues:

> Any serious consideration of a physical theory must take into account the distinction between the objective reality, which is independent of any theory, and the physical concepts with which the theory operates. These concepts are intended to correspond with the objective reality, and by means of these concepts we picture this reality to ourselves.
>
> In attempting to judge the success of a physical theory, we may ask ourselves two questions: (1) "Is the theory correct?" and (2) "Is the description given by the theory complete?" It is only in the case in which positive answers may be given to both of these questions, that the concepts of the theory may be said to be satisfactory. The correctness of the theory is judged by the degree of agreement between the conclusions of the theory and human experience. This experience, which alone enables us to make inferences about reality, in physics takes the form of experiment and measurement. It is the second question that we wish to consider here, as applied to quantum mechanics.
>
> Whatever the meaning assigned to the term *complete*, the following requirement for a complete theory seems to be a necessary one: *every element of the physical reality must have a counterpart in the physical theory*. We shall call this the condition of completeness. The second question is thus easily answered, as soon as we are able to decide what are the elements of the physical reality.
>
> The elements of the physical reality cannot be determined by *a priori* philosophical considerations, but must be found by an appeal to results of experiments and measurements. A comprehensive definition of reality is, however, unnecessary for our purpose. We shall be satisfied with the following criterion, which we regard as reasonable. *If, without in any way disturbing a system, we can predict with certainty, (i.e., with probability equal to unity) the value of a physical quantity, then there exists an element of physical reality*

> *corresponding to this physical quantity*. It seems to us that this criterion, while far from exhausting all possible ways of recognizing a physical reality, at least provides us with one such way, whenever the conditions set down in it occur. Regarded not as a necessary, but merely as a sufficient, condition of reality, this criterion is in agreement with classical as well as quantum-mechanical ideas of reality. [A. Einstein, B. Podolsky, and N. Rosen, "Can Quantum-Mechanical Description of Physical Reality Be Considered Complete?" *Physical Review*, vol. 47, 777–78 (1935).]

We end this inquiry, for the time being, by reminding ourselves of the profound political and social consequences of conflicting presuppositions, even within the West, about human beginnings, as may be seen in the Bible (e.g., *Genesis* 2:18, 11:1 sq.), Plato (e.g., *Symposium* 189C sq.), Aristotle (e.g., *Politics* 1253al sq.), Lucretius, Hobbes/Locke, Jean-Jacques Rousseau, and Charles Darwin. These disparate consequences are reflected in, for example, the status of "individuality," ancient and modern. See Anastaplo, *The American Moralist*, 23. See also notes 62 and 114, above. Such differences may be related, at bottom, to questions about the proper, if not the natural, relation of soul to body. See note 72, above. See also appendix K of this book. These and like questions can become even more acute when Westerners and Easterners attempt to understand each other. See, for example, Anasatplo, *But Not Philosophy* (2002). It could be instructive to consider what the published reception, if any, is of my Commentary, *The Constitution of 1787* (Baltimore: Johns Hopkins University Press, 1989), which is scheduled to be published in China (in a Chinese-language edition) in late 2008.

Appendix G

Shakespeare's Bible*

And therefore the rich poets, as Homer, Chaucer, Shakespeare, and Raphael, have obviously no limits to their works except the limits of their lifetime, and resemble a mirror carried through the street, ready to render an image of every created thing.

Ralph Waldo Emerson

I

Shakespeare's solid use of the Bible is obvious. Many detailed assessments of that use are available. So extensive is the use that commentators can, with some plausibility, say such things as the following (William Burgess, *The Bible in Shakespeare* (Chicago: Winona Publishing Company, 1903), xiii):

> Shakespeare drank so deeply from the wells of Scripture that one may say, without any straining of the evidence, that without the Bible Shakespeare could not be. And if it were possible to suppress every copy of the sacred volume and obliterate its very existence as a book, the Bible in its essence and spirit, its great doctrines of infinite justice, mercy, love and redemption, as well as a vast store of its most precious sayings, would yet live in Shakespeare.

It is also obvious that since Shakespeare's plays draw heavily upon biblical stories, thought, and language, we (who are far less familiar with the Scriptures than Shakespeare's original audiences were) must miss a good deal upon returning to his plays. Nor is this likely to change: we cannot expect soon in the community at large a general revival of that awareness of and devotion to biblical matters which Shakespeare routinely drew upon.

Complicating an understanding, from the beginning, of Shakespeare's use of the Bible has been uncertainty as to what precisely his personal religious beliefs and allegiances were. Especially is this so if Shakespeare is recognized as an extraordinary prophet of a natural understanding of things.

Still, it should be noticed that the stories told in the plays were intended to make considerable sense on their own, no matter what level of information and sophistication there may happen to be in various members of the audience. This is not to deny that one's grasp of what is going on may be deepened by what one brings to a play. Nor is it to deny that one's grasp may, in some cases, be weakened by preconceptions and interests one may happen to have.

II

It should be instructive to illustrate what Shakespeare does with the Bible by examining the use made by him of one biblical character. It is convenient for our purpose on this occasion to take a well-known character who is mentioned almost two dozen times, usually quite briefly, in the New Testament. Our candidate for this exercise is Judas Iscariot, a character whose name is still in common usage in our language as a term of severe reproach. The most recent instance I have come upon was just yesterday, when it was reported that a former associate of the president was regarded as a Judas because of his failure to support the president unqualifiedly in a current controversy. (See Sandra Sobieraj, "Stephanopoulos' Comments Disappoint Loyalists," *Chicago Sun-Times*, February 4, 1998, 3. See also William Klassen, *Judas: Betrayer or Friend of Jesus* [Minneapolis: Fortress Press, 1996], 28f.)

We can be reminded of the biblical account of this man by turning to his entry in the *Encyclopedia Britanica*, which begins:

> *Judas Iscariot* (A.D. 30), one of the Twelve Apostles, notorious for betraying Jesus. Judas' surname is more probably a corruption of the Latin *sicarius* ("murderer" or "assassin") than an indication [as has long been believed] of family origin [or of the town from which he came], suggesting that he would have belonged to the Sicarii, the most radical Jewish group, some of whom were terrorists. Other than his apostleship, his betrayal, and his death, little else is revealed about Judas in the Gospels. Always the last in the list of the Apostles, he was their treasurer. *John* 12:6 introduces Judas' thievery by saying, ". . . as he had the money box he used to take what was put into it."

Whether the term "*betraying* Jesus" is to be preferred either to "*handing over* Jesus" or to "*turning in* Jesus" can be debated, but it is useful to prefer it on this occasion, since *betrayal* is what is assumed by Shakespeare's characters when they do refer to Judas Iscariot. The *Britannica* entry continues with both a description of Judas' most notorious act and suggestions about his motivation:

> He disclosed Jesus' whereabouts to the chief priests and elders for thirty pieces of silver. They provided the armed guard that he brought to the Garden of Gethsemane, near Jerusalem where Jesus went to pray with the other eleven Apostles after the Last Supper. There he identified Jesus with a kiss, addressing him as "master" [or, "rabbi"]. *Matthew* 26:14–16 and *John* 12:6 designate Judas' motive as avarice, but *Luke* 22:3–6 ascribes his action to the entrance of Satan into his body, paralleling *John* 13:27, where, after Judas took the bread of the Last Supper, "Satan entered into him." Jesus then says, "What you are going to do, do quickly." This is the culmination of *John* 6:70–71, which, after Jesus says "Did I not choose you, the Twelve, and one of you is a devil?" discloses that he meant "Judas the son of Simon Iscariot, for he, one of the Twelve, was to betray him."

We are then told:

> There are various traditions about Judas' death. According to *Matthew* 27:3–10, he repented after seeing Jesus condemned to death, then returned the silver and hanged himself (traditionally from the Judas tree). In *Acts* 1:18, he "bought a field with the reward of his wickedness, and falling headlong he burst open in the middle and all his bowels gushed out," implying that he threw himself down, rather than that he died accidentally.

That Judas Iscariot is an intriguing figure is testified to by the attempts that have been made for two millennia now to retell his story in a variety of ways. (See, e.g., Klassen, *Judas*, 38, 74.) I confess to having myself tried, several decades ago, to examine what the motivation could have been of a man who did what Judas evidently did.

That exploratory effort on my part took the form of a play, originally called *The First Christian*, but finally called *The Last Christian*. This shift in titles reflects the complications that await anyone who delves into this character, especially as one reflects upon the general refusal (understandable enough) to make any allowances for Judas. I considered, among other things, what the effect might be on an apparent traitor who is denied the "Christian" response to his conduct that he had yearned for, if not even anticipated. The superhuman effort required in loving one's enemies can become apparent in such circumstances. Did Judas' recourse to suicide testify to the inadequacy of any remorse he felt?

If I recall correctly, it was a painting of the betrayal by Judas that first got me to wondering about him, a painting (which I had seen in a European museum) of Judas tenderly kissing Jesus. (See, for example, Klassen, *Judas*, cover picture. See also *ibid.*, 107–8.) This, and his somewhat mysterious suicide after he learned of the condemnation of Jesus, moved me to do quite a bit of reading about how Judas has been regarded for two millennia—and why. If I also recall correctly, I was able to write this play while my wife (with however many children we had then) was off in Texas visiting her family—which can remind us, I guess, of the dalliances that husbands are capable of when their wives are elsewhere. (Perhaps I was supposed to be working at the time on my dissertation.)

Be all this as it may, the kiss and the evident remorse prompted me to speculate about what might have happened if Judas had seen himself obliged to play a part required for the initiation of cataclysmic events that would lead immediately to the proclamation of the Messiah, if not also to the Last Judgment. That is, one could (as a playwright) wonder whether Judas, as a particularly zealous disciple of Jesus, had tried to hasten the End of Time (perhaps even believing he had been designated by Jesus to do so), only to learn, too late, that he had made a dreadful, indeed fatal, miscalculation. (See, for indications of the range of interpretations available about the career of Judas Iscariot, the addendum to this appendix.)

III

Judas Iscariot is tricky to deal with in any artistic presentation. This may be seen in Shakespeare's *Love's Labor's Lost*. There, in scene ii of act V of that play, some more-or-less common folk are recruited to present, before an irrepressible audience, a series of Nine Worthies, famous characters of antiquity. One of these characters is Judas Maccabees, the Jewish patriot of almost two centuries before Jesus.

Unfortunately, the mischievous audience on the stage of this play-within-a-play insists upon regarding the designated actor not as Judas Maccabees, but rather as Judas Iscariot. This actor's protests and his efforts to correct them are to no avail—Judas Iscariot is referred to a half-dozen times in less than a page of script, so much so that this would-be actor is driven off the "stage," unable to complete the portrayal that he had intended to present of Judas Maccabees. (One can be reminded of the fatal mistaking, in Shakespeare's *Julius Caesar*, of Cinna the poet for Cinna the conspirator. One can also be reminded of the Artemus Ward story, "High-Handed Outrage at Utica." See Anastaplo, *The Amendments to the Constitution: A Commentary* [Baltimore: Johns Hopkins University Press, 1995], 166–67, 436.)

That the Jewish patriot can be derided so unmercifully in this play-within-a-play reflects, I suspect, the low status of Jews generally on the Elizabethan stage, if not in Christendom at large. This may be seen most dramatically, of course, in Shakespeare's *The Merchant of Venice*, with its unrelenting condemnation of a villain depicted as very much a Jew—Shylock—who fiendishly plots against a somewhat Christ-like Antonio. (See Hyam Maccoby, *Judas Iscariot and the Myth of Jewish Evil* (New York: The Free Press, 1992), 116; George Anastaplo, *On Trial: From Adam & Eve to O.J. Simpson* [Lanham, Md.: Lexington Books, 2004], 231.)

I am reminded, by our passage in *Love's Labor's Lost*, of something I was told long ago by one of the rabbis at Hillel House (on the University of Chicago campus). He said that there had once been serious consideration given to using the ancient name of *Judea* by which to call the country we now know as *Israel*, but that it was feared that this name would tend to remind the Christian world of Judas Iscariot. The opening paragraph of a recently published book is instructive here:

> It may seem a strange coincidence that of all Jesus's twelve disciples, the one whom the Gospel story singles out as a traitor bears the name of the Jewish people. The coincidence was not overlooked by Christian commentators, who saw it as a mysterious sign, by which the Judas-role of the Jews was divinely hinted at. I have taken this as the starting-point of a consideration of the part played by the character of Judas Iscariot in the history of Christian antisemitism. As the argument develops, the element of coincidence will tend to disappear, and it will become reasonably clear that Judas was chosen for a baleful but necessary mythological role precisely because of his name. [Maccoby, *Judas Iscariot and the Myth of Jewish Evil*, ix. See Klassen, *Judas*, 199–200.]

The wisdom of the reluctance to use the name *Judea* for the country of the Jews today is suggested by the determined effort in *Love's Labor's Lost* to transform the patriotic Judas Maccabees into the traitorous Judas Iscariot. This is, I am sorry to notice, *not* a transformation that Shakespeare himself seems determined to resist. (Even worse in this respect is what may be seen in Geoffrey Chaucer, as in the prologue to "The Prioress's Tale.")

There are even more prominent uses in Shakespeare's work of Judas Iscariot, the Apostle who can be readily identified as the man "that did betray the Best." (*The Winter's Tale*, I, ii, 418) One use may be seen in *Richard II*, where a desperate king sees himself, in effect, as a Christ-like figure who is betrayed by Judases—not just by the one in twelve that Jesus had to contend with, but rather by twelve thousand of them (IV, i, 168–72):

> Yet I well remember
> The favors of these men. Were they not mine?
> Did they not sometime cry, "All hail!" to me?
> So Judas did to Christ. But he, in twelve,
> Found truth in all but one; I in twelve thousand, none.

Then there is the echo of the Judas story in Shakespeare's *Macbeth*. Macbeth, who is reluctant to assassinate the gracious king who is his guest, finally gives himself the direction that Jesus had given to Judas, that he should do at once what he planned to do (I, vii, 1):

> If it were done, when 'tis done, then 'twere well
> It were done quickly.

It is obvious in these two plays, just as it is in various comments upon betrayal in other plays by Shakespeare, that there is expected to be in the audience an unqualified abhorrence of what Judas Iscariot did. The tradition here is well established and, as we have noticed, can be readily extended to Jews generally, as may be seen in medieval plays. Thus, long before Shakespeare, the Jew was routinely regarded as a betrayer. This is part of a Christian tradition that is pretty much taken for granted and drawn upon by Shakespeare and by others both before and after him, however humanely (if not even sympathetically) Shakespeare's Shylock is presented *up to a point*.

IV

Still another possible use—in some ways the most interesting use—of the Judas Iscariot story may be seen in Shakespeare's *Othello*. I say "possible" because there is among scholars an uncertainty, with respect to the texts we have, as to whether it *is* Judas who is being referred to in the passage I will be examining.

This use may be seen in Othello's next-to-last speech in the play, which is shortly after he has learned that he had been deceived by Iago into killing his innocent wife, Desdemona. This speech by Othello, which concludes with his fatally stabbing himself, includes these lines (V, ii, 353–58):

> Then must you speak
> Of one that loved not wisely but too well;
> Of one not easily jealous but, being wrought,
> Perplexed in the extreme; of one whose hand,
> Like the base Judean threw a pearl away
> Richer than all his tribe.

Many editors read "Indian" rather than "Judean" here. But one of the earliest editions does have "Judean"—and this seems to me to fit in nicely with what Othello says about throwing away a priceless pearl (which can remind an audience of the eternal salvation offered by Jesus). It fits in as well with what

Othello says in kissing Desdemona again as he dies after his awful discovery of what he has been duped into doing (V, ii, 369–70):

> I kissed thee ere I killed thee. No way but this,
> Killing myself, to die upon a kiss.

(See Roy W. Battenhouse, *Shakespearean Tragedy: Its Art and Its Christian Premises* (Bloomington: Indiana University Press, 1969), 94–102. I notice, in passing, that Othello, to the end, still does not know himself insofar as he believes he was *not* "easily jealous.")

It is evident throughout the play that Iago is Satanic in what seems to be the motiveless evil of his relentless effort so to infect the Judas-like Othello that he would destroy the somewhat innocent Christ-like Desdemona, a woman who remains forgiving of her killer to the end. Just as Judas is spoken of in the Gospels as having been corrupted by Satan (despite having been personally chosen by Jesus as one of the Twelve), so Othello's Iago can be spoken of in the play as the Devil. Perhaps indeed one can, because of this play, see even better than one might have seen before, the enormity (as well as perhaps the mystery) of what Judas did in his great betrayal.

V

The uses of the Judas Iscariot story by Shakespeare in *Richard II*, *Macbeth*, and perhaps *Othello* can be said to have sharpened the playwright's portraits of his characters. Also, the nature of the act of betrayal is thereby spelled out. In addition, there is an interesting possibility that one consequence of such uses can even be to promote our reconsideration, sometimes tacitly, of the biblical characters drawn upon. We need not assume that Shakespeare was always aware of this, or that he always did it deliberately. (Much the same, if not even more, can be said about what his characters are aware of in what they say.) That is, it may be poetic inspiration that is at work here, which is not always fully apparent to the artist. (See Plato, *Apology of Socrates*, 22A–C).

Take again, as an example, the artistic use of Judas Iscariot. There is no ambiguity in the most famous accounts about, or references to, him: his betrayal is informed, blatant, and deadly; he is widely, perhaps even uniquely, condemned. This is to be seen in artists of all kinds. Thus, in Dante Alighieri's *Divine Comedy*, Judas is at the very bottom of the Inferno, perpetually mangled by jaws of Satan with the other arch-betrayers, Brutus and Cassius. (We have a curious situation in John Milton's *Paradise Lost*, which finds Lucifer, or Satan, treated better by the poet than is Judas.)

Even so, we can wonder what happens to our sense of Judas when he provides a model for characters as somehow sympathetic as are Othello and Macbeth. I have already indicated that we may be moved to wonder, for example, what it was that Judas was "really" after—and what such elements in the story as his kiss and his suicide may mean.

That is, do we see Judas better after we watch Macbeth and Othello at work? What, we are obliged by the play to ask, *was* Othello "really" after, however jealous, deluded, and homicidal he may have been? Judas is, in some ways, an incomprehensible character, so much so that it has even been asked whether Judas was a betrayer or a friend of Jesus—so much a friend that he sacrificed himself (and his long-term reputation, if not also eternal bliss) in order to drive forward the grand design about which he had learned from his master. (See, for example, Klassen, *Judas: Betrayer or Friend of Jesus*.)

VI

Even so, it should at once be added that whatever some artists (down to our day) have tried to do on Judas' behalf, we need not assume that Shakespeare himself aimed to rehabilitate the Great Betrayer. But, it might be asked, does Shakespeare want us at least to reassess the merits of betrayed innocence (whether in the form of Richard II or Macbeth's Duncan or Othello's Desdemona, if not also in such characters as Cordelia in *King Lear* and Ophelia in *Hamlet*)? (This is a question that does *not* depend upon the substitution of *Judean* for *Indian* in our *Othello* passage.)

There are obvious problems with Richard II: he can easily be seen as too self-centered, if not even as too good for this world. That is, he may not be fit to rule—and so he should be set aside. (Compare Edgar in *King Lear*.) There are serious problems, too, with the mild Duncan in *Macbeth*; it seems to happen again and again, because of that king's trusting spirit, that rebels try to take advantage of him, for which his country pays along with him. (His son Malcolm is much shrewder, more wary, and hence safer than Duncan had been—and thus better for Scotland.)

But what about the Christ-like Desdemona? Should not we have serious reservations about how she treats her family and perhaps her fellow citizens in Venice, contributing to the premature death of her father? This eventually bears upon how far Othello can trust her. Thus, her virtue is compromised, not in the way that Iago claims, but still in an important respect, which can subvert enduring personal relations. These judgments can be consistent with the approval exhibited by "gentle Will" for generous (but firm) forgiveness—as by Prospero in *The Tempest* and by Orlando in *As You Like It*. (Compare the almost sadistic treatment of the murderous Shylock by Portia despite her great "quality of mercy" speech in *The Merchant of Venice*.)

We need not go so far as to suggest that any reservations we develop about more or less "saintly" characters such as Richard II, Duncan, and Desdemona require that we also have reservations about Jesus himself. Jesus is, in these matters, a special case, for obvious reasons. It is not necessary to repudiate *him* in order to notice that imitators of Christ should take account of the circumstances in which hardly-divine human beings find themselves. When the limitations of human beings are truly recognized, Shakespeare can usefully be taken to argue, Jesus may be looked at afresh and hence *seen* for the first time.

VII

Still, it *can* be said that the play's the thing, with all the implications which I have sketched remaining secondary (including reconsideration of the long-established stories and characters that are used by the playwright). Certainly, the effectiveness of the play as drama is necessary if anything else of note is to come of any offering by the playwright.

That effectiveness does depend, in part, upon the language and spiritual resources that must be drawn upon in audiences. Their prejudices and expectations have to be respected, even by those playwrights who would undertake to refine prejudices and redirect expectations. Shakespeare knew that his plays necessarily drew upon the Christian heritage—and that they would tend to be interpreted one way rather than another because of that heritage

Traumatic events do happen to human beings, perhaps again and again, suggesting common patterns. And people naturally try to invest what may be universal stories with majesty and meaning. Since there are recurring patterns in the experiences of the human race, it may be more efficient, if not also more interesting, to work primarily with the archetypes familiar in one's tradition. Shakespeare drew for this purpose upon the biblical heritage, less so perhaps upon the Classical principles that he adapted to Christian settings.

If we are not nourished by thoughtful dramas grounded in a solid moral sense, we will be caught up by more and more sensational stories, in our public life as well as in our theater. Such sensationalism tends to feed upon itself, misleading and corrupting even as it disappoints and impoverishes its audiences.

Shakespeare does continue to have a profound effect, even though less directly perhaps than formerly. He has instilled in the English language various salutary influences from the Bible and from the Classical world, as well as from English constitutional history which is itself illuminated by stories from the Roman Republic, including the story of Brutus and Cassius as martyrs for the republican cause. In this and other ways he may remain essential both to the Anglo-American tradition of responsible liberty and to the most satisfying soul-searching among us.

ADDENDUM

The three passages set forth here suggest the range of interpretations available about the career of Judas Iscariot.

Our first passage is taken from an appendix in *The Holy Bible in Giant Print* (Nashville: Crusade Bible Publishers, 1973), 1842:

> Judas is representative of life and our choice of redemption or destruction.
>
> Judas probably had high hopes that Jesus would establish an "earthly kingdom," which would overthrow the Roman rule.
>
> No doubt, Judas revealed high qualities or he would not have been chosen as a disciple. He was trusted enough to be chosen as the treasurer of the group—distributing the money, to provide for food and rooms to sleep during their travels.
>
> At some point during his spiritual life, greed asserted itself and overcame his spiritual attributes.
>
> At last, Judas betrayed Jesus for 30 pieces of silver. Because Jesus had saved so many others, he probably felt confident that Christ would redeem himself. Finally realizing that he was not going to perform a miracle in his own behalf, he repented and tried to return the silver to secure Jesus' release.
>
> When the chief priests and elders rejected his pleas, Judas was filled with remorse and hanged himself.

Indeed, the passage just quoted, of a Protestant inclination, includes within itself a range of interpretations about Judas.

Our second passage, with even more interpretations, is taken from *The Catholic Encyclopedia* (New York: Robert Appleton Co., 1910), VIII, 541 ("Judas Iscariot" entry):

> But these textual difficulties and questions of detail fade into insignificance beside the great moral problem presented by the fall and treachery of Judas. In a very true sense, all sin is a mystery. And the difficulty is greater with the greatness of the guilt, with the smallness of the motive for doing wrong, and with the measure of the knowledge and graces vouchsafed to the offender. In every way the treachery of Judas would seem to be the most mysterious and unintelligible of sins. For how could one chosen as a disciple, and enjoying the grace of the Apostolate and the privilege of intimate friendship with the Divine Master, be tempted to such gross ingratitude for such a paltry price? And the difficulty is

greater when it is remembered that the Master thus basely betrayed was not hard and stern, but a Lord of loving kindness and compassion. Looked at in any light the crime is so incredible, both in itself and in all its circumstances, that it is no wonder that many attempts have been made to give some more intelligible explanation of its origin and motives, and, from the wild dreams of ancient heretics to the bold speculations of modern critics, the problem presented by Judas and his treachery has been the subject of strange and startling theories. As a traitor naturally excites a peculiarly violent hatred, especially among those devoted to the cause or person betrayed, it was only natural that Christians should regard Judas with loathing, and, if it were possible, paint him blacker than he was by allowing him no good qualities at all. This would be an extreme view which, in some respects, lessens the difficulty. For if it be supposed that he never really believed, if he was a false disciple from the first, or, as the Apocryphal Arabic Gospel of the Infancy has it, was possessed by Satan even in his childhood, he would not have felt the holy influence of Christ or enjoyed the light and spiritual gifts of the Apostolate.

At the opposite extreme is the strange view held by an early Gnostic sect known as the Cainites described by St. Irenaeus (*Adv. Haer.*, I, c. ult.), and more fully by Tertullian (*Praesc, haeretic.*, xlvii), and St. Epihanius (*Haeres*, xxxviii). Certain of these heretics, whose opinion has been revived by some modern writers in a more plausible form, maintained that Judas was really enlightened, and acted as he did in order that mankind might be redeemed by the death of Christ. For this reason they regarded him as worthy of gratitude and veneration. In the modern version of this theory it is suggested that Judas, who in common with other disciples looked for a temporal kingdom of the Messiah, did not anticipate the death of Christ, but wished to precipitate a crisis and hasten the hour of triumph, thinking that the arrest would provoke a rising of the people who would set Him free and place Him on the throne. In support of this they point to the fact that, when he found that Christ was condemned and given up to the Romans, he immediately repented of what he had done. But, as [one critic] remarks, this repentance does not prove that the result had not been foreseen. For murderers, who have killed their victims with deliberate design, are often moved to remorse when the deed is actually done. A Catholic in any case cannot view these theories with favour since they are plainly repugnant to the text of Scripture and the interpretation of tradition. However difficult it may be to understand, we cannot question the guilt of Judas. On the other hand we cannot take the opposite view of those who would deny that he was once a real disciple. For, in the first place, this view seems hard to reconcile with the fact that he was chosen by Christ to be one of the Twelve. This choice, it may be safely said, implies some good qualities and the gift of no mean graces.

But, apart from this consideration, it may be urged that in exaggerating the original malice of Judas, or denying that there was even any good in him, we minimize or miss the lesson of his fall. The examples of the saints are lost on us if we think of them as beings of another order without our human weaknesses. And in the same way it is a grave mistake to think of Judas as a demon without any elements of goodness and grace. In his fall is left a warning that even the great grace of the Apostolate and the familiar friendship of Jesus may be of no avail to one who is unfaithful. And, though nothing should be allowed to palliate the guilt of the great betrayal, it may become more intelligible if we think of it as the outcome of gradual failing in lesser things. So again the repentance may be taken to imply that the traitor had deceived himself by a false hope that after all Christ might pass through the midst of His enemies as He had done before at the brow of the mountain. And though the circumstances of the death of the traitor give too much reason to fear the worst, the Sacred Text does not distinctly reject the possibility of real repentance. And Origen strangely supposed that Judas hanged himself in order to seek Christ in the other world and ask His pardon (*In Matt.*, tract. xxxv).

Our third passage is taken from D. H. Lawrence, *Apocalypse* (New York: Viking Press, 1932), 27:

Judas had to betray Jesus to the powers that be, because of the denial and subterfuge inherent in Jesus's teachings. Jesus took up the position of the pure individual, even with his disciples. He did not *really* mix with them, or even really work or act with them. *He was alone all the time*. He puzzled them utterly, and in some part of them, he let them down. He refused to be their physical power-lord. The power-homage in a man like Judas felt itself betrayed! So it betrayed back again: with a kiss. And in the same way *Revelation* had to be included in the New Testament, to give the death kiss to the Gospels.

NOTE

*This talk was given to the Women's Society of the Hyde Park Union Church, Chicago, February 5, 1998. The epigraph is taken from Ralph Waldo Emerson, *The Poet*.

Appendix H

Countdown to the Millennium: A Look at *The Revelation of St. John the Divine**

Between what matters and what seems to matter, how should the world we know judge wisely?

E. C. Bentley

I

"The reader faced for the first time with the *Book of Revelation*," a Jesuit priest observed in 1993, "is understandably bewildered." (Daniel J. Harrington, S.J., *Revelation* (Collegeville, Minn.: The Liturgical Press, 1993), xiii.) He then added (*ibid.*):

> This book, more than any other New Testament writing, demands commentary. All the more urgently, indeed, as approach of the magical year 2000 fuels expectations of the End. Fundamentalist interest in *Revelation* is bound to heighten during this last decade of our Second Christian millennium.

Among the multitude of biblical commentaries available here is a conservative Protestant reference book that begins its entry on this text, perhaps the most elusive text in the New Testament, with this information (*Zondervan Bible Dictionary*, ed. Merrill C. Tenney (Grand Rapids, Mich.: Zondervan Publishing House, 1963), 721):

> *Revelation, Book of the* (Greek *apocalypses, an unveiling*), sometimes called *The Apocalypse*, is the last book of the Bible and the only book of the New Testament that is exclusively prophetic in character. It belongs to the class of apocalyptic literature in which the divine message is conveyed by visions and

> dreams. . . . The title which the book itself assumes (1:1) may mean either "the revelation which Christ possesses and imparts," or "the unveiling of the person of Christ." Grammatically, the former is preferable, for this text states that God gave this disclosure to Christ that He might impart it to His servants.

The author of *Revelation*, a text evidently written late in the first century of the Christian era, was once believed to have been that John who was one of the twelve disciples of Jesus. Scholars now tend to believe that he was "a well-known character among the churches of Asia Minor." (*Ibid.*) Little seems to be known about him aside from what is indicated in this book. It is believed that he was quite elderly, perhaps even in his nineties, when he finished *Revelation*.

An outline of the *Book of the Revelation of St. John the Divine* introduces us to its contents in this fashion (*ibid.*, 722):

> Introduction: The Return of Christ 1:1–8
> I. Christ, the Critic of the Churches 1:9–3:22
> II. Christ, the Controller of Destiny 4:1–16:21
> III. Christ, the Conqueror of Evil 17:1–21:8
> IV. Christ, the Consummator of Hope 21:9–22:5
> Epilogue: Appeal and Invitation 22:6–21

This outline is spelled out with this account (*ibid.*):

> *Revelation* contains four great visions, each of which is introduced by the phrase "in the spirit" (1:10; 4:2; 17:3; 21:10). Each of these visions locates the seer in a different place, each contains a distinctive picture of Christ, and each advances the action significantly toward its goal. The first vision (1:9–3:22) pictures Him as the critic of the churches, who commends their virtues and condemns their vices in the light of His virtues. The second vision (4:1–16:21) deals with the progressive series of seals, trumpets and bowls, which mark the judgment of God upon a world dominated by evil. The third vision (17:1–21:8) depicts the overthrow of evil society, religion, and government in the destruction of Babylon and the defeat of the beast and his armies by the victorious Christ. The last vision (21:9–22:5) is the establishment of the city of God, the eternal destiny of His people. The book closes with an exhortation to readiness for the return of Christ.

The reader can be reassured here and there that all this is not simply the wild flight of a pathological imagination that it is sometimes taken to be: he is reassured, for example, by the discipline with which the "four great visions" are ordered, insofar as each *is* "introduced by the phrase 'in the spirit.'" Also reassuring, in a way, is the evident reliance by the author upon the *Book of Daniel* as his model in the Hebrew Bible. (Among the memorable stories in *Daniel* is that of Nebuchadnezzar.)

Indeed, much of this fairly short *Book of Revelation* (to say nothing of the entire New Testament) is incomprehensible without at least an awareness of the Jewish things that are repeatedly drawn upon. Mystifying and exasperating as *Revelation* may be, it would be much more so without the reader's sense of its Jewish roots and presuppositions. Even so, no interpretation of it is likely to be definitive for long. Thus, the supposed targets of the most vigorous criticism recorded in the book shift from age to age: it seems once to have been the Roman Empire (characterized as the Harlot of Babylon); at another time, it was the Roman Catholic Church; and still later, it has been modern secularism.

My own sense of how this book is generally regarded was reinforced by a conversation I had on the Illinois Central [Metra] commuter train two days ago. I took advantage of the opportunity available by seating myself next to an elderly African-American woman who was reading a well-thumbed Bible. It was soon evident that this lively woman knew the Bible well and had even annotated parts of it in her own hand. Revelation, she conceded, she found difficult; it is not one of her favorite books. Still, she *had* studied the book, being particularly intrigued by its notion of "End Time." But, she at once added, that definitely does not mean the year 2000; there must be, she pointed out, a number of signs before the End Time comes—and those signs have not yet appeared. (She, by the way, does consider the author to be the John of the original Twelve.) I did not have time to ask her what she believed that the author "actually" saw and heard. But I did talk to her enough to suspect that she herself probably ranked *among the majority* described in a poll last year that has been described in this way (Thomas Hargrove and Joe Bernt, "15 percent of Americans expect doomsday soon," *Chicago Sun-Times*, December 30, 1998, 24):

> A majority of Americans believe that the world as we know it will come to apocalypse as predicted in the Bible, a survey indicates.
>
> But despite the predictions of doomsday-cults fixated on the coming of a new millennium, Americans don't think it will happen soon, according to a poll of 1,027 adults conducted by Scripps Howard News Service and Ohio University.
>
> Most Americans discount imminent end-of-the-world predictions as irrational. The survey found that 15 percent said they believe it is either "very likely" or "somewhat likely" that "the arrival of the new millennium means that the world will come to an end."
>
> But the United States also is the industrialized world's most intensely religious nation, according both to church membership rates and public opinion polls.

The poll told respondents: "The *Book of Revelation* in the Christian Bible makes a prediction that someday the world, as we know it, will be drastically changed by an act of God. Do you, generally, believe in this prediction?"

Seventy-two percent said they believe this Biblical prophecy, 24 percent said they do not, and 4 percent were uncertain.

The poll found that the relatively small number of Americans who believe that the millennium could bring an apocalypse are more concentrated among young adults, people who have not completed a high school education, people in very low-income households, and churchgoers who believe they are spiritually "born again."

But belief that the world's demise will come soon was a minority opinion for all of these groups. [See George Anastaplo, "The Moral Majority," in *The American Moralist* (Athens, Ohio: Ohio University Press, 1992), 327.]

One remarkable feature of Christianity is the extent to which many of its adherents have been guided by *writings* (not merely by an oral tradition) that they *personally* study. My lady on the train conceded that the *Book of Revelation* does not provide any guidance for her, even though she is quite familiar with it. She added that it is to the *Book of Psalms* that she goes most often to learn how she should live.

Another remarkable feature of Christianity, also evident in my fellow passenger, has been the shaping of the sensibilities of its adherents by the notion of End Time. This is a religion that, for two thousand years now, has had looming over it the expectation that "the end is near." This began in its first generation, it seems, with many among the earliest Christians believing that the Second Coming would be seen during the lifetime of some then living. This kind of expectation has been heightened from time to time by Millennial movements stimulated either by special dates (such as the year 1000) or by persuasive prophets (such as William Miller, in the United States, who dramatized the years 1843 and 1844). *Millennium*, we are told by our reference book (*Zondervan Pictorial Bible Dictionary*, 533) is the Latin word for "thousand years." "It comes," we are then told,

from *Revelation* 20:1–15, where a certain period of a "thousand years" is mentioned six times. During this period (1) Satan is "bound" with a "great chain," "locked up" and "sealed" in "the abyss," so that he cannot "deceive the nations;" (2) persons designated as "martyrs" who have been "beheaded," "live" and "reign with Christ."

The "living" of the beheaded persons is declared (by synecdoche) to be "the first resurrection," that is, the resurrection of "those that are Christ's" (1 *Corinthians* 15:23) in contrast with the "living" of "the rest of the dead." "The rest of the dead" did not "live" until the end of the millennial period. After this

> period all the rest of the dead, without exception, are raised to stand before the "great white throne" of God.

That will be the occasion for the Last Judgment, the prospect which continually testifies to the belief that the universe as a whole is neither arbitrarily ruled nor chance-ridden but rather is governed by eternal (and knowable) standards of right and wrong, of good and bad. Contributing to the End Time perspective is the parting quotation from the Lord Jesus, in the next-to-last verse of the *Book of the Revelation*: "Surely I come quickly." (22:20). These are presented as Jesus' very last words in the New Testament.

II

Shortly before these last words there is (also in the closing chapter of the *Book of Revelation*) the statement (again from Jesus): "Behold, I come quickly." (*Revelation* 22:7) A half-dozen verses later, that is expanded into this declaration (*Revelation* 22:12–13):

> And, behold, I come quickly; and my reward *is* with me, to give to every man according as his work shall be. I am Alpha and Omega, the beginning and the end, the first and the last.

Such talk, it can be said, naturally leads some readers to a "countdown," even though it is emphasized in this book and elsewhere in the Bible that there is no way of knowing when *the* end will come. A countdown is a form of numbering—and numbers themselves are made much of in *Revelation*. Much of what I will say on this occasion will work from the numbers with which this book, if not the world itself, is filled.

Among the numbers that figure prominently in this book are 1, 3, 4, 7, 12, 1000, and 144,000. Perhaps the most conspicuous number in the text is 7: there are repeated references to the seven churches, the seven seals, the seven trumpets, etc. The importance of 7 had been established long before in the Hebrew Bible, where it is evidently taken to signify completion, if not even perfection and the divine. As to the numbers just listed, I will say much more about one of them, 1000, as well as about two other numbers that have not yet been mentioned by me and that may indeed be in principle unmentionable, whatever I may seem to say about them. The number 1000 is perhaps the one that is most often associated in the public mind with the *Book of the Revelation*.

A few days before my illuminating conversation with my fellow Illinois Central commuter, I had pursued my *Revelation* inquiry with two distinguished physicists on the University of Chicago campus. I approached them separately, asking each in turn: "Does the number 1000 do anything for you?" Each of these men was firm in dismissing 1000 as of no significance for the physicist. When I went on to ask what number, if any, *was* significant, both of them answered (independent of each other), 137. This number, I was told, is the reciprocal of the fine-structure constant and seems to be critical to quantum-theory accounts of the electrons at the foundation of matter.

The lack of interest in 1000 reflects a substantial change in what can be called "the world view" of physicists—for, as we shall see, that was a number that very much mattered (or so it seemed) to perhaps the greatest of physicists thus far, Isaac Newton. Of course, although 1000 no longer means much if anything to physicists, they do make much of *billions* (whether in miles or in years or even in galaxies). And one of my physicists recalled that a distinguished predecessor, early in this century had made much of 10^{40} (ten to the fortieth power): that was, he had "figured out," the number of atoms in the universe. It could thereafter be recorded, in 1938, that it was "said that there are 10^{77} individual atoms in the universe." I gather that a few more atoms have been found since then. (See, e.g., F. W. Westaway, *Obsessions and Convictions of the Human Intellect* (London: Blackie & Sons, 1938), 325; Sir A. S. Eddington, *Fundamental Theory* (Cambridge: Cambridge University Press, 1949), 105, 216, 265f; C. W. Kilmister, *Eddington's Search for a Fundamental Theory: A Key to the Universe* (Cambridge: University Press, 1994), xi, 4f, 113f, 124f, 146f, 189–90, 198 ("the modern observed number [the fine-structure constant] is 137.036 (to three places)"), 200f ("the 'number of particles in the universe:' At first sight it seems an outrageous claim to be able to calculate such a number"), 214, 231. See also Eric B. Norman, "Are Fundamental Constants Really Constant?" 54 *American Journal of Physics* 317 (1986).)

However cosmic the *Book of the Revelation* may be, it does begin with parochial concerns: the condition and prospects of seven churches in Asia Minor (Ephesus, Smyrna, Pergamos, Thyatria, Sardis, Philadelphia, and Laodicea). Each church is diagnosed and prescribed for in turn. Particularly noteworthy here is not what happens to be said about the churches, but rather the reported fact that it was Jesus himself who thus concerned himself with particular churches. It would be worth investigating whether there is a Christian community in any of these seven places today—and how they regard what could be an overwhelming fact, that the resurrected Jesus had, from Heaven, personally ministered to each of them in turn in their early years.

Another number should be noticed before we turn to the three numbers that we will examine at greater length—and that number has to do with the length of the *Book of the Revelation*: it runs about twenty pages in standard editions of the Bible, making it clearly the shortest of the non-epistolary books of the New Testament. (That is, it is shorter than the four Gospels and the *Book of Acts*. It is, in fact, just about the same length as the *Book of Daniel* in the Hebrew Bible, that book of which the author of *Revelation* is very much aware.)

III

The first of the three numbers we will be examining can be said to be only one-half of a number (just as the second of our numbers can be said to be only two-thirds of a number). I draw here upon what is said in *Revelation* 8:1.

> And when [the Lamb] had opened the seventh seal, there was silence in heaven about the space of half an hour.

This silence—which is in Heaven only, not worldwide—is startling, especially in so "noisy" a book as *Revelation*. (How long a half-hour was then is subject to some debate; it could even be an hour and a half of our time. The book itself can be read in a half-hour.) But however long it was taken to be, is it not an odd pause in the account? Adela Yarbro Collins, of the University of Chicago Divinity School, observes that "after all this turmoil," the silence following upon the opening of the seventh seal is "the most stunning moment in the whole book." She then adds: "It is a prelude to the woes that are to come after the seventh seal is opened." ("Apocalypse Now," *U.S. Catholic*, January 1995, vol. 60, no. 1, 14.)

It is as if the biblical author, if not Heaven itself, must catch a breath before being able to go on. There are, it seems, precedents in the Hebrew Bible for such pauses, designed to dramatize the importance of what is about to be said or done. One can imagine human beings silenced thus, but it *can* seem odd that the Heavenly Host should be immobilized in this way, especially since the account had been so aggressive theretofore. Almost everything else in the book, it seems, is motion, noise, struggle, and upheaval.

Even so, we have in this silence—and so brief a silence at that—a graphic reminder of something evident again and again in this book, that much in the account is keyed to human dimensions, in time, in space, and, above all, in concerns. One cannot help but wonder how this account, which is keyed to the earth with its "attendant" heavenly bodies, is affected by the phenomenal (and, in some ways, unbelievable) expansion of the universe we have witnessed in the twentieth century.

Perhaps it is inevitable that the matters described in *Revelation* have to be tailored to human dimensions if they are to "engage" the reader. This is nicely illustrated by an exchange I had, a few months ago, with the archbishop of Milwaukee when he visited the University of Chicago campus to talk about Gregorian chants. I asked him, during the reception, what the music was that was reported in *Revelation* to have been sung on high. He did not know, which was, I suppose, a reasonable enough answer. But when I pressed him to guess, he said that it must have been Mozart. (A Protestant musician I have similarly queried has nominated Bach.)

Two interpretations of the silence in the opening verse of the eighth chapter of *Revelation* illustrate the varied ways that this entire book has been interpreted by learned scholars. The following report is of a position that is representative of the more restrained approach (Steve Gregg, *Revelation: Four Views* (Nashville: Thomas Nelson Publishers, 1997), 138):

> Albert Barnes writes that the half-hour silence was for effect to mark the solemnity of the events about to be reported, i.e., those resulting from the sounding of the seven trumpets (chs. 8–11). These events follow chronologically after those recorded in the earlier visions [in *Revelation*]. "Of course, this is a symbolical representation, and is designed not to represent a pause in the agents themselves, but only the impressive and fearful nature of the events which are now to be disclosed."

This "of course" is instructive: to regard this merely as "a symbolical representation" dissipates the stunning effect that the passage can have on the unexpecting reader.

A different way of avoiding the effect of an actual silence may be seen in another report (Gregg, *Revelation*, 138):

> Elliott identifies this *silence* with the short period during which the 144,000 were sealed in the previous chapter. It represents the brief interval between the opening of the seventh seal and the first barbarian invasion to be seen in verse 7. This interval is thought to be "the seventy years that intervened between Constantine's victory over Licinius, followed by the dissolution of the pagan heavens, A.D. 324, and Alaric's revolt and the invasion of the empire, consequent on the death of Theodosius, A.D. 395." Elliott calculates that *half an hour* in heaven is precisely equivalent to seventy years of Roman history.

This calculation by Elliott is but a sample of how the history of the world has been found, again and again, in the *Book of the Revelation*.

Still another way of understanding this half-hour of silence is to consider it a guide to how much time there is available for anyone who, on an occasion such as this, might want to talk about the *Book of the Revelation*. That would indeed be a parochial reading of the text.

IV

The second of our three numbers, I have suggested, can be said to be only two-thirds of a number: I refer, of course, to the notorious figure, 666. This is found in *Revelation* 13:18:

> Here is wisdom. Let him that hath understanding count the number of the beast: for it is the number of a man; and this number is Six hundred threescore and six.

If this *is* recognized as two-thirds of the dominant 1000, one might well wonder where the other one-third (or about 333) is.

The suggestions that have been made across the millennia about what or, more precisely, *who* this number (666) stands for are legion, down to our day (with even a recent president of the United States thus designated on the basis of a rather superficial reckoning). An entry in the *Catholic Encyclopedia* reminds us of what can be elicited here (vol. 1, 598):

> The Seer has marked the beast with the number 666. His purpose was that by this number people may know it. "He that has understanding, let him count the number of the beast. For it is the number of a man, and his number is six hundred and sixty-six." A human number, i.e., intelligible by the common rules of investigation. We have here an instance of Jewish gematria. Its object is to conceal a name by substituting for it a cipher of equal numerical value to the letters composing it. For a long time interpreters tried to decipher the number 666 by means of the Greek alphabet. . . . Their efforts have yielded no satisfactory result. Better success has been obtained by using the Hebrew alphabet. Many scholars have come to the conclusion that Nero is meant. For when the name "Nero Caesar" is spelled with Hebrew letters . . . , it yields the cipher 666.

This is a somewhat simplified account of how Greek, Latin, and Hebrew were *combined* to get to *Nero Caesar*. The same conclusion is more simply attained if, instead of 666, the text should read 616—which it evidently does in one or more ancient manuscripts. Of course, one wonders in these matters which comes first, the number or the name. (By the way, the name of Jesus in such a calculation, I am told, can come out as 888).

The use of *Nero* here is understandable if only because of his notorious persecution of Christians. He had died before the book was written, it seems, but he was believed by some either not to have died or to be capable of being resurrected in order to martyr the pious. The *Catholic Encyclopedia* also reports (vol. 1, 598):

> It would be alike wearisome and useless to enumerate even the more prominent applications made of the *Apocalypse* [of the New Testament]. Racial hatred and

> religious rancour have at all times found in its vision suitable and gratifying matter. Such persons as Mahomet, the Pope, Napoleon, etc., have been in turn identified with the beast and the harlot [of Babylon]. To the "reformers" particularly the *Apocalypse* was an inexhaustible quarry where to dig for invectives that they might hurl them against the Roman [Catholic] hierarchy.

(The kind of fanciful "calculation" that can be done in these matters, with a focus instead on the State of Israel, was exhibited recently in the bestselling book, *The Bible Code*.) Among the "villains" detected by interpreters of *Revelation*, we have noticed, has been the Roman Empire, which was succeeded for this purpose in some quarters by the Roman Catholic Church.

However questionable much of what is done in these matters may be, there can be no question, upon examining the *Book of the Revelation* along with the rest of the New Testament, but that the Christian view of the world *is* profoundly Jewish. This can lead one to suspect that if Judaism should ever go, Christianity may not be far behind. It should again be noticed, of course, that the Christian view of the world is also profoundly Greek. The Greek approach to divine matters is reflected in counsel offered by the Platonic Plutarch in the course of a survey of Egyptian religious doctrines and practices (in sections 67 and 68 (377–78) of his essay, *On Isis and Osiris*):

> For God is not something without mind or soul, nor is he subservient to men. Consequently we have regarded as gods the beings who use the products of nature and bestow then upon us, providing us with them constantly and sufficiently; nor do we regard the gods as different among different peoples nor as barbarian and Greek and as southern and northern. But just as the sun, moon, heaven, earth and sea are common to all, though they are given various names by the varying peoples, so it is with the one reason (*logos*) which orders these things and the one providence which has charge of them, and the assistant powers which are assigned to everything: they are given different honours and modes of address among different peoples according to custom, and they use hallowed symbols, some of which are obscure and others clearer, directing the thought towards the divine, though not without danger. For some, erring completely, have slipped into superstition, and others, shunning it like a marsh, have unwittingly fallen in turn over the precipice of atheism.
>
> Therefore in these matters above all we should take as a guide into the mysteries the understanding which philosophy gives, and reflect devoutly on everything said and enacted. Theodorus said that when he proffered his teachings with the right hand, some of his hearers received them with the left. Let us not make the similar mistake of putting a different construction on what established custom has rightly ordered concerning the sacrifices and festivals. For one may assume even from those rites themselves that they are all to be referred to a rational purpose. [See also Plutarch, *On Isis and Osiris*, Section 58 (374–75).]

V

Our third number is, it can be said, the completion of numbers, 1000. Beyond 1000, that is, no other number matters. Thus, the 144,000 of which much is sometimes made is nothing more than 1000 extended, so to speak, by the square of the 12 of the tribes of Israel. Critical to the emergence of 1000 is a vision recorded in chapter 20 of *Revelation*. Here is how this vision has been described (Frederick J. Murphy, *Fallen Is Babylon: The Revelation to John* (Harrisburg, Penn.: Trinity Press International, 1998), 397):

> This vision is in two parts. The first (20:4–6) concerns the thousand-year reign of the messiah, whose reign the martyrs share. The second concerns the release of Satan at the end of the thousand years and his assault on Christ and his people, followed by Satan's defeat and ultimate punishment (20:7–10). Because the messianic reign lasts a thousand years, it is often called the millennium, which, as stated earlier, comes from the Latin words for "thousand," *mille*, and "year," *annus*.

It is the millennium that we [in the year 1999] hear so much of these days—but our millennium (whether the one just concluding or the one coming in a year or two, depending on how one counts) is quite different from the millennium described in chapter 20 of *Revelation*, however much that description has dramatized the notion of *millennium* itself. The biblical countdown begins with a starting point that is *not* connected in the biblical account with any anniversary of either the birth or the resurrection of Jesus. There have been various "countdowns" to the supposed chapter 20 millennium, and there are likely to be many more, with only a few of those keyed to one or two thousand-year intervals since any birth or resurrection. Inasmuch as this is a much less pious time, at least in the Western world, than the time around the year 1000, the most publicized opening today to the mysteries in connection with a millennium takes the form of the Y2K concern: this is a tame, technological version of the much more apocalyptic visions of the past. (The contemporary tameness is rather curious, in part because this is the first time that the human race can be said to have *experienced* the passage of a millennium from its beginning to its ending. "We" did not experience the thousand years leading up to the year 1000, for "we" were not generally aware of the beginning of *that* millennium.)

I return for some useful comments to the scholar I have just quoted (Murphy, *Fallen Is Babylon*, 397):

> Considering the amount of attention the thousand-year reign of Jesus has engendered, one might think that it is the most important part of *Revelation*. Yet it

> occupies only three verses out of the entire book. This reign is not the book's climax. It is only a step along the way to the true climax, contained in chapters 21 and 22. The millennial kingdom has received an amount of attention disproportionate to its place in *Revelation*. . . . At the same time, the millennium does play an important role in the sequence of events leading to the final consummation. Crucial to its interpretation is that it is an *earthly* kingdom and that the martyred faithful share in its rule. It serves as an assertion of God's sovereignty through Christ within the realm of *this* world. Later the present heaven and earth will go out of existence and a new universe will come about in which the boundaries between heaven and earth are effectively abolished (20:11; 21:1–4). Before this happens, God takes control in a definitive manner. Martyred Christians are vindicated for their refusal to accept the counterfeit authority of Rome. Because they rejected Rome's rule, they become the real rulers even before the present world passes away.

Particularly intriguing in all this, or so it seems to me, is the observation with which the first three verses of chapter 20 conclude:

> And I saw an angel come down from heaven, having the key of the bottomless pit and a great chain in his hand. And he laid hold on the dragon, that old serpent, which is the Devil, and Satan, and bound him a thousand years, and cast him into the bottomless pit, and shut him up, and set a seal upon him, that he should deceive the nations no more, till the thousand years should be fulfilled; and after that he must be loosed a little season.

Why is it, one can be moved to ask, that, after the thousand years of messianic rule, Satan "must be loosed a little season"? My lady on the train, when I asked her about this passage, was startled, confessing both that she had never noticed it before and that she had no explanation for what she and I agreed seemed a strange turn of events. She vowed to look into it, first by consulting with her pastor. I am afraid she will not find much satisfaction, except perhaps in the argument that there is something unrelenting about evil. Or, put another way, there may be here also a reliance upon the human perspective in any attempt to grasp the overall order of things, a perspective which itself tends to be afflicted by our everyday awareness of the mutability of the best things that we either observe or make. Perhaps also the approach to such matters of Plutarch should be respected, as when he says (in section 40 (367) of his essay, *On Isis and Osiris*):

> When Isis had recovered Osiris and had nurtured Horus, who was becoming strong through exhalations, mists and clouds, [the villainous] Typhon was indeed overcome, but not destroyed; for the goddess who rules the earth did not allow the substance which is opposed to moisture to be completely destroyed,

but she was lenient and let it go free, wishing the fusion to remain; for the world would not be complete if the fiery element were to cease and disappear. [See also Plutarch, *On Isis and Osiris*, at sections 43, 45–47, 54–57 (368, 369–70, 373–74).]

VI

The difficulties posed by the *Book of the Revelation* can trouble readers. Consider, for example, how D. H. Lawrence can vent his frustration with our text [*Apocalypse* (New York: Viking Press, 1932), 3]:

> *Apocalypse* means simply *Revelation*, though there is nothing simple about this one, since men have puzzled their brains for nearly two thousand years to find out what, exactly, is revealed in all its orgy of mystification, and of all the books in the Bible, they find *Revelation* perhaps the least attractive.

That is the opening paragraph of the Lawrence book. The critique becomes even more severe a little further on (*Apocalypse*, 20–21):

> When we come to read it critically and seriously, we realize that the *Apocalypse* reveals a profoundly important Christian doctrine which has in it none of the real Christ, none of the real Gospel, none of the creative breath of Christianity, and is nevertheless perhaps the most effectual doctrine in the Bible. That is, it has had a greater effect on second-rate people throughout the Christian ages, than any other book in the Bible. The *Apocalypse of John* is, as it stands, the work of a second-rate mind. It appeals intensely to second-rate minds in every country and every century. Strangely enough, unintelligible as it is, it has no doubt been the greatest source of inspiration of the vast mass of Christian minds—the vast mass being always second rate—since the first century, and we realise, to our horror, that this is what we are up against today; not Jesus nor Paul, but John of Patmos.

The Lawrence recourse here to "second-rate minds" has to be challenged, however instructive it may be at first glance. A challenge could well begin with the reminder that one of the most powerful minds in the modern world devoted considerable time and energy to the study of the *Book of the Revelation* along with the *Book of Daniel*. That was Isaac Newton, who would certainly have answered otherwise the question I recently put to two of his successors: "Does the number 1000 do anything for you?" In 1733 there was published Newton's book, *Observations upon the Prophecies of Daniel, and the Apocalypse of St. John the Divine*, a complicated subject he worked at off and on during his life and quite a bit in his closing years. (He died in 1727.)

Here is how one scholar has seen Newton's efforts in this field (Dudley Shapere, *Encyclopedia of Philosophy*, vol. 5, 490):

> Newton devoted a considerable effort throughout his life to such activities as trying to reconstruct the chronology of ancient times by combining astronomical methods with clues from the Bible, and attempting to interpret the Prophecies of Daniel. He did not maintain that the future could be predicted on the basis of Biblical prophecies but only that, once the events had occurred, they could support the Bible by revealing themselves as the events that had been foretold.

Newton's own formulation of what he was doing is, then, more intriguing than that of the typical student of this matter. These biblical prophecies, he suggested, are *not* intended to predict events, but rather, once the events prophesied take place, the prophecies help us understand them, perhaps even testifying thereby to the workings of Providence in the lives of human beings. Is there not something of the scientific stance in this? In astronomy, for example, "prophecies" (or one's accounts of the movements of the heavenly bodies) help us explain what has already happened at least as much as they help us anticipate what is going to happen.

Permit me to add, before I begin to close, that Newton penned by the 1730s the assurance, if assurance it is, that *the* millennium, or the closing down of worldly operations as we know them, would not begin before the year 2060—and it might be considerably after that. (See, for another provocative quotation from D. H. Lawrence's *Apocalypse*, the addendum in appendix G of this book. See, on the writing, publication, and significance of Newton's *Observations upon the Prophecies*, Richard S. Westfall, *Never at Rest: A Biography of Isaac Newton* [Cambridge: Cambridge University Press, 1980], 319–20, 815f, 826f.)

VII

It is curious that so much is offered in *Revelation* of direct quotations from Jesus. (This is dramatically evident in red-letter editions of the Bible.) Some might consider this remarkably presumptuous on the part of the author—or is it that we see here the intimate connection between divine revelation and poetic inspiration?

However cataclysmic the account in *Revelation* may be, it can still assure readers that there *is* a meaning to the whole. After all, our mortality testifies, we have noticed, to our inability to keep things together forever in the forms familiar to us. Meaning can even come, it seems, upon recognizing how villainous our villains are, which makes it necessary that the required purgation be cataclysmic. Even so, our biblical text can soar at times, as may be seen in verses 1–4 and verses 22–27 of chapter 21 in the King James translation:

> And I saw a new heaven and a new earth: for the first heaven and the first earth were passed away; and there was no more sea. And I, John, saw the holy city, new Jerusalem, coming down from God out of heaven, prepared as a bride adorned for her husband. And I heard a great voice out of heaven saying, Behold, the tabernacle of God is with men, and he will dwell with them, and they shall be his people, and God himself shall be with them, and be their God. And God shall wipe away all tears from their eyes; and there shall be no more death, neither sorrow, nor crying, neither shall there be any more pain: for the former things are passed away. . . .
>
> And I saw no temple therein: for the Lord God Almighty and the Lamb are the temple of it. And the city had no need of the sun, neither of the moon, to shine in it: for the glory of God did lighten it, and the Lamb is the light thereof. And the nations of them which are saved shall walk in the light of it: and the kings of the earth do bring their glory and honour into it. And the gates of it shall not be shut at all by day: for there shall be no night there. And they shall bring the glory and honour of the nations into it. And there shall in no wise enter into it any thing that defileth, neither whatsoever worketh abomination, or maketh a lie: but they which are written in the Lamb's book of life.

Perhaps the last word here should be given to a pair of pious British scholars who provided, early in this century, the following summary of the *Book of Revelation* (G. J. Spurrell and C. H. H. Wright, *The Holy Bible* [Cleveland: World Publishing Co., n.d.]):

> *Revelation* is the only prophetic book in the New Testament, and is sometimes called the *Apocalypse*. It gathers up preceding prophecies respecting the coming of the Messiah and the Kingdom of Heaven upon earth, and translates them into anticipation of the new Advent, the new heaven, and the new earth. Its main theme is, "I come quickly." The first three chapters of *w* are comparatively easy to understand, but the intermediate chapters are full of dark visions, the exact meaning of which we are not likely to discover until the Lord comes. There are passages of very great beauty and comparative clearness, and there are also allegories and parables for the interpretation of which we at present lack the means.

It should be evident that we, or at least I, still lack the means to answer some of the vital questions put to us by this challenging book.

NOTE

*This talk was given in 1999 to the Women's Society of the Hyde Park Union Church, Chicago. The epigraph for this talk is taken from E. C. Bentley, *Trent's Last Case* (London: Thomas Nelson and Sons, 1913), 5.

Appendix I

John Locke and *The Reasonableness of Christianity*[*]

> The godly doe not only apprehend the meaning of the words in the Scripture, and are able to discourse of the reasons therein contained, but they discern also the spiritualnesse of the work of grace, that is discovered in the same.
>
> Thomas Hooker (1586–1647)

I

A memorable date, partly because it is so easy to remember—a memorable date in the history of what we call "Church and State" relations is 1600, the year in which Giordano Bruno (who had been born in 1548) was executed in Rome by the Inquisition. This was after a career of often-vigorous encounters by him with people of various religious faiths (all designated as "Christian") in Italy, Switzerland, Germany, France, and England.

Bruno was a learned man of broad philosophical interests. He evidently liked to stir things up. And he may even have been somewhat mad. His challenging cosmology was more Copernican than Ptolemaic—and he could disturb the faithful by speculating about such things as the infinitude of the universe.

Bruno's fate is believed to have had a profound effect upon contemporaries of philosophical inclinations. These included Francis Bacon (1561–1626), René Descartes (1576–1650), and Thomas Hobbes (1588–1679). Bruno, or at least his fate, can also be thought of as having influenced the theological-political speculations of two exceptional thinkers born a couple of generations after the Bruno execution: Benedict Spinoza (1638–1677) and John Locke (1632–1704).

It was obvious by the middle of the seventeenth century that a new intellectual and social era had opened, with the beginnings of what we know as the Enlightenment grounded in the modern scientific enterprise. How "religion" was to be dealt with thereafter was an important concern of thinkers of the time, among whom was, of course, John Locke.

II

How "religion" *was* to be dealt with was not only a question about the demands upon one of one's faith, or about what the philosophic response should be to the claims of religion, but also about how "religion" was to be dealt with as a social and political problem. That that problem was sometimes desperate may be seen in how that period can be described which has Bruno's execution at its midpoint. Here is an account, in a standard reference book, which is provided under the rubric "Religious Wars" (*The World Almanac*, 1998, 562):

> A century and a half of religious wars began with a South German peasant uprising (1524), repressed with [Martin] Luther's support. . . . Radical sects—democratic, pacifist, millenarian—arose (Anabaptists ruled Munster in 1534–35) and were repressed violently. Civil war in France from 1562 between Huguenots (Protestant nobles and merchants) and Catholics ended with the 1598 Edict of Nantes tolerating Protestants (revoked [by Louis XIV] in 1685). Hapsburg attempts to restore Catholicism in Germany were resisted in 25 years of fighting; the 1555 Peace of Augsburg guarantee of religious independence to local princes and cities was confirmed only after the Thirty Years War (1618–1648), when much of Germany was devastated by local and foreign armies (Sweden, France).

Similar strife plagued England as well, epitomized perhaps for the English-speaking peoples by the conflict between Henry VIII (r. 1509–1547) and the pope.

How such strife was to be eliminated, or at least moderated, was a constant concern of thoughtful men and women in the seventeenth century and thereafter. We are reminded of what such contests mean when we encounter the politics of religious fanaticism in various parts of the world today.

III

John Locke's most celebrated discussion of these matters (aside perhaps from what may be found in his solid political works) is *A Letter Concerning Tol-*

eration, a 1689 translation of his *Epistle de Tolerantia*, a letter written in Latin by Locke to a Dutch Arminian friend, during the winter of 1685. Locke was at the time a political exile in Amsterdam, living there "under an assumed name in order to avoid extradition and persecution for his part in the revolutionary activity for toleration in England in 1679–1683." (Locke, *A Letter Concerning Toleration* [Indianapolis: Hackett Publishing Co., 1983], 1.)

We find in this *Toleration Letter* a powerful argument that moves along effectively. It is fairly short, forty or so pages in print. Locke's argument is reflected in, say, Thomas Jefferson's thought on this subject. It is an argument that has been widely accepted in this country, whatever reservations we may now have because of the disabilities assigned (perfunctorily?) by Locke both to known atheists and to Roman Catholics.

The spirit of Locke's argument may be found in one of the most memorable American pronouncements on this subject, the 1785 Virginia Statute of Religious Liberty (promoted by Jefferson), which begins in this fashion:

> Whereas Almighty God hath created the mind free; that all attempts to influence it by temporal punishments or burthens, or by civil incapacitations, tend only to beget habits of hypocrisy and meanness, and are a departure from the plan of the Holy author of our religion, who being Lord both of body and mind, yet chose not to propagate it by coercions on either, as was in his Almighty power to do; that the impious presumption of legislators and rulers, civil as well as ecclesiastical, who being themselves but fallible and uninspired men, have assumed dominion over the faith of others, setting up their own opinions and modes of thinking as the only true and infallible, and as such endeavouring to impose them on others, hath established and maintained false religions over the greatest part of the world, and through all time.

Further on, the Virginia Statute continues thus with its statement of principles, a statement which may include a dubious element or two:

> that our civil rights have no dependence on our religious opinions, any more than our opinions in physics or geometry; that therefore the proscribing any citizen as unworthy the public confidence by laying upon him an incapacity of being called to offices of trust and emolument, unless he profess or renounce this or that religious opinion, is depriving him injuriously of those privileges and advantages to which in common with his fellow-citizens he has a natural right; that it tends only to corrupt the principles of that religion it is meant to encourage, by bribing with a monopoly of worldly honours and emoluments, those who will externally profess and conform to it; that though indeed these are criminal who do not withstand such temptation, yet neither are those innocent who lay the bait in their way; that to suffer the civil magistrate to intrude his powers into the field of opinion, and to restrain the

> profession or propagation of principles on supposition of their ill tendency, is a dangerous fallacy, which at once destroys all religious liberty, because he being of course judge of that tendency will make his opinions the rule of judgment, and approve or condemn the sentiments of others only as they shall square with or differ from his own.

Then it is said, echoing here John Milton's *Areopagitica* (of 1644) and anticipating the arguments thereafter about when, if at all, the freedom of speech or of the press might be limited:

> that it is time enough for the rightful purposes of civil government, for its officers to interfere when principles break out into overt acts against peace and good order; and finally, that truth is great and will prevail if left to herself, that she is the proper and sufficient antagonist to error, and has nothing to fear from the conflict, unless by human interposition disarmed of her natural weapons, free argument and debate, errors ceasing to be dangerous when it is permitted freely to contradict them.

IV

But can even more be done in these matters, at least for the sake of domestic tranquility, than there is done in Locke's *Toleration Letter*? After all, that *Letter* does assume that vital differences among Christian sects will continue—and this means that such differences can at times erupt into violent clashes. (This has been seen in recent years in Yugoslavia.) Should something more than the "political" approach relied upon in the *Toleration Letter* be available here?

Locke's *Reasonableness of Christianity* (a book of some 150 pages, published anonymously in 1695) approaches the problem here from what can be called a theological perspective. Critical to the Locke approach seems to be the recognition that most people do not really choose their religious allegiances. Rather, they tend to inherit them, depending primarily on their families, on their neighborhoods, or on some other such "accidental" factors.

Thus, although people may feel deeply about the religious faith they happen to have, they usually do not truly understand it, or what can be said for it, or even how and why it should be distinguished from other faiths. Their disabilities here are evident to anyone who notices, for example, that most people are not apt to know the original language of their sacred texts or the history of how those texts came to be established in the form they now cherish.

V

One can be reminded here of a provision in article VI of our Constitution of 1787, where it is ordered:

> The Senators and Representatives before mentioned, and the Members of the several State Legislatures, and all executive and judicial Officers, both of the United States and of the several States, shall be bound by Oath or Affirmation, to support this Constitution.

I notice in passing that the alternative provided here of an affirmation itself reflects a compromise developed in religious controversies of earlier years. I also notice that the provision I have just quoted continues in a fashion which can be seen as testimony to the influence of John Locke and his disciples, for it *is* said thereafter in Article VI of the Constitution: "but no religious Test shall ever be required as a Qualification to any Office or public Trust under the United States." That this prohibition is not immediately extended to qualifications for state offices testifies to local divergences at that time in these matters, something evident in the religious establishments that were then still to be found in some states.

But let us return to the Article VI obligation to "support this Constitution." We are not told either here or anywhere else in the Constitution what "support" means. Even more of a puzzle is what "this Constitution" means. That is, what *is* one agreeing to? What is one supposed to hold up for the highest esteem as a citizen, and especially as a citizen entrusted with public office in any of the states of the Union? We can see here the problems inherent in any commonly-held allegiance in a community, especially when most of those who so adhere were born into their "faiths," whether political or religious.

There is even more of a problem when one considers such pledges of allegiance as the Nicene Creed and the Apostles' Creed, venerable pronouncements that are routinely recited (with variations) by hundreds of millions of Christians. (See chapter 16 of this book.) Here, of course, the vocabulary (especially when Trinitarian considerations are involved) is even harder to fathom than that found here and there in our Constitution.

VI

John Locke, in order to promote peace among the many Christian sects of his day, reduces the doctrine that, he insists, Jesus himself had identified as both essential and sufficient for the self-identification of the Christian—he reduces

Christian doctrine to the recognition that Jesus is the Messiah. This, he further insists, is something that people of ordinary capacities can grasp.

The Christian identified in this way may well accept other things that he finds in the Bible. But a recognition of the Messiah-ship of Jesus is (Locke argues) all that is absolutely required. And from this, if one is truly to be a Christian, a proper conduct of one's life follows, conduct which can be guided by precepts provided in the Bible, by Christian communities, and by other influences. It is taken for granted by Locke that most people must be drilled in how to conduct themselves, that they cannot be expected to understand matters as the occasional thoughtful human being does.

It should be noticed that Locke insists here upon the Hebrew term, *Messiah*, not its Greek equivalent, *Christos*, however much he refers in the *Reasonableness* book and elsewhere to *Jesus Christ*. It should also be noticed that Locke does not undertake any extended inquiry into what *Messiah* meant to the Jews during the lifetime of Jesus. I will return, further on in these remarks, to some problems implicit in what Locke does here.

VII

Some of the more passionate Christian partisans of Locke's day did not take kindly to his attempt at peacemaking. However much Locke suggests that other things might well be believed by anyone who does recognize Jesus as the Messiah, he does seem to reduce essential Christian dogma to one affirmation. This was considered by some critics as a form of Deism (or Socianism or Unitarianism), if not even as out-and-out atheism—and certainly not as one of the richly textured professions of faith to which Christians of that day were accustomed.

At the center of the *Reasonableness* book, as determined by its paragraphing, is Locke's emphatic use of the Greek term, *parresia*. This term is used in the New Testament to describe a fitting plainspokenness (without regard to personal consequence) in testifying to one's faith. Locke *presents* himself as plainspoken in this book. Does he, in highlighting *parresia* as he does, tacitly acknowledge that he is not as plainspoken as he presents himself? (See, on the original ambiguities of *parresia*, Anastaplo, *The Constitutionalist*, 275, 781–82.)

Be that as it may, some of Locke's critics doubted his sincerity in the matters presented in the *Reasonableness* book. The most vigorous of these critics, one John Edwards, believed that the unnamed author of that book questioned in effect much of the Christian faith, including what was generally believed about the Creation. Edwards includes, in his denunciation, a challenge as to how the wild freethinkers of his day could possibly account for the existence of the world as human beings have always known it. Are we to believe, he scoffed, that all this came into being merely by chance? Here is a lively passage in which Edwards offers what he obviously considers a commonsensical critique of the unorthodox of his day, having just proclaimed that the "Being or Agent which gave the first motion to things, is *God*" (John Edwards, *Some Thoughts Concerning the Several Causes and Occasions of Atheism* [London, 1695], 16–17):

> If after all they say, that Matter had this Motion by *Chance*, and so was neither from itself or any other, they talk more absurdly and wildly than before; for *Chance* is a Word made to signify only the *unexpected happening of a thing*, but doth not import that there was no Cause or Author at all of it. But however, if they will stand to this (as generally they do) that Matter at first had a strong power by *Chance* to jump into an orderly System of *Heavens*, *Earth*, *Sea*, &c. then I ask them, What is the reason that there hath been nothing of this nature since? What reason can be given why all the Atoms and Effluviums in the several Ages and Successions of Time, ever since this visible World had its being, have not produced some excellent Frame either like this World, or of an other nature? What! is this Lucky Chance quite ceas'd? Is this *Fortunate Lottery* at an end? Is there no probability of a brave fortuitous hit once again?

Edwards's criticism continues with still another question which is followed by a wonderful display (*ibid*., 17–18):

> Is there no such fine piece of work as that of *Sun*, *Moon*, and *Stars*, to be expected once more? No: there is an utter despair of it; for from Eternity (according to them) to this moment, we have had no such Luck, and therefore what reason have we to expect any such afterwards? yea indeed, what ground have these Chance-Philosophers to think that there ever was such thing? What reason have they to declare it to be their firm perswasion that Matter was set into motion from Eternity, and that by the frisking of its Particles, it at last danced into a World? yet this and all the rest they believe and vouch rather than they will hold that the beginning of things was from an *Intelligent* and *Wise Being*.

We can see here the suspicions that someone such as Locke could arouse in his effort to suggest a reasonable plan for a relaxed incorporation of Christian piety in the feverish political order of his day. We can also see how someone such as Locke could arouse among the orthodox of his day a partial resurgence of the passions aroused by Giordano Bruno a century earlier.

VIII

Among the attacks on Locke for his *Reasonableness* book was the charge that he was a covert disciple of Thomas Hobbes, a thinker who had been so imprudent as to invite suspicions of atheism. Hobbes, like Locke after him, had recognized the intellectual (if not also the temperamental) limitations of most citizens—and so *he* advocated that the dutiful citizen should routinely take his lead, in religious matters, from his acknowledged earthly ruler, someone who can call for guidance upon the best minds of the realm.

Hobbes's position here, which is a hardheaded alternative to the determinedly-tolerant position of Locke, has been summed up in this way (Laurence Berns, in *History of Political Philosophy*, Leo Strauss and Joseph Cropsey, eds., third ed. (Chicago: University of Chicago Press, 1987), 417 (emphasis added)):

> The "office of our Blessed Savior," *the Messiah* . . . is threefold: Redeemer, Teacher, and King. Christ on earth was Redeemer and Teacher, not King. He never did anything to call into question the civil laws of the Jews or Caesar, nor gave anyone else warrant to do the same. He is to be the King only after the general resurrection; the kingdom he claimed is to be in another world.

We can see in this passage, with its Hobbesian anticipation of Locke's emphasis upon the Messiah—we can see here how Locke could be considered by the wary to be a tame version of Hobbes—and, as such, requiring greater vigilance on the part of the pious.

Further on, in the Berns summary I have just drawn upon, are these comments on Hobbes's position (*ibid*., 418 [emphasis added]):

> So long as there was no Christian commonwealth, no civil sovereign converted to Christianity, the ecclesiastical power was in the hands of the apostles and those they ordained as ministers. They had no power to command, their office was only to instruct and advise men to believe and have faith in Christ. *That Jesus is the Christ is the sole article of faith necessary for a Christian*. If commanded by an infidel sovereign to profess the contrary with one's tongue, martyrdom is not necessary; confession is but an external thing, a sign of obedience to the law. If commanded by the sovereign to do actions such as worshiping false gods, which in effect, deny the Lord, the sin is not that of the obedient subject but that of the sovereign.

The positions with respect to those matters of both Hobbes and Locke, whatever their differences about resistance to one's ruler, do seem to encourage citizens to be somewhat skeptical (quietly so?) about any political authority that may be claimed by the religious teachers of one's time and place, especially when such claims threaten domestic tranquility.

Should Locke be taken, then, to have said more prudently what Hobbes, perhaps too boldly for his own good, had said about the necessary political supervision of Christian dogmatism? That is, is Locke's reformulation of the Christian creed—something to be accepted not only in England but also on the continent (where his *Toleration Letter* had been published in both Dutch and French)—is Locke's reformulation also grounded not in theology but rather in a reasonable political order?

IX

However astute Locke may have been in his attempt to defuse religious strife by emphasizing as he did the dominance of the Messiah-recognition, he does not seem to have succeeded. I base this judgment on my review of texts in which one might expect to see Locke's influence at work.

One such text is the Book of Common Prayer, the quite substantial prayer book of that Anglican Church in which Locke himself held membership. *Christ*, of course, is used repeatedly, but *Messiah*, rarely. One such use may be found in its catechism, where there is the following brief exchange, which does conform to what Locke argues at great length in his *Reasonableness* book (Book of Common Prayer, New York, 1979, 849):

> Q. What is redemption?
> A. Redemption is the act of God which sets us free from the power of evil, sin, and death.
> Q. How did God prepare us for redemption?
> A. God sent the prophets to call us back to himself, to show us our need for redemption, and to announce the coming of the Messiah.
> Q. What is meant by the Messiah?
> A. The Messiah is one sent by God to free us from the power of sin, so that with the help of God we may live in harmony with God, within ourselves, with our neighbors, and with all creation.
> Q. Who do we believe is the Messiah?
> A. The Messiah, or Christ, is Jesus of Nazareth, the only Son of God.
> [See, also, *ibid*., 187: "Almighty Father, who didst inspire Simon Peter, first among the apostles, to confess Jesus as Messiah and Son of the living God . . ." Confession of Saint Peter.]

Be all this as it may, it should be instructive to compare versions of the Book of Common Prayer, before and after 1700, to see what Locke's influence may have been in these matters.

Even less use of *Messiah* may be seen in texts that reflect the more popular religious sentiments of our own day. Consider, for example, the quite substantial *Sacred Harp* songbook. The uses of *Messiah* in the songs collected there are rare. And it is evident, there as elsewhere, that most Christians today who can speak with veneration of *Christ*, do not readily associate that name with *Messiah* (except perhaps when reminded of this by Handel). Consequently, they may not sense the boldness of the argument that Locke makes about the sufficiency of the *Messiah*-identification, no matter what *Christos* may "really" mean.

It should also be noticed, in accounting for the fortunes of the *Reasonableness* book, that it is perhaps the most tedious of Locke's extended texts. One has to labor through much of it, and even more through the two *Vindications* (of some 250 pages) that he was moved to issue in its defense. This is in marked contrast to the eloquence and persuasiveness of the *Toleration Letter*.

X

The typical Christian today, if not also in Locke's time, does not know much about the specifically Jewish implications of the Messiah tradition. Certainly, as I have indicated, our contemporary Christian is not apt to think "Messiah" when "Christ" is mentioned.

Of course, Locke could argue that the creed he proposes is in effect a tautology: anyone who considers himself a Christian is in effect a Messiah-ist. And so there should be no problem with an emphasis upon Jesus being the Messiah. But, as we have noticed, partisans could wonder whether something more was needed than what might seem to the suspicious as little more than clever wordplay.

The reader who understands Locke's concerns may well observe that to emphasize the Messianic character of Christianity is to recognize, if only tacitly, that the critical problems Locke and others of like mind faced were political, not theological or spiritual. (We should recall, by the way, that the kings of Israel were anointed, not crowned—that is, they were "christened," or made Messiah-like.)

It will not do, Locke indicates, for responsible thinkers to question and thereby to undermine the Christian credentials of a community. Since some religious faith is needed if personal morality and political integrity are to be available in the community at large, whatever religious faith *is* relied upon, it can be expected that it would have to be domesticated politically by the sensible philosopher-statesman who is aware of inherent human limitations. Such domestication of religious faith is called for by a recognition of the fortuitous character of the reliance upon any faith by those who were not themselves privileged to have personally experienced the original revelation vital to their faith.

XI

It is possible that John Locke believed, aside from what he considered politically salutary to promote, that his own understanding of Christianity was superior to that of the conventional theological partisans of his day. He *was*, among other things, quite learned in the Bible.

Even so, he may have been somewhat presumptuous here, especially in the way he used his Messiah argument. Did he, among other things, understand what the Jews both of Jesus' time and since had thought, and thought deeply, about the Messiah? (It can be considered providential that we could be reminded, by a full-page advertisement in the *New York Times* this morning [April 2, 2004, A11], of how some Jews regard the Messiah (*Moshiách*) and the Redemption of the World.)

The Lockean presumptuousness that can be suspected in these matters may also be seen perhaps in another distinguished Englishman of his time, Isaac Newton (1642–1727). He, too, knew the Bible well. Newton dedicated his prodigious intellect, in the closing decades of his life, to (among other matters) an intense study of, and speculation about, prophecies found in the *Book of Daniel* and in the *Book of Revelation*. He wrote at length on what he discovered in those texts, the study of which he believed could provide him at least as reliable a grasp of the spiritual universe as his work in mathematics and physics had provided him and others of the physical universe.

There may be something naive about what both Locke and Newton did in their respective probings of the Bible, assuming that they did take seriously their ostensible teachings. But both of them considered themselves anything but naive in their recognition that it would not have been useful for their reputations and continued public effectiveness to have been identified as Unitarians instead of as Trinitarians, especially since Unitarianism could be considered, by some of the more enthusiastic Christians of their day, to be akin to atheism.

We can suspect that such men might conduct themselves quite differently today. What, for example, would an Islamic Locke identify as the common ground upon which Sunnis and Shiites, for example, could meet in an effort to moderate their sometimes-deadly enmity? Certainly, we on the outside can readily see much more that should unite than should divide the adherents to these two sects of Muslims.

XII

A few more words about Locke's project should be offered here. We have noticed that his critics did suspect that there was something threatening in his recommendations about the fundamentals of the Christian faith.

When one proceeds as Locke did in his *Reasonableness* book, I have suggested, something other than an organized religion is sensed to be relied upon as sovereign, even in spiritual matters. That is, the faithful may well suspect that it is not the "committed" believer who speaks as Locke does, but rather the dispassionate statesman.

Thus, there may be seen here by anyone who is suspicious of what we now know as "intellectuals"—there may be seen here not a heartfelt profession of faith but rather primarily an exercise of rhetoric, albeit in the service of domestic tranquility and other transitory political concerns. And this, it could be feared, depended upon and reinforced a calculated shift away from that primary concern for the salvation of souls that the true believer is apt to hunger for.

XIII

I return, in closing, to the "frisking," or creative dance, of the atoms, which had been ridiculed in 1695 by the Lockean critic, John Edwards (someone to be distinguished, by the way, from Jonathan Edwards of New England).

Consider the challenge posed to the likes of Edwards by the astrophysicists and cosmologists of our day. We are *told* by them that there are at least one hundred billion galaxies in the universe. We begin to get an inkling of what this can mean when we hear that there are one hundred billion suns in our own galaxy alone.

Did John Locke, if not also Isaac Newton himself, assume that there was in the universe only the galaxy of which our solar system is a part? We, on the other hand, can hear scientists speculate not only about an abundance of life elsewhere in the universe but even about the prospects of our creating life here on earth from inanimate materials.

There is, depending on one's perspective and perhaps on one's temperament, something either exhilarating or demoralizing about such speculations, especially as one contemplates, for its practical implications, an "infinity" of worlds elsewhere.

That is, we can see, in what is said to have been already discovered in recent decades about the astonishing extent of the observable universe, a resurrection of the spirit of Giordano Bruno, an intrepid, if not even reckless, explorer, who (unlike the eminently cautious John Locke) could at times trouble not only his enemies but perhaps even more some of his more thoughtful friends.

NOTE

*This talk was given in the First Friday Lecture Series, The Basic Program of Liberal Education for Adults, University of Chicago, Chicago, April 2, 2004. The epigraph is taken from Thomas Hooker's *Application of Redemption, By the Effectual Work of the Word, and Spirit of Christ, for the bringing home of lost Sinners to God*, as quoted in Thomas L. Pangle, "A Critique of Hobbes's Critique of Biblical and Natural Religion in *Leviathan*," *Jewish Political Studies Review* 4:2 (Fall 1992), 25, 35, 56. See also note 67 in this book. See as well appendix K of this book, "Yearnings for the Divine and the Natural Animation of Matter."

William T. Braithwaite, of St. John's College (Annapolis), has been instructive in his study of Locke's *Reasonableness* venture. More can be expected, during the coming decade, from Professor Braithwaite here as elsewhere. It should be instructive to consider, in connection with Locke's approach to these matters, the challenging "General Scholium" with which Isaac Newton concludes his *Principia Mathematica*.

Appendix J

The Holocaust and the Divine Ordering of Human Things*

It is nonsensical . . . to charge a whole people with a crime. The criminal is always the individual. It is nonsensical, too, to lay moral guilt to a people as a whole. There is no such thing as a national character extending to every single member of a nation. There are, of course, communities of language, customs, habits and descent; but the differences which may exist at the same time are so great that people talking the same language may remain as strange to each other as if they did not belong to the same nation. . . .

A world opinion which condemns a people collectively is of a kind with the fact that for thousands of years men have thought and said, "The Jews are guilty of the Crucifixion." Who are "the Jews"? A certain group of religious and political zealots whose relative power among the Jews of that time, in cooperation with the Roman occupation authorities, led to the execution of Jesus. . . .

England, France and America were the victorious powers of 1918. The course of world history was in their hands, not in those of the vanquished. The victor's responsibility is his alone, to accept or to evade. If he evades it, his historical guilt is plain. The victor cannot be entitled simply to withdraw to his own narrower sphere, there to be left alone and merely watch what happens elsewhere in the world. If an event threatens dire consequences, he has the power to prevent it. To have this power and fail to use it is political guilt. To be content with paper protests is evasion of responsibility. This inaction is one charge that may be brought against the victorious powers—although, of course, it does not free us [Germans] from any guilt. In discussing this further, one may point to the peace treaty of Versailles and its consequences, and then to the policy of letting Germany slide into the conditions which produced National-Socialism.

Karl Jaspers

I

There was witnessed in the murderous campaigns by the Nazis across Europe for a decade a recourse to evil that can provide a vindication of the dreadful accounts of the satanic that human beings imagine from time to time. The vicious Nazi programs were probably unprecedented in their ferocity and extent. Particularly singled out for systematic destruction, by the millions, were any Jews that the Nazis could get their hands on.

What the Nazis tried to do—and what they in large measure "succeeded" in doing—made other systematic atrocities we had theretofore heard of pale by comparison. These include such depredations as the conquests by Atilla the Hun, the campaigns of the Inquisition, the African slave trade, the dispossession of North American Indians, the massacres of Armenians, Jews, and others on many occasions, the aerial bombardment of cities during the Second World War, and even the Stalinist Terror. That is, what the Nazi leadership deliberately set out to do *was* in critical respects unprecedented.

Such displays of intrinsically evil acts on so grand a scale do remind us of the worst depravities that the human soul is capable of. Such depravities have at times led pious observers to ask: "Where is God?" The very existence of the divine can be questioned in such circumstances.

II

The decades-long obsession with Jews as the primary object of Nazi hatred can be regarded as a perverse tribute to that ancient "people." Their chosenness by the Nazis, in the twentieth century, somehow mirrored that associated with the divine more than three millennia ago. The only other "people" so distinguished by the Nazis for complete annihilation were the Gypsies, which should make at least the pious wonder whether *that* people might properly be shown more respect than they usually are in Europe.

Why were the Jews butchered as they were? Why were the Nazis so determined to keep killing Jews when it was obviously against the Nazis' military and material interests to do so in the closing year of the war? Did the Nazis somehow sense that the Jews were the critical, if not even the defining, opposites of what Nazism stood for?

The Nazis were essentially atheists who worshiped the state and Germanness (as they conceived them). But they had inherited, and politically exploited, a longstanding theological heritage that was (among many) deeply hostile toward Jews. The Nazis, who were hardly respectful of what Christianity truly yearned for, deepened the hostility they had inherited by refusing to respect conversions by Jews to Christianity during recent generations.

III

My interest in what happened to the Jews at the hands of the Nazis is long-standing. Thus, one of my papers as a law school student, a half-century ago, drew upon my study of the voluminous Nuremberg Trial record (1945–1946). I have returned to the trial from time to time, including in a 1991 public lecture that is incorporated in my 2004 volume, *On Trial: From Adam and Eve to O.J. Simpson*.

I make the following acknowledgment in the Nuremberg Trial discussion in my *On Trial* volume:

> I have found helpful . . . what I learned by taping, for many hours, my [conversations] in 2000–2001 [drawing upon] Simcha Brudno's recollections of his dreadful experiences with the Nazis in Lithuania and in Dachau [during the Second World War]. I hope to be able, some day, to publish these conversations in book form. I was initially drawn to Simcha Brudno, a gifted mathematician and a remarkably resilient human being, when I learned that we are virtually the same age: it was intriguing to explore the radically different effects upon us, as youngsters, of the Second World War.

I had met Simcha Brudno during a teatime preceding the University of Chicago Physics Department weekly colloquia that I have attended for decades. A few minutes after we first began talking he asked me what I thought of the Holocaust, to which I replied that it was "simply unbelievable."

This was an assessment that he emphatically endorsed, recalling that he had spent a year in Dachau, during which time not a day passed but that he found himself unable to believe that *he* was really there. He readily accepted my suggestion that we should talk about these matters in taped conversations, meeting before whatever physics colloquia his health permitted him to attend. There were, over a year, a dozen such conversations that we conducted in a room I had secured for this purpose from the director of the University of Chicago Library.

IV

The quite comfortable Brudno family was part of a substantial Jewish community that had been in Lithuania for centuries. Simcha Brudno grew up in Siauliai, a small city in which his father and mother managed an important leather factory. His father died in Lithuania (of natural causes), his mother in a concentration camp, and he (after being liberated by the American army in May 1945) went to Israel, served in the army there during the founding period of the state, and eventually made his way to the United States (where his sister had gone to live shortly before the war).

Lithuania had to endure, first, a Russian occupation, then a German occupation, and then a return of the Russians. It was the anticipation of that return which led the German army to evacuate Lithuania, taking with it (in July 1944) whatever Jews were still alive after three years of Nazi killings. Thus, there could be seen in Lithuania, as elsewhere in Europe, the disastrous effects of that folly known as the First World War, which had permitted the worst elements to come to power in Russia and Germany, elements that fed off and worsened each other.

Simcha Brudno's mother had an explanation for the miseries to which the Jews of Lithuania were subjected, an explanation that made much of the misconduct tolerated by Jews among themselves. This assessment, by a woman who was scrupulous in obeying the age-old Law of her people, reflected an approach that assumed that there *is* constant divine governance of the universe. Her husband despaired of the prospects of the impending Second World War, anticipating that the Russians would destroy them spiritually and that the Germans would thereafter destroy them physically.

V

The Russian occupation did contribute to a breakdown of respect for law and order among the people of Lithuania, Jews and Gentiles alike. The German occupation included a heartrending round-up (in November 1943) of all the Jewish children who were then shipped off, never to be seen again by their families. But however much the Nazis had railed against the Jews, from well before when they came to power in Germany in 1933, they never described publicly (so far as I have ever heard) what they were doing to the Jews (besides taking control of and harassing them in various ways).

Their remarkable reticence about their systematic slaughter of millions of people reflects the fact that all this *was* "simply unbelievable." That is, what they were doing was, at least for the Nazis, somehow literally unsayable. Whatever might have been suspected by many throughout Germany, it was always evident to the Nazi leaders, however much they could usefully vilify and torment the Jews, that they could not count on the German people explicitly to endorse what was actually being done in the death camps.

All this testifies to the ultimate incomprehensibility of what *was* being done, with most of the routine killings of Jews and others on a large scale relegated "off-stage," so to speak, to occupied Poland. The typical German, it can be suspected, both did and did not know what was going on. But then, it can be argued, even the Nazi leaders themselves did not truly know—"could not really face up to"—what they were doing.

VI

To assess matters thus is to assume (along with, say, the Socratics) that evil is ultimately rooted in ignorance. This teaching, which is *not* widely accepted, is drawn upon, in effect, by Nathan when he confronts King David with respect to the Bathsheba affair. A story *has* to be used by the prophet to help the king to see (truly to see) what he had done.

A more mundane approach to such matters may be seen (as we have noticed) in how Simcha Brudno's mother accounted for the plight of the Jews she knew. Another mundane approach, less grounded in conventional piety, may be seen in the explanation provided by some of Simcha Brudno's fellow townspeople. The Jews of Europe, these Zionists argued, were suffering because they had not gone to the Holy Land when they could have done so.

Some might have added that *that* had been a place provided for them by divine favor. They might have added as well that it was illusory for European Jewry to rely on either the Enlightenment or the emancipation of recent centuries. All this affects how Jews consider themselves obliged to conduct themselves now in the Middle East, having come to believe that they should never again dare rely upon others to protect them.

VII

Most European Jews *were* left, by the civilized nations of the day, to fend for themselves when they were systematically assaulted by the Nazis. It could seem largely a matter of chance who among them survived, once the Second World War began. Some, in considering who did survive, might prefer to recognize here the workings of Providence.

Simcha Brudno argued that a necessary, not a sufficient, condition for survival was both one's evident ability to work and one's apparent willingness to do so. That is, the material self-interest of the Germans could *sometimes* be counted on. It does seem that the Germans even came to regret that they had starved to death hundreds of thousands of Russian prisoners-of-war that they could have used as slave labor in the closing years of the war.

Even so, the Nazi hatred of Jews was such that scarce resources did continue to be used almost to the very end of the war to ship Jews to the camps where they could be killed. Here, too, it can be argued, the Nazis really did not know what they were doing. Some might even see in all this the workings of an inscrutable fate among victims and victimizers alike.

VIII

The inability to see what one *is* doing is not limited to people of modest capacities and in ordinary circumstances. Such an inability may sometimes be seen as well in the most talented. The career of Martin Heidegger, with his much-publicized collaboration with the Nazis in the 1930s, remains instructive.

Heidegger, considered by many scholars the most powerful thinker in the twentieth century, conducted a dalliance with the Nazis that was deeply scandalous. Although he soon discovered that he could not direct and use the Nazis as he had evidently hoped to do, he was never man enough to repudiate publicly what he had tried to do. What he *had* done was done by a man who had had devoted Jewish students of note and who owed much to one of his Jewish teachers.

Indeed, it can be argued, Nazism depended on the influence of prominent Germans across half a millennium, Germans such as Martin Luther and Martin Heidegger. These remarkable men were not as prudent as they should have been in talking either about Jews or about statecraft. That is, they did not consider soberly enough who might exploit in the worst possible ways what they so irresponsibly said and did, as well as what they did not say on critical occasions.

IX

It can, perhaps usefully, be considered providential that the State of Israel could be established when it was. Some might even want to go so far as to suggest that the Nazis, in dramatizing in so awful a manner the constant vulnerability of the Jews, finally compelled "the conscience of the world" to permit Jews to return, after two millennia, to control by them of a Holy Land once said to have been divinely allocated to them. It will probably take generations for Jews to feel, and to act as if, truly secure in their return, just as it has taken generations for Americans to begin to deal properly with the North American Indians and with the slaves by whom they felt themselves threatened.

The hatred encountered by Jews for ages from Christians and during the past century from Arab Muslims is ultimately suicidal for such haters. That is, the divine revelations necessarily relied on by both Christians and Muslims are ultimately grounded in the revelations and history of the Jewish people. In short, Christians and Muslims, when they hate Jews, simply do not know what they are doing to the very foundations of their own faiths—and they, to say the least, should be ashamed of themselves, especially when they are reminded how tiny is the territory that Jews now claim compared to how much Arabs as well as Christians have long possessed in the Mediterranean world.

I kept Simcha Brudno posted, throughout his final hospitalization, about the progress of my preliminary editing of our conversations, something he had urged on me and was very much interested in. When I telephoned him at the hospital, the morning of June 9, 2006, to report that I had just completed my initial edit (which had reduced a thousand-page manuscript to six hundred double-spaced pages), I was informed by a sober attendant that he had "just passed." It was, the pious would be tempted to suggest, almost as if my colleague's indomitable spirit could now take a different, more enduring, form.

NOTE

*This talk was given at the Caxton Club, Chicago, February 9, 2007. The epigraph is taken from Karl Jaspers, *The Question of German Guilt* (New York: Capricorn Books, 1947), 40–41, 91. See further, on Simcha Brudno (who is drawn on here), George Anastaplo, "Our Iraq Follies and the Perhaps Inevitable Search for Scapegoats," *The Greek Star*, Chicago, August 16, 2007, 8. This, too, should be included in the third Anastaplo *September Eleventh* collection. See the note for appendix D, above.

The thousand-page transcription of the Anastaplo-Brudno conversations was prepared by Adam Reinberg while a student at the Loyola University Chicago School of Law.

Appendix K

Yearnings for the Divine and the Natural Animation of Matter*

> [It has been said that there may be] found in the Pythagorean memoirs the following tenets as well. The principle of all things is the monad or unit; arising from this monad the undefined dyad or two serves as material substratum to the monad, which is cause; from the monad and the undefined dyad spring numbers; from numbers, points; from points, lines; from lines, plane figures; from plane figures, solid figures; from solid figures, sensible bodies, the elements of which are four, fire, water, earth and air; these elements interchange and turn into one another completely, *and combine to produce a universe animate*, intelligent, spherical, with the earth at its centre, the earth itself too being spherical and inhabited round about.
>
> Diogenes Laertius

I

It can be wondered what the pervasive human longing for the Divine may mean—that longing evidently encountered always and everywhere, especially when a divinely-prescribed physical order seems to provide support for a proper social order. How is such a longing for the Divine connected to life itself, or at least to self-conscious life? The "Meaning of Life" seems thereby to be testified to—or it can be regarded as something to be sought for and to be guided by.

That "meaning" is sensed by many to be undermined today by, among other developments, the prevailing theory in the Western world of human evolution. Such a challenge can seem to be reinforced by ever more accounts of multitudes of complex galaxies said to be far too numerous to be counted.

The origins of life, according to such theories and accounts, seem to be independent of any Earth-centered divine will, even prompting concerns in many about the meaningfulness of human life and hence of human communities.

The social, political, and legal controversies resulting from such subordination, if not even the elimination, of any divine concern about human affairs take a variety of forms, adapting as they do to constantly changing circumstances. These circumstances include what seem to many to be relentless assaults by modern science upon long-cherished understandings about the nature of human existence and social relations. In short, the very meaning of life, and especially of human life, *can* seem repeatedly to be called into question, especially when it is emphasized that life here and there in the universe may be accidental.

II

I venture to offer in this appendix suggestions about how life itself tends to be regarded (usually "unconsciously"?) by arguably the most rigorous scientists among us, the physicists and astrophysicists of our day. My preliminary suggestions here draw upon my decades-long attendance at the weekly physics colloquia at the University of Chicago. The presenters on those occasions are usually top-notch scientists not only at the University of Chicago but also at other American and European research institutions.

These are people who are generally considered to be as sophisticated about physics and related sciences as any such practitioners in the world today, people who are quite astute in observing and discussing "natural phenomena." Among them is an occasional Nobel Laureate in physics or chemistry. Should it not be expected of such people, therefore, that they would have an instinctive and hence perhaps instructive "feel" for both the materials and the processes they study and are so familiar with?

It can certainly be expected that I personally would not be able to grasp most of what these scientists say between 4:15 and 5:30 (as distinguished from the preceding teatime) every Thursday afternoon (during the academic year). But it may be that my obvious incompetence has itself "liberated" me, so to speak, to notice something that I have not seen commented on, in the materials I have studied (or by the experts I have consulted), about the methods and language of modern science. I have long been intrigued, that is, by the language of the hundreds of physicists I have been privileged to listen to, a language which (it seems to me) presupposes an animation or ensoulment (albeit a somewhat primitive ensoulment) of what these scientists would otherwise routinely regard as thoroughly inanimate matter.

III

I have, over the years, collected scores of instances of physics colloquia language which can be taken to "sense" something animate in the matter and processes being examined (many of which instances should be appended to my *Reflections on Religion, the Divine, and Constitutionalism*). We may be tempted, of course, to dismiss such talk as merely a convenient way of making observations, if not even as no more than careless talk. But the pervasiveness of this kind of talk—it is a rare session during which I do not collect several instances—can encourage the outsider to wonder what may be revealed thus about the very nature of material things by men (and an occasional woman) who are regarded worldwide as among the most competent observers of the "phenomena" being observed and reported on.

The "phenomena" dealt with here range from the most minute things studied by physicists to the most massive things studied by astrophysicists. Casual references can be made to "guys" (say, some electrons) "liking" this or that condition, so much so that the processes described can even *sound* somehow purposive. No doubt, most such scientists would rely on other (rigorously lifeless) language, in addition to the considerable mathematics they routinely use, if what is being said here by me should be called to their attention before they speak.

But should we not try to learn what we can from the "feel" that quite intelligent and sensitive practitioners (both theorists and experimentalists) apparently do have for the materials they seem to "know" so well? Perhaps the most intriguing and suggestive expression long used by physicists (and others) is "Nature abhors a vacuum." Another venerable example, of the kind I am commenting on here, is what is said about bodies either "attracting" or "repelling" each other.

IV

The apparent purposiveness implicit in the language used by physicists can suggest an awareness being somehow exhibited by the very things studied. Such awareness of "others" by material things can (we are told) take apparently weird forms in quantum physics. It is even said that Albert Einstein, who could readily speak of "God" in his less-technical accounts of physical processes, was never comfortable with some of the relations and processes posited by quantum physics.

A more conventional use of "God" can be seen in the work of our greatest physicist, Isaac Newton. But he considered himself limited, as a scientist, to describing the observed relations among the objects of his study as a physicist, most notably perhaps in his accounts of the attractions of bodies to one another throughout the observable universe. The workings of gravity could be measured and predicted by him, but the cause or source of gravitational attraction eluded him (as it still seems to elude his successors ever since).

Newton's accounts of these observable operations could be collected by him in "laws" that should be regarded as applicable everywhere and always. Indeed, the very term "law" treats the matter "governed" thereby as if it were somehow animate, providing still another instance (along with "force"?) of that routine enlivening language of physicists that I venture to suggest should be instructive for all of us. These laws are, of course, never "broken," which may, oddly enough, even suggest to some the limits of whatever animating element may seem to be inherent in matter.

V

Critical to the development of science in the West has been the emergence in our tradition of the idea of *nature*. This is an idea, or a sense of things, that evidently originated only in the ancient Greek world, not in that part of the Western tradition grounded in the Hebrew Bible. Nor, it seems, was the idea of nature ever developed on their own by any of the great civilizations of Asia.

Critical to the idea of *nature*, it seems, is the working of birth-and-growth (something intrinsic to the Greek term *phusis*, from which we get *physics*, *physiology*, etc.), with the development thereafter by the Romans of *natura* to convey the same sense in Latin. *Nature* means, among other things, a governing principle of order and change in things that is independent of any intelligent will. Intrinsic to nature, and its openness to birth-and-growth, seems also to be the prospect of death.

The enlivening of matter in the casual vocabulary of physicists that I have noticed extends (naturally enough?) to how they can speak of "death" in describing things and processes that are usually regarded as inanimate. Thus, one hears again and again of such bodies as "young stars" and of such events as "the death of a star." A particularly dramatic instance of this could be heard in response to recent observations by astronomers of a spectacular explosion (or death on a grand scale) of a supernova.

VI

I have suggested that it seems to be "natural" for physicists to sense (if not even to defer to) life in "things," and hence perhaps even to rely thereby upon an overall intelligence or purposiveness in the universe. It might be difficult otherwise for most people (including many physicists and their audiences) to grasp comprehensive governing principles. The way physicists talk, I have also suggested, reflects an awareness of what "makes sense" in "their world," even if they should appear to be doing no more than using convenient metaphors available from everyday discourse.

I have suggested as well that sophisticated scientists to whom these conjectures are offered would be inclined to point out how limited the capacity is of most people to grasp what physics is really "all about." Many of them are accustomed, for example, to the obvious scientific incapacity of their parents, their spouses, and their children. Such incapacity has to be reckoned with as well in the academic administrators who authorize physics departments and in the government and other agencies that fund them.

None of this is intended by me to disparage our most competent physicists, but rather to try to make use of what they may be particularly well-suited to notice, the capacity, if not even the inherent inclination, of matter for animation. That is, I have noticed in turn that there is, in the vocabulary of our most mechanistically inclined scientists, an awareness of the possible tendency toward life in the "stuff" of the universe. But, I have also noticed, there comes with such an openness to life an awareness as well of the eventuality of death for whatever does manage to exploit that "openness" to life which may be intrinsic to the matter that our physicists have been so adept in subjecting to their remarkable discipline.

VII

Particularly ominous is the talk we do hear from time to time about the "death" of our own sun, especially if such an end takes the form of a cataclysmic explosion that reduces our entire solar system to its constitutive elements. It may be a matter of chance whether the human species (if not already long extinct) will be able to anticipate such a development by having a few of our descendants migrate elsewhere, taking with them memories of human experiences here. Others, of course, are prepared (on the basis of Revelation) to offer a far less tentative form of salvation for every human soul—the "others" here ranging from the more inspired saints we have inherited to such adventurers as the "psychic archaeologists" cautioned against in the September/October 1984 issue of *Archaeology*.

When the Divine is somehow or other derived from the things seen and said from time to time and from place to place, chance may determine what form the Divine will be believed to have. This variety includes the names relied on by peoples, which can even be quite different names here and there for the same divinity. Poets, much more than physicists and historians, may have to be relied on to account for these matters.

Chance may also determine how one's inability to accept the locally prevailing account of the Divine should be regarded. Indeed, it may be difficult, if not impossible, ever to be a thorough atheist in these matters. That is, does the psychic makeup of human beings (and hence language itself) militate against any comprehensive atheism?

VIII

Thus, both the avowed atheist and the true believer may assume more certainty than is available in the all-too-human effort to grasp (or to deny) the Divine. But the physicist, too, may be in need of cautioning. I had occasion, in 1974 (in a recollection of Leo Strauss that drew on Enrico Fermi's spectacular career), to make these suggestions to the physicists of that day:

> What seems to be missing in the current scientific enterprise is a systematic inquiry into its presuppositions and purposes. That is, the limits of modern science do not seem to be properly recognized. Bertrand Russell has been quoted as saying, "Physics is mathematical not because we know so much about the physical world, but because we know so little: it is only its mathematical properties that we can discover." But the significance of this observation is not generally appreciated—as one learns upon trying to persuade competent physicists to join one in presenting a course devoted to a careful reading of Aristotle's *Physics* [where, among other things, an extended examination of the meaning of *cause* can be found]. Is there any reason to doubt that physicists will, if they continue as they have in the Twentieth Century, achieve again and again "decisive breakthroughs" in dividing subatomic "particles"? But what future, or genuine understanding, is there in *that*? I believe it would be fruitful for physicists—that is, for a few of the more imaginative among them—to consider seriously the nature of what we can call the "ultron." What must this ultimate particle be like (if, indeed, it *is* a particle and not an idea or a principle)? For is not an "ultron" implied by the endeavors of our physicists, by their recourse to more and more ingenious (and expensive) equipment and experiments? Or are we to assume an infinite regress (sometimes called progress) and no standing place or starting point? Or, to put this question still another way, what is it that permits the universe to be and *to be* (if it *is*) *intelligible*? [See Anastaplo, *The Artist as Thinker* (Athens: Ohio University Press, 1983), 252–53, 474.]

The suggestion I made about the *ultron*, more than three decades ago (perhaps an echo of the ancient Greek reliance on the *atom*), asked in effect whether physicists truly know what they are looking for (whether they reach for either the smallest things or the entire universe). The suggestions I now make, in this 2007 essay, ask whether physicists recognize properly what they somehow *seem* to know, what they have grasped from their intense, indeed privileged, study of matter. That is, a reconsideration of the everyday (non-mathematical) language, and hence of the routine presuppositions and intuitions, of modern physicists may indeed be instructive.

Such language (I have also suggested on this occasion) indicates that physicists, including the best among them, may have sensed (as do the everyday, perhaps naturally ensouling, metaphors they have inherited) that there is intrinsic to matter a tendency, or disposition, to animation. If so, it can even be wondered whether there might not be, throughout the universe, something that can be called a natural inclination for life. Indeed, the universe may be routinely revealed (to its most sensitive observers) as chockful of life, in various stages of both development and disintegration, so much so perhaps as even to provide somehow a check upon that deadly unending "expansion of the universe" posited by some observers.

IX

It should not be surprising, however, that we have not had direct evidence here on Earth of life elsewhere, billions upon billions of miles away. After all, the peoples of Africa, Europe, and Asia evidently lived for thousands of years without any reliable awareness of the existence of the Western hemisphere, only a few thousand miles away. It is highly unlikely, moreover, that we will ever have meaningful contact with civilizations elsewhere in the universe (unless there indeed is a divine agency at work to this end), especially considering how limited a time there would be in the development of each rational species (both here and "there"), to be able to "communicate" in what is called "real time."

The remarkable discoveries "we" have made, and can expect to continue to make, about both the grandest and the tiniest things, are discoveries that may be vital for what they can help us recognize about ourselves. Among the things to be recognized, of course, is that yearning for the Divine, which has been virtually universal for millennia among the peoples of the Earth, that yearning for a meaningful order which may be vital for an enduring constitutionalism. It remains a challenge to determine what that yearning may be grounded in and what it is "really" looking for.

This challenge has long been apparent to serious students of religion. Far less obvious (I have suggested in this appendix) may be the challenge to determine what our most gifted and accomplished physical scientists both somehow know and instinctively depend upon. However marvelous (as well as threatening) the things are which they have indeed discovered and sometimes harnessed, even more remarkable (and worthy of considerably more thought) is what they may have intuited (without personally recognizing it) about the nature and hence the deeply enlivening propensities of apparently inanimate matter throughout the universe, that *matter* which Aristotle (*Metaphysics* 1036a9) evidently regarded as "unknowable in itself."

NOTE

*This essay was prepared, in 2007, for my volume, *Reflections on Religion, the Divine, and Constitutionalism* (in course of preparation). My most recently published books at that time were *Reflections on Constitutional Law* (Lexington: University Press of Kentucky, 2006) and *Reflections on Freedom of Speech and the First Amendment* (Lexington: University Press of Kentucky, 2007). The epigraph is taken from Diogenes Laertius, *Lives of Eminent Philosophers* (Cambridge, Mass.: Loeb Classical Library, Harvard University Press, 1925), II, 341 (viii, 24–25) (emphasis added). See, on the "besouled body," Aristotle, *De Anima*, Book 2. See, on the ancient hypothesis held by some that "every atom was animated," the Leucippus entry in Pierre Bayle's *Dictionary*. Compare, on the limits of "anthropomorphic language," J. C. Polkinghorne, *The Quantum World* (Princeton, N.J.: Princeton University Press, 1984), 31.

The following abstract of this "Yearnings" essay was prepared on November 13, 2007, for posting on the Internet:

> The points of departure for this Essay are the author's observations, for decades now, of the language used by speakers in the weekly University of Chicago Physics Department Colloquia. That language routinely, if not "naturally," seems to assume, if not even to intuit, an inherent disposition of matter to animation. The implications of such a disposition are offered for further consideration. Questions are suggested about the relation of all this to a pervasive human longing for the divine, as well as questions about the Meaning of Life. Related to such questions is the interest that human beings seem always to have had about the possible existence of life, perhaps even of other rational beings, elsewhere in the universe. Underlying all of these inquiries is what the author posited in 1974 about the *ultron*, which is recalled in this Essay.

One can find, by searching the Internet, a useful comment on this "Yearnings" essay by Larry Arnhart, "Anastaplo on Physics and Religion." Professor Arnhart's publications include *Darwinian Natural Right: The Biological Ethics of Human Nature* (New York: SUNY Press, 1998). One can also find on the Internet later versions of the "Yearnings" essay, such as the Addendum of February 14, 2008.

Endnotes (for Chapters 1–17)

1. A traditional Shaker spiritual. See *The Shaker Spiritual*, Daniel W. Patterson, ed. (Princeton, N.J.: Princeton University Press, 1979), 363. See also note 767, below.

2. The common law, in the Anglo-American tradition, invokes enduring standards of right and wrong. See, on the old-fashioned common law, William T. Braithwaite, "The Common Law and the Judicial Power: An Introduction to *Swift-Erie*," in *Law and Philosophy: The Practice of Theory*, John A. Murley, Robert L. Stone, and William T. Braithwaite, eds. (Athens: Ohio University Press, 1992), II, 744; George Anastaplo, *The Constitution of 1787: A Commentary* (Baltimore: Johns Hopkins University Press, 1989); Anastaplo, "Nature and Convention in Blackstone's *Commentaries*: The Beginning of an Inquiry," 22 *Legal Studies Forum* 161 (1998); note 750, below. William Blackstone's *Commentaries on the Laws of England* was republished by the University of Chicago Press in 1979.

3. Leo Strauss, *Thoughts on Machiavelli* (Glencoe, Ill.: Free Press, 1958), 9. See, on the natural basis for judgments about right and wrong, George Anastaplo, "Natural Law or Natural Right?" 38 *Loyola of New Orleans Law Review* 915 (1993); Anastaplo, "Teaching, Nature, and the Moral Virtues," *The Great Ideas Today*, vol. 1997, 23 (1997). See, for a remarkably useful extensive guide to scholarship influenced by Leo Strauss, John A. Murley, ed., *Leo Strauss and His Legacy* (Lanham, Md.: Lexington Books, 2005). Guidance may be found there to subjects and texts referred to in this book which I have discussed elsewhere.

4. See George Anastaplo, *Human Being and Citizen: Essays on Virtue, Freedom, and the Common Good* (Chicago: Swallow Press, 1975), 46–60, 74–86; Anastaplo, *The American Moralist: On Law, Ethics, and Government* (Athens: Ohio University Press, 1992), 185–98, 367–88. See, on the good, note 67, below.

5. Those traditional notions are evident in the literature we inherit and rely upon for guidance. See, e.g., Richard A. Posner, *Law and Literature: A Misunderstood Relation* (Cambridge, Mass.: Harvard University Press, 1988), 357. See, for a discussion of Judge Posner's readings, George Anastaplo, "Critique," 23 *Loyola University of Chicago Law Journal* 199 (1992). See also William T. Braithwaite, "Why, and How,

Judges Should Study Poetry," 19 *Loyola University of Chicago Law Journal* 810 (1988); Elizabeth Villiers Gemmette, "Law and Literature: An Unnecessary Suspect Class in the Liberal Arts Component of the Law School Curriculum," 23 *Valparaiso University Law Review* 267 (1989). See, on reading the Constitution, note 576, below.

6. Robert H. Henry, "Forward into the Past," 20 *Oklahoma City University Law Review* 1, 15 (1995). See also Anastaplo, *Human Being and Citizen*, 113.

7. Consider the following challenge (which is expanded in the text accompanying note 315, below):

> If the Bible is a work of the human mind, it has to be read like any other book—like Homer, like Plato, like Shakespeare—with respect but also with willingness to argue with the author, to disagree with him, to criticize him. If the Bible is the work of God, it has to be read in an entirely different spirit than the way in which we must read the human books. The Bible has to be read in a spirit of pious submission, of reverent hearing. [Leo Strauss, *Jewish Philosophy and the Crisis of Modernity*, Kenneth Hart Green, ed. (Albany: State University of New York Press, 1997), 359.]

See also *ibid*., 476, n. 1; notes 315, 345, 575, below. See, for a review of this Strauss book, appendix E of this book. (See also appendix A of this book.) See, on "anti-supernaturalism," note 577, below. See, on Homer and Plato, Anastaplo, *The Thinker as Artist: From Homer to Plato & Aristotle* (Athens: Ohio University Press, 1997). See, on Shakespeare, note 8, below. Consider, with respect to the Strauss challenge, "The question of the wise is half an answer," Milton H. Polin, "Ultimately God Will Provide the Solution," *Judaism*, vol. 37, 441 (1988) (quoting Rabbi Shem Tob ben Abraham ibn Gaon). See notes 654 and 748, below.

8. See, on Shakespeare, George Anastaplo, *The Artist as Thinker: From Shakespeare to Joyce* (Athens: Ohio University Press, 1983), 15–61; Anastaplo, *The Constitution of 1787*, 74; Anastaplo, "Critique," 202–4.

9. See Anastaplo, "On Freedom: Explorations,"17 *Oklahoma City University Law Review* 465, 724 (1992). See, for the biblical influences upon Lincoln's Gettysburg Address and Second Inaugural Address, Anastaplo, *Abraham Lincoln: A Constitutional Biography* (Lanham, Md.: Rowman & Littlefield, 1999), 229, 243 (preferred title for this book: *Thoughts on Abraham Lincoln: A Discourse on Prudence*). There is scheduled to be added to this Lincoln book, as a foreword (in any reprinting), Eva T. H. Brann's review of it in 46 *South Dakota Law Review* 666–69 (2001). See also notes 384 and 567, below. I hope to publish in a few years a sequel to my Lincoln book, *Further Thoughts on Abraham Lincoln*. See, for example, the materials gathered in 35 *Valparaiso Law Review* 39–196 (2000).

10. At the same time, students may have experimented with a variety of exotic doctrines. See George Anastaplo, "On the Use, Neglect, and Abuse of Veils: The Parliaments of the World's Religions, 1893, 1993," *The Great Ideas Today*, vol. 1994, 30 (1994). See also notes 47, 58, 209, 212, 651, and 732, below.

11. It can be most instructive for students to observe how the more pious members of their classes (like the public at large) respond to the Scriptures. See, on the effort to adapt ancient teachings (including sometimes "simple gifts") to modern circumstances, George Anastaplo, *The Constitutionalist: Notes on the First Amendment*

(Dallas: Southern Methodist University Press, 1971), 794, n.28. (*The Constitutionalist* was reprinted, with additions (including a foreword by Laurence Berns), by Lexington Books in 2005.)

12. The occasion for each of the discussions below is indicated in the first note for each chapter in this book. See, for other discussions by me of the Bible, Anastaplo, *On Trial: From Adam and Eve to O.J. Simpson* (Lanham, Md.: Lexington Books, 2004); Anastaplo, "Rome, Piety and Law: Explorations," 39 *Loyola Law Review* 1, 39–47 (1993); Anastaplo, "Lessons for the Student of Law: The Oklahoma Lectures," 20 *Oklahoma City University Law Review* 17, 97–112 (1996). See also the Murley bibliography cited in note 3, above.

13. It is hoped that once a student is exposed to a great piece of literature, its magic will have been given an opportunity to do its work. See, on education and educators, George Anastaplo, "Law & Literature and the Bible: Explorations," 23 *Oklahoma City University Law Review* 515, 857 (1998). See also Robert H. Henry, "Anastaplo's Bible as Legal Literature: A Guide to the Perplexed; or a Perplexing Guide," 23 *Oklahoma City University Law Review* 501, 505–9 (1998). Judge Henry is now the Chief Judge on the United States Court of Appeals for the Tenth Circuit. See, for the translations generally used in this book of the Hebrew Bible (the Old Testament) and of the Greek Bible (the New Testament), notes 15 and 41, below.

14. A talk given at a staff seminar of the Basic Program of Liberal Education for Adults, University of Chicago, Chicago, November 9, 1991. See further on prophecy, chapter 12 of this book. See, on the Basic Program, Anastaplo, *The Artist as Thinker*, 284–300. See also notes 27, 144, 183, 300, 391, 482, 534, 573, 589, and 599, below. My association with the Basic Program was on the initiative of Laurence Berns, with Rosary College (Dominican University) on the initiative of Sister Candida Lund, with the University of Dallas on the initiative of Willmoore Kendall, and with the Loyola University Chicago School of Law on the initiative of William T. Braithwaite. See as well Anastaplo, "A Timely Recapitulation, with Some Help from Socrates, Plato, and Aristotle," *The Greek Star*, Chicago, August 9, 2007, 8 (inserted into the Internet by the Hellenic Communication Service in 2007).

15. Numbers 23:19–20. Unless otherwise indicated, quotations in this book from the Hebrew Bible will be taken (sometimes with adjustments by me in capitalization and punctuation) from the translation of the Jewish Publication Society of America (1917, 1953). A few passages in the Hebrew Bible use what is said to be Aramaic. See *Ezra* 4:8–6:18, 7:12–26; *Jeremiah* 10:11; *Daniel* 2:4–7:28. See note 41, below. See also note 308, below; the text accompanying note 604, below. Compare note 75, below. One caution in judging biblical characters is suggested in note 143, below.

16. See Aristotle, *Poetics* 1454a20. See, on Homer, Anastaplo, *The Thinker as Artist*, 13–44, 366–82. See, on Sophocles' *Antigone*, *ibid.*, 391. See also Anastaplo, *On Trial*, 470.

17. See, on Herodotus' Croesus, Anastaplo, *The Thinker as Artist*, 211–52. See, on Sophocles' *Oedipus Tyrannus*, *ibid.*, 400. See also Anastaplo, *On Trial*, 488; Anastaplo, "Critique," 201–2; note 72, below.

18. Letter from John Adams to Thomas Jefferson (February 10, 1812), in *The Adams-Jefferson Letters*, Lester J. Cappon, ed. (Chapel Hill: University of North

Carolina Press, 1959), 298. See, on the Adams-Jefferson correspondence, Anastaplo, *The Amendments to the Constitution: A Commentary* (Baltimore: Johns Hopkins University Press, 1995), 107–24.

19. See, on Delphi, Anastaplo, *The Thinker as Artist*, 93–108, 394. See also notes 148–50, below. See, on Oedipus, note 17, above. See also the text accompanying note 507, below.

20. See, e.g., Aristotle, *Poetics* 1452a6–10. See also chapter 13.

21. See, e.g., 1 *Chronicles* 13:9–10. See also note 61, below.

22. See, e.g., Anastaplo, *Human Being and Citizen*, 18–25. See, on what Socrates did know, Anastaplo, "Freedom of Speech and the First Amendment: Explorations," 21 *Texas Tech Law Review* 1941, 1945–1958 (1990). See also the text accompanying note 728, below.

23. See *Exodus* 7:8–12, 20–22; 8:7, 17–19.

24. See Leo Strauss, "How to Begin to Study *The Guide of the Perplexed*," in Moses Maimonides, *The Guide of the Perplexed*, Shlomo Pines, trans. (Chicago: University of Chicago Press, 1963), xi. See also Anastaplo, *The American Moralist*, 58–79. See, on Leo Strauss, Anastaplo, *The Artist as Thinker*, 249; note 47, below. See also Anastaplo, "Leo Strauss and Judaism"; appendices A and E of this book.

25. See Anastaplo, *The American Moralist*, 139. See also note 224, below.

26. See Letter from John Adams to Thomas Jefferson (May 3, 1812), in *The Adams-Jefferson Letters*, 302.

27. A talk given in the Works of the Mind Lecture Series, The Basic Program of Liberal Education for Adults, University of Chicago, Chicago, April 12, 1992.

28. Strauss, *Jewish Philosophy and the Crisis of Modernity*, 359 ("On the Interpretation of 'Genesis'").

29. Euripides, *Hippolytus*, 612. See Anastaplo, *The Thinker as Artist*, 136–37.

30. See, on the battle of Arginusae, Anastaplo, *Human Being and Citizen*, 13–15, 237, 240. See, on omens and portents among the ancient Romans, Anastaplo, "The Constitution at Two Hundred: Explorations," 22 *Texas Tech Law Review* 967, 985–86 (1991).

31. *Deuteronomy* 4:5–8. See the text accompanying note 90, below. See also the text accompanying note 390, below.

32. See Anastaplo, "On the Use, Neglect, and Abuse of Veils," 41–43. See also chapters 8 and 9.

33. See Strauss, *Jewish Philosophy and the Crisis of Modernity*, 311 ("Why We Remain Jews"). See also note 575, below; the text accompanying note 374, below.

34. See, on Shakespeare's *Macbeth*, Anastaplo, *The Artist as Thinker*, 21–22, 493.

35. See, on the Binding of Isaac, Anastaplo, *On Trial*, 112–34; Anastaplo, *The Thinker as Artist*, 137, 143. See also the text accompanying note 98, below; notes 202 and 252, below.

36. See Eliezer Whatman, "A Look at the Real King Hussein," *Jerusalem Post* (International Edition), March 28, 1992, 8. See also the text accompanying note 55, below; note 444, below.

37. See *Luke* 9:7–9. See, on Jesus' healing, chapter 14. I was told by Monford Harris (of the Spertus College of Judaica) that medieval Hasids went in for faith healings,

more so than did the Jews of biblical times. We recall that Elijah could resuscitate the unconscious, if not also the dead.

38. See, on pollution, Anastaplo, *Human Being and Citizen*, 97–101.

39. See, on the limitations inherent in any investigation of being, Anastaplo, *The American Moralist*, 139; note 369, below. See, on the origins of things, Anastaplo, Book Review, *The Great Ideas Today*, vol. 1997, 448 (1997). See also appendix F of this book, "On Beginnings."

40. See *John* 2:1–11.

41. *Mark* 9:29. Quotations in this book from the Greek Bible (or New Testament) will be taken (sometimes with adjustments by me in capitalization and punctuation) from the King James Version of the Bible. See note 15, above; note 686, below. See also note 317, below.

42. *Exodus* 23:29–30. See also the text accompanying note 376, below.

43. *Exodus* 14:21.

44. John Noble Wilford, "Oceanographers Say Winds May Have Parted the Waters," *New York Times*, March 15, 1992, 12.

45. See, on the origins of Israel, Salo W. Baron, *A Social and Religious History of the Jews* (New York: Columbia University Press, 1937), vol. 1, 32–52. (However the crossing was done, the body of water dealt with is now said to be the Reed Sea, not the Red Sea. See note 260, below.) See also Winston S. Churchill, *Thoughts and Adventures* (London: Odham, 1949), 223–34 ("Moses—The Leader of a People"); George Anastaplo, "Church and State: Explorations," 19 *Loyola University of Chicago Law Journal* 61, 98–99 (1987); note 260, below.

46. See Niccolò Machiavelli, *Discourses on Livy*, vol. I, 56. See also note 64, below. Compare Anastaplo, "Lessons for the Student of Law," 187–98.

47. Anastaplo, *But Not Philosophy: Seven Introductions to Non-Western Thought* (Lanham, Md.: Lexington Books, 2002), 131 (quoting Harry V. Jaffa). See Anastaplo, "Rome, Piety, and Law," 114. See also the texts accompanying notes 510, 519, below. See, on Plato's *Laws*, Anastaplo, *The American Moralist*, 37–50; Anastaplo, *The Thinker as Artist*, 104–6. Compare the text accompanying note 653, below. Compare also the use of Avicenna in the appendix C epigraph.

48. See, on David, Solomon, and the Temple, chapters 10 and 11.

49. *Esther* 4:14.

50. See Monford Harris, *Exodus and Exile: The Structure of the Jewish Holidays* (Minneapolis: Fortress Press, 1992), 103. "In the technical sense, Purim is not a holiday. It is referred to as the 'days of Purim'." *Ibid.* See also Shlomo Riskin, "Hidden in Plain View," *Jerusalem Post*, March 7, 1998, 31. Did the king learn from the Queen Vashti episode *not* to make a similar demand on Queen Esther? Did Esther have any "choice" when called to replace the evidently virtuous Vashti? The character and fate of Vashti should be thought about. See notes 129 and 384, below. See also the quite instructive discussion of the *Book of Esther* in Jules Gleicher, "Mordecai the Exilarch: Some Thoughts on the *Book of Esther*," *Interpretation*, vol. 28, 187 (2001).

51. Carey A. Moore, *Studies in the Book of Esther* (New York: Ktav Publishing House, 1982), XX–XXI.

52. *Ibid.*, XXI–XXII. See, generally, Andre LaCocque, *The Feminine Unconventional: Four Subversive Figures in Israel's Tradition* (Minneapolis: Fortress Press, 1990), 49–83.

53. See chapter 6.

54. Moore, *Studies in the Book of Esther*, XXII, XXIV.

55. LaCocque, *The Feminine Unconventional*, 80, n. 63. See the text accompanying note 36, above.

56. See *Esther* 4:3.

57. See *Esther* 3:8.

58. See, on Ishtar in Mesopotamia, Anastaplo, *But Not Philosophy*, 1 (on the Gilgamesh epic).

59. *Esther* 4:14. One can be reminded of the political consequences of Bathsheba's attractions for David. See the text accompanying note 143, below; chapters 10 and 11. See also William Shakespeare, *The Tempest*, V, i, 203–6.

60. The story of Mordecai and the king, we are told in *Esther* 10:2, is also to be found "in the book of the chronicles of the kings of Media and Persia." Are there available today any remnants of those chronicles? Compare note 238, below.

61. See 1 *Chronicles* 13:9–10; 1 *Samuel* 13:8–14. See also note 21, above.

62. See *Exodus* 20:14; *Deuteronomy* 5:18; *Matthew* 5:27–28. See also Anastaplo, *The Thinker as Artist*, 140–41.

63. See, e.g., *Luke* 6:1–11; *John* 5:1–18.

64. Machiavelli, *Discourses on Livy*, III, 22 (Leo Paul S. de Alvarez, trans.). One can be reminded here of the career of David. See chapter 10.

65. Consider also the institution of ostracism among the Athenians. Consider as well what the high priest, in discussing what should be done with Jesus, is reported to have said about sacrificing one man for the sake of the people. See *John* 11:49–53. See, on the trial of Jesus, Anastaplo, *On Trial*, 155–204.

66. A talk given at Rosary College (now Dominican University), River Forest, Illinois, February 7, 1995. This was the Malcolm Pitman Sharp Memorial Lecture. (I had helped raise in 1980–1981 the endowment for this annual lecture series from alumni of the University of Chicago Law School. My honorarium for this 1995 lecture was donated to Rosary College.)

67. Aristotle, *Nicomachean Ethics*, 1094a1–3 (Joe Sachs translation). See, on the Idea of the Good, Anastaplo, *The Thinker as Artist*, 303. See also note 349, below; the text accompanying note 5, above. Compare note 364, below. Consider also this passage from Thomas Hooker, *The Application of Redemption, By the effectual Work of the Word, and Spirit of Christ, for the bringing home of lost Sinners to God* (London, 1659), 327–28:

> The Will of a Natural man is the worst part about him. The worst thing he hath, and the greatest Enemy he hath, is his own Heart and Will. It follows thus, It is that which maintains al the fitful distempers of his soul, it keeps the whole Army of Corruptions al in their Ranks, that Victuals them, and provides for them, that hinders a man from using the means, or from getting good by al the means of Grace: Its the corrupt wil of a man that keeps him under the power of his sinne, and keeps off the power of an Ordinance, that

> would procure his everlasting good. I speak it the rather to dash that dream of wicked men, when they do ill, and speak ill; yet (say they) my heart is good. Its true, I cannot speak so wel, nor do so wel, nor mak such a shew as others can, but my desires are good. No truly, If thy Life be naught, thy Heart is worse. [Citing *Matthew* 12:34, 35.] There is a treasury of evil in thy heart, variety and abundance of wickedness there.

There may be seen in these quotations (one from Aristotle, the other from the Reverend Thomas Hooker of Hartford, Connecticut) indications of a fundamental difference between ancients and moderns with respect to the natural openness of the human soul to the Good. See also the epigraph for appendix I of this book. See as well note 3, above, notes 384, 462, and 520, below.

68. See Malcolm Sharp, "Aggression: A Study of Values and Law," *Ethics*, vol. 57, 1 (1947).

69. *Ibid.*, 35. A recent review of a book (*Crime Is Not the Problem: Lethal Violence in America* (New York: Oxford University Press, 1997)), co-authored by another of Malcolm Sharp's students, Franklin E. Zimring (with Gordon Hawkins), has elicited these observations in a book review:

> Most developed nations have crime rates equivalent to those of the United States. What separates America from the rest of the industrial world is not the amount of crime but its lethal character in the U.S., the rate of death and life-threatening violence from assaults is 4 to 18 times greater than in other developed nations. . . . [T]he general availability of handguns [is] the single most important factor in our staggering death rate from violence. [Richard Moran, "Making Crime Less Lethal," *Chicago Tribune*, *Books*, September 7, 1997, 1–2.]

See, on Mr. Sharp's career, Anastaplo, "Lessons for the Student of Law," 133.

70. Joseph Campbell, *The Masks of God: Occidental Mythology* (New York: Viking Press, 1964).

71. Gera-Lind Kolarik, *I Am Cain* (Chicago: Chicago Review Press, 1994), 158–59. The one man I have known with the name of Cain, who was then an official of the Chicago Bar Association, always conducted himself, in his dealings with me in a highly controversial matter, as an eminently honorable member of the bar.

72. Robert Sacks, "The Lion and the Ass: A Commentary on the Book of *Genesis*," *Interpretation*, vol. 8, 71 (1980). See note 17, above. Compare Plutarch's treatment of brotherhood and its political significance in his *Moralia*.

73. Anastaplo, *The Amendments to the Constitution*, 1. See, on the devastation of civil war, Laurence Berns, "Thomas Hobbes," in *History of Political Philosophy*, second ed., Leo Strauss and Joseph Cropsey, eds. (Chicago: Rand McNally, 1972), 370.

74. Sharp, "Aggression," 24. I presume to illustrate Mr. Sharp's observations by recalling my letter to the editor of July 4, 2003 commenting on the dreadful consequences of our ill-conceived 2003 intervention in Iraq:

> It is not prudent to assume, as some in the National Administration evidently like to believe, that only Saddam Hussein's continuing influence or the importation of "terrorists" from abroad can account for the deadly attacks these days on American troops in Iraq. For

> more than a decade we battered that country, both militarily and economically—and usually from a safe distance. What should be expected, therefore, from a heavily-armed people of spirit when recognizable agents of a destructive foreign power at last come within range of that people's more primitive weaponry? Frustrated American troops in Iraq talk of never knowing where their next ambush may come from. No doubt, some Iraqis would like to respond that Americans are beginning to learn what besieged Iraqis have felt like for some years as victims both of domestic tyrants and of foreign enemies. There may be seen, on all sides of this unnecessary conflict, the deadly follies that can result from delusions which are not adequately challenged.

See Murley, ed., *Leo Strauss and His Legacy*, 855. See also *ibid.*, 854. See as well George Anastaplo, "September 11th: The ABCs of a Citizen's Responses," 29 *Oklahoma City University Law Review* 165 (2004); Anastaplo, "September 11th, A Citizen's Responses (continued)," 4 *Loyola University Chicago International Law Review* 135 (2006) (with a sequel in volume 5 of this Loyola journal).

75. This translation is taken from Sacks, "The Lion and the Ass," 67–75. (A gap in the received text is indicated by me in verse 8.) Compare note 15, above. Nothing is said about how Eve learned that Cain had killed Abel.

76. *The Encyclopedia of Religion* (New York: Macmillan, 1987), vol. 3, 2.

77. Maimonides, *The Guide of the Perplexed*, II, 30 (347).

78. See *Genesis* 1:28–30, 2:9, 19–20, 3:17–19, 23. See, on Adam and Eve, Anastaplo, *On Trial*, 5–21. Compare *Matthew* 10:16.

79. See William Shakespeare, *Hamlet*, III, iii, 37–47. See, on *Hamlet*, Anastaplo, *The Artist as Thinker*, 18–20.

80. Perhaps, a modern reader might suggest, Cain attacked his brother as a means of venting anger he may have had toward the parents who had lost the Garden for us all. But, then, was not Cain quite capable of getting evicted from the Garden on his own merits? See, on Cain and Abel, Henry, "Anastaplo's Bible as Legal Literature," 509–12.

81. See, on Judas Iscariot, Anastaplo, *The American Moralist*, 4. See also George Anastaplo, *The Last Christian* (an unpublished play); the text accompanying note 616, below. See as well appendix G of this book, especially section II.

82. An observant Jew, I have been told, may go so far in his piety as to refrain from disturbing the order of Creation by killing even a mosquito on the Sabbath, something which one *may* do on other days of the week. See, on innovation, the text accompanying note 100, below. See also note 292, below.

83. *Genesis* 3:9, 4:9.

84. See, on Thomas Hobbes and the suppression of violence, note 73, above. See also note 189, below.

85. See, on Noah, Anastaplo, "Lessons for the Student of Law," 97. See, on Abraham, note 35, above. See, on Moses, chapters 7, 8, and 9. See also the text accompanying note 502, below.

86. Consider for the rebuke to Moses, by his wife, about bloody-mindedness, *Exodus* 4:24–26. See note 267, below. Moses' killing of an Egyptian, after looking to see whether anyone was watching, can be considered an echo of Cain's killing of Abel. See *Genesis* 2:11–15. See also the text accompanying note 240, below.

87. But, it should be noted, Monford Harris discounted this as a biblical preference. Also, he counseled that "omissions" in a biblical text (such as those discussed below) should alert the reader as to the writer's concerns and goals, which can be quite different from those of the modern reader. See the text accompanying note 325, below. Compare references to Jesus as the Good Shepherd.

88. Nor need we be concerned here either about what was said about Cain and Abel in the oral traditions of peoples in that part of the world or about the covenant later developed between God and the Children of Israel. Rather, it is the stripped-down version of the story provided by the author or editor of *Genesis* with which we are primarily concerned on this occasion. Even so, the story does suggest that a detailed prescription of sacrifices moderates competition and makes deadly strife less likely, however formalistic and empty such prescriptions can eventually seem to become in practice.

Oral traditions with respect to Cain and Abel include suggestions about what they talked about in their final encounter. See, e.g., Leonard V. Kaplan, "Unhappy Pierre: Foucault's Parricide and Human Responsibility," 83 *Northwestern University Law Review* 321, 349 (1989). See, for samplings of modern retellings of this story, *Genesis: As It Is Written*, David Rosenberg, ed. (San Francisco: Harper, 1996), 37, 43. See also Giuseppi Gioachino Belli, "Cain," *Poetry*, April 1980, 6. See as well the text at note 548, below.

89. I am told that Cain's very name points (in the Hebrew) to his possessiveness, just as Abel's name points to his ephemeral quality. Plato's great dialogue on virtue, the *Meno*, also has a "hero" who is singularly acquisitive. See, on the *Meno*, Anastaplo, "Teaching," 2. See, on the grounding of the moral virtues in nature, *ibid*., 23; Anastaplo, *Campus Hate-Speech Codes, Natural Right, and Twentieth Century Atrocities* (Lewiston, N.Y.: Edwin Mellen Press, 1999), 127. (An expanded version of this book was published in 1999.) (Laurence Berns and I have prepared a translation of the *Meno*, which was published by the Focus Publishing Company in 2004.) A useful review of that translation was prepared by Dustin A. Gish for the Fall 2007 issue of *Polis*.)

90. *Deuteronomy* 4:6. See the text accompanying note 31, above; the text accompanying note 390, below.

91. See, on capital punishment, Anastaplo, *The American Moralist*, 422; Anastaplo, "The Eighth Amendment and the Punishment of Death," *Chicago Daily Law Bulletin*, April 25, 1998, 23; note 267, below. See, on Mr. Sharp and the *Rosenberg Case* executions, Anastaplo, *On Trial*, 313f, 360f. See also Malcolm Sharp, *Was Justice Done? The Rosenberg-Sobell Case* (New York: Monthly Review Press, 1956). See further, on the *Rosenberg-Sobell Case*, Anastaplo, *Reflections on Freedom of Speech and the First Amendment* (Lexington: University Press of Kentucky, 2007), 253.

92. A talk given for the Committee on Women's Issues, Loyola University of Chicago School of Law, Chicago, February 6, 1984.

93. "I came, I saw, I conquered." See Seutonius, *Divus Julius*, xxxvii, 2; *The Oxford Dictionary of Quotations* (second ed., 1953), 120.

94. Abraham Lincoln, Speech of June 16, 1858, in Abraham Lincoln, *The Collected Works*, Roy Basler, ed. (New Brunswick, N.J.: Rutgers University Press, 1953), II, 461.

95. *Genesis* 5:1–2. Robert Sacks's commentary is instructive about this story as it is about the rest of *Genesis*. See Sacks, "The Lion and the Ass."

96. In the tradition of the Jews, if the mother is "Jewish," so is the child. In this sense, perhaps, the woman transmits the Covenant, not the husband. See *Genesis* 5:2.

97. Isaac informs the weeping Esau: "And by thy sword shall thou live, and thou shalt serve thy brother; and it shall come to pass when thou shalt break loose, that thou shalt shake his yoke from off thy neck." Compare notes 126, 377, below. I do not mean to suggest that the divisions into chapters and verses were in the original text.

98. See note 35, above.

99. Compare Maimonides, *The Guide of the Perplexed*, II, 48 (411): "Likewise when speaking of accidental things due to pure chance, it says in the story of *Rebekah: And let her be thy master's son's wife, as the Lord hath spoken*." See, on Nausicaa, as a would-be Rebekah, Anastaplo, *The Thinker as Artist*, 35–57.

100. See *Genesis* 26:18. Compare *Genesis* 26:19–22, 32–33. See the text accompanying note 82, above.

101. See *Genesis* 25:22.

102. See *Genesis* 25:22–23.

103. See *Genesis* 25:23. Christians can see here a foreshadowing of Mary's relation to the young Jesus. See, e.g., *John* 2:51.

104. See, e.g., Maimonides, *The Guide of the Perplexed*, II, 45 (399).

105. See *Genesis* 25:29–34.

106. See *Genesis* 25:28. See, on the importance of food rationing for political power, chapter 6. See, for an anticipation of the move of Jacob and his family to Egypt, *Genesis* 26:1. See, on the Israelites' associations with Egypt across the centuries, Baron, *A Social and Religious History of the Jews*, I, 32f.

107. See *Genesis* 27:1–4.

108. See, e.g., *The Interpreter's Bible* (New York: Abingdon-Cokesbury Press, 1952), I, 667–69, 680.

109. See *ibid*., I, 681.

110. See, e.g., *Genesis* 31:38–39. Shylock speaks approvingly of this device. See William Shakespeare, *The Merchant of Venice* 1, iii, 69f. Jacob is also like his mother in being smooth of skin. See *Genesis* 27:11.

111. See *Genesis* 27:27–29.

112. See, on the character of Isaac, *The Pentateuch and Haftorahs*, J. H. Hertz, ed. (London, Soncino Press, 1952), 331–32:

> Abraham was an epoch-maker; his life, therefore, was an eventful one. Jacob closes the Patriarchal period, and his life was both rough and eventful. Not so Isaac. He inherits the true belief in God; his is merely the task of loyally transmitting it. No wonder that we hear little of him, and that he repeats some of his father's experiences. . . . Isaac, a patient, meditative men, strong in affection and love, typical of the domestic virtues for which his descendants have throughout the ages been remarkable. He stands as a type of the passive virtues, which have a strength of their own.

Does Isaac use "my son" to indicate that the blessing treats the recipient (whoever he may be) as *the* heir apparent?

113. See *Genesis* 27:41.

114. See *Genesis* 27:42–45. One can be reminded of what happened between Cain and Abel. When Jacob leaves, Isaac gives him, knowing this time who he is, the superior Covenantal blessing. See *Genesis* 28:3–4.

115. See *Genesis* 27:46. See also *Genesis* 26:34–35.

116. See, e.g., *The Interpreter's Bible*, 667, 681–82. See also note 132, below.

117. See, on the limitations of the community and especially of its "leaders," Anastaplo, "The O.J. Simpson Case Revisited," 28 *Loyola University Chicago Law Journal* 461, 484 (1997). See also Anastaplo, *On Trial*, 356–59.

118. See *Genesis* 29:25–30. Compare *Genesis* 26:34–35.

119. See *Genesis* 23:2, 24:67.

120. See *Genesis* 31:18.

121. See *Genesis* 35:29.

122. See *Genesis* 35:38.

123. Johannes Pedersen, *Israel, Its Life and Culture* (Atlanta: Scholars Press, 1991), I, 69. This quotation continues: "No less typical is the example of the clever Abigail, who, behind the back of her husband, tries to atone for his foolishness in relation to the strong captain of the freebooters (1 *Samuel* 25)." *Ibid*. See the text accompanying note 415, below.

124. See, on the need for lawyers to rely much more on negotiation than on battle, Harrison Sheppard, "American Principles & the Evolving Ethos of American Legal Practice," 28 *Loyola University Chicago Law Journal* 237 (1996). See also Harrison Sheppard, *What's Right with Lawyers* (San Francisco: H. Sheppard, 2003).

125. See, on Aeschylus' *Oresteia*, Anastaplo, *On Trial*, 41; Anastaplo, *The Thinker as Artist*, 109.

126. See *Genesis* 33:1–3. How much is Esau materially enriched by Jacob on this occasion?

127. See note 35, above.

128. See *Genesis* 21:9–21.

129. See, on the limits of honor, Aristotle, *Nicomachean Ethics*, I, v, IV, iii. See also note 553, below.

130. On the other hand, if women should move wholeheartedly into the world of men, they should expect some of the genuine disabilities as well as the supposed rewards of men. See Anastaplo, *The American Moralist*, 349. See also note 384, below. See as well appendix F of this book, note 142.

131. See 1 *Kings* 3:16–28, 10:1–13. Monford Harris noticed that there is in the Hebrew Bible the conception of the "wise woman" (see 2 *Samuel* 14:1–2), but perhaps not of the "wise man." See also note 384, below.

132. See Anastaplo, *The American Moralist*, 27.

133. See note 110, above.

134. Lincoln, *Collected Works*, II, 261. See also *ibid*., III, 289; notes 135 and 291, below.

135. See, e.g., Plato, *The Republic*, 414D. See also note 291, below.

136. See, for example, the dedications in Anastaplo, *The Constitutionalist*, Anastaplo, *The Constitution of 1787*, and Anastaplo, *The Amendments to the Constitution*. See also the dedications in my *Artist* books.

137. See Anastaplo, *The Constitutionalist*, 781–82 (on *parresia*); Anastaplo, *The Artist as Thinker*, 75. See also note 132, above.

138. See note 134, above. See also the text accompanying note 63, above; the text accompanying note 642, below.

139. *Genesis* 27:19.

140. *Genesis* 27:22. See also note 110, above; note 337, below.

141. We must leave open the question as to what the rules indeed were among the Israelites about the first-born when we recall the ascendancy of Isaac over Ishmael, of Jacob over Esau, of Joseph over his brothers, of Perez over Zerah, of Moses over Aaron, of David over his brothers, and of Solomon over his brothers.

142. One can be reminded of the complaint lodged by the vanquished Croesus against Apollo. See, on Croesus, Anastaplo, *The Thinker as Artist*, 96, 98–99, 211–12, 234–35, 394. See also note 150, below. My source for the story elaborated upon here is the late William Kilbridge of the Loyola University of Chicago School of Law.

143. See, on Esther, the text accompanying note 59, above. In what ways may our assessments of how Rebekah, Joseph, Moses, and others acted be affected, if not even distorted in their favor, by what we know (which they perhaps could not have known as well except to the extent that they were divinely inspired) about what the Israelites would become? See note 161, below.

144. A talk given at a Weekend Conference of the Basic Program of Liberal Education for Adults, University of Chicago, East Troy, Wisconsin, April 28, 1996.

145. Abraham Lincoln, Speech of January 27, 1838, in Lincoln, *Collected Works*, I, 113–14.

146. *Universal Jewish Encyclopedia* (New York, 1958), vol. 6, 187. Compare Genesis 26:2.

147. The rational element in the story of Joseph seems to be appreciated in Thomas Mann's remarkable retelling of that story in *Joseph and His Brothers*.

148. Nahum M. Sarna, *Understanding Genesis: The Heritage of Biblical Israel* (New York: Jewish Theological Seminary of America, 1966), 212–13. Compare, on the significance of the pairing of dreams, the text accompanying note 168, below. The Sages explain (*B.T. Brahot* 55b): "Three kinds of dreams are fulfilled: a 'morning dream,' a dream which your friend also dreams, and a dream which contains its interpretation within itself. Some add a dream which keeps repeating itself." Shlomo Riskin, "Dreams and Visions," *Jerusalem Post* (International Edition), December 27, 1997, 31. See, on the "polis dream," Anastaplo, *The Constitutionalist*, 767.

149. See Homer, *Iliad*, II, 3–59. Consider also the dream that Iphigenia has that Orestes is dead. This sort of thing contributed, it seems, to personal dreams being supplanted in Greece by official oracles as more reliable sources of revelations. See Euripides, *Iphigenia at Taurus*. See also Anastaplo, *The Thinker as Artist*, 93.

150. One can be reminded of the testing of oracles by Herodotus' Croesus. See Anastaplo, *The Thinker as Artist*, 224, 394. See also note 142, above.

151. The modern musical, *Joseph and the Amazing Technicolor Dreamcoat*, by Tim Rice and Andrew Lloyd Webber (1968), seems to be aptly named. See, on Joseph, Henry, "Anastaplo's Bible as Legal Literature," 508.

152. Sarna, *Understanding Genesis*, 212.

153. See Maimonides, *The Guide of the Perplexed*, III, 29 (514).

154. Does one hear echoes of this story in what is said in the *Gospel of John* 1:5–11 about how another favorite son was rejected by his associates?

155. The Jews may even have had an anticipation here of how their own chosenness came to be regarded by the mean-spirited of the world. See Anastaplo, *Human Being and Citizen*, 155; note 331, below. Compare note 143, above.

156. See *Genesis* 39:12–20. See also the text accompanying note 164, below.

157. See *Genesis* 41:41–43.

158. Even Joseph's doting father was moved to protest, "What is this dream that thou hast dreamed? Shall I and thy mother and thy brethren indeed come to bow down to thee to the earth?" *Genesis* 37:10–11.

159. Sarna, *Understanding Genesis*, 213.

160. See *Genesis* 45:5–8. Compare, in this respect, the productive villainy of Judas Iscariot. See appendix G of this book.

161. It invites speculation that the story of the chaste Joseph should be interrupted by the sensual episode of Tamar and Judah, the precursors of David and Solomon. See *Genesis* 38:13–30. See also *Ruth* 4:12; *Matthew* 1:3; note 422, below. Compare the text accompanying note 241, below. See, on the specialness of Judah, Shlomo Riskin, "Know Your Opponent," *Jerusalem Post* (International Edition), January 3, 1998, 31. Compare this observation:

> The reader is thrown into a quandary since we assume that the *Avot* (Patriarchs) possess the power of *nevu'ah* (prophecy). How could it be in a world of Biblical *nevu'ah* that Jacob, the third and perhaps greatest of all the Patriarchs, would not know the truth that his son Joseph was yet alive? [Sanford H. Shudnow, "What Jacob Didn't Know, and Why," *Chicago Jewish Star*, December 9, 1997, 23.]

See also note 143, above, note 519, below. (Greater even than Abraham?!)

162. See *Genesis* 37:6–7.

163. See *Genesis* 37:6–7, 41:5–7. Joseph and the Pharaoh, it can be said, were sensed by the narrator to be soulmates. See Plato, *Apology of Socrates*, 22B–C. See also note 167, below.

164. See *Genesis* 39:12–20.

165. See Sarna, *Understanding Genesis*, 218.

166. See *Genesis* 40:1–19.

167. Did the baker sense that he was in jeopardy? Is that why he did not dare ask for Joseph's reading of his dream until after the (more confident?) butler had done so and had gotten an auspicious reading? See *Genesis* 40:16–19. The fourth dream interpreted by Joseph, that of the baker, used bread, a product of grain. See the text accompanying note 163, above.

168. See *Genesis* 41:32. The dreams of the butler and the baker can be referred to as connected. See *Genesis* 40:8; the text accompanying note 148, above.

169. See, e.g., *Genesis* 47:20–26.

170. Some scholars refer to seven-year cycles. See, e.g., Sarna, *Understanding Genesis*, 219.

171. See, e.g., *ibid.*, 219.

172. See *Genesis* 41:32–46. One can be reminded of President Nixon's use of Henry Kissinger. Machiavelli counsels the prince against permitting unsolicited counsel from his advisors. See Niccolò Machiavelli, *The Prince*, chapter 23, Leo Paul S. de Alvarez, trans. (Irving, Tex.: University of Dallas Press, 1980). (Is this an instance of unsolicited counsel from Machiavelli himself?)

173. See *Genesis* 37:9–10.

174. See *Genesis* 48:5.

175. See chapter 3, sections VII–IX.

176. See, e.g., *Jeremiah* 27:1, 29:32.

177. See *Genesis* 42:29, 50–14.

178. See, e.g., *Exodus* 16:1–3. After all, not all Jews in the Western world want to live in Israel today. The United States is in *some* respects the modern equivalent of ancient Egypt (another wealthy world power). See chapter 3, end of section VIII. See also Shlomo Riskin, "In the End We Must Choose," *Jerusalem Post* (International Edition), January 10, 1998, 31.

179. See *Genesis* 50:22–25. See also the text accompanying note 186, below. Had Joseph heard, perhaps as a child, what his great-grandfather had been told by God? See note 225, below.

180. Consider, for example, how much is made of the Israelites' Egyptian experience during a Seder gathering. See note 178, above.

181. See, on the need to take advantage of the opportunities one happens to have, Anastaplo, *Human Being and Citizen*, 175; Anastaplo, "'Racism,' Political Correctness, and Constitutional Law: A Law School Case Study," 42 *South Dakota Law Review* 135–36 (1997); Anastaplo, "'McCarthyism,' the Cold War, and Their Aftermath," 43 *South Dakota Law Review* 103 (1998). See also Anastaplo, *The Constitutionalist* (2005 reprinting), xxii–xxiv (on an instructive "racism" controversy and its enduring consequences).

182. See *Matthew* 2:13–15, 19–21.

183. A talk given in the First Friday Lecture Series, The Basic Program of Liberal Education for Adults, University of Chicago, Chicago, October 4, 1996.

184. Machiavelli, *The Prince*, ch. 6. See also the texts accompanying notes 306, 392, 518, below.

185. See *Exodus* 20:11.

186. *Genesis* 15:13–14. See the text accompanying note 255, below. See also the text accompanying note 179, above.

187. 1 *Samuel* 4:8. The dread that God's championing the Israelites would inspire in other peoples is anticipated in *Exodus* 15:14–16.

188. See *Exodus* 32:1. See also the text accompanying note 286, below. Compare *Exodus* 4:12.

189. Is not this the "psychology" that Thomas Hobbes was moved by? See notes 73 and 84, above.

190. *Exodus* 3:6.

191. See Anastaplo, *Abraham Lincoln*, 229. See, for another use of "fourscore," the text accompanying note 359, below. See also note 601, below.

192. See *Genesis* 12:10–20. This Pharaoh was far more receptive to the sanction of a plague than Moses' Pharaoh was. See also the text accompanying note 532, below.

193. In this, it has been suggested, the Haggadah drew upon the Bible's directives. See Everett Fox, *The Five Books of Moses* (New York: Schocken Books, 1995), 251.

194. See *Deuteronomy* 34:6. Compare *Genesis* 50:24–26.

195. One can be reminded of the subtlety of the Confucian *Analects*. See Anastaplo, *But Not Philosophy*, 99.

196. *Exodus* can be considered a second book of origins, bringing the Israelites forth as a people into "history." See also note 39, above. See as well appendix F of this book, part 2.

197. See *Exodus* 2:7–9.

198. Consider what Sigmund Freud presumes to do, and very much in public, with Moses' origins in his *Moses and Monotheism*. See Philo, *On the Life of Moses*, I, 32; Strauss, *Jewish Philosophy and the Critics of Modernity*, 285. See also note 259, below; the text accompanying notes 214 and 242–43, below.

199. See *Exodus* 2:11–12.

200. See *Exodus* 12:29–37.

201. See *Exodus* 4:14.

202. But Abraham does go to war to rescue a kinsman. See *Genesis* 14:13–16. Consider also his apparent willingness to sacrifice Isaac. See note 35, above; note 252, below.

203. See *Exodus* 2:13–14.

204. See *Exodus* 2:12, 15. See also note 86, above.

205. See *Exodus* 2:15–25.

206. *Exodus* 2:14.

207. Do we hear in this challenge an approach to ruling that combines what would later be separated for the Israelites: the king and the judge? See, e.g., 1 *Samuel* 8:5, 22, 12:1–25, 19:19, 24. See also the text accompanying note 254, below; note 366, below.

208. Moses is then asked, "Thinkest thou to kill me, as thou didst kill the Egyptian?" *Exodus* 2:14

209. See *Exodus* 3:2. See also note 260, below.

210. *The Interpreter's Bible*, 870–71. See, on Muhammad and Islam, Anastaplo, *But Not Philosophy*, 175.

211. See *Exodus* 3:2–3, 12; *Exodus* 19:1. See also Umberto Cassuto, *A Commentary on the Book of Exodus* (Jerusalem: Hebrew University of Jerusalem Press, 1967), 225; Hertz, *The Pentateuch and Haftorahs*, 213 ("The spot chosen by God to announce the physical redemption of Israel was also chosen by Him as the place of their spiritual redemption").

212. See, on ancient Egyptian thought, Anastaplo, *But Not Philosophy*, 146. See also note 284, below.

213. See *Exodus* 19:18. See also note 224, below.

214. See, on Abraham's father as an idolater, *Joshua* 24:2. See also the text accompanying note 198, above, the text accompanying note 269, below.

215. This bears upon God's notorious "hardening" of Pharaoh's heart.

216. See *Exodus* 3:19 sq.

217. See *Exodus* 5:1.

218. See *Exodus*, chs. 3–4.

219. *Exodus* 3:11.

220. *Exodus* 3:12. One can be reminded here of what Isaac Newton had to say about biblical prophecy. See appendix H of this book, section VI.

221. *Exodus* 3:13.

222. *Exodus* 3:14. See, for the dubious uses to which the "*I am*" name may be put, *United States* v. *Ballard*, 522 U.S. 78 (1944). See, on the *Ballard Case*, Anastaplo, *The Constitutionalist*, 532, n. 113; Anastaplo, *Reflections on Religion, the Divine, and Constitutionalism* (in course of preparation).

223. See *Exodus* 3:15–22.

224. See, for Thomas Aquinas's guidance here, Anastaplo, *The American Moralist*, 139. See also note 39, above; the text accompanying note 25, above. Thomas Aquinas said that "Good and Being are Convertible Terms." See Harry V. Jaffa, *Storm over the Constitution* (Claremont: The Claremont Institute, 1994), 59. See also notes 520 and 654, below. See, on *I shall be what I shall be*, Shlomo Riskin, "The Fire in Each of Us," *Jerusalem Post* (International Edition), January 17, 1998, 31.

225. *Exodus* 4:1. Would the people be really saying that the Lord had not appeared unto *them*? Is this the objection that Moses himself would have made if he had not personally had the encounter with the Burning Bush? Thus, it had not sufficed for Moses to rely exclusively upon the encounters of Abraham and Jacob with the Lord, let alone upon the encounters of Isaac and Joseph. See note 179, above. Joseph Smith, the founder of Mormonism, indicated toward the end of his life that he himself could not believe the things he had reported if he had not personally witnessed them. See, on Mormonism, Anastaplo, *Reflections on Religion, the Divine, and Constitutionalism* (in course of preparation).

226. See *Exodus* 4:2 sq.

227. See *Exodus* 4:30–31.

228. *Exodus* 4:10.

229. *Exodus* 4:11–12.

230. See *Exodus* 4:13.

231. See *Exodus* 4:14–17.

232. See *Exodus* 4:8–9.

233. See *Exodus* 7:14–25.

234. See *Exodus* 4:22–23.

235. See *Exodus* 12:29–37.

236. I heard Steven Chu, a Nobel Laureate in physics, say something to this effect in a lecture, "Experiments with Single Biomolecules," at the University of Chicago, February 6, 1998. See notes 232 and 235, above. See also the text accompanying note 590, below. See as well appendix K of this book.

237. See *Exodus* 5:1–21.

238. Not so much was done, it seems, to warrant being recorded in the extensive Egyptian records that we happen to have. See Baron, *A Social and Religious History*

of the Jews, 1:6–17. See also the text accompanying note 212, above; the text accompanying note 248, below. See as well note 60, above. The author of *Exodus* referred to here was traditionally believed to have been Moses. See the text accompanying notes 305–8 and 315, below. It can certainly be said that Moses alone of the Israelites could have known much of what is recorded in the Torah. See the text accompanying notes 278 and 280, below. See also the text accompanying note 574, below.

239. See *Exodus* 12:37. Compare *Exodus* 46:26. Modern scholars estimate that the entire population of Egypt at that time may have been no more than five million. Did the author's *three million Israelites* include, in effect, all the Israelites who had lived and died in Egypt across four centuries? Should all of them be considered part of the people eventually liberated in *Exodus*?

240. See *Exodus* 12:1 sq.

241. Compare note 161, above.

242. Fox, *The Five Books of Moses*, 241. See also note 238, above.

243. Strabo, *Geography XVI* (about 20 B.C.E.); H. L. Mencken, *A New Dictionary of Quotations* (New York: Alfred A. Knopf, 1962), 815. See note 198, above.

244. See *Exodus*, chs. 7–11.

245. See, e.g., *Genesis* 35:22–26; 46:8–25, 49:1–28; *Exodus* 1:1–6, 6:14–25. See also Philo, *On the Life of Moses*, I, 96 sq. It is said that there are no less than eighteen different arrangements in biblical listings of the tribes of Israel.

246. Even twentieth-century biologists and epidemiologists have come up with suggestions of natural connections between the plagues. See, e.g., John S. Marr and Curtis D. Malloy, "An Epidemiologic Analysis of the Ten Plagues of Egypt," *Caduceus*, vol. 12, 7 (1996).

247. See, on accounts of origins, note 39, above.

248. See note 238, above.

249. See *Exodus* 4:11–12, 20:8.

250. See *Exodus* 4:13.

251. See *Exodus* 4:14.

252. Moses may usefully be distinguished here from Abraham on the occasion of the Binding of Isaac. See note 35, above.

253. See *Exodus* 32:1–6. See also chapter 8, below.

254. See note 207, above.

255. See *Exodus* 12:40. Compare *Genesis* 15:13; the text accompanying note 186, above.

256. See *Exodus* 14:30. See also note 260, below.

257. See *Exodus* 1:22.

258. See *Exodus* 15:20-21.

259. See *Exodus* 2:4-10. But the specialness of Moses is recognized here by the identification of Miriam as Aaron's sister, not as Moses' sister. See note 198, above; note 384, below. See also note 191, above; note 601, below.

260. See Anastaplo, *The Thinker as Artist*, 303. Consider as well Winston Churchill's prudential assessment of the miracles attendant upon the exodus of the Israelites from Egypt. See Anastaplo, "Church and State: Explorations," 98–99. Were

the wheels of the Egyptian chariots fatally entangled by the reeds in the Sea of Reeds? See note 45, above. Should this be compared to the saving of the infant Moses by placing him among the reeds? It may even be fitting, therefore, that "burning" vegetation is the form in which Moses first encounters God. See the text accompanying note 212, above.

261. A talk given at a roundtable on political philosophy at the Illinois Political Science Association Annual Convention, Rockford College, Rockford, Illinois, November 11, 1995. Instructive guidance to the career of Moses is provided in the *Interpretation* articles by Jules Gleicher (of Rockford College) cited in the headnote for part 2 in appendix F of this book. See also Henry, "Anastaplo's Bible as Legal Literature," 508.

262. *Exodus* 20:1–6. See chapter 9, sections III and IV.

263. *Encyclopedia Judaica*, vol. 7 (1971), 709–10.

264. *Ibid.*, 710.

265. *Ibid.*

266. See, on the *Oresteia*, Anastaplo, *The Thinker as Artist*, 109; Anastaplo, *On Trial*, 41. See also Sophocles, *Ajax*, 1073–79.

267. Thomas Hobbes deplored such a use of power by Moses. Consider, also, what Moses' wife said about her husband, if not also about the Lord, being bloody-minded, upon the occasion of the circumcision of their son. See *Exodus* 4:24–26; note 86, above. See, on capital punishment, Henry, "Anastaplo's Bible as Legal Literature," 511–12; note 91, above.

268. See, e.g., *Numbers* 25.

269. See *Exodus* 32:10. See also the text accompanying note 214, above.

270. Consider the problem of Thomas Becket in T. S. Eliot's *Murder in the Cathedral*. See also Anastaplo, "Rome, Piety, and Law," 138.

271. Would Moses have done as God suggested if God had asked *him* in the way that He had asked Abraham?

272. See Maimonides, *The Guide of the Perplexed*, I, 3 (81). See also the text accompanying note 361, below.

273. *Jewish Encyclopedia* (n.d.), vol. 3, 508 ("Golden Calf").

274. *Ibid.*, 508–9 (quoting *Sanh*, 102). Some argue that the forty years of wandering was due, at least in part, to "the sin of the Calf." It does seem, however, that "the fall of man" (a term to which we have become accustomed) is *not* an ancient Hebrew term. Is there, without the fall of man, any need to distinguish the Second and Third Persons of the Trinity from the First Person? Indeed, without the "fallen" human race is the existence of either the self-sacrificer or the messenger needed? See note 657, below.

275. "Das Goldene Kalb," in *The Complete Poems of Heinrich Heine*, Hal Draper trans. (Cambridge: Suhrkamp/Insel Press, 1982), 586. It may be a mistake, however, to regard "the devil" as involved here. Arnold Schoenberg, in his opera *Moses and Aaron*, imagines an orgy, which involves "sub-orgies of gift-giving and human sacrifice as well as unbridled lust." David Murray, "Moses According to Schoenberg," *Financial Times*, October 6, 1995, 11. See also the text accompanying note 398, below.

Compare Exodus 19:15. See, on Heine, Strauss, *Jewish Philosophy and the Crisis of Modernity*, 346, n. 2.

276. See *Exodus* 32:1.

277. See *Exodus* 32:7.

278. See *Exodus* 32:10. See also note 238, above.

279. See Maimonides, *The Guide of the Perplexed*, I, 36 (82–84). See also *Jeremiah* 2:26–28; the texts accompanying notes 288, 513, and 517, below.

280. See, on the specialness of Moses among all of the prophets, Maimonides, *The Guide of the Perplexed*, II, 35 (367–69). See also note 238, above. We are told that the rabbis who wrote the Haggadah warned against deifying Moses. Did they have the career of Jesus in mind? See notes 388, 515, and 523, below.

281. See *Exodus* 32:7–10.

282. See *Exodus* 32:19.

283. Can the same be said about the long-term consequences of the Fall of Man? Compare note 274, above. Consider also appendix J of this book.

284. See, e.g., *Exodus* 16:3. Compare *Deuteronomy* 8:7–10. Is the Hebrew Bible's reluctance to make much of personal immortality still another hedge against any relapse into those Egyptian ways that were unduly concerned with death and its aftermath? See, on ancient Egypt and the cult of the dead, Anastaplo, *But Not Philosophy*, 31.

285. See, on Hur, *Exodus* 17:10, 12, 24:14.

286. See *Exodus* 32:2–4. Had this gold been taken from the Egyptians when the Israelites fled? See *Exodus* 3:22. See also the text accompanying note 188, above.

287. See *Exodus* 32:5.

288. See the text accompanying note 279, above. See also the note accompanying note 272, above.

289. See, e.g., Maimonides, *The Guide of the Perplexed*, I, i (21): "People have thought that in the Hebrew language *image* denotes the shape and configuration of a thing. This supposition led them to the pure doctrine of the corporeality of God, on account of His saying: *Let us make man in our image, after our likeness* [Genesis 1:26]." See also the text accompanying note 334, below.

290. This was a problem confronted, for example, during the great Iconoclastic Controversy in the Eastern Orthodox Church. See chapter 16. See also note 333, below.

291. The systematic discussion of the political problems here go back to such texts as the account of useful fictions in Plato's *Republic* (414d). See Anastaplo, *The American Moralist*, 27. See also the texts accompanying notes 134 and 135, above. An intriguing use of rhetoric may be seen in how Moses pleaded with God not to wipe out the people of Abraham. See *Exodus* 32:11–13. Consider also the efforts made by Abraham to save Sodom and Gomorrah. See *Genesis* 18:20–33.

292. Consider, for example, the fact that various of the crafts are said to have been developed by the descendants of Cain. See *Genesis* 4:17, 22. See also chapter 4, section IV. Consider as well the challenge posed to divine mastery by the building of the Tower of Babel. See *Genesis* 11:4, 6. Consider further the repeated recourse to

idolatry by the Israelites in the centuries following their deliverance from Egypt. See note 32, above.

293. An odd feature of Aeschylus' play is that we are not told why Zeus was determined to get rid of human beings. Is the natural vulnerability of our species (if not of all species) thereby recognized? Compare appendix K of this book.

294. Particularly troublesome for Zeus is that Prometheus gave *fire* to the human race.

295. See, on *nature*, Anastaplo, *The American Moralist*, 412–15, 616. See also Anastaplo, "Natural Law or Natural Right?"

296. See *Exodus* 32:26–28.

297. See *Exodus* 32:26–29.

298. See *Exodus* 32:9–10, 33–34.

299. We can be reminded here of the issues posed by the *Book of Job*. See chapter 13.

300. A talk given in the Works of the Mind Lecture Series, The Basic Program of Liberal Education for Adults, University of Chicago, Chicago, June 1, 1986.

301. 1 *Kings* 2:2–3.

302. *Deuteronomy* 5:2–5. See, on the significance of the mountain having two names, note 388, below.

303. See *Exodus* 20:1–14.

304. *Deuteronomy* 5:19–28.

305. That tradition is reflected in the rabbinic teachings accumulated over millennia. The Roman Catholic Church, for example, also looks to more than the Scriptures for authoritative guidance. See note 238, above; note 337, below.

306. See the text accompanying note 184, above. See also the text accompanying note 46, above.

307. See the text accompanying note 47, above.

308. *Harper's Bible Dictionary* (San Francisco: Harper & Row, 1985) dates *Exodus* at 451 B.C.E. (Before the Common Era [also known as B.C.]), and dates *Deuteronomy* at 621 B.C.E. See note 319, below.

309. W. Gunther Plaut et al., *The Torah: A Modern Commentary* (New York: Union of American Hebrew Congregations, 1981), 520.

310. *Ibid.*

311. See, e.g., Solomon Goldman, *The Ten Commandments* (Chicago: University of Chicago Press, 1956), 103–4. See, on Delphi, Anastaplo, *The Thinker as Artist*, 93. I myself, while serving in the United States Army Air Corps, passed across the Sinai Peninsula by train in the 1940s, traveling from Cairo to near Jerusalem. Although this trip was at night, making it difficult to see anything outside my railroad car, I do recall sensing that crossing the Sinai was a very strange thing to be doing, and so quickly. (I was turning twenty-one at the time.) See note 355, below.

312. Martin Buber, *Moses: The Revelation and the Covenant* (New York: Harper & Row, 1958), 138–39.

313. *Ibid.*, 139. See, on Martin Buber, Strauss, *Jewish Philosophy and the Crisis of Modernity*, 148–50, 306, n. 1, 353, n. 34.

314. Goldman, *The Ten Commandments*, 129. Compare *Matthew* 3:16–17.

315. Strauss, *Jewish Philosophy and the Crisis of Modernity*, 359–60. See also note 238, above; the text accompanying note 346, below. (The Works of the Mind Lecture Series referred to is at the University of Chicago. See, e.g., notes 27 and 300, above; note 599, below. See also note 183, above.) See, on Leo Strauss, Anastaplo, *The Artist as Thinker*, 249; Kenneth L. Deutsch and John A. Murley, eds., *Leo Strauss, the Straussians, and the American Regime* (Lanham, Md.: Rowman & Littlefield, 1999). See also note 7, above; note 575, below. See as well appendices A and E of this book.

316. Plaut et al., *The Torah*, 531 (citing *Exodus* 34:28 and *Deuteronomy* 4:13, 10:4).

317. *Ibid*., 531. ("C.E.," it should again be noticed, is an abbreviation for "Common Era" (also known as "A.D."). See note 308, above.)

318. This is at *Exodus* 22:17, counting by verses.

319. Plaut et al., *The Torah*, 534. There are seventeen sentences in the Christian versions. *Ibid*. There are 172 words in the Hebrew text, and 156 in the King James English translation. See Goldman, *The Ten Commandments*, 79. See also *Wall Street Journal*, December 11, 1985, 30.

320. See Plaut et al., *The Torah*, 534 (noting the first exception); Goldman, 189 (noting the second exception).

321. See Buber, *Moses*, 119–20.

322. See Plaut et al., *The Torah*, 534–35.

323. *Ibid*. See also Goldman, *The Ten Commandments*, 28.

324. Plaut et al., *The Torah*, 537. "In Roman Catholic depictions (in accordance with the Catholic division of the commandments), three [commandments] are on one tablet and seven on the other." *Ibid*., 537. See note 386, below.

325. See, e.g., Anastaplo, *The Constitution of 1787*, 234. Compare note 87, above. See also note 386, below.

326. *Exodus* 20:2. See, on the translations from the Hebrew used in this book (unless otherwise indicated), note 15, above. Each of the Ten Commandments, when introduced in the discussion that follows, will have its Everett Fox translation provided in its accompanying note. This should help us see better what is being commanded. Thus, the First Commandment has recently been translated by Everett Fox as "I am YHWH your God, who brought you out from the land of Egypt, from a house of serfs." Fox, *The Five Books of Moses*, 369. See also note 329, below.

327. See Plaut et al., *The Torah*, 525.

328. *Exodus* 19:5–6. God, in *Deuteronomy* 9:12, describes the idolatrous people as Moses', and speaks of *Moses* as having brought them out of Egypt. Compare *Deuteronomy* 9:26–28.

329. See, on the Tetragrammaton, *An Encyclopedia of Religion* (New York: Philosophical Library, 1945), 773 ("The four letters of the ineffable name of God, YHWH. This name is never pronounced save with the vowels of Adonai or Elohim."). See also Fox, *The Five Books of Moses*, xxix ("On the Name of God and Its Translation"); the text accompanying note 345, below.

330. *Exodus* 20:3–6.

> You are not to have any other gods before my presence. You are not to make yourself a carved-image or any figure that is in the heavens above, that is on the earth beneath, that is in the waters beneath the earth; you are not to bow down to them, you are not to serve them, for I, YHWH your God, am a jealous God, calling-to-account the iniquity of the fathers upon the sons, to the third and the fourth (generation) of those that hate me, but showing loyalty to the thousandth to those that love me, of those that keep my commandments. [Fox, *The Five Books of Moses*, 369–70.]

331. See note 364, below. An insistence upon such uniqueness is not likely to endear a people to others, unless perhaps the proposition advanced is manifestly preposterous. See note 155, above; note 364, below.

332. See, on the "reading" of works of art, Anastaplo, *The Thinker as Artist*, 335. See also George Anastaplo, "El Greco and His Successors at the Art Institute of Chicago," *The Greek Star*, Chicago, June 28, 2007, 8 (to be included in Anastaplo, *Reflections on Religion, the Divine, and Constitutionalism* [in course of preparation]); note 707, below. See as well appendix D of this book.

333. See, e.g., *Genesis* 9:5. This is also reflected in the prohibition of murder. See, on controversies about the fashioning of images, chapter 16, section VII; note 290, above.

334. See, e.g., note 289, above.

335. See Buber, *Moses*, 115–17. Compare *ibid.*, 125.

336. *Deuteronomy* 4:12.

337. The insistence upon a voice can remind us of Isaac's failure, on the occasion of the blessing, to be guided primarily by Jacob's voice. See *Genesis* 27:22; the text accompanying note 140, above.

338. Strauss, *Jewish Philosophy and the Crisis of Modernity*, 372.

339. Strauss, "How to Begin to Study *The Guide of the Perplexed*," xxi. See *ibid.*, 127. See also note 346, below. Relevant here may be Plutarch's argument, in his essay on superstition, that superstition is worse than atheism.

340. The Israelites should have remembered, for instance, that the first-born of the Egyptians had recently suffered because of their fathers' sins. Compare *Job* 1:5.

341. *Exodus* 20:7. "You are not to take up the name of YHWH your God for emptiness, for YHWH will not clear him that takes up his name for emptiness." Fox, *The Five Books of Moses*, 371.

342. See Buber, *Moses*, 131–32.

343. Compare Plato, *Apology of Socrates*, 21A sq. See Anastaplo, *Human Being and Citizen*, 23.

344. Compare those who make images out of wood and then worship them as they choose. See, e.g., *Isaiah* 37:14–20, 45:18–21; the text at note 513, below. See also Plutarch, *Isis and Osiris*, sec. 66 (end).

345. This is a long way from Moses' first recorded encounter with God. See the text accompanying notes 221–24, above. See also note 329, above. Central to this inquiry is, of course, what it is truly possible for a human being to *know* about God. See note 7, above. See also Henry, "Anastaplo's Bible as Legal Literature," 504.

346. Maimonides insisted upon the moral character as well as the high level of intelligence required in the prophet. See Maimonides, *The Guide of the Perplexed*, II, 36 (369–73) See also Anastaplo, *On Trial*, 822.

347. *Exodus* 20:8–11.

> Remember the Sabbath day, to hallow it. For six days you are to serve, and are to make all your work, but the seventh day is Sabbath for YHWH your God: you are not to make any kind of work, (not) you, nor your son, nor your daughter, (not) your servant, nor your maid, nor your beast, nor your sojourner that is within your gates. For in six days YHWH made the heavens and the earth, the sea and all that is in it, and he rested on the seventh day; therefore YHWH gave the seventh day his blessing, and he hallowed it. [Fox, *The Five Books of Moses*, 371.]

What is understood about the *next* six (or next seven) days for God?

348. Goldman, *The Ten Commandments*, 160. That is, considerable effort (or motion) is needed to provide for rest. This may be witnessed in the remarkable flurry of activity that observant Jews can exhibit upon getting ready for the restful Sabbath.

349. Had God arranged this without an "order," simply because it was good or fitting? But is there not an order intrinsic to goodness? See, on the Idea of the Good, note 67, above. See also note 364, below.

350. See Plaut et al., *The Torah*, 547, 549; Goldman, *The Ten Commandments*, 80.

351. See, e.g., *Exodus* 31:12–117.

352. *Deuteronomy* 5:12 (emphasis added); *Exodus* 20:8 (emphasis added).

353. *Deuteronomy* 5:15.

354. See Goldman, *The Ten Commandments*, 61; Plaut et al., *The Torah*, 533.

355. What does this say about modern five-day or four-day work-week proposals? Related to this development is the importance for us of "the weekend," which tends to be markedly secular, including (I could observe in 1989) in *most* of modern Israel. The Sabbath in the Mandate Territory (Palestine) seemed to me less obviously secular in the 1940s. See note 311, above.

356. See, e.g., Cassuto, *A Commentary*, 9, 224, 245.

357. *Exodus* 20:10.

358. *Exodus* 20:12. "Honor your father and your mother, in order that your days may be prolonged on the soil that YHWH your God is giving you." Fox, *The Five Books of Moses*, 372.

359. Here the male parent is put first. Elsewhere, as in *Leviticus* 19:3, the female parent can be put first. See Plaut et al., *The Torah*, 554.

360. Consider what we know about the significance of nursing homes and what modern mobility does to a healthy (or at least a stable) family life. Consider also what Jesus had to say about turning away from one's parents, as well as from one's spouse, in the singleminded pursuit of personal salvation. See Anastaplo, *The Artist as Thinker*, 75 (discussing John Bunyan's *The Pilgrim's Progress*). Is it possible to have parents properly honored if there should be, as in Plato's *Republic*, an endorsement of a community of wives and children? See note 373, below. See also the text accompanying note 635, below.

361. Deuteronomy 6:4–6. See also the text accompanying note 272, above; the text accompanying note 699, below.

362. Samson Raphael Hirsch, *The Pentateuch* (New York: Judaica Press, 1971), part III, 274. See also Goldman, *The Ten Commandments*, 176. It is not only the Jewish people who depend on "the faithful transmission by parents to children etc." Thus, Mahatma Gandhi (in response to Christian proselytizing?) is reported to have said that conversion was "the deadliest poison that ever sapped the fountain of truth." He is also reported to have declared, "If I had the power and could legislate, I should stop all proselytizing." See Letters to the Editor ("Hindus View Conversion as Anathema"), *Wall Street Journal*, September 29–30, 2007, A7. See, for how Constantine Cavafy examined the troubling tension between the old Pagans and the new Christians, George Anastaplo, "Law & Literature and the Christian Heritage: Explorations," 40 *Brandeis Law Journal* 192, 194–206 (2001).

363. *Exodus* 20:13. "You are not to murder." Fox, *The Five Books of Moses*, 372.

364. Idolatry, too, can be said to be well established among peoples all over the world and across millennia. What does *that* prove? Perhaps that there is in human beings a natural yearning to worship—and perhaps, even, that there exists a Being worthy of worship? See the text accompanying note 511, below. See, on the Idea of the Good, note 67, above. See, on the lessons to be cautiously learned from idolaters, Colleen Smith, "Prayer in a Time of Technological Desolation," *Our Sunday Visitor*, October 19, 1997, 5. See also notes 311, 331, and 339, above; note 705, below.

365. And so a contemporary legal scholar can venture to observe, "[The Ten Commandments], I have always thought, tend to peter out toward the end." Lino A. Graglia, "The Constitution, Community, and Liberty," 8 *Harvard Journal for Law and Public Policy* 291, 292 (1985). See chapter 4. May it be risky to give reasons for *these* commandments? Should they be regarded as "natural"?

366. See Plaut et al., *The Torah*, 544, 587. No "state of nature" theory is assumed, or depended upon, for the sake of understanding. Nor is there a distinction in all this between what we call "church" and what we call "state." See note 207, above.

367. William Blackstone, *Commentaries on the Laws of England*, vol. 4, 178.

368. *Exodus* 20:13. "You are not to adulter." Fox, *The Five Books of Moses*, 372.

369. The Parmenides fragments we have, which celebrate the perfection and permanence of Being, include this observation: "When man and woman mingle the seeds of love / That spring from their veins, a formative power / Maintaining proper proportions moulds well-formed bodies from this diverse blood. / For if, when the seed is mingled, the forces therein clash / And do not fuse into one, then cruelly / Will they plague with double seed the sex of the offspring." Parmenides of Elea, *Fragments*, David Gallop, trans. (Toronto: University of Toronto Press, 1984), 89. See, on being, note 39, above. See also appendix K of this book.

370. Compare the attitude of the Apostle Paul. See Plaut et al., *The Torah*, 554. See, on "The Gospel According to St. Paul," Anastaplo, *On Trial*, 199–204.

371. See, for the traditional notion of Neshamah Yeterah ("additional soul"?), Harris, *Exodus and Exile*, 9, 123. See also note 372, below.

372. See *Exodus* 19:15; Plaut et al., *The Torah*, 523; Buber, *Moses*, 114. Such abstention is *not* required on the Sabbath. Some have even argued that proper sexual activity is to be expected on the Sabbath. See note 371, above.

373. Adultery may also make it difficult both to keep tribes separate and to keep the priestly line pure. See note 360, above.

374. *Exodus* 20:13. "You are not to steal." Fox, *The Five Books of Moses*, 372.

375. See Moshe Greenberg, "Some Postulates of Biblical Criminal Law," in *Yehezkel Kaufmann Jubilee* (1960), 18.

376. *Exodus* 20:12. See also the text accompanying note 42, above.

377. *Deuteronomy* 6:10–12. Other lands, such as those given to the children of Esau and to the children of Lot, are not to be claimed by the Israelites. See *Deuteronomy* 2:8.

378. *Exodus* 20:13. "You are not to testify against your fellow as a false witness." Fox, *The Five Books of Moses*, 372.

379. "Conscience," we should notice, is neither a biblical nor a Classical Greek term. See, e.g., Anastaplo, *The American Moralist*, 607; Anastaplo, *Reflections on Religion, the Divine, and Constitutionalism* (in course of preparation).

380. *Exodus* 20:14. "You are not to desire the house of your neighbor, you are not to desire the wife of your neighbor, or his servant, or his maid, or his ox, or his donkey, or anything that is your neighbor's." Fox, *The Five Books of Moses*, 372.

381. See Plaut et al., *The Torah*, 553.

382. See *Deuteronomy* 5:21.

383. I have been told that, in rabbinic thought, "house" and "wife" came to be used interchangeably.

384. See, on the status of women, Strauss, *Jewish Philosophy and the Crisis of Modernity*, 372; Anastaplo, *The American Moralist*, 349. See also chapter 5; notes 130, 131, 339, and 369, above. However important men might be in founding a religion, women may be central to the routine observances vital to its perpetuation. This may be seen, for example, even in the ferocity of Euripides' *Bacchae*. See note 259, above; note 713, below, and the text accompanying note 636, below. See also the text accompanying note 571, below. See as well appendix F of this book, note 142.

Critical to the status of women, at least in the modern world, may be the influence of Christianity. Consider these remarks by President Lincoln, upon being presented a Bible by "the Loyal Colored People of Baltimore": "In regard to this Great Book, I have but to say, it is the best gift God has given to man. All the good the Saviour gave the world was communicated through this book. But for it we could not know right from wrong. All things most desirable for man's welfare, here and hereafter, are to be found portrayed in it." Lincoln, *Collected Works*, VII, 542. See the text accompanying note 563, below; note 567, below. See also note 767, below. Compare note 67, above; notes 462 and 520, below.

See, on the status of men and their appetite for war, note 74, above.

385. Both of these commandments prove particularly important in the teachings of Jesus, in that he seems to make less of one of them and more of the other than does the Decalogue. See, e.g., note 360, above.

386. The Commandments can be understood as *five* and *five*, even if the tablets are depicted as *three* and *seven* or as *four* and *six*. See, e.g., note 324, above. See, for indications that others before me have evidently worked out some of the things I have about the patterns of the Decalogue (however different they might ultimately have been in many details and perhaps even more in both presuppositions and tone), Goldman, *The Ten Commandments*, 79–80. See also the text accompanying note 325, above.

387. See Goldman, *The Ten Commandments*, 69. See, on numbers, Strauss, "How to Begin to Study *The Guide of the Perplexed*," xxx.

388. See, e.g., Plaut et al., *The Torah*, 520, 537; Buber, *Moses*, 140. The tablets were kept in the Ark, the current whereabouts of which remains a mystery. Was the uncertainty about the name of the mountain designed to keep *its* whereabouts obscure? See note 302, above; note 515, below. See also note 280, above. Would Judaism have become more like Christianity if the whereabouts of both Jerusalem and the *land* of Israel had been obscure? See chapter 3, end of section VIII. See also the text accompanying note 618, below.

389. *Deuteronomy* 5:22–23.

390. *Deuteronomy* 4:5–6. See also the text accompanying notes 31 and 90, above.

391. A talk given in the First Friday Lecture Series, The Basic Program of Liberal Education for Adults, University of Chicago, Chicago, September 1, 1995.

392. Machiavelli, *The Prince*, ch. 13, 56. See also the text accompanying note 184, above; the text accompanying note 405, below.

393. See Serge Schmemann, "Fireworks on Jerusalem's 3,000 Year," *New York Times*, September 5, 1995, A6; Storer H. Rowley, "Israel's Motivation is Criticized as Jerusalem 3,000 Gala Opens," *Chicago Tribune*, September 5, 1995, sec. 1, 4. "About the year 1000 B.C., David, 30 years old, became the King over Judah in Hebron (2 *Samuel* 2:1–4). . . . After a reign of 7 years in Hebron, David was proclaimed king over all Israel (2 Samuel 5:1–5). . . . David died c. 961 B.C. after a reign of 40 years." F. Buck, "David," *New Catholic Encyclopedia* (New York: McGraw-Hill, 1967), vol. 4, 657–58.

394. Robert Alter, *The Art of Biblical Narrative* (New York: Basic Books, 1981), 35.

395. *New Catholic Encyclopedia*, vol. 4, 658. See also the text accompanying note 427, below.

396. *New Catholic Encyclopedia*, vol. 4, 658.

397. This salutation has never been, so far as I know, "Next year in Palestine" or "in the Holy Land" or "in Israel."

398. *The Complete Poems of Heinrich Heine*, 586–87. See the text accompanying note 457, below. See also the text accompanying note 275, above.

399. See 1 *Kings* 2:1. See also the text accompanying note 456, below.

400. Joab can be spoken of as "this toughest of ancient Near Eastern mafiosi." Alter, *The Art of Biblical Narrative*, 102. See note 454, below.

401. The story of Goliath is perhaps Aegean in armament, in the notion of a duel, etc. One can also be reminded of Polyphemos of the *Odyssey*. See appendix B of this book.

402. An instance of this may be seen in the odds faced by the English at Agincourt in Shakespeare's *Henry V*. I say more about Henry V further on. See note 433, below. Consider also the careers of Theseus, Heracles, St. George, and Beowulf.

403. See Mark Twain, *The Adventures of Tom Sawyer*, ch. 4.

404. See 1 *Samuel* 17:40. *Five*, in Hesiod's *Works and Days*, is an inauspicious number. See note 39, above.

405. See the text accompanying note 392, above. Consider also the career of Joan of Arc. See Anastaplo, *On Trial*, 919.

406. See 1 *Samuel* 21:9.

407. One can be reminded of the youthful Robert Maynard Hutchins as president of the University of Chicago. See, on Mr. Hutchins, George Anastaplo, "Freedom of Speech and the First Amendment: Explorations," 21 *Texas Tech Law Review* 1941, 2033–38 (1990); Anastaplo, "September 11th, A Citizen's Responses (Continued)," 4 *Loyola University Chicago International Law Review* 135, 145–46 (2006).

408. See, e.g., 1 *Samuel* 16:23, 18:10.

409. We notice in passing that Saul, as the first king of Israel, follows upon the corruption of the judges who had long ruled the Israelites. See *Judges* 17:6, 18:1, 19:1, 21:25. See also note 423, below.

410. Consider his collecting two hundred foreskins of the Philistines, rather than the one hundred required to win Saul's daughter, Michal. See 1 *Samuel* 18:25–27.

411. See, e.g., 1 *Samuel* 18:6–9. See also the text accompanying note 65, above.

412. See 2 *Samuel* 1:1–16.

413. See note 393, above.

414. See 2 *Samuel* 11:2–27.

415. See, on Abigail, 1 *Samuel* 25:3; note 123, above. See, on Michal, 1 *Samuel* 18:20; note 428, below; the text accompanying note 442, below.

416. Bathsheba, it seems, is prepared to go along with this subterfuge, which might even have had the highly dubious effect of David's sharing of Bathsheba indefinitely with her unsuspecting husband. See note 426, below. Should Uriah's fatal abstinence be considered to have been divinely inspired?

417. See 2 *Samuel* 11:6–13.

418. See 2 *Samuel* 11:14–27. See also the text accompanying note 469, below.

419. See 1 *Samuel* 18:17.

420. See 2 *Samuel* 3:2–3, 15:7, 17:1.

421. This is certainly a question that we would want to consider in, say, a Shakespeare play. See Anastaplo, *The Artist as Thinker*, 15.

422. Among his ancestors are not only Ruth but also the "harlot" who tricks Judah in a good cause. See the text accompanying note 161, above. See also Alter, *The Art of Biblical Narrative*, 36.

423. We can be reminded of the warnings originally issued by Samuel as to how kings will abuse their powers. See 1 *Samuel* 8:4. See also *Deuteronomy* 17:14–15–28:36; note 409, above.

424. One can wonder whether Bernini ever saw the remarkable Hellenistic statue (or a sketch thereof) depicting the brutish executioner sizing up Marsyas for his flaying.

425. See Leo Strauss, *Natural Right and History* (Chicago: University of Chicago Press, 1953), x. See also Alter, *The Art of Biblical Narrative*, 98; Anastaplo, *The American Moralist*, 490.

426. At common law in the (pre-DNA) Anglo-American system, for example, Uriah would have been generally regarded as the father of that son if it had been evident that he had been conceived and born while Bathsheba was still legally married to Uriah. See note 416, above. See also the text accompanying note 460, below. Consider as well the problem (with challenging repercussions down to this day?) of Sarah's attractiveness for the king of the country visited by Abraham and Sarah. See *Genesis* 18:9–15, 20:1–18, 21:1–3. See also the text accompanying note 574, below. See as well note 635, below.

427. See the text accompanying note 395, above.

428. His erotic yearnings are reflected in his relations both with Michal, the daughter of Saul, and with Jonathan, the son of Saul. See 1 *Samuel* 18:1–4; the text accompanying notes 410 and 415, above.

429. See also 2 *Samuel* 18:31, 19:8; Anastaplo, *The Thinker as Artist*, 364.

430. See 1 *Samuel* 21:1, 22:9. One can be reminded of this upon noticing the price paid again and again by those who were loyal to President William J. Clinton.

431. Here is one report of this flare-up following upon David's "rooftops" encounter with Bathsheba:

> An adulterous King of Israel 3,000 years ago is threatening to wreak havoc on the government of Prime Minister Yitzhak Rabin. Jewish Rabbis in Israel's parliament, angry when Foreign Minister Shimon Peres questioned the moral scruples of the biblical King David, are expected to force a no-confidence vote in parliament. . . . Rabbis angry at Peres' position in favor of ceding occupied land for peace cited King David—"a conqueror"—as a real hero of the Jewish people. Peres replied in a statement that launched the storm: "Not everything King David did on the ground and on the rooftops seems to me to be Jewish or appeals to me." ["King David Stirs Israeli Debate," *Chicago Tribune*, December 19, 1994, sec. 1, 6.]

An Israeli political song today has a conservative party leader routinely hailed as "our David."

432. See, e.g., 1 *Samuel* 9:3. Compare 1 *Samuel* 9:15–27, 16:5–23.

433. David is *the* king of the people of Israel (and indeed for many Jews down to our day) somewhat in the way that Henry V can sometimes seem to be *the* king of the English people for Shakespeare. See, e.g., Anastaplo, *The Constitution of 1787*, 74, 86. Henry, too, sees someone he can do without "voluntarily" placing himself in a particularly dangerous part of a battle.

434. See 1 *Kings* 1:1–4. See, on this maiden, the text accompanying notes 445 and 464, below. See also note 462, below. See, on the Messiah, note 488, below. See also appendix I of this book.

435. See 1 *Samuel* 3:1–10. See, on prophecy, chapter 2, above; appendix B of this book.

436. Compare the odd affair of the pestilence chosen by David. See 2 *Samuel* 24:1–25.

437. David can be spoken of as the only previous lyric poet comparable to Sappho. See, on Sappho, Anastaplo, *The Thinker as Artist*, 45–75.

438. 2 *Samuel* 6:12–15.

439. 2 *Samuel* 6:16.

440. 2 *Samuel* 6:20.

441. 2 *Samuel* 6:21–22. See the text accompanying note 466, below.

442. 2 *Samuel* 6:22. See the text accompanying note 415, above. Michal may nevertheless have among her "offspring" such people as the Moral Majority. See, on that conscientious movement (since then known by other names), Anastaplo, *The American Moralist*, 327–37; Anastaplo, *Reflections on Freedom of Speech and the First Amendment*, 313 ("morality, legislation of").

443. A talk prepared for the Law Panels, American Culture Association Annual Convention, San Antonio, Texas, March 29, 1997.

444. Mark Twain, *The Adventures of Huckleberry Finn*, ch. 14 ("Was Solomon Wise?"). See the text accompanying note 478, below. See also Edward Gibbon, *The Decline and Fall of the Roman Empire*, ch. 15: "As those heretics [the Gnostics] were, for the most part, averse to the pleasure of sense, they morosely arraigned the polygamy of the patriarchs, the gallantries of David, and the seraglio of Solomon." Gibbon continues in this way his account of the heretical Gnostics:

> The conquest of the land of Canaan, and the extirpation of the unsuspecting natives, they were at a loss how to reconcile with the common notions of humanity and justice. . . . The Mosaic account of the creation and fall of man was treated with profane derision by the Gnostics, who would not listen with patience to the repose of the Deity after six days' labour, to the rib of Adam, the garden of Eden, the trees of life and of knowledge. . . . The God of Israel was impiously represented by the Gnostics as being liable to passion and to error. . . . They allowed that the religion of the Jews was somewhat less criminal than the idolatry of the Gentiles; but it was [the Gnostics'] fundamental doctrine that the Christ whom they adored as the first and brightest emanation of the Deity appeared upon earth to rescue mankind from their various errors, and to reveal a *new* system of truth and perfection. [*Ibid.*]

See also note 462, below; the text accompanying note 36, above.

445. 1 *Kings* 1:1–4. See the text accompanying note 434, above. See also note 462, below.

446. 1 *Kings* 1:5–10.

447. 1 *Kings* 1:11–14. See, on Nathan, David, and Uriah, chapter 10, section V, above.

448. 1 *Kings* 1:18.

449. 1 *Kings* 1:22–27.

450. 1 *Kings* 1:29–30.

451. 1 *Kings* 1:31. The prospect for David of such immortality here on earth would, of course, have made unnecessary all of these maneuvers by Nathan and Bathsheba.

452. 1 *Kings* 1:34–35.

453. 1 *Kings* 1:40.

454. 1 *Kings* 1:41. We notice, in passing, that Joab rather than Adonijah seems to be in charge here. See note 400, above.

455. 1 *Kings* 1:49–53.

456. 1 *Kings* 2:1–4. See the text accompanying note 399, above.

457. See the text accompanying note 398, above.

458. 1 *Kings* 2:5–6.

459. 1 *Kings* 2:7.

460. 1 *Kings* 2:8–9.

461. 1 *Kings* 2:12.

462. 1 *Kings* 2:13–18. Abishag is sometimes referred to by Christian scholars as David's nurse. See, e.g., *Zondervan Pictorial Bible Dictionary*, 791. It is useful to notice here two sentences in Gibbon immediately following upon the passages quoted in note 444, above:

> The most learned of the [Christian] fathers, by a very singular condescension, have *imprudently* admitted the sophistry of the Gnostics. Acknowledging that the literal sense is repugnant to every principle of faith as well as reason, they deem themselves secure and invulnerable behind the ample veil of allegory, which they carefully spread over every tender part of the Mosaic dispensation. [Gibbon, *The Decline and Fall*, ch. 15 (emphasis added).]

To what extent and in what ways have the principles of reason always been drawn on (often instinctively, perhaps) by believers worldwide in interpreting inherited sacred texts of all kinds? See, on enduring standards of right and wrong, Anastaplo, *Human Being and Citizen*, 46f, 74f; Anastaplo, "Natural Law or Natural Right?" See, on the fundamental limitations of most thought worldwide, Anastaplo, *But Not Philosophy*. See also notes 561, 654, 703, 712, 758, and 761, below. See as well note 384, above; note 520, below.

463. 1 *Kings* 2:20. See the texts accompanying notes 123 and 134, above.

464. 1 *Kings* 2:22–24. See also the texts accompanying notes 434 and 445, above. See as well note 462, above.

465. 1 *Kings* 2:25.

466. 1 *Kings* 2:25–27. See the texts accompanying notes 438–41, above.

467. 1 *Kings* 2:35.

468. 1 *Kings* 2:28.

469. 1 *Kings* 2:32. See the text accompanying note 418, above.

470. 1 *Kings* 2:28.

471. 1 *Kings* 2:30.

472. 1 *Kings* 2:31.

473. See 1 *Kings* 2:35, 4:4.

474. 1 *Kings* 2:36–38.

475. 1 *Kings* 3:39.

476. 1 *Kings* 2:42–43. See, on Adam, Eve, and the Garden of Eden, Anastaplo, *On Trial*, 5.

477. 1 *Kings* 2:46.

478. See 1 *Kings* 3:2–28. See, for reservations about the wisdom of this adjudication, the text accompanying note 444, above.

479. 1 *Kings* 3:1.

480. It is odd that, after his alliance with Pharaoh, Solomon should have burdened the people of Israel with construction projects somewhat as the Israelites had been imposed upon by other Pharaohs in Egypt. See chapter 7. See, on Egypt remaining in the souls of the Israelites, chapter 6, section VII.

481. See, e.g., 1 *Kings* 12:12–17. See also 1 *Kings* 12:28–31. Compare chapter 8. See note 649, below.

482. A talk given in the First Friday Lecture Series, The Basic Program of Liberal Education for Adults, University of Chicago, Chicago, May 4, 1984. See, on prophecy, chapter 2.

483. Augustine, *The City of God*, bk. 21, ch. 8. See, for the Joshua episode, Joshua 10:13. See, for the Hezekiah episode, *Isaiah* 38:8. See also the texts accompanying notes 525 and 526, below.

484. See *Common Values, Common Cause* (a publication of the West German government) (New York: German Information Center, 1983), 60. See also the text accompanying note 533, below. St. Augustine has said: "It is, in fact, God himself who has created all that is wonderful in this world, the great miracles and the minor marvels which I have mentioned; and he has included them all in that unique wonder, that miracle of miracles, the world itself." Augustine, *The City of God*, bk. 21, ch. 10. See note 577, below. Compare appendix K of this book.

485. *Isaiah* 1:1.

486. *Isaiah* 1:2–4.

487. *Isaiah* 66:23–24.

488. See, e.g., *Isaiah* 35:1–10. I have been told that, strictly speaking, *Messiah* is not to be used as an adjective in ancient Hebrew. See, for John Locke's use of "Messiah," appendix I of this book.

489. See, e.g., *Isaiah* 32:13–20, 33:1–24. See also chapter 2; chapter 13.

490. See, especially, *Isaiah* 52:13, 53:12.

491. Samuel Sandmel, *The Hebrew Scriptures: An Introduction to Their Literature and Religious Ideas* (New York: Oxford University Press, 1978), 193. Some twentieth-century Jewish critics believe that the Jewish people is the Suffering Servant.

492. See *ibid.*, 190. Compare Shlomo Riskin, "The Fire in Each of Us," *Jerusalem Post* (International Edition), January 17, 1998, 31.

493. *Isaiah* 53:3–5. At the least, it can be said, this kind of sentiment in ancient Judaism contributed (among the Jews of Jesus' time and their Gentile fellow travelers) to a "Christological" response in those "naturally" inclined in that direction by temperament.

494. See *Isaiah* 44:28, 45:1.

495. See *Isaiah* 1:9, 3:9.

496. See *Isaiah* 10:24–26, 11:15–16.

497. See *Isaiah* 14:12–21. Christians are inclined to use the name of Lucifer here.

498. See, e.g., *Isaiah* 22:22.

499. See *Isaiah* 29:22, 41:8, 51:2.

500. Or so it can seem. See *Isaiah* 43:27, 51:3. See, on Adam, Eve, and the Garden of Eden, Anastaplo, *On Trial*, 5.

501. See *Isaiah* 51:10, 15, 63:11–14. See also chapter 7.

502. See *Isaiah* 54:9–10. See, on Noah, note 85, above.

503. See, on *Jonah*, Anastaplo, *On Trial*, 71.

504. It is said that the poetry of the Koran is also compelling. See, on Islamic thought, Anastaplo, *But Not Philosophy*, 175.

505. Niels Bohr observed: "It is very difficult to make an accurate prediction, especially about the future." See Anastaplo, *The American Moralist*, viii, xiii. See also note 577, below.

506. See chapter 2. See also appendix B of this book.

507. See the text accompanying note 19, above. See also John A. Murley, "Our Character Is Our Fate," *Political Science Reviewer*, vol. 26, 36 (1997).

508. See Aristotle, *Poetics*, ch. 9. Compare Plato, *Republic*, bks. 2, 3, and 10; note 595, below.

509. See, e.g., *Isaiah* 56:1–8, 58:13.

510. See the text accompanying note 47, above; the text accompanying note 519, below. See also the epigraph for appendix C of this book.

511. See note 364, above. See also appendix K of this book.

512. See *Plato, Apology*, 21B–C.

513. See *Isaiah* 2:8, 44:2. See also the text accompanying note 279, above; the text accompanying note 517, below. See as well note 344, above. All this is to be distinguished from how one regards what one has made (or is it discovered?) with one's own mind—from, that is, what one has made with one's life.

514. See chapter 16, section VII.

515. See chapter 8. But Moses could risk breaking even the tablets inscribed by God Himself. Such tablets (though made by God) are not to be worshiped; nor is any human being to be worshiped, however much he or she may be made in the image of God. See notes 280 and 388, above; note 523, below.

516. See, e.g., *Deuteronomy* 5:2–5; the text accompanying note 302, above.

517. See *Isaiah* 44:14–20. See also the texts accompanying notes 279 and 513, above.

518. See the text accompanying note 184, above.

519. See, on prudence, the text accompanying note 47, above. See also note 260, above; note 653, below. There is, however, a rabbinic tradition that Isaiah was tortured to death. Consider, also, the troubles of Jeremiah, another major prophet. See note 161, above. See also the epigraph for appendix C of this book.

520. Is Maimonides (in *The Guide of the Perplexed*) moved by his anti-corporeality campaign even to the extent of denying all divine intervention in human affairs? See the text accompanying note 272, above. Would "divine intervention," in this approach, include commandments and lessons from God? Ralph Cudworth, a seventeenth-century Christian Platonist, argued: "Things are what they are not by will but by Nature." See *The Encyclopedia of Philosophy* (New York: Macmillan, 1967), vol. 2, 272. See also Anastaplo, *The American Moralist*, 139; note 244, above; notes 654, 676, and 700, be-

low. See, as well, notes 67, 384, and 462, above. Consider further appendix K of this book.

521. See *Isaiah* 65:20.

522. See chapter 13. See also note 488, above.

523. And yet, in some ways, Moses is played down. Certainly, as we have seen, he is not to be worshiped. See, e.g., the text accompanying note 193, above; notes 280 and 515, above.

524. See, e.g., chapter 7, section V. See also the text accompanying note 577, below.

525. See *Isaiah* 38:1. See also the text accompanying note 483, above.

526. See 2 *Kings* 20:1–11. This includes the use of a fig-plaster to effect a cure.

527. Are we asked to believe, for example, that a seraphim "actually" touched Isaiah's tongue with a hot coal? See *Isaiah* 6:6. See, on the uses of miracles, chapter 14.

528. See, on Gideon's trials of God, *Judges* 6:36–40. See also the text accompanying note 577, below.

529. The ancients could speak here of the role of the Muses. See, for example, the opening of Hesiod's *Theogony*, of Homer's *Iliad*, and of Homer's *Odyssey*. See note 704, below.

530. See the text accompanying note 508, above. Consider also the remarkable prophecy about the great Elizabeth by Archbishop Cranmer at the end of Shakespeare's *The Life of King Henry VIII*. See George Anastaplo, "Shakespeare's Politics Revisited," in John A. Murley and Sean D. Sutton, eds., *Perspectives on Politics in Shakespeare* (Lanham, Md.: Lexington Books, 2006), 197.

531. Consider, also, the implications of the opinion of the devout Christian that all of *Isaiah* must be written by one author, since Jesus himself evidently regarded it so—and, it will be added, "*He* ought to have known!" See note 577, below. See, on "antisupernaturalism," note 577, below.

532. Pharaoh, for example, could not see properly the signs announced by Moses. See note 192, above.

533. See the text accompanying note 484, above. See, on the twentieth-century Holocaust, appendix J of this book.

534. This talk was given at a Weekend Conference of the Basic Program of Liberal Education for Adults, University of Chicago, East Troy, Wisconsin, November 7, 1993.

535. William Shakespeare, *King Lear*, IV, i, 27.

536. Consider, for example, the high praise of Job in John Milton's *Paradise Regain'd* and of the *Book of Job* in Thomas Carlyle's *Heroes and Hero Worship*. See George Anastaplo, "The Founders of Our Founders," in Harry V. Jaffa, ed., *Original Intent and the Framers of the Constitution* (Washington, D.C.: Regnery Gateway, 1994), 184. See, for a recent retelling of the story of Job, John Berryman, "The Book of Job," in *Poetry*, April 1980, 35.

537. *Encyclopedia of Religion*, vol. 8, 97 (New York: Macmillan, 1989).

538. *Ibid.*, 98.

539. *Ibid.*, 98–99. See, on Mesopotamian thought, note 58, above. See, on Egyptian thought, note 212, above.

540. *Encyclopedia of Religion*, vol. 8, 99–100.

541. *Zondervan Pictorial Bible Dictionary*, 434.

542. *Job* 1:1.

543. *Job* 1:8.

544. See, e.g., chapter 4, section IV.

545. See, e.g., Homer, *Odyssey*, bk. 8. Similarly, the story of Job is evidently referred to in subsequent books of the Bible. See, e.g., *Ezekiel* 14:14.

546. See, e.g., Cervantes, *Don Quixote*, pt. II, ch. 2. Another author had also presumed to provide a sequel to the original Cervantes publication.

547. See, e.g., Anastaplo, *Human Being and Citizen*, 8.

548. See the text accompanying note 544, above. See, on what Cain and Abel knew, and how they knew it, chapter 4 of this book.

549. Herodotus, *History*, II, 3. See also *ibid.*, II, 23, on how Homer or another poet found the name *ocean* and introduced it into his poetry. See, on Herodotus, Anastaplo, *The Thinker as Artist*, 211–52.

550. See *Encyclopedia Judaica*, vol. 2, 12 (1971).

551. See Robert Gordis, *The Book of God and Man: A Study of Job* (Chicago: University of Chicago Press, 1965), 209–18. He does see the book as Hebrew in origin, assigning it to the period between 500 and 300 B.C.E. See *ibid.*, 216, 218. See also *Deuteronomy* 4:6.

552. Does this also mean that Job could not have known what he was doing?

553. The description of the great-souled man in Book IV of Aristotle's *Nicomachean Ethics* is instructive here. See, e.g., Anastaplo, *The Thinker as Artist*, 318–34. See also note 572, below. See as well note 129, above.

554. See, e.g., *Job* 16:11, 30:26. See also note 572, below. Job's afflictions do seem to teach Job instead that we are to the divine as flies are to wanton boys. See Shakespeare, *King Lear*, IV, i, 36. Compare *ibid.*, V, iii, 167. Job's friends insist that there must be something really wrong with Job for him to suffer as much as he does. See *Job* 16:19. They are certainly right in believing that there *is* something unusual, if not extraordinary, in what is going on here. See note 572, below. See also note 667, below.

555. John Flackett, "Panel Discussion—Judge John Noonan's Presentation," 14 *Nova Law Review* 146 (1989) (quoting E. L. Doctorow). See also Anastaplo, *The Thinker as Artist*, 10.

556. See August Weismann, "The Duration of Life," in *The Great Ideas Today*, vol. 1972, 394, 401 (1972).

557. Compare Sophocles, *Oedipus Tyrannus*, 1089–1109.

558. See note 553, above. See also chapter 13, section VII (concluding paragraph).

559. See Anastaplo, *On Trial*, 5.

560. See, e.g., Moshe Greenberg, "Job" in *The Literary Guide to the Bible*, Robert Alter and Frank Kermode, eds. (Cambridge, Mass.: Belknap Press 1987), 286.

561. See Sophocles, *Oedipus Tyrannus*, 739: "What have you designed, O Zeus, to do with me?" See also *ibid.*, 376–79, 497–502. See as well *ibid.*, 903: "O Zeus, if you are rightly called the sovereign lord, all-mastering . . ." See, further, note 462, above.

562. See Anastaplo, "On Freedom," 469–70.

563. See Maimonides, *The Guide of the Perplexed*, III, 22–23 (486–97).

564. See Plato, *Phaedo*, 118. Consider how Socrates regards the constantly sacrificing Cephalus in Book I of Plato's *Republic*. See also *Law and Philosophy*, vol. II, 1038.

565. Compare the African proverb: "When you see water flowing uphill, it means that someone is repaying a kindness [with a kindness]." *African Folktales*, Roger D. Abrahams, ed. (New York: Pantheon Books, 1983), 145. See also Greenberg, *The Literary Guide to the Bible*, 301; Anastaplo, *But Not Philosophy*, 40–41.

566. *The Book of the Dead*, E. A. Wallis Budge, trans. (London: Arkane, 1989), 104–5. See also chapter 16 of this book.

567. It has been noticed that some Christian translations of *Job* favor an expectation of life after death more than the Hebrew text requires. See, on the "workings of divinity," Aristotle, *Nicomachean Ethics*, VII, I ("for just as there is no vice or virtue belonging to an animal, so too neither state belongs to a god, but the one side is something more honorable than virtue, and the other is something of a different kind from vice"). Consider, on the "workings of divinity," these recent remarks by John Van Doren about the *Book of Job*:

> The Voice out of the Whirlwind . . . recreates the world for Job and dares him to find fault with this new rendering of it, in all its splendor—splendor as a work of divine art and divine care. It does this although it never directly answers Job—never proclaims that the world is just or acknowledges that it is unjust. It does point out, with heavy irony, that God knows the difference between good and evil, and can reward the one and punish the other as Job cannot; but it adds, almost scornfully, that this is only a small part of what it can do, and does, to maintain its work.

See note 572, below. Compare note 384, above; note 762, below.

568. See *Job* 42:7.

569. ABC television news broadcast, November 5, 1993.

570. See chapter 2. See also note 46, above.

571. See *Job* 42:14. See also note 384, above.

572. We should not be surprised, in the light of what God had said about Job at the outset to the Satan, that Job was able to hold out as well as he did. Nor should we be surprised that God never reveals to Job the divine challenge put to the Satan and its sequel. Such a revelation, I have suggested, is not needed to understand what happened to Job. After all, such things do happen to exemplary human beings all the time, without any known (*or knowable*) intervention by either God or the Satan. Besides, Job could be understood to have figured out what was or might have been "said" to him by God. See note 567, above. Figuring out a "historical" conversation between God and the Satan requires a quite different kind of work of the mind. Be that as it may, the "happy ending" for the *Book of Job* suggests that the author (or the editor or the public) did not accept the ostensible teaching of the book. That is, it apparently was not acceptable that there need be no correspondence at all between one's virtue and one's worldly condition. Is not this opinion, however, on the brink of a Christian understanding? See note 554, above. See also the text accompanying note 618, below.

573. This talk was given at a staff seminar of the Basic Program of Liberal Education for Adults, University of Chicago, Chicago, February 22, 1975. See, on "The Gospel According to St. Paul," note 370, above.

574. *Genesis* 20:17–18. See note 426, above. See also note 238, above.

575. See, e.g., Strauss, *Jewish Philosophy and the Crisis of Modernity*, 311–56 ("Why We Remain Jews"). It *is* odd, considering how much has been made in recent years of Leo Strauss's Jewishness, that one of the reasons my 1974 eulogy of him was criticized as vigorously as it was (in private) in some quarters was because I had made as much as I did of his Jewishness. See Anastaplo, *The Artist as Thinker*, 475, n. 285. See also appendices A and E of this book. See as well Murley, ed., *Leo Strauss and His Legacy*, 854.

576. See, on the Ten Commandments, chapter 9 of this book. Consider, in reading the United States Constitution, the following questions in this order: Why is there a treason provision at the end of Article III? How does this bear upon the placement of a counterfeiting provision in Article I, Section 8? What does this suggest about the conventional explanation of the purposes of the enumeration of powers in that section? And what does this suggest in turn both about the general powers of Congress and about the reach of a general common law? See, on the Constitution, notes 2, 18, 30, and 136, above.

577. See, on miracles, notes 484 and 528, above. "Anti-supernaturalism" is used by modern critics in assessing the claims made in and for biblical texts. Consider, for example, how the *Book of Daniel* can be discussed:

> Modern criticism . . . overwhelmingly denies the authenticity of *Daniel* as a product of the sixth century B.C. Indeed, as early as A.D. 275 the neo-Platonic philosopher Porphyry had categorically repudiated the possibility of *Daniel*'s miraculous predictions. Anti-supernaturalism must bring the "prophecy" down to a time after the events described . . . or, if the latest possible date has been reached, it must then reinterpret the predictions to apply to other, already-accomplished events. [*Zondervan Pictorial Bible Dictionary*, 199.]

Similar assessments have been made of the *Book of Isaiah*. See chapter 12 of this book. See also notes 7 and 531, above; the text accompanying note 524, above. See as well appendix H of this book. Compare appendix K of this book.

578. See, on how unusual stories should be assessed, Anastaplo, "Lessons for the Student of Law," 187.

579. Deeds, not *Logos*, are emphasized at the outset of *Genesis*. But is not *Logos* implied, as in the perceptions of *goodness* recorded in *Genesis* 1:10, 12, 18, 21, 25, 31? See, on the ideas and the good, notes 67 and 349, above.

580. See, e.g., *John* 10:37–42. See, for the New Testament translation usually used in this book, note 41, above. Compare note 15, above.

581. See *John* 2:1–11, 4:46–54.

582. See *John* 2:2–11.

583. See *John* 4:46–54.

584. See *John* 5:29.

585. See *John* 6:1–14. See, on the centrality of this miracle, the text accompanying notes 593 and 594, below.

586. See *John* 6:16–21.

587. See *John* 9:1–41.

588. See *John* 11:1–54.

589. See *John*, chs. 18–20. See, on the trial of Jesus, Anastaplo, *On Trial*, 155, 172.

590. See *John* 2:2–11, 11:1–54. See also the text accompanying note 236, above. I again notice that my list here does *not* include the "super-miracles" of the Incarnation and the Resurrection. Nor does my list include either miracles *not* described at length or miracles reported to have been performed by Jesus after the Resurrection. See, e.g., *John* 8:59, 18:5–6, 21:1–14. See the texts accompanying notes 672 and 673, below. See also chapter 16, sections V and VII.

591. See *John* 4:46–54, 9:1–41.

592. See *John* 5:2–9, 6:16–21.

593. See *John* 6:1–14. See also *John* 21:1–14.

594. It should be recalled that the first of the temptations in the wilderness by the Devil was that Jesus command that "stones be made bread." *Matthew* 4:3. Would not that have been a radically different thing from what Jesus is recorded to have done in *John* 6:1–13? Was the stone-into-bread temptation given first place in *Matthew* because the supplying of material needs is for most men quite impressive, contributing as it does to self-preservation? Is this how one gets men's attention on a large scale? (Consider the Grand Inquisitor episode in Fyodor Dostoyevsky's *The Brothers Karamazov*. See, for example, the essay on that episode in George Anastaplo, *Reflections on Life, Death and the Constitution* (in course of preparation).) Does the author of *John* somehow spiritualize this temptation from the Devil? Compare *John* 6:26.

It should also be noticed that when Jesus discusses signs with perhaps skeptical Jews, he is told by them that Moses had provided them manna in the desert. Jesus offers to provide them even better sustenance, albeit at a price. See *John* 6:30–65. It is then recorded: "From that time many of his disciples went back, and walked no more with him." *John* 6:66. The implications of the miracle of the loaves and fishes do seem central to Jesus' career in *John*. See note 585, above.

595. The prudent would have us recall here the discovery by Socrates that poets are not always able to explain (that is, to understand?) the fine things they have made. Compare the text accompanying note 580, above.

596. *John* 21:21–22.

597. *John* 21:23.

598. *John* 21:25. "I suppose" suggests a "personal" account?

599. This talk was given in The Works of the Mind Lecture Series, The Basic Program of Liberal Education for Adults, University of Chicago, Chicago, April 12, 1987.

600. 2 *Samuel* 12:19–24. See the text accompanying note 730, below. The relations of David and Bathsheba are discussed in chapter 10, sections I, V, VI, and VII. See, on Solomon and Bathsheba, chapter 2, sections III and VI.

601. See, on the Gettysburg Address, Anastaplo, *Abraham Lincoln*, 229.

602. Cullen Murphy, "Who Do Men Say That I Am?" *Atlantic Monthly*, December 1986, 43 (quoting Albert Schweitzer).

603. *Ibid.*, 50 (quoting Hans Kung).

604. See Brian E. Beck, *Reading the New Testament Today* (Atlanta: John Knox Press, 1978), 11. See also note 15, above.

605. See *ibid.*, 141.

606. See, on the development of the New Testament canon, *The New Oxford Annotated Bible* (New York: Oxford University Press, 1962), 1167–70.

607. See *The Jerome Biblical Commentary*, Joseph A. Fitzmyer and Raymond E. Brown, eds. (Englewood Cliffs, N.J.: Prentice Hall, 1968), 144.

608. The prayer, at *Matthew* 6:9–11, reads:

> Our Father which art in heaven, hallowed be thy name. Thy kingdom come. Thy will be done in earth, as it is in heaven. Give us this day our daily bread. And forgive us our debts, as we forgive our debtors. And lead us not into temptation, but deliver us from evil: For thine is the kingdom, and the power, and the glory, for ever. Amen.

See note 646, below. See, for the translation used in this chapter, note 41, above. Compare note 15, above.

609. The prayer, at *Luke* 11:2–4, reads:

> Our Father which art in Heaven, hallowed be thy name. Thy kingdom come. Thy will be done, as in heaven, so in earth. Give us this day by day our daily bread. And forgive us our sins; for we also forgive every one that is indebted to us. And lead us not into temptation, but deliver us from evil.

See note 646, below. Some understand "from evil" to be "from the Evil One." See note 666, below.

610. Beck, *Reading the New Testament*, 11.

611. See Raymond E. Brown, *New Testament Essays* (Milwaukee: Bruce Publishing Company, 1965), 220. See also *Harper's Bible Dictionary*, 388–89.

612. See *A Catholic Commentary on Holy Scripture*, Bernard Orchard et al., eds. (New York: Nelson, 1953), 954. For convenience I refer to the authors of these two gospels as "Matthew" and "Luke," whoever they may have been.

613. See Beck, *Reading the New Testament*, 5.

614. Augustine, *The City of God*, X, 11, 18. See Anastaplo, "Teaching, Nature, and the Moral Virtues," 21. See also the texts accompanying notes 595, above, and 745, below. Compare note 751, below.

615. All this bears on the use that has been made in our public schools of the Lord's Prayer as a "non-sectarian prayer" for school children to recite. See *School District of Abingdon* v. *Schempp*, 374 U.S. 203 (1963). See, on the Religion Clauses of the First Amendment, Anastaplo, *The Amendments to the Constitution*, 47–76; Anastaplo, *Reflections on Religion, the Divine, and Constitutionalism* (in course of preparation).

616. Thomas Paine, *Age of Reason*, in *The Life and Works of Thomas Paine*, William M. Van der Weyde, ed. (New Rochelle: Thomas Paine National Historical Association, 1925), vol. 8, 11.

617. See Murphy, "Who Do Men Say That I Am?" 51. See also note 81, above.

618. *Ibid.*, 44. Compare chapter 3, section VIII. See also note 388, above.

619. *Harper's Bible Dictionary*, 399. See also *Jewish Encyclopedia*, vol. 10, 471.

620. See *The New English Bible* (Oxford Study Edition), *Matthew* 3 (1970).

621. See Brown, *New Testament Essays*, 222–23.

622. *A Catholic Commentary on Holy Scripture*, 863.

623. See, e.g., *Anchor Bible Commentary* (New York: Doubleday, 1964), 900.

624. *Jerome Biblical Commentary*, 74.

625. *Ibid.*, 73.

626. See Brown, *New Testament Essays*, 220, n. 7.

627. See, on individualism, Anastaplo, "Individualism, Professional Ethics, and the Sense of Community: From Runnymede to a London Telephone Booth," 28 *Loyola University Chicago Law Journal* 285 (1996). See also note 756, below.

628. See *Luke* 11:1.

629. See *Zondervan Pictorial Bible Dictionary*, 491.

630. *A Catholic Commentary on Holy Scripture*, 863.

631. Beck, *Reading the New Testament Today*, 121. See also *ibid.*, 141.

632. Murphy, "Who Do Men Say That I Am?" 53 (referring to uses of "Father" in *Mark* and in the *Epistles of Paul*). See also *Romans* 8:15; *John* 16:25f.

633. See *Matthew* 10:31–38.

634. See *Matthew* 12:46–50.

635. *Matthew* 23:9. All this points up the ambiguous position of Jesus' earthly father. Compare chapter 9, section VII. Compare also note 426, above.

636. See *Matthew* 22:23–30. See also *Mark* 12:25. See as well the text accompanying note 674, below.

637. See Beck, *Reading the New Testament Today*, 14; appendix H of this book. Is it possible that the same event could be seen by Jews and Christians so differently? Practice in reconciling troublesome dualities may be seen in chapter 16, sections V and VI. See also the text accompanying note 652, below.

638. See *ibid.*, 142. See also chapter 14, section VII.

639. *The Jerome Biblical Commentary*, note 607, above, at 144.

640. See, e.g., *Matthew* 4:22, 5:3, 17, 6:33, 7:21, 8:12, 9:13, 35, 10:7, 11:12, 12:28, 13:11, 13:19, 24f, 31–32, 33f, 44, 45, 47f, 16:28, 18:1, 4, 23, 19:12, 11f, 20:20f, 21:31f, 43, 22:2f, 24:14f, 25:1f, 31, 28:18f.

641. *Matthew* 6:33.

642. See chapter 14.

643. See *Matthew* 4:3–4. This Satan is *not* the skeptical figure seen in the *Book of Job*. See chapter 13.

644. See, e.g., *Matthew* 6:25f, 7:9, 14:13f, 15:32f, 26:26f. See also the text accompanying note 593, above.

645. See note 594, above. See also the text accompanying note 614, above.

646. There are in Greek, depending on how one counts, fifty-seven or fifty-eight words in the *Matthew* version of the Lord's Prayer. There are thirty-eight words in the *Luke* version. The King James translations of the prayer may be seen in notes 608 and 609, above.

647. See *A Catholic Commentary on Holy Scripture*, 863. See also Beck, *Reading the New Testament Today*, 141–42.

648. We can be reminded of the (revealing?) redundancy of sorts in *Genesis*, where for example God provides that the earth should "grass grass." *Genesis* 1:12.

649. This is consistent with various urgings by Jesus that his disciples not concern themselves as others do for the future with respect to material things. For example: "Consider the lilies of the field, how they grow; they toil not, neither do they spin: and yet I say unto you, that even Solomon in all his glory was not arrayed like one of these." *Matthew* 6:28–29. See also *Matthew* 10:9, note 572, above.

650. Ernest Lohmeyer, *The Lord's Prayer* (London: Collins, 1965), 303. See, on *epiousion* and related matters, *ibid*., 134–59.

651. Compare "Hindu Thought: *The Bhagavad Gita*," Anastaplo, *But Not Philosophy*, 67. See also note 732, below.

652. Is *ousia* somehow superimposed upon *ousia* to get the *epiousion*? See note 637, above.

653. *Matthew* 13:35. See also *Matthew* 11:25. Compare the text accompanying note 47, above.

654. Aristotle's god is not an active one, in the ordinary sense, and hence not one to whom one is likely to pray, whatever divinities Aristotle might expect to be provided for the community at large. See notes 7 and 520, above. See as well note 462, above. See, on the Doctrine of the Ideas, Anastaplo, *The Thinker as Artist*, 303. See also note 718, below.

655. See, on Aristotle's *Nicomachean Ethics*, Anastaplo, *The American Moralist*, 20; Anastaplo, *The Thinker as Artist*, 318–34.

656. See, e.g., Anastaplo, *The Artist as Thinker*, 228.

657. Judaism, too, assumes that it is possible for a human being here on earth to be truly virtuous, that is to say, fully righteous, albeit primarily in his deference to the commands of God. See notes 274, 554, and 572, above; note 749, below. See, on the yearning for immortality, chapter 17.

658. See *Matthew* 16:23–24. See, on the self, note 756, below.

659. See Anastaplo, "Teaching, Nature, and the Moral Virtues," 14.

660. See Brown, *New Testament Essays*, 224, n. 23. See, on Tertullian, Anastaplo, "Rome, Piety, and Law," 47.

661. See, for a contrite heart, *Psalms* 51:1.

662. See, e.g., *Matthew* 5:7, 22, 12:14–15, 18:21–35.

663. See *Matthew* 7:12; *Luke* 6:27–31. See also *James* 2:8. The Golden Rule may be found, in effect, in the Hebrew Bible as well. See, e.g., *Leviticus* 19:18. See also *Tobit* 4:14; "Golden Rule, The," *The Jewish Encyclopedia*, vol. 6, 21–22 (n.d.).

664. See *Matthew* 22:34–40. See also *Matthew* 19:16.

665. John Bartlett, *Familiar Quotations* (Boston: Little Brown & Co., 1955), 663. See the text accompanying note 723, below.

666. See also *Matthew* 12:38f, 16:1–4. See, as well, 1 *Corinthians* 10:13. See appendix H of this book, section IV. See also note 609, above.

667. See Mortimer J. Adler and Charles Van Doren, *Great Treasury of Western Thought* (New York: Bowker, 1977), 1395 (#41).

668. See Anastaplo, "Teaching, Nature, and the Moral Virtues," 23–36.

669. See chapter 9; chapter 16.

670. Consider, for an elaboration upon the Lord's Prayer, Dante Alighieri, *Purgatorio*, Canto XI.

671. Compare Moses' slaughter of three thousand of the idolaters (an action that even the authority-minded Thomas Hobbes found questionable). See chapter 8, sections II and VI.

672. See, e.g., *Matthew* 7:29. See also *Matthew* 28:11f. Two quite different accounts can be tacitly recognized here as available to account for all of the evidence.

673. Beck, *Reading the New Testament Today*, 147.

674. See Adler and Van Doren, *Great Treasury of Western Thought*, 234. See also the text accompanying note 636, above.

675. See Thomas Hobbes, *Leviathan*, ch. 10.

676. The Declaration of Independence is drawn upon here. See, on divinity in the Declaration, Anastaplo, *Abraham Lincoln*, 31f; Anastaplo, *The Constitution of 1787*, 21. The concluding lines of Homer's *Odyssey* suggest how divinity can be understood as brought down to earth among human beings. This suggests also what divine intervention may mean. See the text accompanying note 520, above.

677. This talk was given at a symposium on Hellenic-American identity, Chicago, September 30, 1979. Its original title was "The Orthodox Church: Its Meaning for Greek Americans." I benefited, in preparing this talk for its original publication, from suggestions by Fotios Litsias, Kostas Kazazis, and Malcolm Sharp.

678. See Cicero, *The Nature of the Gods*, Horace C. McGregor, trans. (Baltimore: Penguin Books, 1978), 194–95. See, on the Stoics, Anastaplo, "Samplings," *Political Science Reviewer*, vol. 27, 394 (1998). See, on Cicero, Anastaplo, *The American Moralist*, 83.

679. See, on Eastern Orthodoxy and its history, Timothy Ware, *The Orthodox Church* (Baltimore: Penguin Books, 1963).

680. Robert Donus, "Greek Orthodox Protestants," *Logos*, March 1971, 54.

681. See, e.g., Ware, *The Orthodox Church*, 30–31. Nor are we familiar as Americans with the kind of faith that proclaims, in the words of St. Athanasius, "What God has spoken through the Synod of Nicaea [the First Ecumenical Council, C.E. 325] endures forever." *Ibid*., 29. (Consider also the ending of the Gettysburg Address.) St. Athanasius also argued: "God became man that we might be made god." *Ibid*., 29. (Is Mormonism anticipated here?) See also *ibid*., 224, 226. See as well notes 691 and 707, below.

682. Ware, *The Orthodox Church*, 203. Thus, Constantine Cavafy could have a (non-believing?) narrator (a millenium and a half ago) say, in his poem, "In Church":

> I love the church—its hexapteriga,
> the silver of its sacred vessels, its candlesticks,
> the light, its icons, its pulpit.
>
> When I enter a church of the Greeks,
> with its fragrances of incense,
> with its voices and liturgical choirs,
> the stately presence of the priests
> and the solemn rhythm of each of their movements—
> most resplendent in the adornment of their vestments
> my mind goes to the high honors of our race,
> to the glory of our Byzantine tradition.

The Complete Poems of Cavafy, Rae Dalven, trans. (New York: Harcourt Brace Jovanovich, 1961), 42. See also Anastaplo, "Ancients and Moderns: On Cavafy's 'Thermopylae'," *Greek Star*, Chicago, January 14, 1999, 7; Anastaplo, "Law, Education, and Legal Education: Explorations," 37 *Brandeis Law Journal* 585, 763 (1998–1999). See as well Murley, ed., *Leo Strauss and His Legacy*, 876.

683. Ware, *The Orthodox Church*, 208.

684. See, on the Lord's Prayer and American "theology," the text accompanying note 671, above.

685. See, on Greekness and Christianity, Erhart Kaestner, *Mount Athos: The Call from Sleep* (London: Faber and Faber, 1961), 88–89. Fotis Kontoglou, the noted iconographer and author, said: "The Orthodox Christian faith and the fatherland are for us Hellenes fused into one thing. And whoever fights against one of these is fighting against the other, too, and let him not deceive himself." *Hellenic Chronicle*, March 27, 1979, 4.

686. See Ware, *The Orthodox Church*, 208. One can be reminded here of how some Protestant fundamentalists, at least in the United States, regard the King James English translation of the Bible as divinely inspired. See note 41, above.

687. I have, with the assistance of Theodora and Themi Vasils (of Chicago), adapted for use here a standard translation of the Nicene Creed. See note 690, below.

688. See note 681, above; note 692, below.

689. Thomas Herbert Bindley, *The Oecumenical Documents of the Faith*, 4th ed., rev. by F. W. Green (London: Methuen, 1950), 13.

690. "Very God of Very God" could also be "True God of True God." See note 687, above.

691. See Ware, *The Orthodox Church*, 29:

> Christ must be fully God and fully man. Each heresy in turn undermined some part of this vital affirmation. Either Christ was made less than God (Arianism); or His manhood was so divided from His Godhead that he became two persons instead of one (Nestorianism); or He was not presented as truly man (Monophysitism, Monothelitism).

692. Thus, Alfred North Whitehead could report: "The Reformation, for all its importance, may be considered as a domestic affair of the European races. Even the Christianity of the East viewed it with a profound disengagement." Alfred North Whitehead, *Science and the Modern World* (New York: Pelican Mentor Books, 1948), 1.

693. The central words, in the Greek text of the Nicene Creed, are "Pilate, and."

694. 1 *Corinthians* 15:14–17. Compare note 707, below.

695. See chapter 14, section V.

696. See, on Christian paradoxes, Francis Bacon, *Works*, James Spedding and Robert Leslie Ellis, eds. (New York: Hurd and Houghton, 1864), vol. 14, 143. Consider also "[The Christian] believes himself to be precious in God's sight, and yet loathes himself in his own." *Ibid.*, 144.

697. See Cicero, *The Nature of the Gods*, 141. See also the text accompanying note 717, below. See, on Maimonides and the non-corporeality of God, note 24, above.

698. Compare Theseus' response to Hippolyta, William Shakespeare, *A Midsummer Night's Dream*, V. i, 2–22.

699. See *Deuteronomy* 6:4. See also the text accompanying notes 361 and 515, above.

700. There is also the problem of whether such a divinity cares for, or ever intervenes in, human affairs. See note 520, above. The gods of the ancient Greeks were both attractive and vulnerable because they had "personal" histories. See, e.g., Plato, *Republic*, bks. II–III.

701. See, on the *filioque*, Ware, *The Orthodox Church*, 54, 58–60, 62–65, 71, 80, 218–23, 235, 322; Bindley, *The Oecumenical Documents of the Faith*, 88; *A Select Library of Nicene and Post-Nicene Fathers of the Church* (New York, 1900), vol. 14, 165; Charles Augustus Briggs, *The Fundamental Christian Faith* (New York: C. Scribner's Sons, 1913), 267; Deno J. Geanakoplos, *Byzantine East and Latin West* (Oxford: Blackwell, 1966), 99; F. J. Badcock, *The History of the Creeds* (London: Society for Promoting Christian Knowledge, 1930), 189, 191, 192, 209.

702. See, on the Trinity, William Shakespeare, *The Phoenix and Turtle*.

703. See Paul T. Fuhrmann, *An Introduction to the Great Creeds of the Church* (Philadelphia: Westminster Press, 1960), 37; *Nicene and Post-Nicene Fathers of the Church* (1897), vol. 4, 150. The philosophical tradition is reflected in Cicero. See, e.g., the texts accompanying notes 678 and 697, above; the text accompanying note 717, below. See also note 462, above; note 712, below.

704. See Ware, *The Orthodox Church*, 221. The contending divinities of the opening pages of Hesiod's *Theogony* come to mind, as do those of Homer's *Iliad* and *Odyssey*. See also note 712, below. See, on the *Theogony*, appendix F of this book.

705. Is the Nicene Creed somehow related to the controversy about Julian the Apostate? See Bindley, *The Oecumenical Documents of the Faith*, 70. See, on the Emperor Julian, Anastaplo, "Rome, Piety, and Law," 68. See also note 364, above.

706. Is Arianism (a kind of monotheism) reemerging today among "Christians"? See, e.g., notes 32–33 and 209, above; note 748, below.

707. Indeed, little, if anything is said about the Jews (except by implication, with the reference to the mother of Jesus, and with the use of the names, "Jesus," "Christ," and "Mary").

> In 1950 the pope declared the dogma of the Assumption of Mary, that is, that Mary's body did not decompose in the grave, but was reunited by God to her soul soon after she died. Roman Catholic theologians now openly refer to Mary as the "Co-creator" and the "Co-redemptrix" of the [human] race. None of these post-apostolic developments have any support in Scripture. [*Zondervan Pictorial Bible Dictionary*, 515.]

See George Anastaplo, "Liberation Pedagogy," *Cross Currents*, vol. 39, 463 (1989) (numerous corrections of unauthorized editorial changes are needed in this article). See also note 681, above; the text accompanying note 694, above. See as well note 332, above.

708. Thomas Aquinas, when he discusses this matter in the *Summa Theologica*, seems to me to be somewhat flexible on this issue, as if he recognizes (and perhaps wants to hint) that his church's position is not all that it should be here.

709. See, for recent developments in attempts to bridge the centuries-old schism, Steve Kloehn, "Orthodox Leader [Ecumenical Patriarch Bartholomew] Sees Wider Christian Split," *Chicago Tribune*, October 22, 1997, sec. 1, 3; Steve Kloehn, "Local Prelates Seeking Bridge Across Ancient Schism," *Chicago Tribune*, February 7, 1999, sec. J, 8. See the text accompanying note 723, below. Papal statements on this subject in 2007 seem to confirm a split.

710. See Ware, *The Orthodox Church*, 38–42. The Iconoclastic Controversy may have anticipated within Eastern Orthodoxy some of the reforms seen later in the Reformation of Western Christendom.

711. See *ibid.*, 38–42; Kaestner, *Mount Athos: The Call from Sleep*, 90.

712. See Plato, *Republic*, bks. II, III. See also notes 703 and 704, above. There can be a serious question about how much was understood of the philosophical tradition by anyone in authority in the church (in the East or in the West) by this time. See note 462, above.

713. A special role is assigned to the Empress Theodora in the restoration of the icons, which restoration (in 843) is celebrated annually on "Orthodoxy Sunday," the first Sunday in Lent. See Ware, *The Orthodox Church*, 39. See also note 384, above; note 767, below.

714. George J. Tsoumas, "Religious Question Box," *Hellenic Chronicle*, March 15, 1979, 4.

715. *Ibid.*, 4.

716. See George J. Tsoumas, "Religious Question Box," *Hellenic Chronicle*, May 31, 1979, 4.

717. See Cicero, *The Nature of the Gods*, 141; the text accompanying note 697, above, the text accompanying note 760, below. There is also to be found in Cicero the suggestion that the order of the universe, which we can all see, is in effect an icon of the divine. See Cicero, *The Nature of the Gods*, 144–45.

718. The word from which "idea" comes is related to the physical shape and hence the appearance that a thing has. See, on the Doctrine of the Ideas, note 654, above. It

is also important to remember that, as it has been reported, after the iconoclastic crisis monastic life increased in fervor, becoming more mystical and emotional, and less intellectual. See Kaestner, *Mount Athos: The Call from Sleep*, 60; Ware, *The Orthodox Church*, 45–48.

719. See *ibid.*, 38.

720. See, on Islam, note 209, above.

721. Roy Larson, Column, *Chicago Sun-Times*, January 14, 1978, 22.

722. *Ibid.*, 22.

723. See note 709, above. See also the text accompanying note 665, above.

724. James Joyce, *A Portrait of the Artist as a Young Man* (New York: Viking Press, 1957), 243–44.

725. See, on Leo Strauss and a sense of honor, note 33, above.

726. See, e.g., Anastaplo, *Human Being and Citizen*, 203. See also the text accompanying note 678, above; the text accompanying note 760, below; appendices C and D of this book.

727. It is apt to be forgotten in this connection that Socrates was killed by a democratic regime, some leaders of which felt vulnerable before him.

728. See, on the trial of Socrates, Anastaplo, *Human Being and Citizen*, 8. See, on what the constantly-inquiring Socrates *did* know, Anastaplo, "Freedom of Speech and the First Amendment: Explorations," 21 *Texas Tech Law Review* 1941, 1945 (1990).

729. This talk was given at the Lenoir-Rhyne College Hickory Humanities Conference on the Quest for Meaning, Wildacres Retreat, Little Switzerland, North Carolina, May 14, 1992. This college is Lutheran in its orientation.

730. *Ecclesiastes* 9:5. See the text accompanying note 600, above.

731. A. Conan Doyle, "The Adventure of the Retired Colourman" (emphasis added). We return to this "client" in the text accompanying note 766, below.

732. *Encyclopedia Britannica*, "Buddhism" (fifteenth ed.). See, on Buddhism, Anastaplo, *But Not Philosophy*, 147. See also note 572, above. Is Gautama's charioteer somehow comparable to Arjuna's charioteer in the *Bhagavad Gita*? See note 651, above. See, for another account of the serenity of monks, Robert Browning, "Soliloquy of the Spanish Cloister."

733. See the text accompanying notes 738 and 739, below.

734. See the text accompanying notes 747 and 748, below. See also note 728, above.

735. See, e.g., the text accompanying note 730, above. See also chapter 2.

736. See Leo Tolstoy, *Master and Man, and Other Stories* (Baltimore: Penguin Books, 1977). See also the text accompanying note 741, below.

737. See the text accompanying note 740, below. See also chapter 13.

738. Thomas Aquinas, *Summa Theologica*, I–II, Q.5, Art. III.

739. *Ibid.*

740. See, e.g., *Job* 1:1, 8. See also chapter 13.

741. See note 736, above.

742. See, e.g., Anastaplo, "Church and State: Explorations," 183; note 651, above. See also note 732, above.

743. See, for an instructive introduction to Thomas Aquinas' commentary on the *Nicomachean Ethics*, Harry V. Jaffa, *Thomism and Aristotelianism* (Chicago: University of Chicago Press, 1952).

744. See, e.g., Anastaplo, *The Thinker as Artist*, 318.

745. See the text accompanying note 614, above.

746. See, e.g., Jaffa, *Thomism and Aristotelianism*, 182.

747. See Plato, *Apology*, 40C. See also notes 726 and 728, above.

748. See, on natural theology, Strauss, *Jewish Philosophy and the Crisis of Modernity*, 117, 129. See also note 7, above; the text accompanying note 767, below. See as well appendix K of this book.

749. See, e.g., Anastaplo, *The American Moralist*, 413–15. Compare the implications of Jewish teachings about the thirty-six righteous men who (despite their anonymity) keep the world going. See note 657, above.

750. See, e.g., *Erie Railroad Company* v. *Tompkins*, 304 U.S. 64, 79 (1938) (quoting Oliver Wendell Holmes, Jr.). See also Anastaplo, *The Constitution of 1787*, 128–37, 320 n. 95; note 2, above. Compare note 762, below. The questionable *Erie* doctrine is discussed as well in Anastaplo, *Reflections on Constitutional Law*. See, e.g., Philip A. Dynia's review of this *Reflections* volume in *Law and Politics Book Review*, an electronic periodical of the American Political Science Association, vol. 17, no. 4, 286–89 (2007). (The recently-reprinted *Constitutionalist* volume is reviewed by Clifford Angell Bates, Jr., *Law and Politics Book Review*, vol. 17, no. 4, 724–26 (2007).)

751. See, on the good, the true, and the beautiful, Anastaplo, *The Artist as Thinker*, 275. Compare the text accompanying note 614, above.

752. See, e.g., Anastaplo, "Natural Law or Natural Right?"

753. See, e.g., chapter 3, sections VII, VIII, and IX. See also note 728, above.

754. Compare Aristophanes' memorable story in Plato's *Symposium*. See Anastaplo, *The Thinker as Artist*, 171.

755. See, e.g., Anastaplo, "Teaching, Nature, and the Moral Virtues," 4.

756. See, on the self, Anastaplo, *Human Being and Citizen*, 87; *The American Moralist*, 620; *Campus Hate-Speech Codes*, 111. See also note 627, above; the text accompanying note 658, above.

757. See notes 651, 732, 742, above.

758. Consider this passage from Strauss, *Thoughts on Machiavelli*, 298:

> Modern man as little as pre-modern man can escape imitating nature as he understands nature. Imitating an expanding universe, modern man has ever more expanded and thus become ever more shallow. Confronted by this amazing process, we cannot cease wondering as to what essential defect of classical political philosophy could possibly have given rise to the modern venture as an enterprise that was meant to be reasonable.

See, on an expanding universe, appendix F, part 3 (e.g., note 64) and appendix K of this book.

759. See, e.g., Anastaplo, *The Thinker as Artist*, 178.

760. See, e.g., the text accompanying notes 697 and 726, above. See also note 728, above.

761. We may also sense that our talents, discipline, and temperaments, more than our finite life spans, determine how much we can learn about the most important things. More and more "input" does not necessarily enhance our capacity to think and to understand. This should become evident as we struggle to liberate ourselves from the seductive plentitude of such mixed blessings as the Internet, email, and the cellular telephone, all of which tend to enslave the typical user. See note 758, above. See, on death and dying, Anastaplo, *Human Being and Citizen*, 214.

762. See, on will, reason, and rightness in God, Thomas Aquinas, *On Truth*, Q. 23, Art. 6, c. See also Anastaplo, *The American Moralist*, 139. Compare note 750, above. Compare also note 567, above.

763. Compare the insistence, in 2 *Peter* 1:16, that the Christians (unlike the pagans?) have *not* fashioned "cunningly devised fables."

764. See Plato, *Republic*, bks. II, III. See also Anastaplo, "Samplings," 426; note 39, above.

765. A. Conan Doyle, *The Adventure of the Norwood Builder*.

766. See the text accompanying note 731, above.

767. See, e.g., note 528, above. See also note 748, above. See, on what is truly good and enduring, Colmo, *Breaking with Athens*, chap. 7 ("Alfarabi, Islam, and the Hereafter"). See, on piety and statesmanship, Anastaplo, *The Thinker as Artist*, 104. See also the text accompanying note 47, above. Central to the concerns of statesmanship today with respect to an effective use of piety (especially in an age when gifted atheists seem to be divinely inspired to disdain prudence and ordinary sensibilities on principle) may be a reconsideration of the place of women in the religious life as well as in the political life of the community, especially when that community is likely to continue to be pervaded by a yearning for "the valley of love and delight." See, e.g., note 384, above. See also note 142 in appendix F of this book. See as well the text accompanying note 1, above.

Index

*An unabidged version of this index is available from the author.